Insurance Aspects of Cross-Border Road Traffic Accidents

Insurance Aspects of Cross-Border Road Traffic Accidents

Luk De Baere
Frits Blees

eleven
international publishing

Published, sold and distributed by Eleven International Publishing
P.O. Box 85576
2508 CG The Hague
The Netherlands
Tel.: +31 70 33 070 33
Fax: +31 70 33 070 30
e-mail: sales@elevenpub.nl
www.elevenpub.com

Sold and distributed in USA and Canada
Independent Publishers Group
814 N. Franklin Street
Chicago, IL 60610, USA
Order Placement: +1 800 888 4741
Fax: +1 312 337 5985
orders@ipgbook.com
www.ipgbook.com

Eleven International Publishing is an imprint of Boom uitgevers Den Haag.

ISBN 978-94-6236-958-0
ISBN 978-94-6274-730-2 (e-book)
NUR

Preface

As most of you are drivers, I can easily imagine that you have, at some point of your lives, been involved in a car accident. If this is the case, I sincerely hope it was only a minor collision without any serious consequences. On a daily basis, thousands of road traffic accidents occur and a substantial part of them are characterised by a cross-border element in one way or another.

Since the inception of the Green Card system in the middle of the twentieth century, international organisations, national governments and the motor insurance industry have cooperated and searched for possibilities to support victims in their attempts to obtain compensation for damage caused by cross-border road traffic accidents. Since the beginning of the Green Card system, the Council of Bureaux (CoB), has played a coordinating role in the cooperation between national Motor Insurers' Bureaux and, later, also between Compensation Bodies, Guarantee Funds and Information Centres.

As Secretary General of the CoB, together with the other members of the CoB Secretariat, we are privileged to be able to actively participate in this coordinating role between these organisations, which on a daily basis strive for the protection of cross-border road traffic victims.

At the same time, we are also confronted with the complexity of the systems and of the rules governing the handling of cross-border motor insurance claims. The strong protection offered to victims can result in highly complex claims handling processes. Based on my experience, I can say that many people, including professionals from the insurance sector, struggle with the numerous rules and their concrete application in the case of cross-border road traffic accidents. Indeed, questions are regularly submitted to the Council of Bureaux and to other organisations regarding the compensation of victims of cross-border accidents.

Bearing in mind those aspects, initiatives to reinforce the knowledge about the protection mechanisms for road traffic victims seem useful and even imperative in order to ensure that professionals have sufficient knowledge and expertise regarding the applicable rules. I hope that the book you now have before you will help increase the necessary knowledge about the claims handling of cross-border motor traffic accidents, be it in the framework of the Green Card system, the European Motor Insurance Directive or rules relating to private international law.

I am delighted that the organisations working together in the Council of Bureaux have supported the initiative to create this book and, consequently, have contributed to the exchange of knowledge. I wish to explicitly thank all the Members of the Council for having allowed Luk De Baere to devote some of his working time to writing this book and I wish to particularly thank Frits Blees for his willingness to dedicate so many hours on the book while being retired and profiting from his post-professional life. Also the team of the Council of Bureaux' Secretariat in Brussels have given a helpful hand in the realisation of this work. Thank you all, dear colleagues, for your help!

But most of all, thank you, dear reader, for picking this book from the shelf and reading it. By doing so, you are sharing knowledge on the handling and settling of claims resulting from cross-border road traffic accidents. Nobody wishes to be a victim of such an accident but those who have suffered an accident deserve to be treated well and to be compensated in a correct way. Let us work together to increase knowledge and thus to protect the victim!

I wish you all pleasant reading.

Greet Floré
Secretary General, Council of Bureaux, Brussels.

Table of Contents

1 Introduction

1.1 Insurance aspects of cross-border road traffic accidents

Every year, hundreds of thousands of people in Europe and neighbouring countries are confronted with the consequences of minor or serious road traffic accidents. A limited, but definitely not negligible number of these accidents are of an international or cross-border nature.[1] This may be, for example, because the accident was caused by a foreign vehicle or because the accident occurred in a state of which the victim was not a resident. In whatever way the cross-border nature of the accident makes itself felt, it always leads to the 'injured' party (whether only sustaining material damage or also suffering bodily injury) wondering about how to be properly compensated. All kinds of practical issues, not least the language and communication aspects, can increase the complexity of dealing with such claims.

Europe has quite a number of rather small countries and a relatively highly developed motor vehicle use. Due to the continent's geography, motor vehicle traffic is not limited within the national borders of the various countries, and international traffic accidents are not at all exceptional.

Although cross-border vehicle traffic can lead to complex loss incidents and leads to important environmental damage, it (still) remains a necessity for strong economic growth and constructive international contacts within Europe and neighbouring countries.

In order to ensure consistency between cross-border vehicle traffic and the proper protection of the victims of the consequent road traffic accidents, various international organisations have attempted to find solutions to reconcile both aspects. In the first instance, the United Nations provided the necessary impetus. In a second

1. In 2017 the total number of cross-border accidents involving motor vehicles in Europe was over 400,000.

phase, the European Union (or more specifically its legal predecessors) increased the level of that protection, albeit with a more limited geographical coverage.

The aim of this book is to investigate how legally compulsory motor vehicle insurance, and the associated protection mechanisms, lead to simplified international travel by road, without reducing the protection of road accident victims.

1.2 Justification

The protection mechanisms introduced by the United Nations and the European regulators did not just come about in a single action. They are a gradual evolution that has been in progress for several decades and have not yet reached their final stage.

In the past, various articles and books were devoted to claims handling as a result of international road traffic accidents. These are often not available in English and, due to the numerous changes, may be out of date.

As the authors of this book, we believe that Europe lacks a proper overview of the insurance aspects of cross-border road traffic accidents. At present, there is no up-to-date English-language book describing the functioning of the Green Card system and the European Motor Insurance Directive.

A few years ago, the second author defended a doctoral thesis on this subject.[2] We wanted the book that you are now reading to be a work that is largely inspired by that thesis but differs from it in various respects. First of all, the thesis was written in Dutch and is therefore inaccessible to the larger part of our readers. Secondly, we do not have any academic aspirations. Our work is written for practitioners. And last but not least: developments, both in the field of legislation and jurisprudence as well as in the international organisations of insurers have not stopped since 2010; a new and updated study is therefore warranted.

1.3 Target audience

This book is a general introductory work and is intended for anyone who is involved, in a professional capacity, in dealing with cross-border loss incidents: insurance companies (and more specifically, insurers operating in the Motor Third Party Liability (MTPL) insurance sector), legal assistance insurers, claims handling offices, lawyers, representatives of road accident victims, judges, loss adjusters,

2. F.J. Blees, De weg naar schadevergoeding in het internationale gemotoriseerde verkeer, PhD thesis Erasmus University Rotterdam, Kluwer – Deventer 2010.

international Motor Insurers' Bureaux, Guarantee Funds, Compensation Bodies, Information Centres and any other interested parties.

1.4 Restriction of the field

This book is intended to provide an analysis of the protection mechanisms developed for injured parties in cross-border road traffic accidents. These are mainly the European Green Card system and the European Motor Insurance Directive. It focusses on the insurance aspects that can contribute to paving the way for the injured party to obtain compensation for the (material and/or bodily) damage sustained.

In the case of *cross-border road traffic accidents*, we will be dealing with accidents caused by a foreign vehicle in the victim's country of residence. Inversely, it could be an accident that takes place in what is, for the victim, a foreign country (not their country of residence). In every case, such road traffic accidents must involve a motor vehicle. Claims resulting from road accidents in which no motor vehicles are involved (such as accidents with pedestrians, cyclists, horse riders, roller skaters etc.) are, in principle, beyond the remit of this book. Moreover, we shall restrict ourselves to road accidents; air and waterborne transport will not be considered.

There are three other legal aspects which will not, in principle, be addressed by this book:

- *Liability law:* this determines who is obliged to compensate the 'loss' sustained. This obligation may not only be based on the tortious behaviour of the person who caused the accident (tortious liability) but can equally derive from one of the many national no-fault or risk liability systems that offer increased protection to vulnerable road users (and, in some cases, vehicle passengers); or even from a breach of contract, such as a carriage agreement. Liability rules are of vital importance to the successful handling of a road traffic accident claim. However, they fall outside the scope of this book because they belong within the national civil law of individual countries; they also differ from each other in fundamental respects. It would be impossible even to describe the basic principles of liability in every individual state. Not only are there already enough valuable works on the subject; but also liability law goes beyond the field of insurance aspects of cross-border road traffic accidents.
- *Compensation law:* this determines to what extent the damage sustained can be remedied or, if complete redress is impossible, compensated. These rules also fall under national law and are therefore virtually unaffected by rules of international or supranational law. These national rules are similarly excluded from the scope of this book.

- Rules of *national insurance law*: Although the supranational legal order, essentially the European Union, has had a significant influence on the rules of international insurance law, there remains ample scope for national policy. In some parts of Europe, this can even involve international or non-European policy. For example, the national rules of motor vehicle insurance in the three Benelux countries are based on principles laid down in the context of the Benelux Agreement.[3] However, it is mostly a matter of national rules and, for that reason, we do not take them into consideration.

Aspects of liability law, compensation law and/or national insurance law may be dealt with indirectly, but in that case mainly by way of illustration or clarification of certain international or supranational provisions. Furthermore, the growing influence of the European legal order on issues of liability and compensation law cannot be ignored. Since the European Motor Insurance Directive determines what cover must be provided by MTPL insurance, the link to liability law is becoming ever closer. As will be apparent from chapter 6, the jurisprudence of the Court of Justice of the European Union is also making the dividing line between insurance cover and national liability law ever narrower.

The principles of subsidiarity, proportionality and conferral of competences, as laid down in the Treaties of the European Union, continue to militate against the harmonisation of liability and compensation rules at European level.

Since injured parties in road traffic accidents are key to the study of insurance aspects of cross-border road traffic accidents, we will restrict ourselves to the motor insurance that offers protection to the injured parties of road traffic accidents. It concerns the insurance that covers the statutory civil law liability that can arise from the use of motor vehicles in road traffic (motor third party liability or MTPL insurance). That legally mandatory insurance is not only in the interest of the insured or the liable keeper or driver of the vehicle; it also protects the injured party of an accident. A triangular relationship, as it were, is created between the insurance company, the person who may be liable (the insured, keeper or driver of the vehicle) and the injured party.

From the historical perspective, MTPL insurance was originally intended primarily to protect the insured's assets against potential compensation claims from injured parties in accidents. Gradually, third-party insurance would come to be considered as a necessary protection for injured parties, who no longer had to seek compensation only from the liable motorist, but could also make a claim directly against the liability insurer. In that way, the injured party is no longer dependent on the sol-

3. The Benelux is comprised of Belgium, the Netherlands and Luxembourg.

vency of the liable motorist for obtaining compensation but can also make a claim directly against an insurance company; this, in principle, should ensure the availability of the required funds. The protective function of third-party motor vehicle insurance for the injured party has led to European states gradually making that insurance mandatory.

The insurance market does offer other products associated with the use of a vehicle, and which are not compulsory at law:

- *Comprehensive insurance:* this is primarily intended to compensate the material damage sustained by the insured vehicle even if the insured is the unintended cause of such damage. Subject to the policy terms and conditions, comprehensive insurance will compensate all kinds of accidental damage, even if they are caused by *force majeure.* Unlike MTPL insurance which is intended to protect the injured party and is therefore subject to much tighter legal regulation, comprehensive insurance leaves the parties to the contract (insurer and insured) considerably greater freedom to agree the policy terms between themselves. This has led to several subcategories, where the insurance cover can be restricted or expanded depending on the wish of the parties ('mini' comprehensive arrangements that are limited to theft and fire; the introduction of lower or higher excess clauses, where the insured persons have to accept to bear part of the damage themselves etc.);
- *Legal assistance insurance*: this provides legal assistance or guarantees payment for legal assistance to the insured in order to claim compensation or cover the costs associated with calling on external legal assistance (such as a lawyer) to uphold the said insured's interests;
- *Road Assistance insurance:* this offers technical or logistical support after an accident or in the event of a breakdown while on the road.

Since these three insurance products are not intended to protect the injured third-party, little or no further attention will be devoted to them in this book.

Finally, we shall similarly not be considering the protection of the potentially liable driver in a road traffic accident. Since this book primarily focusses on compulsory Motor Third Party Liability insurance, the injury sustained by the liable driver due to a road accident, will equally be disregarded. There are insurance products that cover such injury, either as a separate (stand-alone) insurance product or as supplementary and optional cover within an existing insurance product (for example an MTPL or comprehensive policy). The protection mechanisms discussed in this book (the Green Card system and the European Motor Insurance Directive) in principle do not involve protection of the liable driver since this falls outside the field of civil liability. There is also national legislation where the injured driver must be covered by the respective own liability insurance (a sort of first-party insurance or traffic insurance). Indeed this is the case in some Scandinavian countries and in Finland; but these mandatory protection rules are excluded from the mechanisms of the Green Card system and the European Motor Insurance Directive.

1.5 Acknowledgements

The authors sincerely wish to express their strong feelings of gratitude towards the following persons for their support and their help in the realisation of this book:

- The Council of Bureaux for its general and financial support;
- The Secretary General and the colleagues at the Secretariat of the Council of Bureaux, for their patience and support whenever we disturbed them with our questions;
- All the colleagues in the national Motor Insurers' Bureaux, Compensation Bodies, Guarantee Funds and Information Centres for their willingness to give us information about rules and practices in their respective states;
- Mr John Attard (Malta) and Mr Paul Yaghmourian (United Kingdom), for the many hours they spent in proofreading the English text of this book and for their valuable suggestions for improving the language used. Not being native English speakers, we would not have been able to write this book without the help of John and Paul;
- Our families who refrained from complaining every time we were discussing the topics dealt with in this book or writing the text of the manuscript.

It is worth dedicating this book to each and every person mentioned above for their well-appreciated help in its realisation. Nevertheless, if any dedication is to be actually made, this must be to the persons we had constantly in mind during the writing process: the far too numerous victims of road traffic in Europe and other continents of the world. Firstly, we hope that every vehicle driver will take road safety seriously and endeavour to avoid any accidents. Secondly, we would like politicians, public authorities, car manufacturers, insurers and all other involved stakeholders to prioritise road traffic safety in order to decrease the number of accidents and victims as much as possible. Thirdly, we dare to hope that initiatives like the realisation of this book may be a tiny contribution to the improvement of victims' rights and may help them in receiving a fair compensation.

The text of this book has been completed on 1 March 2019. Later developments in legislation and jurisprudence have only occasionally been incorporated.

2 Historical development

2.1 Introduction

The body of this book consists of a description and analysis of the complex system of supranational and international legislation and of private agreements between organisations of insurers and governmental bodies that facilitate the cross-border traffic of motor vehicles in Europe. Over decades these systems have matured into a complex and intertwined fabric of rules, agreements and practices that cannot be easily understood without having at least some basic knowledge of their conception, birth and adolescence. This chapter provides that basic knowledge.

Although the larger part of this book is dedicated to the so called Green Card system, that came into life in the period between 1949 and 1953 and to the legislation emanating from at first the EEC, later the EC and – since the Treaty of Maastricht of 1992 – the EU, we have to start earlier, well before World War II. Then we will describe the start of the Green Card system and its development, the beginning of the intervention of the European legislator and the broadening scope of European influence on motor insurance, culminating in the Protection of visitors Directive – the 4th Motor Insurance Directive – in 2000, the 5th Directive of 2005 and the codified Directive of 2009.

2.2 Motor insurance, its early years

The first motor insurance policies have been brought to the market very soon after the first industrially manufactured motor vehicles were appearing in the streets.[1] Compulsory insurance against the liability for damage caused by these dangerous contraptions comes only later. But not much later, although the requirements vary widely from country to country. The first compulsory motor insurance legislation in Europe is introduced in 1919 in Denmark. Finland follows in 1925 and Norway is the next country in 1926. When World War II erupts, such schemes are additionally introduced in Switzerland, Austria, Sweden, the UK, Luxembourg and Ger-

1. Schmitt, Das System der Grünen Karte, Basel 1968, p. 4.

many. If these schemes are covering all types of motor vehicles, in other countries only part of the vehicle fleet is subject to compulsory insurance, mostly public transport and commercial vehicles. Examples of such legislations are to be found in Belgium, Bulgaria, France, Yugoslavia, Poland and Romania. After the war developments go fast, but not everywhere: compulsory motor insurance legislation is only introduced in the Netherlands as late as 1965, in Hungary in 1970, in Italy in 1971[2] and in Greece in 1976.[3]

With vehicle fleets growing, not only accidents become more frequent, international travel by car also becomes more popular and as a consequence insurance issues have to be resolved. When a country requires its motorists to take out insurance against liability in the interest of potential victims, it is only logical that foreign visiting motorists are subject to the same requirement. Usually, visitors will be required to buy a policy at the border: a frontier policy providing insurance cover for the vehicle in the visited country. Obviously this policy, issued by a local insurer, will meet the requirements of the legislation of the visited country.

But what if the motorist already has a policy covering not only his own country of residence but also the visited country? That is already a fairly common practice in several countries even before the Second World War. Then the motorist would be paying double premium for the same risk, if he would have to take out a frontier policy despite the cover he already benefits on the basis of his 'home' policy. Insurers – in collaboration with their governments – develop various solutions. And one of these solutions will serve as the source of inspiration and the model for the Green Card system that only comes into being *after* the War. It even can be regarded as a model on which the 1st Motor Insurance Directive was built in 1972!

As early as the late 1920s compulsory motor insurance legislation is in force in the four Nordic countries Denmark, Norway, Sweden and Finland. The rather intensive cross-border traffic between these countries necessitates a practical solution, their shared culture facilitates finding it.

The fact that all vehicles in the Nordic countries have to be insured, that this obligation is also applicable to visiting vehicles and that insurance companies provide cover for all four countries make it possible to allow vehicles from one of the neighbouring countries to cross the border simply because they are presumed to be insured.[4] The criterion to be allowed to enter the country without being checked on

2. Shortly before the publication of the 1st Motor insurance directive in 1972.
3. Schmitt, o.c. p. 4 ff; Blees, De weg naar schadevergoeding in het internationale gemotoriseerde verkeer, Deventer 2010, p. 18 ff.
4. This was the situation since 1937, when Finland as the last Nordic country introduced compulsory insurance for foreign vehicles.

insurance is: the registration plate.[5] The problems of cross-border claims handling are resolved by entrusting the insurance associations with this task on behalf of the foreign insurer involved: the basic structure of the Green Card system.

Visitors from other (non-Nordic) countries still have to take out a frontier insurance policy, but especially German insurers find a way around that practical obstacle as well. On the basis of an agreement between the German insurers and the insurers' associations in the Nordic countries, they are allowed to provide their insured person with a certificate which is recognised by the border authorities and which provides a guarantee of cover and a structure for claims handling. The colour of the document? Green. *Nil novi sub sole.*

A separate and totally different approach to find a solution is pursued by *Unidroit*, the Rome institute for the unification of private law, in the second half of the 1930s. Two preparatory studies are published. The first study under the title *'Responsabilité civile des automobilistes'* analyses the law on liability in motor traffic in a wide range of countries.[6] The study demonstrates that these national systems differ considerably. The second study, entitled *'Assurance obligatoire des automobilistes'* shows the lack of international harmonisation. In their report *'Unification internationale en matière de Responsabilité et d'Assurance obligatoire des automobilistes'*.[7,8] *Unidroit* publishes a preliminary draft of a uniform code on the liability of motorists and of uniform legislation regarding motor insurance, both to be implemented by national legislators. Needless to say that the war makes all these efforts completely useless. And after the war developments go in a totally different direction. With much more success.

2.3 The period between 1949 and 1953: the conception and birth of the Green Card system

When, after the war, Europe has to be rebuilt again and international relations normalise, international motor traffic builds up and even intensifies in comparison with the pre-war world.

An increasing number of countries introduce legislation protecting victims of motor traffic accidents. This protection often takes the shape of special liability rules and in several of these countries also of compulsory liability insurance. Since an increasing number of countries also require visiting motorists to be insured, problems at the frontiers arise: delays and additional costs for the motorist.

5. The regime of the 1st Motor insurance directive of the European Economic Communities of 1972, as will be described in detail in para 3.5.2.
6. *Unidroit études XVII*, doc. 1, Rome 1935.
7. *Unidroit études XVII*, doc. 8, Rome 1936.
8. *Unidroit études XVII*, doc. 31, Rome 1940.

The intensified international motor traffic makes a solution for these insurance related problems even more urgent and the issue is picked up by the Economic Commission for Europe of the recently founded United Nations, the *UNECE*. This Commission invites insurance organisations in the various countries in Europe to try and come with a solution. The organisations of motor insurers of initially 12, soon 14, countries meet in London in 1949 and decide to develop a scheme along the principles of the system in the Nordic countries of the 1930s.

The scheme that is developed can be described as follows. In each of the participating countries a central organisation of motor insurers is either set up or recognised under the name of *Bureau*. This Bureau fulfils a double role: it takes up responsibility for the handling and settling of claims resulting from accidents for which visiting motorists bear liability, in accordance with the existing liability and insurance legislation and on behalf of the liability insurer of the visiting motorist. On the other hand it stands as a guarantor that the outlays of the Bureau of the country of accident will be reimbursed.

In order for this scheme to function properly a certain number of conditions has to be fulfilled. First and foremost insurers in the participating countries will have to provide cover abroad. And this cover will have to comply with the legal requirements in the visited country. Equally important: the authorities of the visited country will have to accept that cover provided by foreign insurers as sufficient. And thirdly: proof that the liability of the visiting motorist is adequately covered will have to be presented.[9] That proof of cover is the international certificate of insurance, commonly known as the Green Card which will be accepted as proof of cover by the national border control authorities.[10] And lastly: the governments of the participating countries must refrain from imposing restrictions on the export of currency, since the Bureau in the country of accident has to be reimbursed in its own currency.

The national insurers' organisations – collectively operating under the name *Council of Bureaux* with their seat in London – present this approach to the UNECE in Geneva. The UNECE soon agree with the proposals and lay them down in a *Recommendation* to its Member countries.[11] Although modified several times over the

9. We deliberately avoid the expression 'insured' in this context, for reasons that will be explained in detail later. Essentially the 'proof of cover' does not prove the existence of a valid policy of insurance but only the existence of a guarantee that a potential victim is compensated and that the Bureau that provided that compensation is fully reimbursed.
10. The system is, as we already observed, inspired by the Nordic system of the 1930s. Even the colour of the certificate is borrowed from the Nordic example.
11. Recommendation no. 5, adopted on January 25, 1949 (Recommendation on Insurance of Motorists against Third Party Risks E/ECE/TRANS 145, E/ECE/TRANS/SCI/39).

years and now having the legal form of a *Resolution,* its essence remains unchanged.[12]

The Bureaux lay down their mutual relations in standard agreements. For many years these agreements were the bilaterally concluded so called *Uniform Agreement between Bureaux.* The close relationship between the *Recommendation/Resolution* on the one hand and the agreements between Bureaux on the other is demonstrated by the fact that both documents refer to one another. These agreements between Bureaux – which currently are laid down in the *Internal Regulations* but which in their essentials are unchanged – contain on the one hand a mandate to the Bureau of the country of accident to handle and settle claims on behalf of the Bureau of the country of origin of the liable motor vehicle and on the other hand a guarantee that any outlays of the former Bureau will be reimbursed by the latter. The Bureaux are in that double capacity usually referred to as *handling Bureau* and *guaranteeing Bureau.*[13]

The Green Card system thus provides a solution for two different problems: it simplifies cross-border traffic by replacing checks on insurance policies by the simple check on the existence of a uniform and internationally recognised and accepted document. And it offers adequate victim protection by putting at their disposal a solvent party in their own country with whom they can negotiate and settle their claims for compensation.
This system officially becomes operational as of 1 January 1953.

2.4 From 1953 to the first motor insurance directive of the EEC

This period is characterised by two developments: on the one hand a strong geographical growth and on the other attempts to simplify insurance cross-border formalities even further.

When the Green Card system was conceived in the late 1940s, insurance organisations from 14 countries, mostly in Western Europe, participated in the negotiations. In the early 1970s the Council of Bureaux has as many as 27 member organisations. Whereas in 1949 from the Member States of the Eastern Bloc only Czechoslovakia participated in the discussions that led to the creation of the Council of Bureaux, in 1972 the Council counts 29 members, 6 of which are 'Socialist States'. A number of

12. Revised Consolidated Resolution on the Facilitation of Road Transport (R.E. 4), adopted by the Inland Transport Committee of UNECE on its 66th session (17 – 19 February 2004).
13. The designation *handling Bureau* is not entirely adequate, since in general Bureaux do not handle claims themselves. The actual claims handling is in the large majority of cases entrusted to so-called *nominated correspondents,* who act in the name of the Bureau of the country in which they are active and on behalf of the insurer of the vehicle. For practical reasons however we will use the term 'handling Bureau'.

non-European countries also join the Council of Bureaux. And soon we will see that this is by far not the end of the geographical expansion.

A second development is the reaction of governments and insurers on the growth of international motor traffic. Although the introduction of a uniform and internationally recognised certificate as proof of cover at the frontier means a substantial reduction of border formalities, in a Europe that is increasingly internationally connected by road traffic the procedures to verify the existence and the validity at the borders become more and more inconvenient.

Alternatives are investigated and introduced. Again the 1930s' Nordic approach of the use of the registration plate attached to the vehicle as sufficient proof of cover serves as an example and model. In the Council of Bureaux a Committee under the chairmanship of the President of the German Bureau, Mr. Hans-Heinrich Brumm, develops proposals along the same lines, the *Zürich Recommendations,* as early as 1959. The idea is that Bureaux bilaterally agree to abstain from the requirement of a Green Card as the basis for claims handling and reimbursement. The effectively enforced compulsory insurance, with cover for the country of the other signatory of such an agreement, enables the assumption of cover and of a valid Green Card. A model for such bilaterally concluded agreements accompanies the *Recommendations.*

More or less parallel to each other, systems along these lines are set up for vehicles registered in the Federal Republic of Germany, Austria, Czechoslovakia and Hungary for their mutual traffic and in the Benelux countries. In the latter this is based on an Agreement of 1966 between the three countries which also closely harmonises their legislation on compulsory Motor Third Party Liability insurance (MTPL insurance).

But then the European Economic Community (EEC) steps forward, takes over the initiative and in 1972 the first Motor Insurance Directive (MID) sees the first light of day.[14]

> *From European Communities to European Union*
> A short description of the development of the European Union since their foundation in the early 1950s may prove useful.

14. Council Directive 72/166/EEC of 24 April 1972 on the approximation of the laws of Member States relating to insurance against civil liability in respect of the use of motor vehicles, and to the enforcement of the obligation to insure against such liability, OJ L 103, 2.5.1972, p. 1.

The initial three Communities of 1951 (European Coal and Steel Community) and 1957 (European Atomic Energy Community or EURATOM and European Economic Community) started with six Member States: Belgium, Germany, Italy, France, Luxembourg and the Netherlands.
The first geographical enlargement was realised in 1973 with the accession of Denmark, Ireland and the United Kingdom of Great Britain and Northern Ireland. Greece followed in 1981 and in 1986 Portugal and Spain also joined the European construction. In 1995 the number of Member States increased to 15 with the accession of Austria, Finland and Sweden. The biggest enlargement was realised in 2004 when ten new Member States joined the existing 15: the Czech Republic, Cyprus, Estonia, Hungary, Latvia, Lithuania, Malta, Poland, the Slovak Republic and Slovenia. Three years later, in 2007, Bulgaria and Romania followed. The last European enlargement dates from 2013, when Croatia joined the European construction. In March 2017, the United Kingdom of Great Britain and Northern Ireland activated Article 50 of the Treaty on the European Union, expressing their determination to leave the European Union. Following this step, both parties started negotiating the modalities of the United Kingdom's departure, which initially would have resulted in the withdrawal of the country at the latest in March 2019 (see also para 3.2.2). However at the time of the completion of the manuscript of this book, the ultimate date of the withdrawal is highly uncertain.
In the meantime, the three initial communities have merged into one single organisation, the European Union (EU), the political goals of which have expanded much larger than the initial economic aims of the 1950s.

The 1972 Directive instructs the – then six – Member States to introduce compulsory motor third party liability insurance.[15] Cover has to be provided for the entire territory of the Communities. Once that has been achieved, the Bureaux of the six countries can conclude agreements in which they undertake to guarantee the compensation of any damage caused by vehicles originating from one of the other Member States, according to their national legislation. Once such agreements have been concluded and under the condition that this guarantee also extends to uninsured vehicles, insurance checks on the Green Card at the frontiers can be abolished as far as vehicles originating from the Member States are concerned. This not only applies to checks at internal borders but also at the external borders of the EEC. For vehicles from third countries, the checks on the Green Card in principle stay in place, but once they have entered the EEC they would no longer be checked at the internal borders.

The concept of 'normally based' is introduced to determine from which Member State a vehicle is originating. The registration plate – as in the original Nordic

15. We call to mind that this type of insurance was already compulsory in five of the six founding Member States, Italy being the only country where it still had to be introduced in 1971.

example – is the criterion. If certain types of vehicles are not required to be registered but bear an insurance plate or other distinguishing sign, that sign determines the country in which it is normally based. In the absence of even an insurance or other plate, the Member State of the domicile of the person who has the custody of the vehicle is the decisive criterion. In the course of the years to come, this criterion is repeatedly refined but not its fundamentals: a vehicle is admitted without checks on a Green Card if it bears the registration plate or the insurance or other plate of a Member State, or in the absence of such plates if the custodian is domiciled in another Member State.

The agreements that facilitate the abolishment of border checks initially are referred to as *Supplementary Agreements*. Supplementary to the Uniform Agreements which also remain applicable in the relations between the Bureaux of the Member States. The criterion to determine whether an accident falls within the scope of a *Supplementary Agreement* is the same as under the Directive: a vehicle is normally based in a Member State if it bears a registration plate of that State. The rules about vehicles bearing insurance plates or other distinguishing signs, or no plate at all, are also copied in the Agreements.

The fact that Germany has similar agreements with Austria, Czechoslovakia and Hungary, countries which at that time did not adhere to the EEC, makes it necessary – or at least highly desirable – to extend the system to these three countries. The admission of Denmark in 1973 (simultaneously with the UK and Ireland) makes a similar agreement with Norway, Sweden and Finland a necessity, in view of the arrangements already in place between these four countries since the 1930s. A failure to extend the system to these third countries would obviously have as a consequence that the 'old' checks on Green Cards would have to be reintroduced at the borders of these non-EEC countries with the Member States.

2.5 From 1972 until 1990: 2ND and 3RD Motor Insurance Directives

The abolishment of the checks on Green Cards at the internal borders of the EEC are a very practical and concrete step forward towards an internal market, an area of free movement of persons, goods, services and capital. But other aspects of a less direct nature also can be seen as impediments to such free movement, especially of persons.

Although insurance is compulsory in all Member States, the policy conditions as required under the national legislations are far from being harmonised. Sums of cover, policy conditions, rights of victims against the insurer, opposable policy exceptions, every country has mixed its own cocktail. Harmonisation is seen as a means to bring the internal market forward.

The 1st Directive only contains the provision that a policy of motor insurance has to provide cover in the entire Communities. The 2nd Motor Insurance Directive takes the first material step.[16] Both material damage and bodily injury have hence forthwith to be insured. The Directive also introduces minimum amounts insured (the amounts will remain unchanged until the 5th Directive of 2005).

A further improvement is a restriction to apply legal or policy exclusions or limitations in the relation between insurer and the person injured: the insurer may not exclude or limit the compensation of bodily injuries of members of the family of the person insured, the driver of the vehicle or any other person whose liability is covered under the policy, merely on grounds of their family relationship.

Another 'novelty' – although not in all Member States since several of the Member States already know the concept – is the introduction of the Guarantee Fund, with the mission to intervene for the consequences of accidents caused by uninsured or unidentified vehicles. The minimum protection of the Guarantee Funds (accidents caused by uninsured and unidentified liable parties, damage to property, although with serious restrictions, bodily injury and the concept of subsidiarity of the Guarantee Funds) remain in broad terms the basis of their work until the present day.

In 1990 the EEC takes a further step on the road to harmonised cover. The 3rd Motor Insurance Directive brings more restrictions to the possibility for the insurer to apply legal or policy restrictions against the third party victim.[17] Bodily injury of all persons in the vehicle with the exception of the driver has to be covered. The provision of the 1st Directive that the policy should cover the entire Communities is clarified in the sense that this cover will have to be insured at a single premium. In view of the fact that the sums insured vary widely from one Member State to another – some countries provide only the minimum amounts under the 2nd Directive, others give unlimited cover, at least for bodily injury – a new provision states that the policy should provide cover for the amounts prescribed by the legislation of the Member State of the accident, unless the cover under the legislation of the country in which the vehicle is normally based is higher, in which case the latter amounts are applicable.

It is important to emphasise that all Directives provide for a minimum level of harmonisation. Member States may provide for higher protection for victims and

16. Second Council Directive 84/5/EEC of 30 December 1983 on the approximation of the laws of the Member States relating to insurance against civil liability in respect of the use of motor vehicles, OJ L 8, 11.1.1984, p. 17.
17. Third Council Directive 90/232/EEC of 14 May 1990 on the approximation of the laws of the Member States relating to insurance against civil liability in respect of the use of motor vehicles, OJ L 129, 19.5.1990, p. 33.

insured persons and that is common practice in the Member States. In a European Union (substituting the earlier EEC) which is today composed of 28 countries which show substantial differences in economic, cultural and historic development this is only logical.[18]

2.6 Freedom of services in motor insurance

The freedom of movement, which is one of the main instruments of the Communities to realise the internal market, has more aspects than physical border crossings of persons and goods. Capital and services should also be able to cross-borders freely. Insurers already can establish themselves by way of subsidiaries or branch offices in other Member States.[19] In 1990 the time is ripe to enable consumers (motorists) to take out their compulsory MTPL insurance with insurance undertakings established in other Member States. Directive 90/618/EEC ensures that under certain conditions insurers may offer their policies in other Member States than the one of their establishment.[20] These conditions are mainly related to victim protection, which is one of the main objectives of compulsory MTPL insurance: an insurance undertaking intending to provide MTPL in freedom of service will have to give a notification to the authorities in the Member State of service, will have to join the Green Card Bureau of that country, must financially contribute to the Guarantee Fund and will have to nominate a representative. The latter provision ensures that victims of accidents in the country of service will have an entity in their own country to discuss and settle their claim.

> Despite the good intensions of the EEC, it seems to us that cross-border insurance under freedom of service never was enthusiastically embraced by the public in general, except perhaps with multinational enterprises with vehicle fleets in several countries and lease and car rental companies. The reason for this lack of enthusiasm both with insurers and potential insured persons is that, notwithstanding the obvious attempts to harmonise the playing field, MTPL insurance still is a branch of insurance that is predominantly governed by national factors, such as the economic situation, legislation on liability and compensation, local competition on the insurance markets, the influence of social security and, last but not least, cultural aspects related to claims handling. All these factors are essential to set premium rates and technical reserves. For an insurer established abroad they are complicated to assess properly. On top of that, potential insurance buyers – motorists – perhaps also tend to hesitate to trust 'foreign' companies.

18. Following Brexit, the EU will comprise 27 Member States.
19. Council Directive of 24 July 1973 abolishing restrictions on freedom of establishment in the business of direct insurance other than life assurance (73/240/EEC), OJ L 228, 16.8.1973, p. 20.
20. Council Directive 90/618/EEC of 8 November 1990 amending, particularly as regards motor vehicle liability insurance, Directive 73/239/EEC and Directive 88/357/EEC which concern the coordination of laws, regulations and administrative provisions relating to direct insurance other than life assurance, OJ L 330, 29.11.1990, p. 44.

2.7 Developments in the Council of Bureaux

In the early 1970s, the Council of Bureaux counts 27 members, the majority of which are Bureaux of non-EEC Member States. In 2002, that number has already increased to 42. The growth in members in that period is mostly the result of two factors: the end of the Soviet Union, which led to a number of countries which from then on could act in the international playing field as independent nations. The Baltic states, Belarus, Ukraine and Moldova are examples of such new members of the Council of Bureaux.

The second factor is the troubles on the Balkan, which led to the end of Yugoslavia. The former federal republics which together made Yugoslavia, enter the Green Card system as independent members: Slovenia, Croatia, Bosnia-Herzegovina and the Former Yugoslav Republic of Macedonia – since 12 February 2019 the Republic of North Macedonia – are admitted as members, as is some years later Serbia-Montenegro (Montenegro would in 2012 become a member in its own right).

On the level of the Agreements between Bureaux, the Supplementary Agreements are replaced in 1994 by the Multilateral Guarantee Agreement; the Uniform Agreement, although periodically modified, remains basically the same.

2.8 2000: Protection of visitors (4th directive)

It is crucial to note that the Green Card system concentrates on one part of the problems of cross-border victims: it protects only the national victim of an accident provoked by a visiting motorist. The reverse side of the medal – the visitor of another country who meets with an accident and, on his return to his country of domicile, wishes to claim his damages – seems to be neglected. The legislation of the European legislator as described in the previous paragraphs also fails to address the serious issues a visiting victim will meet. It is true that the visiting victim is also in a sense facilitated by the increased level of protection that is provided by especially the 2nd and the 3rd MID. But many practical difficulties remain: he will have to identify the insurance company of the liable motorist, he will have to communicate with that company abroad, probably in a foreign language, in case of a dispute he will have to start legal proceedings in another country. As late as 2000 a solution will be provided with the 4th MID.[21]

21. Directive 2000/26/EC of the European Parliament and of the Council of 16 May 2000 on the approximation of the laws of the Member States relating to insurance against civil liability in respect of the use of motor vehicles and amending Council Directives 73/239/EEC and 88/357/EEC (Fourth motor insurance Directive), OJ L 181, 20.7.2000, p. 65.

It is an interesting question why it has taken so long for the EU to take action. Several answers are possible. One must bear in mind that – historically – a liability insurance was intended to protect the interests of the liable party and, although the increasing emphasis on victim protection has of course broadened the scope of this form of insurance, for a long time this historic aspect played a role in the background. It was also long felt that the victim of an accident provoked by a visiting motorist needed more protection than a visiting victim: one cannot choose the nationality of the opposite liable party. But the choice to travel abroad is of a different nature: if one takes the risk to visit another country one can also buy protection through travel insurance, comprehensive cover for one's vehicle etc.

But is it not true that the issue was first and only addressed by the EU. In the mid-1990s the attention of the Council of Bureaux was drawn to the problem of the protection of visitors, following a question from the European Commission. As a consequence, a working group was created that studied the various aspects of the issue. One of the findings of the Working Group was that a full solution could not be achieved through the Council of Bureaux alone since a number of member Bureaux were restricted in their possibilities to assume responsibilities outside the scope of the Green Card system. Those Bureaux could not act in a capacity comparable to their Green Card role. More specifically they could not take up financial responsibilities and stand as a guarantor for their counterparts in other countries.

The Council of Bureaux' ambitions were therefore too high and the Bureaux had to land with both feet on the ground again. A model agreement – the Protection of visitors Agreement – was created that could be signed bilaterally by those Bureaux that were interested in creating a form of protection of visiting victims. In its basic form the signatories agreed to exchange, following a request of the victim, information related to accidents such as insurance data, police reports, medical information. In an optional section 2 of the Agreement, Bureaux could mandate each other to handle and settle claims on their behalf or on behalf of their member insurance companies with the victims after their return to their country of residence. Although the agreement in its basic form was signed by a substantial number of Bureaux, that was not the case with section 2. Because the basic agreement was of very little help to victims, the success of the Protection of visitors Agreement was – to put it mildly – very moderate.[22] The result was the intervention of the EU on an initiative of the European Parliament. Willi Rothley MEP, Vice-Chair of the Committee on Legal Affairs and Citizen's Rights of the European Parliament, played an essential role in the development and adoption of this new Directive.

22. It is interesting to note that a new version of the Protection of visitors Agreement has been developed in 2012. The purpose is to offer (some) protection to those visiting victims who do not benefit from the fourth Directive, because the accident falls outside the scope of the Directive, for example because the victim is a resident of a non-Member State or the accident takes place in a third country. See *infra*, para 5.8.

The solutions of the 4th Directive are not only different from the ones of the Green Card system, they are also relatively complicated to understand. Basically, the intention of the Directive is to provide the victim of an accident in – primarily – another Member State than the one of their domicile with an access point they can approach to present their demand for compensation, a 'fall back scenario' if the negotiations fail, and a safety net for situations where either the liable motorist or their insurance undertaking cannot be identified within a reasonable span of time.

In order to achieve this, the Directive introduces new 'functions', such as claims representatives and Compensation Bodies, that have some similarities with existing roles such as those of the Bureaux or the Guarantee Funds and nominated correspondents, but with significant differences. The geographical scope of the Directive is also narrower than the Green Card system. And last but not least: the protection of visiting victims – or rather the applicability of the Directive – depends on a series of factors, such as the country of the accident, the domicile of the victim, the country of registration of the liable vehicle and the Member State of establishment of the insurer.

Victims usually can present their claim to the claims representative of the 'liable' insurance undertaking. But under certain circumstances they can or should, on their return, address their claim to the Compensation Body in the Member State of their domicile. In its turn, that body will have a claim for reimbursement on either the Compensation Body or the Guarantee Fund of the Member State where the liable vehicle is normally based, where the insurance company that insured the vehicle is established or of the Member State of the accident. Such a right of recourse can only function properly on the basis of agreements between the entities involved. Therefore, as was the case with the 1st Directive, the 4th Directive states that it only enters into force after the conclusion of such agreements between the Compensation Bodies and the Guarantee Funds of the Member States. Such Agreements were in fact concluded in 2002.

2.9 Developments since 2002

First the developments on EU level. In 2004 and later in 2007 and 2013 a total of 13 new Member States are admitted to the European Union. Quite a number of new independent states in central and eastern Europe join the Union, as well as a number of countries in southern Europe, such as Cyprus and Malta. At the time of completion of this work the EU counts 28 Member States.[23]

23. The decision of the UK to leave the Union will reduce the Membership to 27. It is useful to note that the UK will continue its membership of the Green Card system.

The membership of the Council of Bureaux also increases to 47 since 2016, the new members being mostly countries in eastern Europe. The most significant development within the Council of Bureaux is the replacement of the two sets of Agreements that govern the relations between Bureaux – the Uniform Agreement and the Multilateral Guarantee Agreement – by one single document: the Internal Regulations. The benefit is that the rules that apply to all Bureaux, independently of the nature of their relationship and which deserve an identical interpretation and development can be combined in a common chapter. The rules that differ – because they either deal with the Green Card as a document or with the normally based principle – are brought together into two separate Sections.

In the field of legislation, there are further developments as well. With the coming into force of the 4th Directive, the structure of protection of visitors of cross-border traffic accidents within the European Union seems in broad terms complete: in the large majority of situations, victims can apply to an entity in the country of their residence – being it an insurer, a Bureau, its agent, a nominated correspondent, a claims representative, a Guarantee Fund or a Compensation Body – in order to receive compensation for their damages.
Several loose ends exist however in the eyes of the European legislator and they are addressed in the 5th Directive in 2005.[24] This Directive is a mixed tot of modifications of the previous four Directives with a topping of a few new 'inventions'.

The most important modification is the new method of calculating and determining the minimum amounts of cover. Since the 2nd Directive the amounts have remained unchanged and in the light of inflation the existing amounts are felt to be quite inadequate. The new regime not only increases the levels but also provides for a periodical indexation mechanism.

A novelty is a procedure for an insurance regime for vehicles that are dispatched from one Member State to another.[25] Buyers of – often second hand – vehicles in another Member State than that of their residence frequently meet problems to find insurance cover for the period – usually weeks – during which they go through the procedure of bringing over the vehicle to their home State and reregistering their new property. Insurers in the Member State of origin are not eager to take an unknown foreigner as a customer, whereas insurers in the Member State of desti-

24. Directive 2005/14/EC of the European Parliament and of the Council of 11 May 2005 amending Council Directives 72/166/EEC, 84/5/EEC, 88/357/EEC and 90/232/EEC and Directive 2000/26/EC of the European Parliament and of the Council relating to insurance against civil liability in respect of the use of motor vehicles, OJ L 149, 11.6.2005, p. 14.
25. Within a single market without internal borders, goods can no longer be 'exported'. Hence, the use of the term 'dispatched'.

nation (i.e. the Member State of domicile of the buyer) cannot and may not provide cover for a vehicle with the registration plate of another country.

The new regime, which will be analysed in detail in paragraph 6.2.5.6, is in our opinion as complicated as it is unworkable in practice. It is administratively burdensome and it does not resolve the basic problem: reluctance of insurers.

A third provision worth mentioning is the treatment of deregistered vehicles or vehicles with false, withdrawn or suspended plates. In 1993, the Council of Bureaux, following the *Fournier* decision of the EU Court of Justice, had developed an Agreement dealing with the issue of false plates as a result of which the financial burden of an accident provoked by a vehicle with a false plate would ultimately rest on the insurance market of the Member State of the last genuine registration.[26,27] Not all member Bureaux of the Council of Bureaux were satisfied by that solution and they found a willing ear with the EU. Under the 5th Directive the Guarantee Fund of the Member State of the accident will have to deal with accidents caused by vehicles provided with registration plates which do not or do no longer correspond with the vehicle. The problem is that according to the services of the European Commission, the concept of 'no longer corresponding' encompasses a wide range of situations including cancellation or suspension of the registration or withdrawal of the plate. And since the triggers for cancellation, suspension or withdrawal vary widely from one Member State to another, the result is much confusion in the field of claims handling (see further para 6.2.5.4).

The 5th Directive contains quite a number of other, minor modifications which will be discussed in detail in the following chapters.

In 2009 all previous Directives are brought together into one single document: the codified Directive.[28] The idea behind this operation is to facilitate the use of the existing legislation by the citizen. The content of the Directives is to remain unaltered.

The question is whether this goal can be achieved in the approach of the European legislator: in fact all the previous texts have been put in one document in their chronological order of development. And the result is a rather illogical sequence of provisions. The succession of the various paragraphs of the Directive appear to show very little or no deeper

26. CJEU, Judgment of 12 November 1992, *Fournier*, C-73/89, EU:C:1992:431.
27. CoB Agreement between Signatory Bureaux of the Multilateral Guarantee Agreement concerning vehicles with false registration plates (Agreement signed in Stockholm on 17 September 1993).
28. Directive 2009/103/EC of the European Parliament and of the Council of 16 September 2009 relating to insurance against civil liability in respect of the use of motor vehicles, and the enforcement of the obligation to insure against such liability (codified version), OJ L 263, 7.10.2009, p. 11.

> thought. Provisions of a totally different nature have been put together in a single chapter. The only real advantage is that all EU rules on motor insurance can now be found in one single document. One still has either to go through the entire document to find the provision one is looking for, or be an expert.

The codified Directive is also not to be the end of developments. In May 2018 the European Commission published a proposal for a new Directive, amending the codified Directive, following a public consultation. Whether these proposals will be an improvement for victims, insurers and the Bureaux, Guarantee Funds and Compensation Bodies remains to be seen for the time being.

In this work we will consistently refer to the Articles of the codified Directive and only where a reference to the previous texts can be helpful to understand their background and meaning, we will quote the original Directives.

3 THE GREEN CARD SYSTEM

3.1 THE BASIC PRINCIPLES OF THE GREEN CARD SYSTEM

3.1.1 *The goals of the Green Card system*

As discussed in detail in chapter 2, the Green Card system seeks to fulfil a dual objective:

- On the one hand, the United Nations wished to support and allow further development of cross-border motor traffic. International travel by road was not, of course, considered as an end in itself but as a means to facilitate the economic reconstruction of the European continent in its slow recovery from the devastation brought about by the Second World War. At a later stage, the facilitation of cross-border traffic could also be extended to countries outside the European continent with which Europe has strong ties.
- On the other hand, the United Nations wanted to prevent any reduction in the protection of victims of road traffic accidents. A victim of a road accident, caused by a foreign vehicle, cannot be in a less favourable position than a victim of a road accident caused by a vehicle registered in the country of the accident. We would reiterate that the remit of the United Nations Economic Commission for Europe (UNECE) is restricted to the protection of victims in the country of the accident. UNECE did not intend to provide any protection under the Green Card system for a victim of a road traffic accident in a foreign country.

In that regard, UNECE addressed its Recommendation No. 5 to the governments of the participating countries. This recommendation enshrined the basic principles on which the Green Card system is still based today. In 2004, the content of Recommendation No. 5 was replaced by a new text (Annex 1 of the Revised Consolidated Resolution), which still comprised the same basic principles.[1]

1. Annex 1 of the Revised Consolidated Resolution on the Facilitation of Road Transport (R.E.4) adopted at the sixty-sixth session (17 – 19 February 2004) of the Inland Transport Committee of the Economic Commission for Europe.

3.1.2 National Bureaux

UNECE's Recommendation No. 5, and the new Annex 1 of the Revised Consolidated Resolution, call on the governments of the participating countries to set up a Bureau in each country, which all MTPL insurers are required to join. In turn, that Bureau must join the Council of Bureaux; this is the umbrella organisation for the Green Card system, which acts under the aegis of UNECE.

A Bureau, based on the principles of Recommendation No. 5 and Annex 1 of the Revised Consolidated Resolution, must undertake the following tasks:

- The Bureau must issue insurance certificates (Green Cards) which are valid for one or more states; these are to serve as confirmation that MTPL insurance is in force in respect of the vehicle whose particulars are shown on the Green Card. The Bureau may also authorise its Member insurers to issue Green Cards on its behalf.
- The Bureau guarantees the reimbursement of all compensation paid in another country under the said Green Card.
- The Bureau settles claims for compensation in respect of accidents occurring in the territory for which it is responsible, caused by a vehicle from another country if that vehicle has a Green Card. This claims handling task may be delegated to an agent or correspondent acting on behalf of the Bureau (cf *infra*).

Though the national Bureau must be recognised by the government of the country for which it is responsible, it must equally be able to act and to decide independently. Both the government as well as its Member insurers must respect such autonomy.

The Bureau must be funded by its members, which are all Motor Third Party Liability (MTPL) insurance companies authorised to issue Green Cards under the authority of the said Bureau; all member insurers are jointly and severally liable for the Bureau's obligations.

Example

Let us illustrate the working of the Green Card system and the role of national Bureaux by means of a practical example.

A French resident wants to go on holiday in Italy by car. Before the introduction of the Green Card system, it was not certain that the insurer of the French vehicle would have covered the vehicle while it was in Italy. Even so, it was equally uncertain that such cover would be recognised by the Italian border control authorities. The French traveller would therefore have to take out a so-called frontier insurance at the border; this would cover the vehicle while on Italian soil. If the Frenchman wanted to drive to

Italy through Switzerland, he would similarly have to purchase frontier insurance for that country.
Thanks to the Green Card system, the French traveller can purchase a Green Card in France, providing cover for Italy. The French national Bureau can issue this Green Card and it would serve as international confirmation that the French traveller's vehicle is covered by MTPL insurance. Frontier insurance would no longer be required as the Green Card would be recognised at the Italian border. In case of an accident in Italy for which the French traveller is liable, an Italian victim need not claim compensation from a foreign insurance company in France; rather, such compensation can be sought directly from the Italian national Bureau. This Bureau would assume the role of a 'handling Bureau' in the country of the accident providing compensation in accordance with the relevant Italian legislation. Equally important is the fact that all exchanges between the victim and the Bureau would take place in the victim's native language.
Once the claim is settled, the Italian Bureau (handling Bureau) will then seek full reimbursement from the French insurer of the French vehicle. If, for whatever reason, such reimbursement is not effected, the French Bureau, acting as the 'guaranteeing Bureau', would itself reimburse the Italian Bureau. In this way, the French Bureau delivers the guarantee associated with the Green Card issued under its authority to the French traveller.
As explained later in paragraph 3.4.1, this example shows that the Green Card provides documentary evidence of a guarantee that the claim payment would be refunded, irrespective of the possible invalidity of the underlying insurance cover.

3.1.3 *Conditions for adherence to the Green Card system*

Before being able to access the Green Card system, a country and its Bureau must satisfy a number of conditions. These are described in the Constitution of the Council of Bureaux together with a number of criteria that the Council has listed. A country's candidature, and that of its Bureau, are assessed by a specially established committee within the Council of Bureaux; this is designated as the Application Committee. The latter will evaluate the Constitution of the candidate Bureau and screen the national legislation on compulsory MTPL insurance for motor vehicles before issuing an opinion to the Council's decision-making bodies.

3.1.4 *Relations between national Bureaux: the Internal Regulations*

In paragraph 2.4 we already explained how the original agreement – the Uniform Agreement between Bureaux – was amended by Supplementary Agreements following the introduction of the first European Motor Insurance Directive. These

Supplementary Agreements were, in turn, replaced in 1991 by the Multilateral (Guarantee) Agreement.

In the early years of the millennium, the members of the Council of Bureaux (all national Bureaux participating in the Green Card system) decided to integrate the *Inter-Bureaux Uniform Agreement* and the *Multilateral Agreement* in a single all-encompassing Agreement: the *Internal Regulations.*

The two preceding separate Agreements governed the cooperation between national Bureaux in the context of the two operational variations within the Green Card system in existence since 1972: on the one hand, the Green Card system based on the actual existence of a Green Card; and, on the other hand, the Green Card system based on the presumption of insurance (see para 3.2). With the merger of the two Agreements previously in existence, the Bureaux were seeking a reconciliation of the divergent rules in order to avoid the said agreements being interpreted differently in the two operational variations within the Green Card system.

Unlike the preceding Agreements, the Internal Regulations were not enshrined in an agreement to be subscribed by all participating Bureaux; rather, they were outlined as a set of rules with which the Bureaux had to comply following a binding decision on all member Bureaux made in accordance with the Constitution of the Council of Bureaux. In our opinion, the Internal Regulations can also be considered as a sort of 'General Terms and Conditions' that apply to the implementation of the bilateral agreement between Bureaux. The Internal Regulations were adopted unanimously at the General Assembly held on 30 May 2002 by the Council of Bureaux in Rethymno (Greece).

The decision, not to enshrine the rules for cooperation between Bureaux in an agreement but to require a decision of the General Assembly of the Council of Bureaux for the applicability of the Internal Regulations, offers greater flexibility for subsequent amendments of the document. The decision-making rules of the Council of Bureaux allow the Internal Regulations to be amended by a majority vote. In practice, amendments do seem to have been approved unanimously, or supported by an overwhelming majority. Since their initial approval in 2002, the Internal Regulations have been amended by the General Assembly of the Council of Bureaux in 2008, 2013, 2016 and 2017. New amendments are foreseen to be adopted in 2019.

Article 1 of the Internal Regulations states that the purpose of the regulations is "to govern the reciprocal relations between National Insurers' Bureaux thereby enforcing the provisions of Recommendation No. 5 (…)." It is important to point out, in this regard, that the Internal Regulations only deal with relations between Bureaux.

When agents are acting on behalf of a national Bureau, they are similarly bound by the provisions of the Internal Regulations.[2] The Internal Regulations do not affect relations between other parties involved in cross-border claims.

That refers to insurance companies and correspondents as well as third parties: injured parties and liable persons (whether they are insured or not).[3] Insurance companies and correspondents are free, in principle, to decide for themselves the rules of their reciprocal relations; that is part of their freedom of contract. They may make reciprocal arrangements or rules about the way in which they wish to communicate and the periods within which a response is expected; about the arrangements and the deadlines for repayment of compensation; about the level and method of calculation of management fees etc.

In reaching those agreements, insurance companies and correspondents must observe the basic principles of the Green Card system. They should be encouraged to do so by the national Bureaux, which are expected to convert these principles into the Constitution of the Bureaux and into the cooperation charters that Bureaux enter into with correspondents.

In principle, injured parties and liable persons cannot invoke the Internal Regulations. Their rights and obligations must be defined in national legislation. The Internal Regulations make no provisions concerning any right of recourse of national Bureaux against uninsured liable parties (drivers or keepers of uninsured vehicles). Such right of recourse also needs to be laid down in national legislation.[4]

In practice, the Internal Regulations serve as a reference text for insurance companies and correspondents involved in handling claims resulting from cross-border road traffic accidents. Insurers and correspondents can refer to the Internal Regulations when describing their reciprocal relations in separate agreements. On certain points, it is possible to derogate from the Internal Regulations, as long as the basic principles of the Green Card system are observed.

In order to provide the necessary interpretation, supported by background information, of the Internal Regulations, the Council of Bureaux supplemented this document with an *Explanatory Memorandum to the Internal Regulations*. As its designation implies, this document delivers detailed explanations and background information about the various provisions of the Internal Regulations, and for some rules, provides information about the motivation for introducing them. In this way, the Explanatory Memorandum is a useful instrument for the application and

2. For the role of agents: see para 3.7.3.
3. For the role of correspondents: see para 3.7.4.
4. Cf CJEU, Judgment of 15 June 2017, *Dockevičius*, C-587/15, EU:C:2017:463.

the interpretation of the Internal Regulations. Furthermore, during the routine handling of claims in the context of the Green Card system (which entails about 400,000 claims a year!), questions regularly arise about the correct interpretation of the Internal Regulations. If deemed to be sufficiently important for the day-to-day running of the Green Card system, such issues of interpretation are initially submitted to the relevant Committees within the Council of Bureaux. If the General Assembly of the Council of Bureaux subsequently reaches a consensus on a specific interpretation of an Article of the Internal Regulations, then this decision is integrated in the Explanatory Memorandum. In this manner, the Explanatory Memorandum has steadily become a compilation of decisions which have been taken by the Council of Bureaux at their General Assemblies, which decisions are of importance to the Green Card system and the proper interpretation of the Internal Regulations.

The Court of Justice of the European Union, in a judgment dated 15 June 2017, ruled that it was not competent to interpret the Internal Regulations.[5] Therefore, the Council of Bureaux continues to retain the freedom to decide on the interpretation of the Internal Regulations which, it should be repeated, govern only the relations between the national Green Card Bureaux.

> The facts of the case leading to decision C-587/15 are relevant for a better understanding of the Court's judgment.
> In 2006, an uninsured Lithuanian vehicle caused an accident in Germany, resulting in a German citizen suffering damage. The German Green Card Bureau compensated the German victim and, afterwards, claimed reimbursement from the Lithuanian Bureau. Since both Germany and Lithuania are Member States of the European Union, their cooperation is based on 'deemed insurance cover'; this means that the Lithuanian Bureau has to guarantee all compensations paid by Green Card Bureaux in other EU Member States in respect of accidents caused by vehicles normally based in Lithuania, whether they are validly insured or not. The Lithuanian Bureau immediately respected this obligation under the Green Card system and reimbursed the German Bureau for the compensation paid. Subsequently, it tried to recover its outlay from the Lithuanian driver, owner or holder of the uninsured vehicle.
> In their attempt to secure reimbursement, the Lithuanian Bureau referred to the Internal Regulations of the Council of Bureaux. The uninsured person contested the Bureau's right of recourse and questioned the compensation paid by the German Bureau to the German injured party.
> The conflict between the Lithuanian Bureau and the uninsured person resulted in legal proceedings that escalated to the Lithuanian supreme court; in its deliberations, the latter decided to submit a number of preliminary questions to the European Court of Justice. Such preliminary questions related to the interpretation of the Charter of Fundamental

5. CJEU, Judgment of 15 June 2017, *Dockevičius*, C-587/15, EU:C:2017:463.

Rights of the European Union and of the EU Motor Insurance Directives as well as to the interpretation of the Internal Regulations.
The latter brought to the fore the issue of whether the European Court of Justice actually had jurisdiction to interpret the Internal Regulations. According to Article 267 of the Treaty on the Functioning of the European Union, the Court has jurisdiction "to give preliminary rulings concerning (a) the interpretation of the Treaties, and (b) the validity and interpretation of acts of the institutions, bodies, offices or agencies of the Union." Part of the discussion before the Court was therefore the question whether the Internal Regulations can be considered as an "act of the institutions, bodies, offices or agencies of the Union."
The Advocate General was of the opinion that the Internal Regulations had been subject to evolution, resulting in their gradual incorporation into EU law; this would give the Court the necessary jurisdiction to rule on their interpretation. In his written opinion, the Advocate General described why the context within which the Internal Regulations operate today differ from the time when the Court had ruled in a comparable case on its jurisdiction to interpret an agreement concluded in the framework of the Council of Bureaux.[6]
The Court did not follow the Advocate General's opinion and ruled that it did not have jurisdiction on the interpretation of the Internal Regulations of the Council of Bureaux.

In its ruling, the Court confirmed the private law character of the Internal Regulations; therefore the Council of Bureaux remains the only body competent to interpret the provisions of the Internal Regulations.

The Internal Regulations and the Explanatory Memorandum are both easily accessible on the website of the Council of Bureaux (www.cobx.org).

3.1.5 Conditions for the application of the Green Card system: bilateral agreements between Bureaux

Participation of a national Bureau in the Green Card system, in itself, does not imply that all Member Bureaux are automatically contractually linked to all other Members. Although a national Bureau does become a member of the Council of Bureaux and pays an annual membership fee to the Council, there is no formal, multilateral agreement that is signed with all the other Member Bureaux. Once a Bureau has joined the Green Card system and the Council of Bureaux, it is immediately bound by the Internal Regulations; but in order to make the Internal Regulations applicable to relations between individual Bureaux, separate agreements are required.

6. CJEU, Judgment of 6 October 1987, *Demouche and others*, C-152/83, EU:C:1987:421.

Recommendation No. 5 and Annex 1 of the Revised Consolidated Resolution require the signature of such agreements between Bureaux. Annex 1 assigns a facilitating role to the Council of Bureaux in reaching those agreements. The negotiation and signature of such bilateral agreements are laid down in Article 16 of the Internal Regulations:

> "Bureaux may conclude bilateral agreements between themselves whereby they undertake within the context of their reciprocal relations to abide by the mandatory provisions of these Internal Regulations, as well as the optional provisions specified herein."

The remaining text of Article 16 lays down the practical arrangements to be followed when entering into bilateral agreements.

Signature of bilateral agreements is a logical step when joining the Green Card system and it is to be expected that a new member shall enter into such bilateral agreements with all other members of the Council of Bureaux. As can be deduced from the use of the words 'may conclude', signature is not an obligation. So there are a limited number of national Bureaux that participate in the Green Card system without having entered into agreements with one or more other Bureaux. The consequence is that the Internal Regulations and the operation of the Green Card system cannot apply between the two countries in question.

> If the Bureaux of countries A and B have not signed a bilateral agreement, the insurance companies of both countries cannot specify country A or B respectively on their insurers' Green Cards as a country where the Green Card is valid. If a driver from country A wants to travel to country B, it would be necessary to take out frontier insurance as in the past. That is why it is preferable that, if at all possible, Bureaux should sign agreements with all other members of the Council. National political issues may make it difficult for a Bureau to sign an agreement with another specific Bureau. Examples of this are Iran and Israel.

3.2 The Green Card system in two variants

3.2.1 Introduction

We have so far discussed the Green Card system in the way it was initially conceived by the UNECE: a system facilitating travel between participating countries on the basis of a mutually recognised document, the Green Card. This system, however, still necessitates that at each border crossing, the vehicle is physically stopped, a Green Card is shown and its validity (in respect of the territory being visited) controlled. It goes without saying that such a system is still excessively burdensome and creates a lot of administration. In a continent like Europe, with so many relatively small countries and a tradition of easy cross-border traffic, the physical control of Green Cards at each border crossing would today lead to huge traffic jams and endless waiting lines at the frontiers.

For this reason the European Union, or more correctly its predecessor the European Economic Community (EEC), tried to develop the Green Card system by simplifying it. Inspiration was found in cooperation schemes that were already operational in a number of countries. Instead of admitting vehicles on the basis of a Green Card, the Member States of the European Union accepted that vehicles can travel freely within the entire territory of the European Economic Area, without physical checks at the borders.[7]

When a vehicle causes an accident in the territory of a Member State other than the State from where it originates, the Bureau of the country of the accident would be competent to handle the claim and compensate the injured parties. But in order to determine which Bureau is to reimburse the compensation paid (and – prior to that – whether a vehicle will be admitted to a country without the validity of its Green Card being checked), the handling Bureau will no longer require a Green Card but will establish *where the foreign vehicle is normally based.* Special rules have been developed in order to determine the state where a vehicle is normally based (see further para 3.5.5); but it can be generally affirmed that the registration plate of a vehicle would, in probably more than 95% of the cases, be the criterion.

The major difference between this new system and the existing one lay in the treatment of accidents caused by uninsured vehicles. The guaranteeing Bureau (of the country where a vehicle is normally based) would have to guarantee the consequences of accidents caused by all vehicles normally based in the territory of its competence, whether these vehicles are insured or not. In other words, the new system is based on an (albeit unrealistic) presumption that all vehicles normally based on the territory of a Member State are validly insured. The system is therefore referred to as 'cooperation based on deemed insurance cover'. If a vehicle turns out to be uninsured, then the Bureau of the country where that vehicle is normally based would guarantee the consequences of the accident caused by that vehicle.

Example

Let us explain the difference between both systems again by means of the example, given earlier, of the French citizen wishing to go on holiday in Italy.

7. For the difference between the European Union and the European Economic Area: see para 3.2.2.

Since both France and Italy participate in the European Economic Area, the Green Card of the French vehicle will no longer be controlled at the border between France and Italy. The French vehicle will simply be allowed to enter the Italian territory on the basis of it being registered in France. If the French vehicle causes an accident in Italy and an Italian citizen suffers damage from that accident, the Italian injured party will be able to submit a claim for compensation to the Italian Bureau. The Italian Bureau will communicate with the Italian injured party in Italian and will pay compensation in accordance with the applicable Italian legislation. Once the required compensation has been made, the Italian Bureau will recover its outlay from the French insurer. If the insurer does not reimburse the Italian Bureau on time or if the vehicle turns out to be uninsured, the French Bureau will have to guarantee the reimbursement, no longer on the basis of a Green Card being issued under its authority but on the basis of the liable vehicle being normally based in France.

The system of deemed insurance cover was introduced by the European Economic Community in 1972; that is, nearly twenty years after the initial entry into force of the Green Card system. The 'original' system was however not replaced in all countries; consequently, today both systems co-exist simultaneously and have different territorial scopes of applicability (see further para 3.2.2).

A separate Section of the Internal Regulations (see para 3.1.4) has been specifically dedicated to each of the two different variants of the Green Card system. Whereas the preamble and sections I, IV, V, VI and VII are common to both systems, the following two sections are dedicated to the two variants:
- Section II (Articles 7, 8 and 9) relates to the original Green Card system: 'Specific rules governing contractual relations between Bureaux based on the Green Card';
- Section III (Articles 10 to 15) relates to the system of deemed insurance cover: 'Specific rules governing contractual relations between Bureaux based on deemed insurance cover'.

The following paragraphs will describe the two main variants and the principles and rules of the Green Card system itself in detail.

After describing the geographical scope of the system, we will briefly revert to the insurance cover for cross-border motor traffic in the absence of a Green Card. If no Green Card is available, a motorist can still enter the territory of a country after having purchased a frontier insurance policy. How this is done and what kind of cover is offered by frontier insurance will be described briefly in paragraph 3.3.
After that, the two different variants will be described in paragraphs 3.4 and 3.5; these will tackle the guarantees offered by a Green Card.

Once the specificities of the two variants have been illustrated, we will focus on the operational rules common to both systems. We will describe how the guarantee offered by the system can be invoked (para 3.6) as well as how and by whom the injured party would be compensated for the damage suffered (para 3.7). We will subsequently examine how the body that compensated the injured party can recover its outlay from the insurer concerned or from the guaranteeing Bureau (para 3.8). Finally, we will discuss the importance of financial discipline and financial stability for the continuity of the Green Card system (para 3.9).

3.2.2 *Geographical scope of the Green Card system*

Following the adoption of Recommendation N° 5, in 1953 the Green Card system was operational in thirteen participating countries.[8] Step by step, additional states joined the system; today, the Green Card system operates in 51 countries, for which 47 Bureaux, members of the Council of Bureaux, are competent. The reason for the difference between the number of countries and the number of competent Bureaux lies in the fact that certain Bureaux are competent for more than one territory. The Swiss national Bureau operates also as national Motor Insurers' Bureau for Liechtenstein. The French Bureau is competent for France and Monaco, whereas the Italian Bureau also is additionally competent for San Marino and Vatican City. Andorra, on the other hand, was initially serviced by the Spanish Bureau but is now a member of the Council of Bureaux on its own right since 1996.

Mainly conceived as a European 'structure', the Green Card system operates also in a number of non-European countries, such as Iran, Morocco and Tunisia. The geographical scope of the Green Card system has been defined by the Council of Bureaux as applying to countries lying to the West of the Ural Mountains and the Caspian Sea as well as states bordering the Mediterranean Sea. Taking into account the existing members of the Council of Bureaux, the following countries lie within the scope of the Green Card system and are potential Members:

- Countries lying to the West of the Ural Mountains and the Caspian Sea: Armenia, Georgia and Kazakhstan;
- Countries bordering the Mediterranean Sea: Algeria, Egypt, Lebanon, Libya and Syria.

8. Belgium, Denmark, Finland, France, Germany (at that time only the Federal Republic of Germany ('West Germany'); the German Democratic Republic ('East Germany') joined the system only later), Greece, Ireland, Luxembourg, the Netherlands, Norway, Sweden, Switzerland (the Bureau of which also operates for Liechtenstein) and the United Kingdom. Czechoslovakia was one of the 'founding fathers' of the Council of Bureaux, actively participating in the discussions in London between 1949 and 1953, but for political reasons the Bureau could only activate its membership in 1956.

The second variant of the Green Card system, the system of deemed insurance cover, is characterised by a comparatively smaller geographical scope, focussed on the European continent. As will be described in more detail in paragraph 3.5, the system of deemed insurance cover is based on the Motor Insurance Directives of the European Union which are applicable in the European Economic Area (EEA). The EEA is comprised of:

- The 28 Member States of the (pre-Brexit) European Union;
- Iceland, Liechtenstein and Norway, which are the three states of the European Free Trade Association (EFTA) that decided to participate in the EEA. Switzerland, also a member of the EFTA, decided in a referendum in 1992 not to take part in the EEA.

Countries not participating in the EEA can, on the basis of a special agreement, participate in the system of deemed insurance cover. This is at the moment the case of Andorra, Serbia and Switzerland. Together with the 31 states of the EEA, these three countries have concluded the so-called Multilateral Agreement, resulting in the applicability of the system of deemed insurance cover (based on the territory in which a vehicle is normally based) as per 1 March 2019 in the following 34 states:

- The 28 Member States of the European Union: Austria, Belgium, Bulgaria, Croatia, Cyprus, the Czech Republic, Denmark, Estonia, Finland, France, Germany, Greece, Hungary, Ireland, Italy, Latvia, Lithuania, Luxembourg, Malta, the Netherlands, Poland, Portugal, Romania, the Slovak Republic, Slovenia, Spain, Sweden and the United Kingdom;
- The three countries of the EFTA participating in the EEA: Iceland, Liechtenstein and Norway;
- Three other European countries outside the EEA having signed the Multilateral Agreement: Andorra, Serbia and Switzerland[9].

It should be emphasised that, although all countries of the Multilateral Agreement are today situated on the European continent, nothing withholds the system of deemed insurance cover to be applicable in non-European countries as well. It is therefore theoretically possible that countries such as Morocco or Tunisia could adhere to the system by becoming a signatory to the Multilateral Agreement.

The entry of vehicles coming from Andorra, Serbia or Switzerland into the territory of the EEA without any control on the existence of insurance (or rather the existence of a valid Green Card or frontier insurance) necessitates a specific decision of

9. In 2019, the Bureau of Bosnia and Herzegovina became a signatory of the Multilateral Agreement, resulting in the system of deemed insurance cover also being applicable in that country as of the date that will be decided by the European Commission.

the European Commission. This is stipulated in Article 8 of the codified Motor Insurance Directive (see further para 3.5.1).[10,11]

On 29 March 2017, the United Kingdom of Great Britain and Northern Ireland activated Article 50 of the Treaty on the European Union. Depending on the negotiations between the United Kingdom and the European Union, this should have resulted in this country no longer being a Member State of the European Union after 29 March 2019. At the time of finalising the manuscript of this book, the political process in the UK has made the actual date of activation of Brexit highly uncertain. Moreover, it is not yet clear how the future relationship between the United Kingdom and the European Union will be shaped and in what form the Green Card system will be applicable in the United Kingdom.

Even if the United Kingdom will no longer be part of the European Union and, probably, no longer participate in the EEA either, it will continue to be a signatory of the Multilateral Agreement. Unless of course the decision would be made that the British Motor Insurers' Bureau (MIB) would withdraw from the Multilateral Agreement. In the latter case, the United Kingdom will fall back on Section II of the Internal Regulations and a Green Card or frontier insurance policy would be necessary to enter or leave the United Kingdom. On the other hand, if the MIB opts to remain a signatory of the Multilateral Agreement, a specific European Commission decision would be required, in accordance with the said Article 8 of the codified Motor Insurance Directive, before UK vehicles can enter the territory of the EEA without their insurance cover being checked.

An overview of all the existing countries taking part in the Green Card system, together with the year of their adherence can be found in Annex 1. A map of the system and the different countries is also available on the website of the Council of Bureaux: www.cobx.org.

10. Directive 2009/103/EC of the European Parliament and of the Council of 16 September 2009 relating to insurance against civil liability in respect of the use of motor vehicles, and the enforcement of the obligation to insure against such liability (codified version), OJ L 263, 07.10.2009, p. 11.
11. For Andorra: Commission Decision of 29 November 2005 on the application of Council Directive 72/166/EEC with regard to checks on insurance against civil liability in respect of the use of motor vehicles, OJ L 315, 1.12.2005, p.16; for Serbia: Commission Implementing Decision of 22 November 2011 on the application of Directive 2009/103/EC of the European Parliament and of the Council with regard to checks on insurance against civil liability in respect of the use of motor vehicles, OJ L 310, 25.11.2011, p. 17; for Switzerland: Commission Decision of 28 July 2003 on the application of Council Directive 72/166/EEC relating to checks on insurance against civil liability in respect of the use of motor vehicles, OJ L 192, 31.7.2003, p. 23.

3.3 Cross-border traffic without Green Card: frontier insurance

One of the preconditions set by the Council of Bureaux and UNECE for a country to participate in the Green Card system is the existence of compulsory MTPL insurance. It follows that a vehicle arriving at the border of such a country will require a valid Green Card for the territory to be visited. If this is not available, the motorist must provide evidence of adequate MTPL insurance before being allowed to enter the territory. Different possibilities exist, depending on the situation and the country to be visited:

- The vehicle originates from a third country and wishes to enter a country participating in the Green Card system, which is not a signatory of the Multilateral Agreement. The motorist can purchase frontier insurance providing cover exclusively for the country visited. In case cover is required for a wider geographical scope of countries that are participating in the Green Card system, a Green Card will have to be delivered, providing cover for the countries that the motorist would be visiting;[12]
- The vehicle originates from a country participating in the Green Card system and wishes to enter the territory of another country similarly forming part of the Green Card system. The simplest way would be for the motorist to purchase a Green Card in their country of origin. Alternatively, the motorist can purchase frontier insurance at the border, to which a Green Card can optionally be added, depending on the territories to be visited;
- If the vehicle (whatever country of origin) arrives at the border of a non-EEA country the Bureau of which is however a signatory of the Multilateral Agreement (e.g. Serbia), it would still be possible to obtain frontier insurance exclusively for that country. Once the vehicle arrives at the border of a country participating in the EEA however (e.g. Croatia), the motorist would be obliged to obtain Green Card cover (by means of frontier insurance) for the entire territory of the EEA. Since there are no insurance checks at the internal borders of the EEA, a Green Card providing cover for Croatia would, by law, have to provide cover for all the other EEA states;
- Frontier insurance may also be necessary for a vehicle for which a Green Card has been issued but not for the country that the motorist wishes to enter. If, for instance, a Russian vehicle for which a Green Card was obtained providing cover exclusively for Ukraine arrives at the border between Ukraine and Moldova and wishes to enter that country, the Russian motorist would have to buy frontier insurance providing cover for Moldova. If the same vehicle with the same Green Card (valid only for Ukraine) arrives at the border with Hungary, it will need Green Card cover (which can be bought by means of frontier insur-

12. This is one of the few exceptions where a Bureau can issue Green Cards for vehicles that are not registered in the Bureau's country. See further para 3.4.3.1.

ance) for the entire territory of the EEA, since Hungary belongs to the EEA. Insurance cover cannot be provided for Hungary exclusively; entering that country necessarily requires MTPL insurance cover for the entire EEA territory.

3.4 The Green Card system based on the existence of a Green Card

3.4.1 *The Green Card as a guarantee document*

The Green Card is essentially a guaranteeing document. It guarantees that any compensation for harm, caused by the vehicle for which the Green Card is issued, will be reimbursed to the body that has initially compensated the damage caused.

Since the Green Card is a guaranteeing document, it cannot be considered as proof of MTPL insurance. Obviously, a Green Card should only be issued in respect of a vehicle for which a valid MTPL insurance has been purchased, valid for all the countries indicated on the Green Card. But the guarantee related to the Green Card will not be subordinated to the validity of the underlying insurance cover. A contractual deficiency of the underlying insurance contract (for instance, because the insured consciously described the risk in a wrongful way or because the policy has been cancelled due to non-payment of premium) will not have any influence on the guarantee provided by the Green Card. Conceived from the outset as a guarantee document, the entity handling a specific claim must necessarily have the guaranteed certainty that any claim compensated under coverage of a Green Card shall be reimbursed on the basis of that Green Card.

The provisions under Section II of the Internal Regulations (contractual relations between Bureaux based on the Green Card) require the presence of an identified Green Card before the claims handling process can start. In the absence of an identified Green Card, the handling entity will not be allowed to initiate any claims handling activities. This is one of the main differences with the guarantee provided under the system of deemed insurance cover, where the presence of a Green Card is not required for the claims handling process to commence. The concept of an identified Green Card will be discussed later in paragraph 3.6.2.

If a Green Card cannot be provided by a motorist at the site of the accident, the Bureaux still cooperate between themselves in order to determine whether any Green Card was issued for the vehicle in question. In such cases, the Bureau of the vehicle's state of origin will try to find in the relevant databases any trace of a Green Card issued for that vehicle. The compulsory deadlines to give such information, as provided in the Internal Regulations, will however not apply in case of the absence of an actual Green Card. If it is clear that no Green Card has ever been issued for the vehicle liable for the accident, the provisions of the Green

Card system will not be applicable and the guarantee provided by a Green Card cannot be relied upon. In that case the vehicle will, in most countries, be considered as an uninsured vehicle and the victim of the accident will have to rely on other forms of compensation. In all probability, the Guarantee Fund of the country of the accident will be competent to handle the case; however, national legislation may provide for limitations in the protection scheme offered by the Guarantee Fund in such circumstances (for the intervention of Guarantee Funds in case of uninsured vehicles: see chapter 4).

Since the Green Card is a guarantee document delivering the certainty that any damage caused will be compensated in accordance with the rules applicable in the country of the accident, the guarantee applies equally to false or unauthorised Green Cards. The checks on the presence and validity of a Green Card, carried out by the border control authorities, cannot provide a detailed and exhaustive inspection of the Card itself. Therefore, even falsified Green Cards will have to be guaranteed by the Bureau under the authority of which the Card is purported to be issued. The precise modalities of this guarantee for false or unauthorised Green Cards will be further discussed in paragraph 3.6.2.2.

3.4.2 The nature of the guarantee offered by a Green Card

The Green Card, as a guarantee document, does not only provide a guarantee for the benefit of the Card holder but also for the benefit of the victim of an accident caused by the vehicle for which the Card had been issued:

- The holder of the Green Card may rely on the said guarantee in order to be confident that any damage caused will be compensated and reimbursed by the insurer to which a premium was paid in return for the Green Card cover. The injured party may still make a claim directly to the liable party but the latter can rely on the guarantee offered by the Green Card to make sure that any compensation to be paid will be covered by the insurance and/or the guarantee provided by the Green Card;
- The injured party, on the other hand, will have the certainty that any damage will be compensated in accordance with the rules of liability and of compensation applicable in the country of the accident. The cover that will be offered by the Green Card will be the cover that is required under the legislation on MTPL insurance of the country of the accident, independently of the cover that is provided for in the country of the origin of the vehicle.

The latter principle is one of the basic characteristics of the Green Card system: the Green Card guarantees that the cover provided to both the Card holder and the injured party will be the mandatory cover provided in the country of the accident. By crossing the border under the protection of a Green Card, the motorist will immediately benefit from the compulsory cover provided in the visited country; and this in accordance with the compulsory MTPL insurance legislation applicable in that country. This is equally applicable even though the compulsory insurance cover required in the visited country would be higher than in the Green Card holder's country of origin.

Example
We return to the earlier example of a French motorist travelling to Italy. As from the moment the French motorist enters the Italian territory, the respective vehicle will be covered by the compulsory third party insurance requirements applicable in Italy, whatever the requirements applicable in France, the country of origin, may be.
The same principle will obviously apply inversely; that is for an Italian motorist travelling to France. The maximum amount of cover applicable in Italy in respect of third party personal injury, is (on 1 March 2019) € 6,070,000. In France, however, there is no capping on the maximum amount of cover under French legislation on MTPL insurance in case of personal injuries; the cover for bodily damage must be unlimited. Once the Italian vehicle enters the French territory, the comparatively higher French insurance cover will be applicable. The Italian motorist will benefit from the unlimited cover for third party personal injuries in case of an accident on the French territory. At the same time, the injured party in France will not be subject to the limitations of insurance cover applicable in Italy, but will have the guarantee to benefit from the unlimited cover for personal injury as required by French legislation.

In addition to the applicable amounts of insurance cover the rules on liability and on compensation of damage will normally be those applicable in the country of accident. In this way, the victim of an accident caused by a foreign visiting vehicle will not be in a less favourable position when compared to the victim of an accident caused by a vehicle originating from the country of the accident itself. There are exceptions to this rule of the *lex loci delicti commissi* (the law of the place of the accident will be the applicable law), but these will be discussed in chapter 8 (Aspects of Private international law).

As already stated, the cover provided by the Green Card will be the one in force mandatorily in the state where the accident occurred, even if the latter is higher than that in the country of origin of the vehicle concerned. But what if the situation is reversed? What if the cover to be provided in the country of the accident is comparatively lower than the mandatory cover in the vehicle's country of origin? This question will be relevant if the damage caused in the visited country will be higher than the maximum cover applicable in the country of the accident. In that case, the Bureau, agent or correspondent in the country of the accident will have to notify the insurer of the vehicle about the part of the damage that exceeds the limits applicable in the country of the accident. This is stipulated, as far as it concerns Bureaux and agents, in Article 3(5) of the Internal Regulations and will be explained in more detail in paragraph 3.7.2.[13]

> **Example**
> If the French vehicle, benefiting in the country of origin from an unlimited cover for bodily injury, causes an accident in Italy, the 'limited' Italian amount of cover will be applicable. If the compensation awarded however exceeds the amount of € 6,070,000 as applicable in Italy, the injured party could, for the amount in excess of the Italian capped limit, address a claim directly against the French liable driver. Since, however, the French driver should normally benefit in France from the availability of a higher cover (and should have already paid premium for that higher cover in France), it seems logical that the handling entity (Italian Bureau, agent or correspondent) would take liaise with the insurer concerned in order to make the necessary arrangements enabling the French driver to continue benefitting from the comparatively higher French cover for which the policyholder paid premium.

3.4.3 *Issuance, form and content of the Green Card*

The issue and delivery of Green Cards is determined by Article 7 of the Internal Regulations. The format of a Green Card is stipulated in Article 2(11) which describes the content of the Card.

3.4.3.1 *Issue and delivery of the Green Card*

Article 7(1) of the Internal Regulations:

> "Each Bureau shall be responsible for printing its Green Cards or shall authorise its members to print them."[14]

This provision clearly places the responsibility for the issue and delivery of Green Cards on the national Motor Insurers' Bureaux. A number of Green Card Bureaux still 'centralise' the issue of Green Cards under their exclusive control as the sole body responsible to issue, print and deliver the guarantee document. However,

13. A related provision can be found in Article 14 of the codified MID. See further para 6.2.10.4.
14. The text of Article 7(1) of the Internal Regulations is likely to be modified after the completion of the manuscript of this book in the annual meeting of the Council of Bureaux in June 2019 in the following way: "*Each Bureau shall be responsible for establishing the rules on the issuance and delivery of Green Cards under the Bureau's authority.*" The new wording clarifies that it is also permitted to provide policyholders with Green Cards in a digital format such as a pdf document, allowing them to print the document themselves. See *infra* para 3.4.3.2.

Article 7(1) also provides for the possibility (not the obligation) for a Bureau to mandate insurers, members of the Bureau, to print the Green Cards and to deliver them to the insured. Nevertheless, in that case, the issuing authority remains the national Motor Insurers' Bureau, under the authority of which the Green Card has been issued and which will still remain the final guaranteeing body in the Green Card system. Moreover, an insurer can, in turn, be authorised by its national Bureau to mandate insurance intermediaries (brokers, agents, ...) to print and deliver Green Cards. Once again, this outsourced mandate will not alter the responsibility of the insurance undertaking nor the guarantee to be delivered by the Bureau under the authority of which the Green Card is issued. At the end, the Green Card document specifically states (in box 2) "issued under the authority of", followed by the official name of the national Motor Insurers' Bureau.

It goes without saying that, when Insurers or insurance intermediaries are authorised to print and deliver Green Cards, they will have to respect the official model or models as proposed by the Council of Bureaux and approved by the United Nations Economic Commission for Europe (UNECE).

Bureaux and insurance undertakings may only issue Green Cards for vehicles registered in the country for which the Bureau is competent (Article 7(2) Internal Regulations). This means that:
- The Bureau or its member insurers may only deliver Green Cards for vehicles registered in or bearing the registration plate of the country for which the Bureau is competent. The Romanian Bureau or a Romanian insurer cannot, for instance, issue any Green Card for a vehicle registered in Bulgaria;
- The Bureau or its member insurers can only deliver Green Cards for vehicles registered in the country for which the Bureau is competent and which is recognised as such by the United Nations. Since the Council of Bureaux is operating under the aegis of the United Nations Economic Commission for Europe, it is logically bound by the borders of the countries as they are internationally recognised by that organisation.

There are two exceptions to Article 7(2) of the Internal Regulations, according to which Green Cards can only be delivered for vehicles registered in the territory of a Bureau's competence:
1. According to Article 7(3) of the Internal Regulations, and in conjunction with the text of the Explanatory Memorandum pertaining to that Article, the Council of Bureaux can agree that member insurers of a given Bureau can be authorised to issue Green Cards for vehicles registered in any country where no Bureau exists. The authorisation is, however, subject to the requirement that the insurer wishing to issue Green Cards in such country is established in that country.

An 'establishment' is, according to the Explanatory Memorandum, to be understood as any office, branch or subsidiary in the country concerned which is officially approved by the authorities for the transacting of motor insurance in that country. In short: a permanent presence. This requirement to have an establishment in the so-called 'third state' can be justified by the need of a 'contact point' for policyholders in their country of origin.
A number of other criteria are taken into consideration before the Council of Bureaux accepts that a certain Bureau can authorise its members to deliver Green Cards for vehicles in a country where no Bureau exists. These criteria can be found in the Explanatory Memorandum under Article 7(3) of the Internal Regulations.
It goes without saying that the approval by the Council of Bureaux to issue Green Cards in such third country is limited to vehicles registered in that country only and cannot be extended to any other third country if no approval was issued for it. Moreover, the authorisation to issue Green Cards for vehicles registered in a country where no Bureau exists may result in a substantially larger exposure of the Bureau in question for false and unauthorised Green Cards (see further para 3.6.2.3).

Example
As an example, the Bureau of Russia has the possibility, after having received the approval of the Council of Bureaux, to authorise Russian member insurers to issue Green Cards for vehicles registered in Georgia. Since Georgia does not participate in the Green Card system and the Georgian Motor insurers' Bureau is not a member of the Council of Bureaux, Georgian motorists can obtain a Green Card from a Russian insurer, duly authorised by the Russian Bureau, on condition that this Russian insurer has an establishment in Georgia. If Georgia, which lies within the geographical scope of the Green Card system, would eventually join the Green Card system, such possibility will come to an end, since the condition that there may be no Bureau (member of the Council of Bureaux) in Georgia will no longer be fulfilled.
The authorisation to issue Green Cards for vehicles is limited in this case to Georgia and cannot be considered as granted, for instance, for Armenia.

2. A second exception to the principle that a Bureau may only issue Green Cards for vehicles registered in the territory for which it is competent, is to be found in the provision of frontier insurance (see *supra* para 3.3). As discussed earlier, if a vehicle arrives at a border without any Green Card valid for the country the driver intends to visit, the motorist can purchase frontier insurance for the country or for a number of other countries. In the latter case, the frontier insurance will be combined with a Green Card, issued under the authority of the

Bureau of the country the driver wishes to visit but linked to a vehicle that is not registered in the territory of that Bureau's competence. Moreover, if the country in question forms part of the European Economic Area (EEA), the entry to that country will automatically result in an authorisation to enter all the other states of the EEA. The reason is that the EEA is to be considered as one common territory without internal border controls; consequently, insurance cover for one state automatically entails insurance cover for the entire territory of the EEA. As a result, if frontier insurance is delivered for one EEA state, it will have to be combined with a Green Card issued for the foreign vehicle concerned and with cover for the entire EEA.
It is relevant to emphasise that this constitutes also an exception to the principle that Green Cards may only be delivered to vehicles registered in countries where no Bureau exists. A Polish frontier insurance (with additional Green Card) may be delivered to a Russian vehicle, although Russia has a Bureau and is a member of the Council of Bureaux.

3.4.3.2 Form of the Green Card

The Green Card, as a guarantee document, should be easily recognisable and should allow border control authorities to verify the content of the Card quickly. In order to achieve this goal, the Green Card must correspond to one of the two fixed models (portrait or landscape layout) and should contain a number of easily verifiable data entries. The content of the Card, displayed in the different boxes or headers, will be described in paragraph 3.4.3.3.

The format of the Green Card was developed by the Council of Bureaux and then submitted for approval to UNECE. The specific body competent for the approval of the Green Card model is the Working Party on Road Transport of the Inland Transport Committee of UNECE.

Article 14 of Annex 1 of the Revised Consolidated Resolution on the Facilitation of Road Transport (see earlier para 3.1.1) stipulates the following conditions regarding the format and language of the Green Card:

> "The Green Card shall conform in colour, content and layout to the models referred to in paragraph 3 above. The dimensions of the Green Card may be varied, provided that the format is not changed, but the overall size of the document shall not be larger than A4. The Green Card shall be made out in the language of the Bureau of issue and its title shall also be given in English and French. All data on the Green Card shall be recorded in the Latin alphabet with the option, if desired, to additionally record the same data in other alphabets."

This text clarifies that each Bureau is free to decide on the dimensions of the Green Card, as long as it does not exceed the A4 format (A4 paper size in accordance with the ISO 216 standard: 210 mm x 297 mm). Moreover, Bureaux are also free to produce the document in portrait or landscape layout.

The standardised format, with different data entries displayed in separate boxes or headers each with a specific number, facilitates a better understanding of the document, even if not drafted in one common language. Only the first header, displaying the name of the document, must be written in the official language of the issuing Bureau as well as in English (*International Motor Insurance Card*) and French (*Carte internationale d'assurance automobile*). All the other headers are only displayed in one language; that is, the official language of the Bureau under whose authority the Green Card is issued. It is surprising that both the Revised Consolidated Resolution and the Explanatory Memorandum to the Internal Regulations remain silent on the situation of countries where more than one official language exists. It may be presumed that the Bureaux concerned also have the freedom to give directions regarding the use of languages on the Green Cards issued under their authority.

Today, the 47 Bureaux participating in the Green Card system still operate and interact on the basis of a Green Card document which does not deviate much from the originally conceived document brought into circulation in 1952-1953. It is still a green-coloured paper document that has not been replaced (yet) by any electronic means. Since the document needs to be controlled at many border crossing points and needs to be checked by police authorities in case of accidents, the transition to a digitalised format of the Card is not yet possible today.

The Bureaux participating in the Green Card system have always been aware of a paper document's 'easy' exposure to forgery. However, the extent of such exposure has obviously increased as a result of the technological advancements taking place since the introduction of the Green Card. In the early years of the Green Card system, the relatively low cost of purchasing Green Card cover did not justify the 'investment' and the risk necessary to falsify the green paper document.[15] With the technological progress that has since taken place, it is of course no big deal anymore to duplicate an official Green Card. This is one of the reasons why the Council of Bureaux is considering a transition towards a more modern 'carrier' for the guarantee provided by the Green Card system (see further chapter 9: Future Devel-

15. The difference in approach can be illustrated by a letter written by the Chairman of the Council of Bureaux in 1951 to the Chairman of the Dutch motor insurance association, concerned with the risk of counterfeit in relation to Green Cards: "When one remembers the class of persons who tours the Continent and the fact that a Green Card will be obtained so easily without cost, it is difficult to see why anybody should take the trouble to run the risk of forging a card. Even a crook will not run the risk of forgery for the sake of saving three Swiss Francs." The latter amount was the price imposed at the border of Switzerland to obtain insurance cover in that country and taken as an indication of the costs of a Green Card.

opments). Nevertheless, the new format must be acceptable to all participating Bureaux and their insurer members.

Meanwhile, insurers are searching for ways to reduce the operational costs related to the printing and distribution of Green Cards. In this regard, consideration was given to the possibility of providing Green Cards in a standardised electronic format (for instance pdf) to their insured persons and allowing them to print the guarantee document themselves. The Council of Bureaux, in principle, does not want to hinder such development and leaves national Bureaux the possibility to approve this practice. But one simple and logical condition must be met: the Green Card must be coloured green. That entails the obligation on the insured to either print the document on green paper or to print it in green colour. A 'Green' Card displayed black on white will not be considered by national Bureaux and border control authorities as a valid Green Card.[16]

The issue of finding easy ways to provide Green Cards to motorists is all the more relevant in countries where the Green Card is not only an international guarantee document but is, by law, also recognised as the compulsory national proof of insurance. For instance, in countries like Belgium, the Czech Republic and France, the Green Card is a compulsory document that must be available in the vehicle (registered in the country in question) in case of checks on (compulsory MTPL) insurance.

Whenever the format or content of the model Green Card changes (e.g. when a new country is admitted to the Green Card system and the respective country code is to be added to the Green Card model), the 'old' existing Green Cards still remain valid for a period of two years. Green Cards issued in accordance with the 'old' model are still recognised during that transitional period but since the new country is not mentioned on that 'old' Card format, cover within the 'new' country will be denied as long as it is not mentioned on the Card. Once the two-year period is over, the old Green Cards are no longer considered to be valid.

3.4.3.3 Content of the Green Card

As already mentioned, the Green Card format is made up of eleven different headers or boxes. These eleven items in the order as they appear on the Green Card are the following:

16. At the time of finalising this manuscript, the possibility to deviate from the obligatory green colour was discussed in the Council of Bureaux. It is possible that 'Green' Cards printed black on white will be accepted in the near future. Moreover, the possibility granted to individuals to print their Green Cards themselves may result in these Green Cards not always being printed recto-verso, another mandatory formal requirement. Therefore, the Council of Bureaux is considering making the reverse side of the Green Card optional.

1. **The title of the document** (in capitals): 'INTERNATIONAL MOTOR INSURANCE CARD'. As explained above, this title must appear in English and French ('CARTE INTERNATIONALE D'ASSURANCE') as well as in the official language of the issuing Bureau. The order in which the main languages appear on the document is at the discretion of the national Bureaux. As also mentioned in Article 14 of Annex 1 of the Revised Consolidated Resolution (see *supra* para 3.4.3.2), the text must be in the Latin alphabet.
2. **'ISSUED UNDER THE AUTHORITY OF'**: the identity of the issuing Bureau is to be specified. The official name of the Bureau, in the language of the Bureau (but also in the Latin alphabet as required by the Revised Consolidated Resolution), is to be used.
3. **'VALID FROM ... TO ...'**: the period of validity of the certificate must be stated, specifying the day, month and year of the first and last validity date.
   The Explanatory Memorandum specifies the validity period to include entire calendar days (00:00 – 24:00 hrs). This may initially seem a minor detail; but without this specification fraud and abuse would be facilitated. Every professional in the motor insurance business will be acquainted with the 'risk' of uninsured drivers trying to purchase an insurance contract on the very same day of an accident, in an attempt to have it covered 'retroactively' by the insurance policy. After the occurrence of the accident, they approach an insurer or an insurance broker and have the vehicle insured against MTPL. If the insurer (or broker) is not vigilant and provides cover without specifying its starting time on the policy document, the uninsured accident might fall within the insurance cover. As the Green Card does not allow the specification of a starting time while stipulating (under the same header 3) that both dates mentioned are inclusive, the Green Card cover must be considered as starting at 00:00 hrs. It would therefore be good business policy to have Green Card cover incepted on the day following the start of the related policy cover.
   Article 7(4) stipulates that Green Cards are deemed to be valid for at least fifteen days from their date of inception. Even if the Green Card were to specify a shorter validity period, the Bureau, under whose authority the Green Card has been issued, must guarantee it for a minimum period of fifteen days from the initial validity date. The reason behind this minimum period of validity is that the Green Card is an international certificate, granting access to the territory of a state. Once the border is crossed and the validity period would turn out to be too short, the guarantee provided by the document would no longer be applicable; this would render the vehicle uninsured on the visited territory and the Guarantee Fund of that state would be responsible for any third party damage or injury caused (subject to the rules of intervention of the Guarantee Fund; see chapter 4: Guarantee Funds). Therefore, Bureaux have agreed that a minimum period of fifteen days must be guaranteed, even if the period of validity specified on the Green Card would be shorter.

The Internal Regulations do not provide for a maximum period of validity of a Green Card. It is again left to the discretion of the Bureaux (or their member insurers if the Bureau doesn't impose any rules in this regard) to decide what period of validity they want to provide cover for (provided that it is longer than fifteen days). Whether it is advisable to provide persons insured with Green Cards valid for a longer period than the period for which the insurer received premium is another matter. The Green Card remains valid, even in case of non-payment of premium; retrieving such a Green Card would, in practice, often be impossible.

4. **'Country Code/Insurer's Code/Number'**: Under this header, the proper identification of the document is made possible. This identification must start with the issuing Bureau's country code (unless the Green Card is issued for a vehicle not registered in the country for which the Bureau is competent, in accordance with Article 7(3) of the Internal Regulations). The country codes used are the *UNECE Distinguishing Signs Used on Vehicles in International Traffic*. For the country codes: see Annex 1.
5. **'Registration No. (or if none) Chassis or Engine No.'**: The registration (plate) number is the most appropriate way to identify the vehicle for which cover is granted. Only if there is no registration number or if it is unknown, the chassis number (Vehicle Identification Number or VIN) can be used to identify the vehicle covered by the Green Card.
6. **'Category of vehicle':** this box allows the issuer of the Green Card to choose one of the categories mentioned at the bottom of the Green Card. The list contains the following options: A. car, B. motorcycle, C. lorry or tractor, D. cycle fitted with auxiliary engine, E. bus, F. trailer, G. others. The Explanatory Memorandum to the Internal Regulations specifies that "the words 'and trailer' or 'and caravan' can be added to this case if the law on compulsory insurance of the country visited does not require a separate Green Card to cover trailers and caravans. It is left to the individual insurer to assess which option is most suitable for certain types of vehicles."
7. **'Make of vehicle':** This box identifies the make of the vehicle for which the Green Card is issued. Often, not only the make of the vehicle is specified but also the model, providing in that way a more detailed identification of the vehicle covered.
8. **'TERRITORIAL VALIDITY':** this is a very important box, specifying the countries for which the Green Card is valid. Box eight mentions the abbreviation of all the participating countries' Bureaux. The issuing entity can strike out (cross over) the countries for which the Green Card is not valid. Consequently, the vehicle in question will not be authorised to enter the countries that have been crossed out on the Green Card. If the vehicle circulates in a country which is crossed out on the document, the Green Card will not be considered valid for that country and the guarantees related to the document will not be applicable.

It is important to emphasise that all the countries of the European Economic Area (EEA) are displayed in one and the same frame; this means that they have to be considered as one common territory. Indeed, because of the rules on deemed insurance cover (see para 3.2.1 and, more in detail, para 3.5), the whole territory of the EEA must be considered as one territory. It is impossible to give cover only for one or more of the countries of the EEA without covering them all.

For the different countries, their abbreviation and their status in the Green Card system: see Annex 1.

9. **'Name and Address of the Policyholder (or User of the vehicle)':** This header does not require much explanation. The name, as well as the address of the person to whom the document has been issued, are to be stated here.
10. **'This Card has been issued by':** In addition to the (compulsory) insertion of the name and the address of the insurer of the vehicle, it is also possible (optionally) to add extra information about the said insurer: such as, the logo of the insurance company; a phone and/or fax number; an e-mail address and the insurer's website. The Explanatory Memorandum specifies that "the insertion, deletion or any other modification of a Bureau's logo can never be deemed as constituting the falsification of the Green Card itself."[17]
11. **'Signature of Insurer':** The Green Card must be signed by the insurer concerned. This does not necessarily need to be a physical signature, made on each document individually, but may also be a scanned signature.

3.5 The Green Card system based on deemed insurance cover

3.5.1 Influence of the European Union

The Green Card system, as originally conceived by the United Nations, started to operate in 1953; that is, a few years after the adoption of Recommendation N° 5 by UNECE. In 1951, exactly in between the issuance of Recommendation N° 5 (1949) and the start of the Green Card system (1953), the first cornerstones of the European Union (EU) were being laid. On 18 April 1951, the Treaty establishing the European Coal and Steel Community was signed in Paris. In the years to follow, new Communities were created: the European Atomic Energy Community and the European Economic Community, both established in 1957. The European 'con-

17. This text leads to confusion between the terms Bureau and insurer. On the one hand, the model of the Green Card specifies that under this heading information about the insurer must be given, whereas the Explanatory Memorandum, on the other, mentions in this context that "the insertion, deletion or any other modification of a Bureau's logo can never be deemed as constituting the falsification of the Green Card'. This sentence seems to imply that the Bureau's logo may be added to box 10. However, the model of the Green Card provides only for an optional logo at the top of the document. Whatever choice a Bureau or an insurer wishes to make, it must be remembered that a Green Card is in all circumstances issued 'under the authority of a Bureau'.

struction' started in the 1950s with six Member States and enlarged gradually until it reached its present number of 28 cooperating states.[18]

One of the primary goals of the European 'concept' was to develop and establish an internal borderless market in which four 'freedoms' would be guaranteed: the free movement of capital, goods, persons and services. Moreover, from a geographical perspective, this internal market was to cover not only the 28 existing Member States of the European Union but also the three states of the European Free Trade Association (EFTA) that participate in the European Economic Area or EEA: Iceland, Liechtenstein and Norway. In that way, the internal market comprises the territory of 31 EEA states.

It is obvious that creating an internal market where capital, goods, persons and services can freely circulate within the territory of the EEA is closely related to the facilitation of cross-border motor traffic. It would therefore be unthinkable that the European Union would not have shown its interest in the functioning of the Green Card system. Although the initial double goal of the Green Card system (facilitation of cross-border motor road traffic and the protection of victims of accidents caused by such cross-border motor road traffic) was completely in line with the aims of the European internal market, the physical checks on the existence of a Green Card at the internal borders of that internal market was considered as too heavy an administrative burden, hindering the free interstate traffic and, as such, the development of the internal market itself.

In a first step, the European Union improved the existing Green Card system by replacing the physical checks on insurance with a structure based on deemed insurance cover. This was then followed by a gradual harmonisation of the protection offered by MTPL insurance; and this through a number of insurance Directives.

A Directive is a legal instrument, used by the European institutions, to impose legally binding obligations on the Member States through the respective national legislation. A Directive defines the result that is to be achieved by the Member States but leaves the same Member States free as regards the form and method to achieve the desired goal. A directive needs to be transposed or implemented into a Member State's national legislation; this safeguards the achievement of the goals formulated in the Directive itself. In order to harmonise the national legislation on Motor Third Party Liability (MTPL) insurance, the European Union has, until today, always used the legal instrument of directives.

18. See also *supra* para 2.4.

Article 288 of the Treaty on the Functioning of the European Union defines the legal instruments at the Union's disposal to realise its political goals. Apart from directives, the European Union can adopt regulations, decisions, recommendations and opinions. Article 288 defines these instruments as follows:

- "A regulation shall have general application. It shall be binding in its entirety and directly applicable in all Member States.
- A directive shall be binding, as to the result to be achieved, upon each Member State to which it is addressed, but shall leave to the national authorities the choice of form and methods.
- A decision shall be binding in its entirety. A decision which specifies those to whom it is addressed shall be binding only on them.
- Recommendations and opinions shall have no binding force."

The first Directive adopted by the European Union in order to harmonise MTPL insurance in the initial six Member States, was published in 1972 and required the implementation into national legislation at the latest by 31 December 1973.[19] In this book, we will use the term First Motor Insurance Directive, or 1st MID, to refer to the 1972 legal instrument. The 1st MID was later complemented by additional Directives. Between 1983 and 2005, four more Directives were issued, ensuring a more harmonised and higher level of protection to European 'consumers' (policyholders and victims or injured parties of road traffic accidents).[20] The 1st MID will be described in paragraph 3.5.2, whereas the innovations of the 2nd, 3rd and 5th Motor Insurance Directives (MIDs) will be handled in chapters 4 and 6. A separate chapter 5 will be devoted to the specific protection scheme introduced by the 4th MID in 2000.

The several Directives not only introduced new provisions and protective measures; often, they also changed the provisions of the preceding Directives in order to improve existing mechanisms. Such new provisions and modifications gave rise to

19. Council Directive of 24 April 1972 on the approximation of the laws of the Member States relating to insurance against civil liability in respect of the use of motor vehicles, and to the enforcement of the obligation to insure against such liability (72/166/EEC), OJ L 103, 2.5.1972, p. 1.
20. Second Council Directive of 30 December 1983 on the approximation of the laws of the Member States relating to insurance against civil liability in respect of the use of motor vehicles (84/5/EEC), OJ L 8, 11.1.1984, p. 17; Third Council Directive of 14 May 1990 on the approximation of the laws of the Member States relating to insurance against civil liability in respect of the use of motor vehicles (90/232/EEC), OJ L 129, 19.5.1990, p. 33; Directive 2000/26/EC of the European Parliament and of the Council of 16 May 2000 on the approximation of the laws of the Member States relating to insurance against civil liability in respect of the use of motor vehicles and amending Council Directives 73/239/EEC and 88/357/EEC, OJ L 181, 20.7.2000, p. 65; Directive 2005/14/EC of the European Parliament and of the Council of 11 May 2005 amending Council Directives 72/166/EEC, 84/5/EEC, 88/357/EEC and 90/232/EEC and Directive 2000/26/EC of the European Parliament and of the Council relating to insurance against civil liability in respect of the use of motor vehicles, OJ L 149, 11.6.2005, p. 14.

a 'puzzle' of legal texts that had to be integrated in order to have a precise overview on the current applicable rules. In order to bring more order in that 'puzzle', the European Commission took the initiative, in 2009, to codify all the existing Directives into one single and coordinated document, Directive 2009/103/EC.[21] In this book, we will refer to this document as the codified Motor Insurance Directive, the codified MID or, even in a more abbreviated manner, the MID or the Directive.

In 2017, the European Commission started the procedure for a legislative proposal in view of the fact that a new Motor Insurance Directive was in the pipeline. This initiative was part of the Commission's so-called REFIT programme intended to verify whether existing European legislation is effective, efficient and at minimum cost.[22] A public consultation was launched, focussing on the functioning of the Motor Insurance Directive. On 24 May 2018, the European Commission published a *Proposal for a Directive of the European Parliament and of the Council amending Directive 2009/103/EC of the European Parliament and the Council of 16 September 2009 relating to insurance against civil liability in respect of the use of motor vehicles, and the enforcement of the obligation to insure against such liability.*[23]

The Commission's proposal for a new Directive is not the end stage of the legislative process but is only the start of a procedure in which the European Parliament and the Council of the European Union have the deciding power. On 1 March 2019, the legislative process was far from being finished.

The Commission's proposal focuses on five different issues and these will be treated in different paragraphs in this book:
- Scope of the Directive, the risks to be covered under MTPL insurance and the definition of the use of a vehicle: para 6.2.4;
- Risks due to uninsured driving and checks on insurance: para 4.3.2;
- Insolvency of an insurer and the protection of injured parties in case of the insolvency of an insurance undertaking or the lack of cooperation of an insurance undertaking: para 4.3.6 and 7.4.5;
- Minimum amounts of cover: para 6.2.10;
- Claims history statements: para 6.3.7.

21. Directive 2009/103/EC of the European Parliament and of the Council of 16 September 2009 relating to insurance against civil liability in respect of the use of motor vehicles, and the enforcement of the obligation to insure against such liability (codified version), OJ L 263, 7.10.2009, p. 11.
22. REFIT = the European Commission's Regulatory Fitness and Performance Programme.
23. COM(2018) 336 final.

3.5.2 *The First European Motor Insurance Directive*

In 1972, nearly twenty years after the entry into force of the Green Card system, the predecessors of the European Union adopted the First Motor Insurance Directive or 1st MID, thereby substantially influencing the existing Green Card system.[24]

In order to move towards the creation of an internal market, in which vehicles can freely circulate from one Member State to another, the European legislator further built on the existing variants within the Green Card system. Inspiration was found in a system that was, prior to the adoption of the 1st MID, functioning already in a more or less comparable way in the countries of the Benelux (Belgium, Luxembourg and the Netherlands), in the Nordic countries, (Denmark, Finland, Norway and Sweden) as well as in a number of Central-European countries (Austria, Czechoslovakia, Germany and Hungary). The new system would enable a vehicle to travel from one Member State to another without any physical check, at the border, of the vehicle's insurance status.

In all of the six Member States, the insurance against civil liability arising from the use of motor vehicles (MTPL insurance) was made compulsory. Starting from this obligation to have vehicles insured, the European legislator introduced a presumption that each and every vehicle circulating in one of the Member States is legally insured. Obviously, everybody knows (including the European institutions) that such a presumption is, unfortunately, an illusion. Still today, too many vehicles circulate on European roads without being insured against the civil liability that a road traffic accident could result in. This presumption is called 'deemed insurance cover'. Thanks to this concept, national authorities may now presume that each national and foreign vehicle is legally insured for MTPL; consequently, they do not have to be concerned about controlling each and every vehicle entering the respective territory via an internal border of the common market. Border control on insurance could therefore be abolished at the internal borders of the internal market.

If a vehicle from one Member State causes an accident on the territory of another Member State, the Green Card system will apply in order to guarantee a correct compensation to the injured party or parties. Such compensation will, as earlier under the original Green Card system, be guaranteed by the national Motor Insurers' Bureau of the Member State where the accident occurred. This Bureau will, however, no longer be dependent on the actual existence of a Green Card to start taking action but will only check whether the vehicle involved in the accident is

24. Council Directive of 24 April 1972 on the approximation of the laws of the Member States relating to insurance against civil liability in respect of the use of motor vehicles, and to the enforcement of the obligation to insure against such liability (72/166/EEC), OJ L 103, 2.5.1972, p. 1.

normally based in the territory of another Member State of the European Union (or nowadays in the territory of a state participating in the EEA).
After having compensated the injured party, the Bureau of the Member State where the accident occurred (the handling Bureau) will recover its outlay from the insurer of the vehicle or from the Bureau of the Member State where the vehicle in question is normally based (the guaranteeing Bureau). The latter will have to provide its guarantee regardless of whether the liable vehicle is validly insured or not. The only criterion to trigger such guarantee would be the vehicle being normally based in the territory of the guaranteeing Bureau's competence.

In the vast majority of cases, a vehicle will be normally based in the Member State of which it bears the registration plate. There are however other criteria to determine in which Member State a vehicle is normally based and these will be examined further in paragraph 3.5.5.

Example
The main principles of the deemed insurance cover concept were already explained earlier, when describing the two variants of the Green Card system (in para 3.2.1). The said concept was illustrated by means of an example, which can here be reiterated to illustrate the proper functioning of the concept as introduced by the 1st MID.
Both France and Italy participate in the European Economic Area; this means that the Green Card of a French vehicle, travelling to Italy, will no longer be controlled at the border between the two countries. The French vehicle will simply be allowed to enter the Italian territory on the basis of it being registered in France. If the French vehicle causes an accident in Italy, the Italian injured party will be able to address a claim for compensation to the Italian Bureau. The Italian Bureau will communicate with the Italian injured party in Italian and will pay compensation in accordance with the Italian law. After the compensation has been paid, the Italian Bureau will recover its outlay from the French insurer. If the said insurer does not reimburse the Italian Bureau in time or if the vehicle turns out to be uninsured, the French Bureau will have to guarantee the reimbursement; and this no longer on the strength of a Green Card issued under its authority but on the basis of the liable vehicle being normally based in France.

It is interesting to note that, for the achievement of the goals pursued by the 1st MID, the European legislator has completely relied on the existing mechanism of the Green Card system, with the existing institutional framework of national Motor Insurers' Bureaux. As we will describe in chapter 5, this has not been the case with the 4th Directive, in which the European legislator wanted to provide special protection to the victim of an accident that occurred in a Member State other than the victim's Member State of residence; this is the concept of the 'visiting victim'. In order to achieve this goal, the European legislator created a whole new institutional network of claims representatives, Compensation Bodies and Information Centres.

3.5.3 Necessary conditions

More than for the 'pure' Green Card system, based on the actual physical existence of a Green Card, the concept of deemed insurance cover requires the fulfilment of a number of conditions in all of the participating countries. These conditions must be respected in their entirety; therefore, they have to be considered as cumulative.

– The term 'deemed insurance cover' logically necessitates the *existence of compulsory MTPL insurance*. Even if the presumption is, as explained earlier, based on an illusion that each and every vehicle is validly insured, the concept cannot function if MTPL insurance is not mandatory in all the participating countries. Article 3 of the codified Motor Insurance Directive requires that

> "Each Member State shall, subject to Article 5, take all appropriate measures to ensure that civil liability in respect of the use of vehicles normally based in its territory is covered by insurance."

  The text of this provision clearly illustrates the nature of the legal instrument of a directive: an instruction, which binds the Member States as to the result to be achieved, while leaving it to the national authorities of the Member States to choose the form and methods to attain that goal. The aim is to have the use of vehicles insured against civil liability. The Directive remains silent on how that result is to be achieved; it only stipulates that each Members State shall take all appropriate measures.

  Another characteristic of European legislation is that each directive has to be translated in all of the (currently 24) official languages of the European Union. The translation of the provision cited above has led to substantial differences between the distinct languages. The English text, requiring that civil liability in respect of *the use of vehicles* be covered by MTPL insurance, seems to have a much wider scope of obligation than that stated in a number of other languages, where the link with *traffic* is much closer. In this regard, it is interesting to observe the French and Spanish versions, where the insurance obligation is imposed for '*la responsabilité civile relative à la circulation*' or '*la responsabilidad que resulta de la circulación de vehículos*'. And those texts then again differ from the German version where not only the notion of *traffic* seems to have been discarded but even the term *use* has been omitted: '*die Haftpflicht bei Fahrzeugen*'. How much these language differences can have an influence on the exact interpretation of the Directive is illustrated by a judgment of the Court of Justice of the European Union in the *Vnuk* case.[25]

- The compulsory MTPL insurance must necessarily *cover the entire territory of all the participating countries* (Article 14 of the codified MID). Since the aim of the system is to abolish insurance checks at the borders, vehicles must be able to freely circulate, not only within the national territory of the respective originating state but also within the territories of all the states participating in the system of deemed insurance cover. This means that MTPL insurance, issued for the territory of one participating state, is automatically valid for the territories of all the other participating states; and this without any additional premium. An insurer, wishing to limit the risks related to MTPL insurance, will therefore not be allowed to exclude certain countries (or parts of countries) from the cover that is offered to the insured. For instance, a clause in the insurance policy stating that the cover is not valid in Germany would therefore be invalid. In the same way, any other less defined territorial restrictions, such as 'mountainous roads' or 'roads at an altitude higher than 1500 meters', are equally unacceptable. The entire territory to be covered by the MTPL insurance issued in accordance with Article 14 of the MID will be described more in detail in paragraphs 3.5.4 and 6.2.8.1.
- Closely related to the preceding concept is the requirement that the MTPL insurance, covering the territories of all countries participating in the system of deemed insurance cover, must necessarily do so at *one single premium* (Article 14 of the codified MID).[26] An insurer is not allowed to differentiate the premium payable in respect of the geographical territory covered. Since the entire territory needs to be covered, no additional premium can be charged for the cover in certain geographical areas. An insurer cannot request a higher premium if a vehicle leaves its national territory or travels to one or more Member States or areas thereof. An illustration of the obligation of a single premium, stipulated in Article 14 of the MID, is to be found in the *Litaksa* judgment of the Court of Justice of the European Union.[27]

  Although the concept of a single premium, covering the entire territory of all participating states in the system of deemed insurance cover seems to be an evident condition, it was not included as an obligation in the 1st MID. Only with the adoption of the 3rd MID in 1990, the principle of the single premium was incorporated in the obligations of the Motor Insurance Directives (as it can now be found in Article 14 of the codified MID).

25. CJEU, Judgment of 4 September 2014, *Vnuk*, C-162/13, EU:C:2014:2146. See also *infra* para 6.2.4.
26. See also *infra* para 6.2.8.2.
27. CJEU, Judgment of 26 March 2015, *Litaksa*, C-556/13, EU:C:2015:202.

Strangely enough, prior to the 3rd MID, the obligation of a single premium was not incorporated in the texts and it was common practice, for instance in the United Kingdom, to require an additional premium for cover beyond the national borders. The scope of application of such a requirement must then have been restricted to the relationship between the insurer and the policyholder, without impinging on the right to compensation of the injured party. In case a driver would cause an accident outside the territory of the United Kingdom, in the absence of an additional premium being paid for the cover abroad, the injured party would still be compensated in accordance with the guarantees offered by the Green Card system; but the policyholder would most probably have been 'exposed' to a right of recourse exercised by the insurer concerned. Such practice is no longer allowed since the implementation of the 3rd MID.

- *Elimination of insurance control at the borders.* Strictly speaking, this is not a requirement for the concept of deemed insurance cover to apply. It is rather a (possible) consequence. But since this was a means to come closer to the European internal market and exactly the aim pursued by the European legislator, it was considered so important that it was inserted as an obligation in the Motor Insurance Directive. The current Article 4 provides that

"Member States shall refrain from making checks on insurance against civil liability in respect of vehicles normally based in the territory of another Member State and in respect of vehicles normally based in the territory of a third country entering their territory from the territory of another Member State."

It is surprising that the Directive excludes any kind of checks on insurance and does not only limit this restriction to border checks. Most probably, such a general requirement was made in order to avoid that Member States would circumvent the restriction on border checks by performing systematic road checks a few kilometres further inside the border.
Article 4 however mitigates the restriction in the following way:

"However, they may carry out non-systematic checks on insurance provided that those checks are not discriminatory and are carried out as part of a control which is not aimed exclusively at insurance verification."

In view of the objectives pursued by the 1st MID in 1972, this provision is perfectly understandable. Today, more than forty years later during which considerable technical progress has taken place, the restriction on systematic insurance checks is seen as an important hindrance to an effective fight against uninsured driving. Contrary to the situation in 1972, the insurance status of a vehicle can now be checked without having to systematically stop every vehicle and ask for the vehicle's papers. Systematic insurance checks can be performed by means of automatic number-plate recognition (ANPR) using special cameras, avoiding in that way any traffic jams caused by the systematic physical control of vehicles and drivers. In this context, the modification of Article 4 of the MID seems appropriate in order not to restrict the systematic (camera-based) checks on the insurance status of a vehicle. In the proposal for a new Motor Insurance Directive, published in May 2018, the European Commission suggests modifying Article 4 in such a way so as to allow non-discriminatory checks on insurance that do not require any vehicle to stop.[28]

3.5.4 *Geographical scope*

The Motor Insurance Directive, including all the obligations and harmonisation measures as explained in more detail in the following chapters 4, 5 and 6, is applicable on the entire territory of the European Economic Area (EEA).

As already described in paragraph 3.2.2, the territory of the EEA consists of:
- The 28 Member States of the (pre-Brexit) European Union: Austria, Belgium, Bulgaria, Croatia, Cyprus, the Czech Republic, Denmark, Estonia, Finland, France, Germany, Greece, Hungary, Ireland, Italy, Latvia, Lithuania, Luxembourg, Malta, the Netherlands, Poland, Portugal, Romania, the Slovak Republic, Slovenia, Spain, Sweden and the United Kingdom of Great Britain and Northern Ireland. For the repercussions on the Green Card system of the United Kingdom's decision to leave the European Union: see *supra* para 3.2.2 and *infra* para 9.2.
- The three states of the European Free Trade Association (EFTA) participating in the EEA: Iceland, Liechtenstein and Norway. Switzerland is also part of the EFTA but it decided not to participate in the EEA after a national referendum held in 1992.

As also set out in paragraph 3.2.2 the system of deemed insurance cover has been extended to three additional third countries: Andorra, Serbia and Switzerland. The Bureau of Bosnia and Herzegovina became a signatory of the Multilateral Agreement in 2019. For the system of deemed insurance cover to become applicable in that country, a formal decision of the European Commission is required. At the moment of concluding the manuscript of this book, the Commission decision was not adopted yet.

The 31 countries of the EEA, together with Andorra, Serbia and Switzerland, have together concluded the Multilateral Agreement in order to implement the system of deemed insurance cover in their reciprocal relations.

28. See also *infra* para 6.2.8.4.

It is to be emphasised that only the provisions of the MID, relating to deemed insurance cover and to the territory in which a vehicle is normally based, are relevant for the three non-EEA states participating in the Multilateral Agreement (Andorra, Serbia and Switzerland). All the other provisions of the MID, relating to the insurance cover to be provided for the protection of the insured and the injured party, are only binding for the EEA states and not for Andorra, Serbia and Switzerland.

An interesting question is whether the three non-EEA states are bound by the jurisprudence of the Court of Justice of the European Union regarding the interpretation of the notion 'territory in which a vehicle is normally based'. In our opinion this question is, strictly speaking, to be answered in the negative. It is hard to imagine that countries would be bound by the jurisprudence of a court to which they have not committed themselves. Bear in mind that the Multilateral Agreement was only signed by the national Bureaux of these countries and not by their respective governments. But since the 'normally based notion' is a means by which the three countries bind themselves to the 31 other countries, which do have to follow the interpretation given by the European Court of Justice, it is at the same time difficult to imagine that these three countries would give a different interpretation to the term normally based than the 31 countries of the EEA. It may be interesting to make the following distinction:

- Traffic from the three non-EEA States (signatories of the Multilateral Agreement) towards the EEA: according to Article 8 of the Motor Insurance Directive, these vehicles are "treated as vehicles normally based in the Community." As a consequence, the interpretation given by the European Court of Justice to the notion 'territory in which a vehicle is normally based' will also apply to such vehicles;
- Traffic from the EEA States to the three non-EEA States (signatories of the Multilateral Agreement): having regard to the reciprocal character of the Multilateral Agreement, it seems normal that the same interpretation is given in the three non-EEA States to the notion of 'territory in which a vehicle is normally based'. Even if it is difficult to defend the position that these States should be bound by the jurisprudence of the Court of Justice of the European Union, the reciprocity of the Multilateral Agreement would require the interpretation to be identical.

Finally, it is important to mention that the Motor Insurance Directive has made the entry into force of the system of deemed insurance cover conditional upon the conclusion of the Multilateral Agreement. This is stipulated in Article 2 of the codified Directive.

3.5.5 *The concept of the territory in which a vehicle is normally based*

In order for the system of deemed insurance cover to function well, it is important to determine where a vehicle originates from; in other words, to establish in which territory of a Member State is the vehicle in question 'normally based'. The term appears both in the Directive and in the Internal Regulations. The content of the 'normally based concept' in the Directive is analysed in paragraphs 6.2.5.2 to 6.2.5.5. This paragraph is dedicated to the 'normally based' concept according to the Internal Regulations.

The Internal Regulations govern the reciprocal relations between national insurers' Bureaux, both as regards the 'basic' Green Card system (requiring the physical existence of a Green Card) and as regards their cooperation on the basis of deemed insurance cover. The second variant, based on deemed insurance cover, is regulated by Section III of the Internal Regulations. This section needs a definition of the notion 'territory in which a vehicle is normally based' in order to determine which Bureau is to guarantee the consequences of a cross-border road traffic accident caused by a motor vehicle.

Article 11 of the Internal Regulations copies, in almost identical terms, the definition of the territory in which a vehicle is normally based from that found in Article 1(4) of the codified Motor Insurance Directive:

> "**Article 11 The normally based concept**
> 1. The territory of the State in which the vehicle is normally based is determined on the basis of any of the following criteria:
> 1.1. the territory of the Member State of which the vehicle bears a registration plate, whether this be permanent or temporary;
> 1.2. where no registration is required for the type of vehicle but the vehicle bears an insurance plate, or a distinguishing sign analogous to a registration plate, the territory of the State in which the insurance plate or the sign is issued;
> 1.3. where neither registration plate nor insurance plate nor distinguishing sign is required for certain types of vehicles, the territory of the State in which the person who has custody of the vehicle is permanently resident.
> 2. If a vehicle required to bear a registration plate bears no plate or bears a registration plate which does not correspond or no longer corresponds to the vehicle has been involved in an accident, the territory in which the accident occurred shall, for the settlement for any resulting claim, be deemed to be the territory where the vehicle is normally based."

In the vast majority of cases, the determining factor will be the registration plate of a vehicle. Situations where a vehicle is not required to bear a registration plate are rare and, moreover, such vehicles will only rarely cross the national borders. A little bit more frequent, but still a minority, will be the cases falling within the criterion outlined in Article 11(2), where there is a deficiency in the registration status of the vehicle.

In this way the uniformity of the concept, both in the European legal order and in the rules of the Green Card system, is safeguarded. This uniform and harmonised approach is, however, not an absolute necessity. The European Motor Insurance Directive is a legal text, upholding the principles of the European internal market and, at the same time, protecting the interests of the policyholder and the injured parties of a road traffic accident. The Internal Regulations, on the other hand, only envisage regulating the reciprocal relations between national Insurers' Bureaux. Whether and how these Bureaux organise their relations, the guarantees to be provided and the reimbursements of compensations to be made, belongs to their contractual freedom. As long as the interests of policyholders and/or of the injured parties are not harmed, Bureaux can deviate from the rules on how to determine the concept of territory in which a vehicle is normally based.[29] Though today the concept is defined in an almost identical way, that has not always been the case. In the past, Bureaux had at a certain moment decided to apply another concept than the one defined in the Directive and as interpreted by the Court of Justice of the European Union. That will be explained more in detail in paragraphs 6.2.5.2 and 6.2.5.3.

3.6 Examination of the guarantee within the Green Card system

3.6.1 *Introduction*

We have explained what the Green Card system is about (in essence a system of guarantee between national insurers' Bureaux) and how it has historically developed in two variants: the 'basic' Green Card system, requiring the physical existence of a Green Card, and the Green Card system based on deemed insurance cover, under the influence of the European legislator.

But the Green Card system is of course not a theoretical construction in itself. As already discussed, the aim of the system is not only to facilitate cross-border road traffic in Europe; it is also designed to protect the victims of accidents caused by such cross-border road traffic. Therefore, we will gradually turn our attention to the handling of claims resulting from accidents in which a foreign vehicle is involved.

29. See CJEU, Judgment of 6 October 1987, *Demouche and others*, C-152/83, EU:C:1987:421 and CJEU, Judgment of 12 November 1992, *Fournier*, C-73/89, EU:C:1992:431; see also *infra* para 6.2.5.3.

Before the actual claims handling activity – including the correct compensation of the injured party – can start, the handling entity (a Bureau, agent or correspondent, as will be examined under paragraph 3.7) needs to determine whether the condition for the Green Card system to apply is fulfilled; namely, that a guaranteeing Bureau actually exists. How the existence of such guarantee can be verified depends on which of the two variants is applicable and according to which variant the claims handling entity is performing its task:

- If the claim falls under Section II of the Internal Regulations, or, in other words under the 'basic' Green Card system based on the actual existence of a Green Card, the handling entity will have to establish whether there is a valid Green Card and, in the absence thereof, whether the conditions to rely on a Bureau's guarantee for false Green Cards are fulfilled. This will be the subject of paragraph. 3.6.2;
- If the claim falls under Section III of the Internal Regulations and the system of deemed insurance cover is applicable, the handling entity will have to determine where the liable vehicle is normally based. The request for confirmation of the territory in which a vehicle is normally based will be examined in paragraph 3.6.3.

3.6.2 *Examination of the guarantee within the Green Card system based on the existence of a Green Card*

3.6.2.1 *The request for confirmation of the validity of a Green Card*

An accident has taken place in a country participating in the Green Card system. The driver of the liable vehicle presents a Green Card. The injured party submits a claim to the Motor Insurers' Bureau in the country of the accident and that Bureau will initially have to determine whether it can start handling the claim. For that purpose, an *identified Green Card* is required.

a. What is an identified Green card?

The text of the Explanatory Memorandum, relating to Article 8 of the Internal Regulations, lists the following three elements that are indispensable for a Green Card to be identified:[30]

i. the name of the (issuing) Bureau or country code;
ii. the insurer's name and/or code;
iii. the serial number of the Green Card.

It is specified that all three elements must necessarily be available in order for a Green Card to be considered as identified.

30. For the Explanatory Memorandum: see para 3.1.4.

In earlier times, it was common that a Green Card was issued jointly with an official duplicate that could be handed over in case of an accident. If the handling entity has an original, a duplicate or a (certified) copy of the Green Card, the identification is easy. The currently available technological means (such as smartphones) also allow the easy identification of a Green Card by means of a photo. Nevertheless, despite the lack of an original, a duplicate, a photocopy or a photo, a Green Card can still be identified on the basis of the above-mentioned three elements being integrated in an accident statement or in a police report.
Once the Green Card has been identified, its *validity* must be checked; and this as concerns the date and the country where the accident occurred.

b. How can a handling entity ascertain that an identified Green Card is valid?
In the first place, the handling entity will have to verify whether the Green Card is valid on the date of the accident and in the country of the accident. In case an original, duplicate, copy or photo of the Green Card is available, that is of course easy on the basis of boxes 3 ('valid from ... to ...') and 8 ('territorial validity'). If that information immediately results in the Green Card not being valid on the date and/or in the country of the accident, the handling entity will have to end its intervention. Depending on the applicable rules, the claim can then be forwarded to the Guarantee Fund of the country of the accident (see further chapter 4). But even if the Green Card meets the required date and the country of the accident, its validity will still have to be confirmed.

The validity of the Green Card needs to be confirmed by the Bureau under whose authority the Card was issued. The handling Bureau or the agent (see further para 3.7.3) therefore sends a 'request for confirmation of the validity of a Green Card'. This is a formal request that needs to be answered within six weeks by the Bureau to which it is addressed (Article 8 of the Internal Regulations). The Council of Bureaux has developed a template for this request, which must be sent (and replied to) in an electronic form. In future, the exchange will take place via an online communication platform between Bureaux. In case the Bureau to which the request was addressed does not respond within six weeks, the Green Card will be deemed to be valid. The guaranteeing Bureau cannot revoke that silent confirmation afterwards. This explicit or silent confirmation of validity ensures that the guarantees, characterising the Green Card system, have their full effect. It will avoid that a handling Bureau or an agent be hindered in their handling activity by the possible inertia or passivity of the guaranteeing Bureau. If the latter denies the validity of the Green Card, it will have to substantiate the denial by means of a reasoned reply.

The strict deadline of six weeks will only apply if the handling entity has the information required to identify the Green Card. It is however conceivable that one or more of the three parameters outlined above is unavailable and the Green Card cannot be considered to be identified. In such circumstances, the Explanatory Memorandum of the Internal Regulations stipulates that the solution can be found through the cooperation between Bureaux. The handling entity can still contact the possible guaranteeing Bureau in order to verify whether a valid Green Card exists for the liable vehicle. The majority of Bureaux are able, through national databases, to find out whether a valid Green Card exists for a certain vehicle of which the registration plate is known. The Explanatory Memorandum explicitly refers to the "spirit of cooperation in good faith, existing between members of the System" to motivate them to adopt a cooperative approach in case of an accident by a vehicle bearing an unidentified Green Card. The only difference is that for the cooperation between Bureaux in the absence of an identified Green Card, the six weeks' deadline to confirm the validity of a Green Card will not apply. For this deadline to apply, an identified Green Card must be available.

Finally, even in the absence of an identified Green Card, Bureaux can still exchange information on the insurance status of the vehicle in question. Even if the guarantees of the Green Card system cannot be relied on due to the absence of an identified Green Card, the insurance status of the vehicle can be established and communicated. If the vehicle turns out to be validly insured and the insurance covers the date and the country of the accident, the injured party will be able to claim compensation from the insurer concerned.[31]

Since the request for confirmation of the validity of a Green Card is described in Article 8 of the Internal Regulations and since the Internal Regulations mainly govern the contractual relations between Green Card Bureaux, the handling activity of correspondents falls outside that provision. In practice, however, the claims handling activity of Green Card claims will often be in the hands of correspondents, acting on behalf of foreign insurers and representing these insurers in the state of the accident (see further para 3.7.4). When these correspondents are confronted with a claim, submitted by an injured party following a road traffic accident caused by a vehicle insured by their principal, the correspondent will contact directly the foreign insurer concerned. In practice, very often the foreign insurer will confirm insurance cover for the vehicle concerned and for the country where the accident took place. With such confirmation in hand, the correspondent will start handling the case and will compensate the victim, without the formal procedure of Article 8 being invoked.

31. In order to reinforce and formalise this cooperation between Bureaux, a new Article 8(2) of the Internal Regulations is being developed and will most probably be adopted in 2019.

Problems may occur, however, if the correspondent acted on the basis of the confirmation given by its principal and, subsequently, there seems to be a complication with the Green Card cover. If the foreign insurer declines to reimburse the correspondent, will the correspondent then be entitled to invoke the guarantees offered by the Green Card system? Is a Bureau, in the absence of a formal confirmation of the validity of a Green Card based on Article 8, bound by the confirmation of cover given by a member insurer? This question seems to be answered in the positive. A Bureau is bound by the confirmation of insurance cover given by an insurer. This principle can be derived from the following statement in the Explanatory Memorandum under Article 3(2), point (1) of the Internal Regulations:

> "The guaranteeing Bureau is bound by the confirmation of cover given by the Intermediary acting on behalf of the insurance company, and in particular when the insurance company is wound up, and the guaranteeing Bureau has to substitute for it in obligations arising out of the claim."

If a Bureau is bound by the confirmation of cover given by an intermediary, this should *a fortiori* apply equally to a confirmation of cover given by the insurer itself.

Example

A citizen from Ukraine drives a vehicle (registered in Ukraine) into Moldova and causes an accident there. Before starting to handle the claim, the Moldovan national Bureau will ask the injured party to either present a copy of the Green Card or to provide the necessary data to identify a Green Card.

If the Green Card gives cover for Moldova on the date of the accident, the Moldovan Bureau will submit a request for confirmation of the validity of the Green Card to the Ukrainian Bureau. The Ukrainian Bureau has six weeks to either confirm or reject the validity of the Green Card. In case it rejects the validity, it should specify the reasons for the rejection. In case the Ukrainian Bureau gives no answer within the six weeks' period, the Moldovan Bureau may presume the Green Card to be valid and handle the claim (in the capacity of handling Bureau).

If the necessary data for the identification of the Green Card is not available, both Bureaux can still cooperate in good faith to determine whether Green Card cover actually exists (e.g. on the basis of other data such as the registration plate) and/or to find out whether insurance cover exists for Moldova.

3.6.2.2 *The guarantee for false or unauthorised Green Cards*

It has already been stated and emphasised earlier: in essence, the Green Card system is a system based on guarantees. Based on the availability of a Green Card, border control authorities will grant access to the territory of their country, without requiring the subscription of insurance valid for the country visited. The Green Card provides sufficient guarantee that any damage, recognised in the visited country as falling under the scope of MTPL, will be compensated in accordance with the law of the country visited.

In order to avoid that the control of valid insurance would give rise to endless border checks on the validity of a Green Card being presented, the guarantee for Green Cards is not only limited to valid Green Cards but also extends to Green Cards that seem to be valid, initially, for the period and the country visited but subsequently turn out to be false or unauthorised.

Article 9(1) formulates this principle as follows:

> "Any false or unauthorised Green Card presented in a country in which these Internal Regulations are applicable, purporting to be valid and issued under the authority of a bureau shall be guaranteed by that bureau."

Article 9(1) relates to false or unauthorised Green Cards. The Explanatory Memorandum to the Internal Regulations specifies both terms more in detail.

- *False Green Cards* are:
  - either genuine Green Cards that have been illegally altered (including stolen genuine templates that have illegally been completed)
  - or counterfeited cards which intend to (re)produce or replace an original Green Card or give that impression.
- *Unauthorised Green Cards* are genuine Green Cards that have been issued in breach of the Internal Regulations, even if that was done by mistake (for instance when an insurer, member of a national Bureau, issues a Green Card to a vehicle registered in another country where a Green Card Bureau already exists).

An important distinction between the guarantee for valid Green Cards and the guarantee for false or unauthorised Green Cards is that the latter assumes the physical existence, at the time and the location of the accident, of a document which apparently has the characteristics of a Green Card. This assumption stems from the word 'presented' used in Article 9. Indeed, it seems logical that the Bureau, under the authority of which the Green Card is purported to be issued, should be granted the possibility to control whether, *prima facie*, the Green Card seems to be valid, thus activating its guarantee. The original, a duplicate, a copy or a photo of the Green Card should at least be available. The three elements listed in paragraph 3.6.2.1 and necessary to identify a Green Card cannot cause a Bureau's guarantee for a false or unauthorised Green Card to be put in doubt. It is however possible that the police were present at the scene of the accident and that a police report was drafted. Since the presence of the police ensures a better guarantee for the avoidance of any fraud, a false or unauthorised Green Card shall be deemed to have been physically presented if the essential elements for the identification of a Green Card are mentioned in the police report: the name of the Bureau or country code, the insurers' name and/or code and the serial number of the Green Card. However, in this case, the period of validity must also be mentioned.

In paragraph 3.6.2.1, the procedure to request the confirmation of the validity of a Green Card was described. In the reply to this request, the guaranteeing Bureau can deny the validity of the Green Card (providing the reason(s) for such denial) and, at the same time, confirm that it will guarantee the Green Card on the basis of Article 9(1) cited above.

It is relevant to point out that the extended guarantee for false and unauthorised Green Cards applies to Green Cards that seem, 'at first sight', to be valid. This means that a Bureau's guarantee cannot, on the basis of this extended guarantee, be invoked for a Green Card that is not valid for the day of the accident (because it does not fall within the period of validity displayed in box 3) or for the country visited (because the country in question is crossed out in box 8). Moreover, Green Cards that manifestly appear to be invalid should not activate any guarantee.

The Explanatory Memorandum formulates the limitations as follows:

> "Experience has shown that there are some obvious cases of falsification where the guarantee could be denied on that basis. Those false documents not considered as Green Cards and which, consequently, do not engage the responsibility of the Bureau in the name of which they purport to have been issued:
>
> - purported Green Cards from which the identity of the guaranteeing Bureau cannot be clearly ascertained (e.g. the name of the Bureau does not correspond to the country code);
> - purported Green Cards the format of which does not correspond to (whether in terms of size or layout or both) the model recognised by the Working Party on Road Transport of the Inland Transport Committee of the UNECE;
> - purported Green Cards not having one of the following data: vehicle identification data (registration plate or V.I.N. number), the territorial validity or the period of validity.
>
> In the listed cases the Bureau may deny its guarantee in accordance with the procedure outlined above. Under these exceptional circumstances, the guarantee may also be denied for 'Green Cards' purporting to have been authorised under Article 7.3."

3.6.2.3 *The limitation of the guarantee for false or unauthorised Green Cards under Article 9(2) of the Internal Regulations*

A Bureau's guarantee for false Green Cards cannot be unlimited. We have already explained how easier it is nowadays to falsify Green Cards (which are mere paper documents printed on green paper) in comparison to the early days of the Green Card system's introduction in 1953 (see para 3.4.3.2). A Bureau cannot be expected to guarantee any document that has been falsified and that happens to carry the name of the Bureau in question, even if it is presented by the driver of a vehicle registered in a completely different country.

For that reason, Article 9(2) of the Internal Regulations limits the guarantee for false Green Cards to vehicles that are legally registered in the country of the Bureau under whose authority the Card is purported to be issued:

> "However, the bureau's guarantee shall not apply where a false Green Card relates to a vehicle which is not legally registered in that bureau's country, with the exception of the circumstances specified in Article 7.3."

It is to be emphasised that this limitation only relates to false Green Cards and does not extend to unauthorised Green Cards. That is logical when one observes the definition of unauthorised Green Cards: "genuine Green Cards issued in breach of the Internal Regulations, even if by mistake." The Explanatory Memorandum gives, right after this definition, the example of an insurer issuing a Green Card to a vehicle registered in a country where a Green Card Bureau already exists. It is evident that in such case, where an insurer has given cover in return for a premium, the Bureau must guarantee the Green Card in question, even if issued for a vehicle that is not registered in the territory of the Bureau's competence. A valid Green Card, issued in breach of the rules of the Green Card system and for which premium has been received, must be guaranteed.

Contrary to the system of deemed insurance cover, the 'basic' Green Card system, based on the physical existence of a Green Card, has in principle no link with the registration status of a vehicle. The determining factor for the guarantee is the existence of a Green Card. With this provision of Article 9(2), however, a link is established with the registration system applicable in the participating states. Article 9(2) does not simply refer to the registration but requires that the vehicle for which the guarantee may be denied is not *legally* registered in the Bureau's territory. In this way, the question arises, also in the 'basic' Green Card system, about what is to be understood by the concept 'legally registered vehicle'. Registration procedures are not harmonised in the Green Card system. Rules of registration and deregistration of vehicles are mainly of national competence. As a result, the question of whether a Bureau can 'escape' the guarantee to be given for a false Green Card on the basis of the vehicle not being legally registered in the Bureau's territory depends on the national regulations governing vehicle registration and deregistration, as applicable in the Bureau's legal system.

As an illustration, the Explanatory Memorandum, under Article 9(2) of the Internal Regulations, specifies the following instances where a vehicle can be considered as not legally registered in the territory of the presumed guaranteeing Bureau:

- its registration plate was issued or purports to have been issued under the authority of another country;
- it bears no registration plate despite the obligation to have them in the country of the presumed guaranteeing Bureau;
- the registration plate does not correspond or no longer corresponds to the vehicle;
- it has never been registered in that country.

The Explanatory Memorandum also specifies that it is the entire responsibility of the Bureau invoking Article 9(2) of the Internal Regulations to provide evidence that the vehicle in question is not legally registered in the Bureau's territory. A mere statement that the vehicle is not or no longer legally registered in the Bureau's competent territory cannot be accepted as sufficient.

The last phrase of Article 9(2) refers to Article 7(3) of the Internal Regulations. It is relevant to point out that, under that provision, Bureaux can be allowed to authorise their member insurers to issue Green Cards for vehicles registered in countries where no Bureau exists (see para 3.4.3.1). Since, under that provision, Green Cards will be issued for vehicles registered in a state other than the state for which the Bureau is competent, it is evident that a Bureau can no longer invoke Article 9(2) in order not to give a guarantee for vehicles registered outside the territory of its competence. The inability to invoke Article 9(2), if a Bureau has received the approval to authorise member insurers to issue Green Cards for vehicles registered in a country where no Bureau exists has however far-reaching consequences. The Bureau's obligation to guarantee false Green Cards will not only extend to vehicles registered in the territory for which the Bureau is competent and to vehicles registered in the country for which this authorisation has been given; but it will extend to *any* false Green Card purported to be issued under the authority of the Bureau concerned, irrespective of where the vehicle in question is registered. This is an important extension of the guarantee that is to be taken into account by any Bureau wishing to obtain an approval under Article 7(3) of the Internal Regulations.

3.6.2.4 *The consequences of a Green Card for which no guarantee can be provided*

If no Bureau is prepared, based on the Green Card system, to provide a guarantee for an accident which occurred in the handling entity's territory and caused by a foreign vehicle, it should not necessarily leave an injured party without any compensation.

Several reasons could trigger the lack of a guarantee being provided by a Bureau: the driver of the liable vehicle managed to enter the country without the Green Card being controlled; the period of validity of the Green Card has expired (and the border control authorities have not detected that deficiency) or the period was still valid on the date of entry but subsequently expired before the vehicle concerned exited the territory; the Green Card is false and the vehicle is registered in a different state than the one for which the Bureau, mentioned on the false Green Card, is competent.

Usually this will result in the vehicle being considered as uninsured. One of the criteria taken into consideration by the Council of Bureaux in respect of an applicant Bureau to attain its membership and to participate in the Green Card system is the existence in the country for which the Bureau is competent of a compensation scheme for accidents caused by vehicles for which the insurance obligation has not been respected. In practice, this means that in most cases there is a Guarantee Fund, competent to intervene and provide compensation for the consequences of an accident caused by an uninsured vehicle. The modalities of intervention can however differ from country to country. Moreover, the Guarantee Fund's intervention can be subject to a minimum limit (a deductible or a threshold to be applied to the compensation paid) and/or an upper limit (a maximum amount of compensation). These limitations are subject to national regulations of (insurance) law.

In the states of the European Economic Area (EEA), however, the intervention of the Guarantee Funds for accidents caused by uninsured vehicles will be much more harmonised; and this due to the influence of the provisions imposed by the European Union in the codified Motor Insurance Directive. But equally in that case, important differences remain because the Motor Insurance Directive allows Member States to regard the intervention of Guarantee Funds as subsidiary. Chapter 4 will go into more details of the Guarantee Funds operating in the EEA states and the possibility of subsidiarity.

At the end of this section, it is important to emphasise that all the rules described to determine whether a Green Card is identified, valid, false or unauthorised and whether the rules of the Green Card system apply or not, are based on the Internal Regulations and the Explanatory Memorandum. As already stated earlier, these rules govern the contractual relations between Bureaux and are not binding on policyholders or injured parties. In case of accidents caused by foreign vehicles, it will be the national courts that can decide, on the basis of the national legislation, whether a Green Card is to be considered as valid or not and whether the Bureau of the country of the accident is to intervene for the compensation of the damage caused or not. If a national court, based on national legislation, rules that a Green

Card is valid, this decision will be binding on the handling Bureau and the latter will not be able to contradict that judgment on the basis of the Internal Regulations.

An interesting question is whether in that case, the guaranteeing Bureau, under whose authority the Green Card is (purported to be) issued, must provide a guarantee and must reimburse the handling Bureau all the compensation paid by the latter to the injured party. The national court decision, concerning the validity of the Green Card, is not binding on the (foreign) guaranteeing Bureau and it may be expected that the latter will only be willing to reimburse the handling Bureau if the Green card is to be considered valid in accordance with the rules of the Internal Regulations. If, based on the Internal Regulations, the Green Card is not valid, the guaranteeing Bureau will not find itself compelled to reimburse the handling Bureau, merely on the basis of a national court decision. If the handling Bureau does not agree with the point of view of the guaranteeing Bureau, the dispute will ultimately be settled by mediation or arbitration.

3.6.3 Examination of the Guarantee within the Green Card system based on deemed insurance cover

3.6.3.1 Introduction

Contrary to the 4th MID (see later chapter 5), where a complete new institutional framework was created, the system of deemed insurance cover is entirely built on the existing cooperation between national Motor Insurers' Bureaux in the framework of the Green Card system. The claims handling activity within the system of deemed insurance cover will therefore remain in the hands of Bureaux, agents and correspondents.

Before starting to process a claim, the handling entity will have to ascertain whether it is allowed to act on behalf of a foreign entity (Bureau or insurer). Similarly to the variant of the 'basic' Green Card system, the handling entity will need to receive a confirmation. This time, the confirmation will no longer be related to the validity of a Green Card but to the existence of insurance cover and to the question whether a vehicle is normally based in the territory for which a Bureau is competent.

The rules on how such confirmation can be given are to be found in Section III of the Internal Regulations ('Specific rules governing contractual relations between Bureaux based on deemed insurance cover').

3.6.3.2 *The request for the confirmation that a vehicle is normally based in a Bureau's territory*

Where Article 8 of the Internal Regulations focusses on the submission of a formal request for confirmation of a Green Card's validity, a comparable procedure is foreseen in Article 13 related to the cooperation between Bureaux based on deemed insurance cover.

Article 13 gives a handling Bureau the possibility to ask for the confirmation that a vehicle is normally based in the territory of the country for which the Bureau receiving the request is competent. The same deadline of six weeks is foreseen within which the Bureau, receiving the request, must provide an answer. In the absence of a reply within the foreseen time period, the vehicle in question will be deemed to be normally based in the country for which the Bureau, receiving the request, is competent. The latter Bureau will then be required to provide a guarantee for the vehicle in question.

In the framework of their cooperation within the Council of Bureaux, the national Bureaux have created templates to be used for sending out a request for confirmation based on Article 13 as well as to reply to such request.

The template for the "reply to the request for confirmation of the territory in which a vehicle is normally based" grants Bureaux the possibility to reply in three different ways:

- The Bureau can confirm that the vehicle described in the request is normally based in the Bureau's territory of competence. Such confirmation automatically grants the handling Bureau the authorisation to handle the claim in the name of the replying Bureau which, through this confirmation, becomes the guaranteeing Bureau. The template also specifies that the claims handling activity must be performed in accordance with the rules of the Internal Regulations.
- The Bureau can, within the same template, also indicate the insurer of the vehicle in question. This information allows the handling Bureau to take further steps in the claims handling process and, in case the insurer has appointed a correspondent in the country of the accident, forward the claim to the correspondent concerned. Technically, it is even possible that the responding Bureau indicates the insurer of the vehicle in question without formally confirming that the vehicle is normally based in its territory of competence. Such a provisional reply allows the handling entity to contact the insurer concerned and, based on the latter's information, to start the handling process. At the same time, the responding Bureau can start or continue any possible investigation of the registration status of the vehicle as to determine whether confirmation can be given that the vehicle is normally based in its territory of competence. It is however recommended to limit this option (of only indicating the

insurer without formally confirming the normally based status) to a strict minimum. It should only be done in cases where the responding Bureau has justified doubts about the registration of the vehicle. In any case, if the Bureau only indicates the insurer on the reply template, it should still, afterwards, formally confirm or deny that the vehicle is normally based in the territory for which it is competent. It is relevant to highlight the fact that, in the absence of an explicit confirmation or denial of the normally based status, the six weeks' period continues to run; the failure to respond by the end of this period shall signify that the vehicle concerned shall be deemed to be normally based in the territory of the responding Bureau.
- The Bureau can deny that the vehicle is normally based in its territory of competence. Such denial should, however, be substantiated. The template provides for a number of qualified reasons that can be invoked by the responding Bureau to deny that the vehicle is normally based in its territory. A mere denial of the normally based status, or even merely confirming that the registration plate does not correspond or no longer corresponds to the vehicle in question, cannot be considered as sufficient.

As was the case with the 'basic' Green Card system, the concept of deemed insurance cover envisages that cases can be handled and injured parties can be compensated without a formal request for confirmation, based on the Internal Regulations, being sent out. If a claim is addressed to a national Bureau and the handling Bureau can, on the basis of the information available in the claim documents (e.g. an accident statement) identify the insurer of the foreign vehicle involved in the accident, it can start the claims handling process. If the said insurer confirms cover for the vehicle in question, no formal request on the basis of Article 13 of the Internal Regulations is necessary.

In the case of deemed insurance cover, the question of territorial validity actually becomes irrelevant. The handling entity does not have to enquire whether the insurer has given cover for the country in which the accident occurred. This is because both the country of origin of the vehicle and the country where the accident occurred belong to the area where the Multilateral Agreement is applicable. That means that any insurer is bound to provide MTPL cover in the territory of each signatory Bureau; hence, the question of territorial validity becomes irrelevant.

For that reason, in the vast majority of cases handled in the framework of deemed insurance cover, the handling process will start without any formal request based on Article 13 of the Internal Regulations being sent and replied to.

3.6.3.3 Not corresponding or no longer corresponding registration plate

In paragraph 3.5.5, we have examined the criteria put forward in the Internal Regulations to determine in which country a vehicle is normally based.[32] The last point of these criteria refers to "cases where the vehicle does not bear any registration plate or bears a registration plate which does not correspond or no longer corresponds to the vehicle"; it stipulates that in such cases, the vehicle in question will be considered to be normally based in the territory where the accident took place.

This means that no foreign Bureau will be required to guarantee the consequences of an accident caused by such a vehicle. Again, similarly to the situation where no valid Green Card is available for a foreign vehicle, the vehicle in question will most probably be considered as uninsured and the injured party will, subject to national rules of intervention for uninsured vehicles, have to address a claim to the Guarantee Fund. In many countries this will, in practice, not make a significant difference because the functions of Bureau and Guarantee Fund are performed by the same organisation. But there are also several countries where Bureau and Guarantee Fund are separate institutions. And in any case, even if both functions are taken up by the same organisation, the rules of intervention of the Guarantee Fund can be subject to certain limitations or rules of subsidiarity. The intervention of Guarantee Funds is discussed in chapter 4.

Example

For deemed insurance cover, we can again refer to the same example of a French citizen driving a vehicle registered in France and causing an accident in Italy.

For the claims handling process, no physical Green Card will be necessary; the French registration plate will be sufficient. An ideal document to increase the efficiency of the claims handling process is the European Accident Statement, developed by the European insurers. On this accident statement, the registration plate and other essential or useful information is elicited so as to allow the involved professionals to take the necessary action.

The Italian injured party (or their representative) will be able to address a claim directly to the French insurer, or to the correspondent of the French insurer in Italy (if a correspondent was appointed) or to the Italian national insurers' Bureau.

Based on the information available, the Italian Bureau will either forward the claim to the correspondent of the French insurer in Italy or start handling the claim itself. In the latter case (or in any case where there may be uncertainty about the correct registration status of the French vehicle), the Italian Bureau may address a formal request to the French Bureau seeking confirmation that the vehicle is normally based in its territory.

32. The criteria of the Directive with respect to the normally based concept are described in para 6.2.5.2 to 6.2.5.5.

The French Bureau has six weeks to answer that request; failing which, the vehicle will be deemed to be normally based in France. This allows the Italian Bureau to handle the case in accordance with the Internal Regulations.
If the French Bureau denies that the vehicle concerned is normally based in its territory, this denial will have to be based on one of the qualified reasons already envisaged in the template related to Article 13 of the Internal Regulations. In case of denial, the Italian Bureau will then have to determine whether the vehicle may, possibly, be normally based in any other Member State.
In case the vehicle is not normally based in any other Member State, then it will have to be considered to be normally based in Italy, which is the country of the accident.
Even when the vehicle is not validly registered in France and must be considered to be normally based in Italy, it can still be validly insured in France. In that case, the identified French insurer can still compensate the injured party or authorise its Italian correspondent to do so.
In case the vehicle is neither normally based in France nor validly insured, the case will have to be handled by the Italian Guarantee Fund, in accordance with Italian legislation on accidents caused by uninsured vehicles. Since the Bureau and the Guarantee Fund are two separate institutions in Italy and they are even based in two different cities, the file will move from Milan to Rome.

3.7 The claims handling process with the injured party

3.7.1 *General remarks*

In the preceding sections, we have explained the basic principles of the Green Card system, highlighting the two characteristic variants: the 'basic' Green Card system based on the physical existence of a Green Card and the system of deemed insurance cover. We have also explained how, in both variants, the claims handling activity can be based on either the existence of a valid (or false or unauthorised) Green Card or on the confirmation that a vehicle is normally based in the territory for which a Bureau is competent.

Once the existence of a Green Card is ascertained or the territory being confirmed, the actual claims handling activity can start. In this regard, we revert to the earlier provisions of the Internal Regulations; namely, Articles 3 and 4.

An accident has occurred and an injured party seeks compensation for the damage suffered. It will, therefore, submit a claim to the handling entity. The latter will be expected to take the necessary steps in the claims handling process in accordance with the rules applicable in the country of the accident. The claims handling entity may have to appoint experts to assess the damage or may have to examine the expert report submitted by the injured party. It may have to follow up the evolution of the damage. Certainly in case of bodily injury this can be a relatively long process. Once the damage has been determined with certainty, compensation will have to be provided; and this with the goal of returning the injured party – as much as reasonably possible – to the situation immediately prior to the accident. The payment of such compensation will be made either on the basis of an amicable settlement or after a court has pronounced itself on the matter. When compensating an injured party, it is important to underline the fact that the handling entity must advance the compensation payments. Under no circumstances can the handling entity delay compensation payments until being paid by the reimbursing entity (the foreign insurer or the guaranteeing Bureau). All these claims handling activities form part of the national rules on liability, insurance law and compensation of damage; these are topics which fall outside the scope of this book (see the introduction in chapter 1).

When having to determine the right claims handling entity, one will in the first place think about the Motor Insurers' Bureau of the country in which the accident occurred.

Motor Insurers' Bureaux can have a claims department integrated within their organisation; this would be capable of handling a claim as well as providing the correct compensation to the injured party, in accordance with the applicable rules of the country of the accident. Several Bureaux, however, do not have such a department; they therefore entrust the claims handling activity to an agent, appointed by the Bureau for that purpose.

Right from the start, however, the Green Card system has also provided for the possibility to outsource the claims handling activity to a correspondent, chosen by the insurer and approved by the Bureau of the country in which such correspondent is acting.

The three bodies, able to take up the role of a claims handling entity, will be described in the following sub-sections:

- the handling Bureau (para 3.7.2);
- the agent (para 3.7.3);
- the correspondent (para 3.7.4).

3.7.2 *Claims handled by the handling Bureau*

Even in the absence of any claim being addressed by the injured party to the Bureau of the country in which the accident occurred, the Internal Regulations already impose a task on that Bureau. Article 3(1) of the Internal Regulations formulates it as follows:

> "When a bureau is informed of an accident occurring in the territory of the country for which it is competent, involving a vehicle from another country it shall, without waiting for a formal claim, proceed to investigate the circumstances of the accident. It shall as soon as possible give notice of any such accident to the insurer who issued the Green Card or policy of insurance or, if appropriate, to the bureau concerned. Any omission to do so shall however not be held against it."

In practice, it will only happen exceptionally that a Bureau is informed about an accident if no claim is received. The French system of 'Trans PV' operates in such a way that when a French police report is drafted in respect of an accident in which a foreign vehicle is involved, a copy is automatically forwarded to the French Motor Insurers' Bureau (*Bureau central français*).

When the insurer of the liable vehicle has appointed an approved correspondent in the country of the accident, the Bureau shall forward the information about the accident or the claim promptly to the said correspondent (see further para 3.7.4).

When no correspondent had been approved for the insurer concerned, the Bureau will be responsible for handling the claim. The Bureau will then have the option to handle the claim itself or to entrust the handling activity to an agent (see further para 3.7.3).

The possible scenarios can be illustrated as follows:

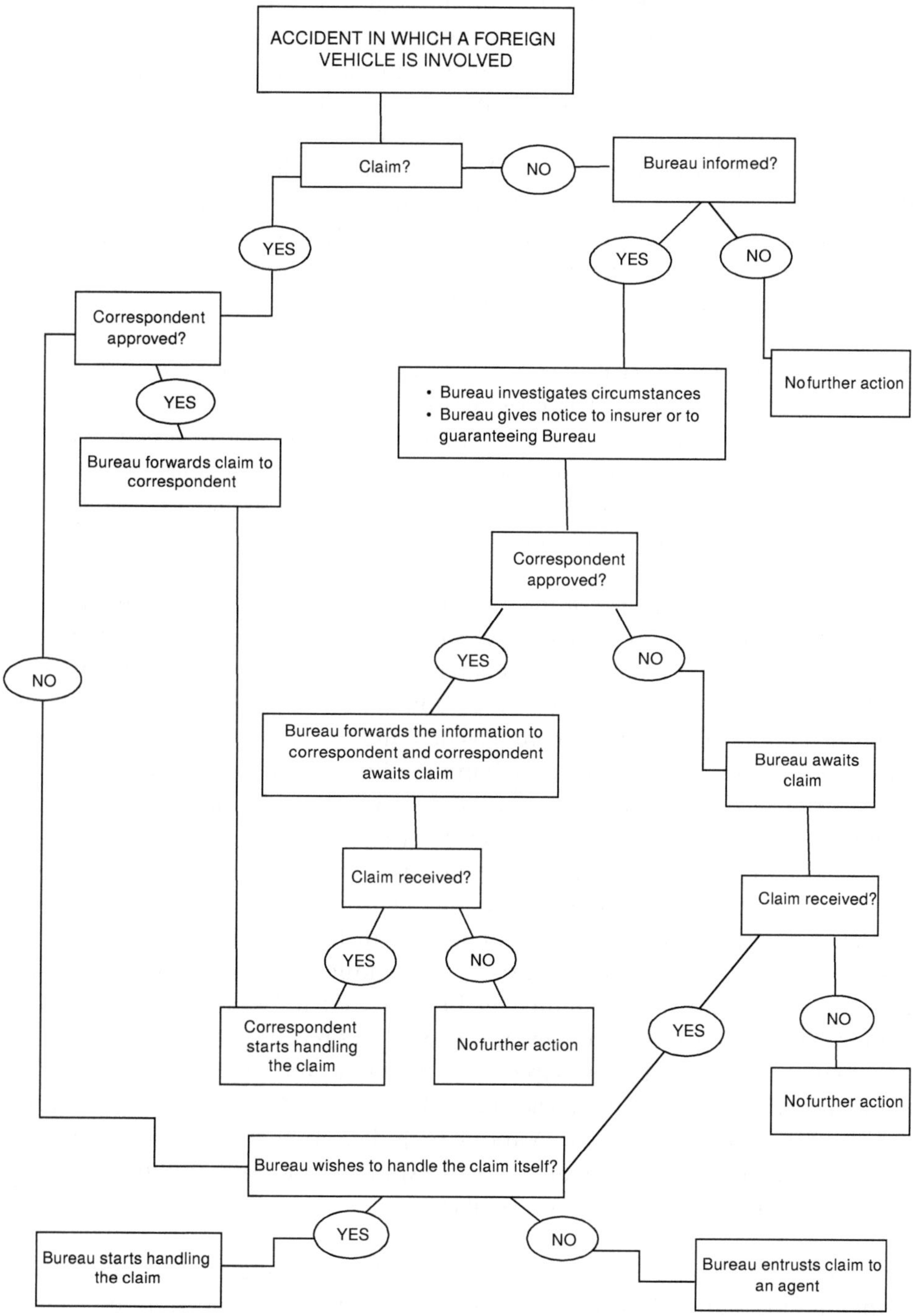
ACCIDENT IN WHICH A FOREIGN VEHICLE IS INVOLVED
Claim?
NO
Bureau informed?
YES
NO
YES
NO
Correspondent approved?
No further action
YES
• Bureau investigates circumstances
• Bureau gives notice to insurer or to guaranteeing Bureau
Bureau forwards claim to correspondent
Correspondent approved?
YES
NO
NO
Bureau forwards the information to correspondent and correspondent awaits claim
Bureau awaits claim
Claim received?
Claim received?
YES
NO
Correspondent starts handling the claim
No further action
YES
NO
No further action
Bureau wishes to handle the claim itself?
YES
NO
Bureau starts handling the claim
Bureau entrusts claim to an agent

Since the compensation that will be paid in the course of the claims handling activity will have to be reimbursed by the foreign insurer and will have to be guaranteed by the foreign Bureau, it is evident that the insurer and the guaranteeing Bureau must be kept well informed about the case by the handling Bureau. Therefore, the Internal Regulations require the latter Bureau to provide essential information to the said insurer and/or the guaranteeing Bureau; and this in order to allow them to make a reasonable estimate of the possible financial impact of the claim, in terms of technical provisions or reserves. Because of the importance of this information, the Internal Regulations have recently been modified on this specific topic and now read as follows (Article 3(2), point (2)):

> "Whenever dealing with a claim, the Bureau or its agent shall inform the insurer or the Bureau concerned about its best estimate of the expected claims amounts so that the addressee can set up an appropriate technical provision. It shall attach essential and relevant documentation and update the information as well as the documentation whenever substantial changes occur to it. This obligation is without prejudice to any other obligation of the Bureau or its agent in the country of accident arising from this Article. '

Despite the fact that the insurer or the guaranteeing Bureau will eventually have to reimburse the compensation paid and even if it is therefore so important that they are well informed and equally well documented about the envisaged claim settlement, this does not mean that they will be able to decide – or to have a say – on whether the injured party is to be compensated and, if so, to what extent. The accident has occurred in the country of the handling Bureau and any resultant claim is to be settled in accordance with the laws of the country of the accident. Therefore, the handling Bureau is the most suited to determine and decide on the liabilities, the steps to be taken in the claims handling process and the compensation to be paid. It is also the handling Bureau's autonomous decision to try to reach an amicable settlement with the injured party or to submit the liability issue and/or the compensation to the competent courts. The handling Bureau should keep the insurer concerned and the guaranteeing Bureau well informed about the major steps in the handling process; however, it should not receive any 'instructions' (or interference) from them. This principle is referred to as the *handling autonomy of the handling Bureau*; it is one of the basic rules of the Green Card system (see Article 3(4) of the Internal Regulations). Without prejudice to such autonomy, the said insurer or the guaranteeing Bureau can still explicitly ask the handling Bureau to be informed before any final decision is taken.

When handling a claim in accordance with the Internal Regulations, the Bureau concerned is still required to act *in the best interests* of the insurer or of the guaranteeing Bureau; and this in terms of Article 3(4) which concerns its handling autonomy.

The guarantees of the Green Card system safeguard the principle that a vehicle, when entering the territory of a country for which it is insured (either by means of a valid Green Card or by the system of deemed insurance cover), benefits from the compulsory MTPL cover as applicable in the visited country. If, however, the insurance conditions in the vehicle's country of origin are more beneficial than in the country visited, and the settlement envisaged by the handling Bureau is in excess of the conditions applicable in the country of the accident, the Internal Regulations provide for a consultation to be held by the handling Bureau with the insurer concerned in relation to the part of the claim that exceeds the conditions applicable in the country of the accident.

Example

The maximum amount of cover for personal injuries applicable in Moldova is MDL 1,000,000 per victim, which corresponds to approximately € 50,000. In Belgium, to the contrary, there is unlimited cover for personal injuries.

If a Belgian vehicle travels to Moldova, it will benefit from the compulsory MTPL insurance cover as applicable in Moldova on entry.

If the Belgian vehicle causes an accident with personal injury in Moldova, the total amount of which is estimated to be around € 250,000 the Moldovan Bureau will have to consult with the Belgian Bureau in order to determine whether, when effecting compensation, the higher cover as applicable in Belgium can be taken into consideration.

In accordance with Belgian law, the Belgian insurer will confirm that the Belgian driver or policyholder may indeed benefit from the higher cover available in Belgium.

The situation is different if the accident takes place in a Member State and involves a vehicle normally based in another Member State: under Article 14, point (b) of the codified Motor Insurance Directive the cover to be provided in such a case is that of the Member State of the accident, unless the compulsory cover in the Member State where the vehicle is normally based is higher. That implies that the Bureau of the Member State of the accident is not required to ask for authorisation to take into account the higher cover.

3.7.3 *Claims handled by an agent*

As explained above, the handling Bureau has the choice, in the absence of an approved correspondent for a certain insurer, either to handle claims for that insurer itself or to forward such claims to an agent. It is also the Bureau's choice how to organise the distribution of claims to agents. It can decide to centralise all claims against a certain insurer with the same agent or it can apply a rotation scheme by entrusting claims to different agents. The handling Bureau is free to determine who can operate as an agent, but this will usually be member insurers of the Bureau and/or specialised claims handling offices.

In any case, the Bureau will have to determine, when forwarding a claim to an agent, that the agent in question has no financial interest in the claim. If the agent were to have any such interest, the Bureau will have to entrust the claim to another agent or to seek the prior written consent of the insurer concerned before entrusting the claim to that specific agent. Article 3(6) provides for a sanction if this obligation is not observed in that the handling Bureau will only be allowed to receive half of the sum that would be recoverable if the obligation would have been respected.

Example

A citizen of Hungary, insured with the Hungarian insurance company Hungaria, travels to Germany and causes an accident in that country resulting in damage being suffered by a German citizen. The German victim's vehicle has full comprehensive (casco) insurance with the German insurance company Germania. The German citizen reports the damage to Germania and receives compensation in accordance with the terms and conditions of the comprehensive insurance contract. Germania is subrogated in the German citizen's claim against the Hungarian tortfeasor and can address a claim to the German Motor Insurers' Bureau.

The German Bureau, which does not directly handle claims itself, will entrust the claim to an agent; but when doing so (possibly on the basis of a rotation scheme), the Bureau will have to make sure not to entrust this specific claim to Germania.

When an agent is requested to handle a claim on the request of a handling Bureau, the agent will have to act as if it was the handling Bureau. The agent has no contractual relationship with the insurer concerned describing the modalities of the claims handling and reimbursement process. It only has a contractual relationship with the handling Bureau and it is therefore recommended that the Bureau and the agent make clear, written arrangements concerning the way in which the agent will execute the task and be remunerated for it. Those arrangements will clearly have to refer to the Internal Regulations, which are to govern the way in which the agent has to handle the claim and communicate with the foreign insurer. That is the reason why the Internal Regulations always refer not only to the Bureau but also to the agent.

Contrary to what is applicable to the Bureau, in most countries it will not be possible to start legal proceedings against the agent. These will have to be issued against the Bureau in whose name the agent acts.[33]

3.7.4 *Claims handled by a correspondent*

Although designed as a cooperation mechanism between Motor Insurers' Bureaux, the Green Card system has, right from the beginning, provided the possibility that insurers can choose to centralise all their claims in another Green Card country in the hands of a correspondent. This is a possibility and not an obligation. In the absence of any appointed and approved correspondent, the claims handling activity will be in the hands of the Motor Insurers' Bureau of the country of the accident (which can, subsequently, decide to entrust the handling activity to an agent, as explained above). Moreover, the fact that an insurer appoints a correspondent in one Green Card country does not mean that it will have to appoint correspondents in all the other Green Card countries. It is perfectly possible that an insurer chooses to work with a correspondent in, for instance, 15 countries, whereas it leaves the claims handling process in the hands of the national Bureaux (or agents) in all the other countries.

A correspondent can be either an insurer or any specialised claims handling office. If the correspondent is an insurer, it can either be an insurance undertaking belonging to the same group or holding of insurance companies as the mandating insurer or it can be an insurer without any ownership links. Claims handling offices can be companies acting in one single country as a specialist in claims handling activities in that specific market, or they can belong to an international group or network of claims handling entities. A claims handling office can also be a legal office or a loss adjusting company, acting as Green Card correspondent.

Since correspondents act in the country of the accident and they do so in the name of the handling Bureau, their nomination is subject to the approval of the handling Bureau. The Internal Regulations require each national Bureau to "set out the conditions under which it grants, refuses or withdraws its approval to correspondents established in the country for which it is competent" (Article 4(1)). In this way, transparency in the approval process is safeguarded, while at the same time respecting the Bureau's autonomy to approve correspondents.

33. In practice the situation occurs that a vehicle initially seems to be insured with an insurance company that has nominated a correspondent. If the correspondent has started handling the claim, but subsequently the vehicle turns out to be uninsured (which means that the Bureau itself is responsible for the handling of the claim), the Bureau can ask the correspondent to proceed with the handling of the claim in a capacity of the Bureau's agent.

A number of Bureaux require correspondents which are not insurers/members of their Bureau to provide the name of an insurer who is willing to act as a 'fronting company' for that correspondent. This construction reinforces the link between the Bureau and the correspondent of the foreign insurance company.

In the interest of a qualitative claims handling process, Bureaux have the right to exercise control over correspondents acting in the country for which they are competent (Article 4(1) of the Internal Regulations). Certain Bureaux indeed organise regular audits over the claims handled by correspondents.

> Since 2010, the Swiss Bureau operates a control mechanism on correspondents operating within the Swiss market. The system is characterised by a combination of both an internal audit and an external audit.
> For the internal audit, which takes place every year, each agent and correspondent has to examine 5% of the files closed during the current calendar year, with a minimum of 20 claims and a maximum of 100 claims. One third of the claim files submitted to the audit have to be personal injury claims. The audit is performed with the help of an online tool, which is embedded in the intranet of the Swiss Bureau and contains a questionnaire on the quality of the handling process. A report on the audit is generated automatically by the system at the end of the review period.
> For the external audit, an external independent expert in foreign claims is selected. This external auditor is regularly (normally once every four years) requested by the Swiss Bureau to perform a quality control on 2% of the claims (with a minimum of 20 and a maximum of 50) handled and closed during the previous calendar year by each correspondent operating on the Swiss market. One third of these claims must be files which were already audited by the correspondent in the framework of the internal audit system.
> Far less than being considered as an external control, the audit system in Switzerland is perceived by Swiss insurers and correspondents as a means of cooperation in order to improve the quality of the claims handling process. The experiences are positive and seem to realise the objectives targeted when establishing these audit mechanisms.

It is normal that insurance companies, belonging to insurance groups that are internationally active, would want to appoint their sister, mother or daughter companies in other countries as their Green Card correspondent. In order to safeguard that possibility, the Internal Regulations provide that

> "this approval [*of a correspondent by the handling Bureau, the authors*] shall be granted when requested in the name of a member of another Bureau for any establishment of this member in the country of the Bureau receiving the request provided that such establishment transacts insurance against civil liability in respect of the use of motor vehicles."

An insurer, wishing to obtain the approval of its chosen correspondent in a specific country cannot simply send the request for such approval directly to the Bureau of that country but has to obtain the approval through its own national Bureau of which the insurer is a member. The latter Bureau then has to submit the request to the Bureau of the country in which the correspondent is to be approved. The request must be supported by proof that the proposed correspondent accepts the requested nomination. The Bureau of the country in which the correspondent is to be approved, has to respond to the request within a period of three months; failing which the request will be deemed to have been approved.

Example
If the Estonian insurer Estins wishes to obtain the approval of the correspondent Fincor in Finland, it will have to send a request to the Estonian Bureau. The Estonian Bureau shall then send a request for approval of the said correspondent to the Finnish Bureau. This request must be supported by proof that Fincor accepts the requested nomination.
If the Finnish Bureau does not reply to the request within three months, the approval will be deemed to have been given.

In practice, it happens quite often that the formalities for sending out the request, together with the proof that the correspondent accepts the requested nomination, are prepared by the correspondent in question. After all, acting as a correspondent is often considered as a commercial activity and correspondents are in search of insurers they can represent. Therefore, they will give all possible support to an insurer that wishes the correspondent to represent it in a specific country.

An insurer can nominate only one correspondent per country.
Once approved, a correspondent will act in the name of the Bureau that approved it and on behalf of the insurer that requested its approval. The Internal Regulations do not explicitly grant the same handling autonomy to a correspondent as that envisaged for a handling Bureau in Article 3(4); but Article 4(4) of the Internal Regulations stipulates that a correspondent

> "shall handle all claims in conformity with any legal or regulatory provisions applicable in the country of accident relating to liability, compensation of injured parties and compulsory motor insurance."

This implies that the insurer that requested the correspondent's approval shall not give instructions to the correspondent and must respect the correspondent's decisions as to the way in which claims are being dealt with. Any clauses written in contracts between insurers and correspondents, requiring the insurer's prior approval to any envisaged settlement, must therefore be considered in breach of the principles of the Green Card system and of the Internal Regulations.

When a Bureau has given its approval to a correspondent acting on behalf of a foreign insurer, this approval must of course be respected. The Bureau is therefore held to forward to the correspondent concerned any claims related to accidents in which an insured of the foreign insurer is involved. Having regard to the fact that the correspondent acts in the name of the Bureau, the latter has the right at any time to take over the handling and settlement of a claim from a correspondent, without having to justify that decision (Article 4(5) of the Internal Regulations). It goes without saying that such a right is to be exercised with due care and should only be invoked in exceptional circumstances. The Explanatory Memorandum to the Internal Regulations states that the revocation of a claim should be exercised "solely for the purpose of ensuring the efficient handling of claims."

In case a handling Bureau has to compensate the injured party (after the withdrawal of a claim file from a correspondent on the basis of Article 4(5) or for whatever other reason), that Bureau shall not have to send a demand for reimbursement to the insurer concerned but shall be directly reimbursed by the guaranteeing Bureau (Article 4(6) of the Internal Regulations). The details of such reimbursement procedures will be examined in more detail under paragraph 3.8.

Insurers and correspondents benefit from the contractual freedom to determine their modalities of mutual cooperation. As long as their terms of cooperation are not in contradiction with the basic principles of the Green Card system or with the conditions imposed by the Bureau responsible for approving the correspondent, insurers and correspondents are free to negotiate how they shall communicate with each other and how the compensations paid to injured parties are to be reimbursed. One of the main elements in these negotiations will be the 'fee' that will have to be paid to the correspondent in return for its claims handling activity. This reward or consideration for the work done is called a 'handling fee' and will be treated in more detail in paragraph 3.8.2.2. The amount of the handling fee and its calculation are subject to the contractual freedom between the insurer and the correspondent. Whilst stipulating and respecting this contractual freedom, the Internal Regulations state however that these modalities of cooperation between insurers and correspondents shall not be enforceable against any Bureau. In case a Bureau has to act in place of a correspondent, it shall do so in accordance with the provisions of the Internal Regulations. Article 4(7) of the Internal Regulations formulates this principle as follows:

> "Subject to the provisions of Article 4(4), the correspondent is free to agree with the insurer that requested its approval the conditions for reimbursement of sums paid to injured parties and the method for calculating its handling fees which agreement, however, shall not be enforceable against any Bureau."

In the interest of a qualitative claims handling process and in the interest of the insurer, it is strongly advised that correspondents and insurers make clear arrangements on how to inform each other about the relevant specificities of claims being handled by the former on behalf of the latter. Whilst respecting the handling autonomy of the correspondent, insurers should be kept well informed by the former about the specificities of a claim, the number of injured parties and the nature of their damage; more importantly, the insurer should be informed about the extent of the impact of the claim on its financial exposure. Therefore, insurers and correspondents should agree on contractual provisions comparable to Article 3(2), point (2) of the Internal Regulations. Such clauses would compel the correspondent to inform the insurer about the best estimate of the expected claim amount(s), enabling the insurer to set up appropriate technical provisions. Additionally, correspondents and insurers can agree to provide essential and relevant documentation related to the claim presented.

The Internal Regulations also provide for rules in case the relation between an insurer and a correspondent comes to an end. Three different scenarios can be envisaged and are dealt with in the Internal Regulations.

a. ***The Bureau (in whose name a correspondent operates) withdraws the approval of the correspondent to act for the foreign insurer.***
   If a Bureau decides to withdraw its earlier approval, this will probably mean that serious problems have occurred in the claims handling process and/or the way in which injured parties are compensated.
   In order to guarantee full transparency, the Internal Regulations require in such a situation that the Bureau (that initially granted the approval of the correspondent and is now withdrawing it) informs the guaranteeing Bureau, which is the Bureau of the country of the insurer, of its decision. In that way, the guaranteeing Bureau can then inform its member insurer that the approval of the correspondent concerned has been withdrawn. The Bureau shall also determine the date when the withdrawal of the approval will take effect.
b. ***The correspondent wishes to stop the representation activity for the foreign insurer.***
   Various reasons may cause the correspondent to end its relationship with the foreign insurer. The correspondent may wish to end all claims handling activities or may only want to end the activities with one specific insurer because of the latter's continuous lack of respect for the rules of the Green Card system.

Also in this case, the Bureau, which initially issued the correspondent's approval, will inform the other Bureau of which the insurer concerned is a member. It will again determine the date when the end of the correspondent's appointment will take effect.

c. ***The insurer wishes to end the relationship with the correspondent.***
In this case, two 'sub-scenarios' are possible:
   i. *The insurer no longer wishes that the claims handling activity is performed by any correspondent.*
   In this case, the handling activity will no longer be exercised by a correspondent but will be the entire responsibility of the handling Bureau. The latter can either decide to deal with claims for the foreign insurer itself or outsource the claims to be handled by an agent. The Bureau will, again, determine the date when the correspondent's activities will cease.
   ii. *The insurer wishes to replace the existing correspondent by a new correspondent.*
   This 'sub-scenario' will, in practice, be more likely to occur than the preceding one. As the choice of a correspondent is at the discretion of an insurer (provided that the correspondent is approved by the Bureau concerned), an insurer may wish to replace an existing correspondent with a new one because of expected better cooperation or more advantageous terms and conditions that can be negotiated. But it is also possible that the insurer's wish to replace a correspondent is in reality an attempt of the insurer to escape its responsibilities towards the existing correspondent. In 2013, the Council of Bureaux has introduced the current Article 4(9) of the Internal Regulations in order to put an end to the approach of certain insurers to change correspondents in certain countries mainly to try to escape their existing financial obligations (such as, reimbursements of compensations already paid to injured parties) towards the existing correspondent. In order to eliminate such practices, the current Article 4(9) requires Bureaux, when determining the appointment date of the 'new' correspondent, to take the following two factors explicitly into consideration:
      - The outstanding debts of the insurer towards the preceding correspondent;
      - The way in which the insurer and the 'old' correspondent have respected the rule that the damage is to be assessed and compensated in accordance with the laws applicable in the state of the accident, as determined in Article 4(4). This rule includes the principle that the correspondent should ignore any 'instructions' of the insurer when effecting compensations.

These two rules allow the Bureau to postpone the effective date of the change of correspondent until any outstanding debts towards the 'old' correspondent are settled. It has to be taken into consideration, however, that the 'old' correspondent, after becoming aware of the end of its (commercial) relationship with the insurer concerned, may be disappointed and not motivated to inform the Bureau of any possible outstanding debts or, alternatively, to overestimate such outstanding payments. In order to offset such reaction, a discretionary power is granted to the Bureau to determine the effective date of the change of correspondent.

Now that the different provisions of the Internal Regulations relating to the operation of correspondents have been explained, let us focus our attention on the status of a correspondent, representing a foreign insurer in a specific country. As specified in Article 4(4) of the Internal Regulations, the correspondent acts 'in the name of the Bureau that has approved it and on behalf of the insurer that requested its approval'. Blees describes this dual representation by the correspondent as 'serving two masters'.[34]

- On the one hand, the correspondent represents the foreign insurer in the country where it was approved. From a legal perspective, this representation can probably best be described as a mandate. As already explained, the correspondent is free to negotiate the conditions of this representation with the insurer concerned, as long as the basic principles of the Green Card system are not violated. This includes the important provision, as worded in Article 4(5) of the Internal Regulations, giving the correspondent a degree of handling autonomy when compensating the injured party without having to follow any possible 'instructions' of the insurer. Any compensation paid by the correspondent will have to be reimbursed by the insurer; failing which, the correspondent will be able to fall back on the guarantee provided by the handling Bureau (see further para 3.8.5).
- On the other hand, the correspondent acts in the name of the Bureau that approved it. Any compensation paid by the correspondent to the injured party will discharge the Bureau's responsibility towards the latter. This relationship can be qualified as a mandate. If the correspondent does not respect its obligations towards the injured party or if the latter is not satisfied with the compensation proposed and wants to incept legal proceedings, the final responsibility will then rest with the handling Bureau. For that reason, in most countries it is not possible to initiate legal proceedings against the correspondent but only against the Bureau.[35]

It is also because of this final responsibility of the handling Bureau that it is important that the Bureau makes clear and detailed contractual arrangements with the entities that can be approved as correspondents. The Council of Bureaux has pre-

34. F.J. Blees, De weg naar schadevergoeding in het internationale gemotoriseerde verkeer, p. 161.
35. Even if the Bureau is, formally speaking, the defendant in the court proceedings, it is in practice often the correspondent who coordinates the proceedings and decides how the defence will be organised.

pared a 'Model for a Correspondents' Charter' on which Bureaux can base themselves to establish the rules governing their relations with the correspondents in the territory of the Bureau's competence. The model is not a compulsory text but can be used, entirely or in part, by Bureaux to implement it in their markets.

3.8 The recovery of outlays in the framework of the Green Card system

3.8.1 Introduction

In paragraph 3.7, we have spoken about claims handling and about the entities responsible for providing a correct compensation for the injured party's damage. Once the injured party has received a correct compensation in accordance with the applicable law, it is obvious that the handling entity will seek reimbursement of its outlays from the insurer of the vehicle liable for the accident; or, if that insurer is unwilling or unable to pay, from the entity (a Bureau) required to guarantee such reimbursement, as per the rules of the Green Card system. It was explained earlier that the Green Card system is, in essence, a guarantee system providing certainty to the entity that compensated the injured party of a road traffic accident, caused by a foreign vehicle, to be reimbursed for its outlays.

In this overall guarantee mechanism, different relations need to be examined in detail and these will be the subject of the next sections. We will successively examine the following scenarios:
- The handling Bureau claims from the foreign insurer (para 3.8.2);
- The handling agent claims from the foreign insurer (para 3.8.3);
- The correspondent claims from the foreign insurer (para 3.8.4);
- The correspondent invokes the guarantee of the handling Bureau (para 3.8.5);
- The handling Bureau claims from the guaranteeing Bureau (para 3.8.6).

In case of delayed payments, the Internal Regulations provide for the possibility to invoke the guarantees offered by the Green Card system, namely: the guarantee call, as described in Article 6. This will be examined in more detail in paragraph 3.8.7. Reimbursement of the compensations paid will also have to be guaranteed in case of the insolvency of the foreign insurer; this will be the subject of paragraph 3.8.8.

Finally, there may be situations where the guaranteeing Bureau will not be the final debtor since this Bureau may wish to reclaim its outlay, in a second instance, from a third debtor. This may be the case when a Green Card has been falsified or when the Bureau had to intervene in respect of an uninsured accident and the system of deemed insurance cover was applicable. But the Bureau may also wish to recover its outlay from a member insurer in cases where the latter did not respect its reimbursement obligations in the framework of the Green Card system. This aspect will be examined, albeit shortly, in paragraph 3.8.9.

3.8.2 *The recovery between the handling Bureau and the insurer*

3.8.2.1 *General remarks*

Here, we will examine the situation where the insurer, providing cover for the liable vehicle in a cross-border accident, is not represented by a correspondent in the country of the accident. In this case, the Bureau (established in the country of the accident) can either handle the claim itself or entrust an agent with the claims handling process. We will now examine the situation where the Bureau itself deals with the claim. The second possibility (an agent dealing with the claim on behalf of the Bureau) will be debated in the next paragraph 3.8.3.

Example

Let us, in order to illustrate the reimbursement mechanisms of the Green Card system, revert to the example that we already gave at the beginning of this chapter: a French resident leaves by car for a holiday in Italy and causes an accident in that country. An Italian citizen suffers material damage resulting from this accident. A car expert calculates the damage to the Italian victim's vehicle at € 1,000. Moreover, the Italian victim suffers very limited bodily injury as a result of the accident, which can be estimated at € 500.

The injured party addresses a claim for reimbursement to the Italian Bureau. In case the French insurer is not represented by a correspondent in Italy, the Italian Bureau handles the case and compensates the injured party.

The Italian Bureau wants to be reimbursed for these outlays and therefore addresses a demand for reimbursement to the insurer in France.

It is however to be emphasised that many of the principles, described in this paragraph 3.8.2 may be transposed – mutatis mutandis – to the relations between other partners involved in the claims handling process, as described in the subsequent paragraphs 3.8.3 to 3.8.6.

The handling Bureau will advance the compensations to be paid to the injured parties and, after having compensated the damage caused, ask for reimbursement. First of all, it is to be emphasised that the term 'reimbursement' necessarily implies that the compensation of the injured parties has been advanced by the handling entity. Since one of the two main goals of the Green Card system is to provide an adequate and timely compensation to the injured party, it includes as a basic principle that handling entities may not first request an advance payment from the insurer or the guaranteeing Bureau concerned before compensating the injured party. The handling entity must first compensate the person suffering damage and may only afterwards claim its outlay back. This principle implies that any handling entity – a Bureau, an agent or a correspondent – must at all times have sufficient financial means to make advance payments.

> Unfortunately, it still happens that handling entities wait for the payment by the insurer or the guaranteeing Bureau before compensating the injured party. It even happens that injured parties are informed by the handling entity that no compensation can be paid yet because the paying entity has not yet transferred the necessary funds. This is to be considered as a serious violation of the basic principles of the Green Card system and should not be accepted.

After having effected the agreed compensation, the handling Bureau will address a *demand for reimbursement* to the insurer or to the guaranteeing Bureau (as applicable).

The Internal Regulations specify, in a rather detailed way, all the elements that a demand for reimbursement must contain (para 3.8.2.2). Moreover, they are quite strict regarding the period within which the demand for reimbursement is to be sent (para 3.8.2.3) and to be settled by the paying entity (para 3.8.2.4). Finally, the said Regulations specify instructions regarding the method of communication to be used for delivering a demand for reimbursement (para 3.8.2.5). Some remaining topics, relating to the reimbursement obligations listed in the Internal Regulations, will be handled in para 3.8.2.6.

3.8.2.2 The content of a demand for reimbursement

A number of elements that must necessarily be included in the demand for reimbursement, cannot be found in the Internal Regulations themselves but result from a Council of Bureaux decision taken in 2011. These are listed in the text of the Explanatory Memorandum, under Article 5(1) of the Internal Regulations. Any demand for reimbursement must necessarily contain the following information:

1. The date of the demand;
2. The name of the entity addressing the demand (the handling entity, which is either the handling Bureau, an agent or a correspondent. In case of a correspondent, however, the relations between the correspondent and the insurer are primarily to be governed by their mutual contract);
3. The name of the entity to which the demand is addressed (the insurer or the guaranteeing Bureau);
4. The number or reference of the file by which the case is known to the insurer and/or the guaranteeing Bureau;

5. The date and the country of the accident. If the exact place of the accident is known, this should also be mentioned;
6. Information regarding the liable party:
   a. For claims handled according to Section II of the Internal Regulations (claims based on the existence of a Green Card): the number of the Green Card (and, if available, the number of the insurance policy);
   b. For claims handled according to Section III of the Internal Regulations ('deemed insurance cover'): one of the criteria that determine the territory in which the vehicle is normally based (the registration number of the vehicle, the insurance plate or the place of permanent residency of the holder of the vehicle).
7. The sums that the final debtor must reimburse;
8. The compulsory information arising out of paragraph 1 of article 5(2) of the Internal Regulations;
9. Details regarding the bank of the handling entity.

As regards item 7 of the list (the sums that the final debtor must reimburse), Article 5(1) of the Internal Regulations provides more details about the three basic elements that these sums can be composed of (Articles 5(1) (point 1), point (2) and point (3)):

> "5.1.1. The sums paid as compensation to injured parties under either an amicable settlement or a court order."

It is to be reminded that the compensation for the damage suffered is to be advanced by the handling entity and that it must be in accordance with the rules of the applicable law. In chapter 8 (Aspects of private international law), we will explain how the applicable law is to be determined. In the vast majority of cases, this will be the law of the country of the accident or, in other words, the law of the country where the handling Bureau is operating. It is also to be reminded (refer earlier in para 3.7.2) that the applicability of the law of the country of the accident justifies the handling autonomy given to the Bureau that handles the case (Article 3(4) of the Internal Regulations).

The compensation paid to the injured party can only be contested *after* having settled the demand for reimbursement. This is the application of the principle *'pay first, argue later'*; this is another basic principle of the Green Card system which is to be seen as a direct consequence of the guarantees characterising it.

The handling autonomy does not preclude the reimbursing entity from requesting supporting documentation about the claims handling process or about the compensations paid. In cases where adequate information or supporting documents have not yet been provided in accordance with Article 3(2) point (2) of the Internal Regulations (see *supra* para 3.7.2), Article 5(4) gives the reimbursing entity the right to request these and even specifies that evidence can be demanded to confirm that the injured party has been compensated prior to the demand for reimbursement being sent out. It is to be emphasised that the request for such information, supporting documentation or proof may not delay the reimbursement ('pay first, argue later').

Example

In the example given earlier, it is obvious that the material damage to the Italian victim's car (€ 1,000) as well as the bodily injury (€ 500) will fall under the first heading: the sums paid as compensation to injured parties.

The total amount of compensation paid by the Italian Bureau (€ 1,500) will be specified on the demand for reimbursement addressed to the French insurer of the liable vehicle.

Article 5(1) point (2) reads as follows:

> "5.1.2. The sums disbursed for external services in the handling and settlement of each claim and all costs specifically incurred for the purposes of a legal action which would have been disbursed in similar circumstances by an insurer established in the country of the accident."

Depending on the complexities and the peculiarities of the case, the handling entity may feel the need to involve one or more external experts in the claims handling activity. If the precise circumstances of the accident are unclear and the declarations of the parties do not allow the determination of the liability, a traffic expert may have to be hired to examine the circumstances and check the parties' declarations with the evidence found at the place of the accident. The material damage caused to the vehicle will probably have to be assessed by a loss adjuster. In order to establish the precise injuries of the victim, their causal link with the accident and their impact on the professional activities and the daily life of the victim, a medical expert will be necessary. Moreover, if the claim cannot be settled out of court and legal proceedings are incepted, the external costs will increase through the involvement of attorneys. There are other external costs that can be incurred; for example, the involvement of fraud specialists if the circumstances of the accident or the characteristics of the claim give rise to suspicions of insurance fraud.

It goes without saying that all these possible (external) partners involved in the claims settlement process are not working for free and will have to be remunerated. Additionally, these costs will initially be borne by the handling entity; subsequently, they will be passed on to the insurer by integrating them in the demand for reimbursement.

It is to be emphasised that only the reimbursement of *external* costs may be demanded from the insurer. The handling Bureau cannot, under this item, ask for compensation in respect of the work carried out by the Bureau staff while handling the claim in question. These *internal* costs are deemed to be compensated by the handling fee that may be requested in accordance with Article 5(1), point (3) of the Internal Regulations.

In practice, it may often be difficult to distinguish between internal and external costs. Certain Bureaux may have their own claims experts and damage assessors. The respective costs of these members of staff should be considered as compensated by the handling fee. But if the Bureau were to opt for external experts, the respective cost would obviously be integrated in the demand for reimbursement. The same may apply to either hiring external fraud investigators or using own specialised employees. The criterion is: would these costs also have been made by an insurer in similar circumstances?

Example
Referring to the example of the accident caused in Italy, if the claim can be settled without legal proceedings, then it may be expected that the following costs for external services are to be reimbursed:

- A technical expert for the evaluation of the material damage to the vehicle: € 50;
- A medical expert for the evaluation of the personal injuries suffered by the victim and the impact of these injuries on the victim's professional activities and daily life: € 150.

Article 5(1), point (3) of the Internal Regulations reads as follows:

> "5.1.3. A handling fee to cover all other charges calculated under the rules approved by the Council of Bureaux."

In compensation for the material work invested in the claims handling activity (internal costs), the handling Bureau is allowed to charge a handling fee. The calculation of the handling fee is determined by the Council of Bureaux. On 1 March 2019, the handling fee chargeable between Bureaux (and between handling Bureaux and insurers) amounts to 15% of the sums mentioned under Article 5(1), point (1) of the Internal Regulations – that is, the overall compensation to injured parties under either an amicable settlement or a court order – with a minimum amount of € 200 and a maximum amount of € 3,500.

The *15% handling fee* may be calculated only on the sums paid as compensation and not on the sums disbursed for external services as described in Article 5(1), point (2) of the Internal Regulations.
As long as these costs have, right from the outset, been paid by the handling entity, there will be less cause for discussion. There can, however, be discussion when the costs of external service providers (such as, experts or attorneys) have first been paid by the injured party (direct victim or subrogated party) and afterwards reimbursed by the handling entity. Are these costs then to be considered as part of the sums paid as compensation or as sums disbursed for external services as described in Article 5(1), point (2) and on which the 15% handling fee may not be calculated? The answer to this question depends on how these costs are regarded by the applicable rules of national law on compensation of damage. If the national law considers these costs, initially borne by the injured party, as part of the damage to be compensated, they will fall under Article 5(1), point (1) (and the 15% handling fee may also be calculated on these costs). In case they are, however, considered by the applicable law as external costs, they will then fall under Article 5(1), point (2) and should not be included in the calculation of the 15% handling fee.

The *minimum handling fee of € 200* will be applicable:

- In case the calculation of 15% on the compensation paid to the injured party amounts to less than € 200; that is, in cases where the compensation paid is less than € 1,334;
- In case the claim would – in accordance with the applicable rules on liability, compensation of damage and insurance law – be rejected by the handling entity and this rejection is either accepted by the injured party or confirmed by a court decision. In such cases, it is possible that external costs were incurred by the handling entity (expert fees, costs for attorneys,...) and these will also have to be reimbursed.
  This principle of reimbursement of external costs and payment of the minimum handling fee is stipulated in the second paragraph of Article 5(1), point (3) of the Internal Regulations:

  > "When claims arising out of the same accident are defended and settled without any compensation being paid, such sums as provided in 5.1.2 above and the minimum fee fixed by the Council of Bureaux in conformity with 5.1.3 above may be claimed."

No handling fee may be claimed in cases where an accident has not resulted in any claim for compensation (Article 5(7) of the Internal Regulations). This may initially seem strange; but there are cases where a Bureau is made aware of an accident involving a foreign vehicle whereas no claim is submitted to the Bureau. This can, for instance, be the case when an injured party chooses not to rely on the rules of the Green Card system to obtain compensation but prefers to address a claim directly to the foreign insurer. It is relevant to point out that the protection mechanisms of the Green Card system are not mandatory for injured parties; the latter retain the option to discard these mechanisms and to claim directly from the tortfeasor or from the (foreign) insurer. There are also cases, as described in paragraph 3.7.2, where a Bureau automatically receives police reports of accidents involving foreign vehicles. If it is obvious that no liability exists for the foreign vehicle and no claim results from the accident, then the handling Bureau cannot ask for a handling fee whatsoever, not even for the minimum amount.

The *maximum handling fee of € 3,500* will apply when the 15% of the compensation paid to the injured party exceeds the amount of € 3,500; that is, in cases where the compensation paid exceeds € 23,333.

Example
Referring to the example of the Italian Bureau, handling a claim resulting from an accident caused by a person driving a French vehicle in Italy, the Italian Bureau will include the following items in its demand for reimbursement:
- Sums paid as compensation to injured parties: € 1,500;
- Costs for external services: € 200;
- Handling fee: 15% of € 1,500 = € 225.

It is once again relevant to point out that the handling fee calculation, as established by the Council of Bureaux, only applies in the following 'relationships': Bureau-Bureau, Bureau-insurer, agent-insurer and agent-Bureau. In the 'relationship' between correspondents and insurers, both parties are free to agree the conditions for reimbursement and the method for calculating handling fees (Article 4(7) of the Internal Regulations; cf. para 3.7.4). In practice, the calculation and the amount of handling fees is one of the main factors of differentiation between business entities operating as correspondents. The same Article 4(7) provides, however, that the agreement between insurer and correspondent is not enforceable against any Bureau.

Apart from all the elements mentioned above, the demand for reimbursement must also contain information regarding the period within which the reimbursement is to be made. This is stipulated in Article 5(2) of the Internal Regulations and will be further described in paragraph 3.8.2.4, where we will speak about the period within which the demand for reimbursement must be settled.

3.8.2.3 The period within which the demand for reimbursement must be sent

Article 5(1) of the Internal Regulations obliges the handling Bureau to send the demand for reimbursement to the paying entity *within a maximum period of one year from the date of the last payment made in favour of an injured party.*

One year may initially seem a rather long period; nevertheless it is advisable for handling Bureaux or other handling entities to insert an automatic system of reminders in their software platform in order to avoid that the one-year time period may elapse without any demand for reimbursement being sent out. Especially in complex claim files, there may be several payments in favour of injured parties. The situation can easily arise in which a handling entity makes what it believes to be a final payment since, in its view, the entire damage has been compensated. If the injured party does not agree and insists on additional payments being made, a discussion may ensue between the latter and the claims handling entity which may require time to resolve. The risk for the claims handling entity is that it would focus its entire attention on the ongoing discussion and, once this is concluded, it would discover that more than a year has elapsed since the last payment in favour of the injured party with no demand for reimbursement being sent to the insurer concerned. The tough consequence is that the handling entity loses the right to obtain reimbursement! For that reason, it is important to install an 'automatic' internal warning system which reminds the claims handler when the one year period is getting near.

The period within which a demand for reimbursement must be sent out is calculated from the date of the last payment made in favour of an injured party. Nevertheless, there will be cases where no payment will be made to the injured party because the handling entity does not accept the liability for the accident or because no real damage can be determined. Similarly, when an investigated claim is identified fraudulent, there will be no payment in favour of the claimant. In those situations, the Explanatory Memorandum to the Internal Regulations in the context of Article 5(1) provides for an alternative date from which the one year period is to be calculated:

> "Where the claim has not resulted in compensation being paid, sums disbursed for external services and costs of legal proceedings may be claimed as well as the minimum handling fee as approved by the Council of Bureaux.
> In this case, the demand for reimbursement of sums disbursed for external services and costs of legal proceedings as well as the demand for payment of the minimum handling fee shall be addressed:
> – Within a period of maximum one year after the last negative response that a Bureau or the agent it has appointed has given to the claimant and that has remained without further reaction or that no legal action was taken by the injured party, or

- Within a period of maximum one year after the decision of a court or any other competent body, refusing any compensation to the claimant, has become final and irrevocable or after that the decision has been rendered if, according to the applicable legal rules and proceedings, it is possible that such decision does not become final or irrevocable."

The process of compensating damage may sometimes be particularly lengthy, especially in complex cases with severe bodily injury or where court cases are in progress. It is then normal – and even indispensable – to pay (substantial) provisional payments to the injured party, enabling the latter to face the most significant and urgent costs resulting from the accident. If, in such cases, the handling entity necessarily has to advance several provisional payments to the injured party and can only request reimbursement after the last payment made, that could result in the handling entity receiving reimbursement after many years of having periodically advanced significant sums of money. Therefore, the Internal Regulations foresee that provisional reimbursements may be requested, even if the entire damage has not been compensated yet. Article 5(5) of the Internal Regulations states the following:

"Reimbursement of all sums cited in Articles 5.1.1 and 5.1.2 above may be claimed in accordance with the conditions set out in this article notwithstanding that the Bureau may not have settled all claims arising out of the same accident. The handling fee provided for under Article 5.1.3 above may also be claimed if the principal sum which is the subject of the reimbursement is in excess of the amount fixed by the Council of Bureaux."

As regards the last sentence relating to provisional demands for handling fees, the Council of Bureaux has decided, in 2003, that

"If the disbursements calculated under the rules of Article 5.1.1 of the Internal Regulations result in a provisional demand for reimbursement of € 1 500 or more, then a handling fee may be claimed. If the provisional demand for reimbursement is less than € 1 500, then no handling fee may be claimed."

Provisional demands for payment of handling fees may, however, not exceed the maximum handling fee per file, which is set at € 3,500.

Moreover, it is once again to be emphasised that provisional demands for reimbursement or provisional demands for payment of handling fees may never breach the basic rule that the injured party must first be compensated before reimbursement can be requested from the paying entity. No demand for reimbursement can ever be sent prior to the injured party having been compensated by the amount specified in the demand for reimbursement.

3.8.2.4 *The period within which the demand for reimbursement must be settled*

The reimbursement of the sums paid to the injured party are an essential component of the guarantee mechanisms of the Green Card system. Hence, Article 5(2) of the Internal Regulations sets a clear time period within which the reimbursement is to be made, sanctioned by a high interest rate in case of late payment:

> "The demand for reimbursement shall specify that the amounts due are payable in the country and in the national currency of the beneficiary, free of costs, within a period of two months from the date of demand and that, on expiry of that period, late interest at 12 % per annum on the amount due from the date of the demand until the date of receipt of the remittance by the bank of the beneficiary shall apply automatically. In the event of a guarantee call according to Article 6 resulting from the demand for reimbursement, the application of late interest shall accrue until the date of issuance of that guarantee call.
> The demand for reimbursement may also specify that amounts expressed in the national currency are payable in euro, at the official rate of exchange current in the country of the claiming bureau at the date of the demand.'

All in all, the period offered to a reimbursing entity to settle the demand for reimbursement may still be considered as lengthy. The paying entity has two months within which to make the reimbursement of the amount requested by the handling entity, which amount it cannot contest ('pay first; argue later'). The Council of Bureaux has repeatedly discussed the possibility of reducing the period of reimbursement. Until now there is no majority of Bureaux in favour of such reduction. Bureaux and insurers contend that the receipt of the demand for reimbursement is, in many instances, the first time that they have a complete overview of the exact circumstances of the accident, the nature of the damage, the extent of the claims and the entire financial impact on their business. Only at that moment is the paying entity able to make a correct evaluation of the consequences of the claim file; it therefore requires sufficient time to examine the file in detail and make the payment that is demanded. It is in this context that the Council of Bureaux has, in 2016, inserted the duty of information exchange between Bureaux more explicitly in the Internal Regulations. With the introduction of the specific Article 3(2), point (2), a quicker and better communication is envisaged between handling and paying entities, obliging the former to provide the latter with a best estimate about the expected claims amounts (enabling the setting up of proper technical provisions) and to forward any relevant documentation about the claim (cf. *supra* para 3.7.2). The Council of Bureaux will assess whether this improved exchange of information can give the paying entity a better and earlier understanding of the claim, which, in turn, could justify a shorter reimbursement period.

Once the reimbursement period of two months is not respected, the Internal Regulations impose late payment interest at 12% per annum, calculated from the date of the demand for reimbursement until the date of receipt of the remittance by the bank of the beneficiary. In the current days of low interest rates, it goes without saying that this sanction should be high enough to motivate Bureaux and insurers to make their payments on time.

The reimbursement should be received by the beneficiary free of costs. The Explanatory Memorandum to the Internal Regulations gives more detail on what this exactly implies for the practicalities of the payments being made.

Since, in accordance with Article 4(7) of the Internal Regulations, correspondents and insurers are free to agree the conditions for reimbursement of sums paid to injured parties, the time period within which a demand for reimbursement is to be settled can freely be agreed between them. Such agreement is however, again in accordance with the same Article 4(7), not enforceable against any Bureau.

3.8.2.5 *The method to communicate a demand for reimbursement*

Article 5(1) of the Internal Regulations requires the demand for reimbursement to be sent by fax or e-mail. In reality, the communication method used most often will be e-mail. The main aim of this provision is to avoid that demands for reimbursement be sent through the post; this would only lead to more costs, increased administration and a possibly lengthy difference between the date of despatch and the date of receipt of the demand for reimbursement. For the future, the Council of Bureaux is developing an online tool of communication; this would allow demands for reimbursement to be exchanged via this platform.

Again, the means of communication between insurers and correspondents can be freely agreed between them, but such agreement is not enforceable against any Bureau (Article 4(7) of the Internal Regulations).

3.8.2.6 *Other topics related to the reimbursement obligations listed in the Internal Regulations*

Article 5(1), point (4) of the Internal Regulations was inserted in 2016; and this after certain Bureaux were confronted with an increasing amount of funds being blocked on their account or having to be deposited. Such actions can be imposed by court decisions as a provisional measure in order to safeguard the compensation to be paid to the injured party. If, for instance, a court orders a handling Bureau to pay compensation to an injured party and the Bureau contests the court decision by initiating appeal proceedings, the Bureau may be ordered to deposit the contested amount or to have the amount blocked on its account. If these amounts are considerable (the Internal Regulations foresee a minimum of € 10,000), the handling Bureau may request reimbursement of the blocked amounts, even if the injured party has not been compensated yet. In that way, the Bureau's liquidity is safeguarded. Once the court proceedings result in a final decision, the real costs of the claim have to be set off against the amounts already paid by the paying entity on the basis of Article 5(1), point (4) of the Internal Regulations.

Article 5(3) of the Internal Regulations reflects the principle that the Green Card system only relates to Motor Third Party Liability (MTPL) insurance and cannot apply to payments that go beyond its scope. No fines, bail bonds or other financial penalties, imposed upon the tortfeasor following an accident, can be included in the amounts to be reimbursed.

Article 5(6) of the Internal Regulations deals with the possibility of re-opening claim files after a (final) demand for reimbursement had already been sent and honoured by a paying entity. As long as claims arising out of an accident do not become legally prescribed, new claims can be submitted by new claimants who had not presented themselves earlier or by existing claimants who are confronted with aggravation or deterioration of their personal injuries related to the accident that had not been taken into account in the initial settlement. If the handling entity is compelled to re-open the file and to pay additional compensation, new demands for reimbursement may be formulated and additional handling fees may become due if the maximum handling fee of € 3,500 has not been reached.

One final provision of the Explanatory Memorandum to the Internal Regulations still deserves some attention and is related to the practice of certain insurers to *outsource* foreign claims to external service providers. Due to the complexity of the rules relating to cross-border claims handling, some insurers prefer not to handle these claims in-house but to delegate them to external partners such as claims handling offices. We are not referring to the situation where insurers entrust claims handling activities in a certain country to a correspondent, but to the situation where an insurer does not have the necessary know-how about cross-border accidents and outsources *all* activities related to accidents that occur in a foreign country (including the communication with the correspondent handling the case in the country of the accident). As the insurer still remains the main debtor of the demand for reimbursement, the Council of Bureaux decided, in 2010, that demands for reimbursements must be addressed to the insurance undertaking itself; and this even if the latter has outsourced the claims handling process.

3.8.3 The recovery between the agent and the insurer

The function and task of an agent has already been described in paragraph 3.7.3. Under that heading, we explained that a handling Bureau can choose not to perform any claims handling activity itself but to entrust such activity to an agent, acting under the Bureau's responsibility. When an agent handles a claim in the name of a Bureau and on behalf of a foreign insurer, the said agent would have no contract with the foreign insurer and will therefore be bound by the provisions of the Internal Regulations.

What is true for the claims handling activity also applies to the rules on reimbursements to be settled between the agent and the foreign insurer. For that reason, the first provision of Article 5 starts with the words "when a bureau or the agent it has appointed for the purpose…." All the different provisions of Article 5 of the Internal Regulations, pertaining to the relations between the handling Bureau on the one hand and the foreign insurer or the guaranteeing Bureau on the other hand can be transposed to the relation between the agent and the foreign insurer or the guaranteeing Bureau. The agent will therefore have to observe all the rules, formalities and deadlines applicable to the demand for reimbursement as stipulated in the Internal Regulations and the Explanatory Memorandum when requesting the guaranteeing Bureau or foreign insurer for reimbursement of the compensation made in favour of the injured party.

3.8.4 *The recovery between the correspondent and the insurer*

Many aspects of the relationship between a correspondent and an insurer have already been explained in paragraph 3.7.4. As regards the reimbursement obligations between the approved correspondent and the foreign insurer on behalf of which the former handles claims, the most important provision is again Article 4(7) of the Internal Regulations:

> "Subject to the provisions of Article 4.4, the correspondent is free to agree with the insurer that requested its approval the conditions for reimbursement of sums paid to injured parties and the method for calculating its handling fees which agreement, however, shall not be enforceable against any Bureau."

All modalities regarding the reimbursement obligation are subject to the contractual freedom of insurers and correspondents; but it is again to be kept in mind that such agreements cannot be binding on a Bureau and should not violate the basic principles of the Green Card system. This includes the principle that the injured party should first be compensated before any payment can be requested from the insurer concerned.

On the basis of Article 4(7), insurers and correspondents will be able to enter into agreements regarding:
- the data or information that should be included in the demand for reimbursement;

- whether the correspondent needs to provide proof that the compensation amounts have been paid to the injured parties and how this proof is to be delivered;
- the supporting documentation that should be attached to the demand for reimbursement;
- the timeframe within which the insurer has to settle the amounts mentioned in the demand for reimbursement;
- the amount and the method of calculation of the handling fees.

In order to ensure that the basic principles of the Green Card system are respected in the relationship between correspondents and insurers, these should be reflected in the legal instruments adopted by the Bureau setting out the obligations for correspondents. In this regard, the Council of Bureaux has developed a 'Model for a Correspondents' Charter' in which a Bureau can find inspiration to devise a document outlining the respective obligations of insurers and correspondents within the Green Card system.

3.8.5 *The correspondent invokes the guarantee of the handling Bureau*

We cannot emphasise enough that the Green Card system is, essentially, a guarantee system providing the certainty to the handling entity that any compensation paid to the injured party will be reimbursed. Concerning the compensations paid by the correspondent, however, the Green Card system is characterised by an unexpected peculiarity. When observing the relationship between correspondent – handling Bureau – foreign insurer – guaranteeing Bureau, one would expect that if the correspondent is, for whatever reason, not reimbursed in time by the foreign insurer, the said correspondent would be able to rely on the inherent guarantees of the Green Card system to obtain reimbursement from the guaranteeing Bureau. Nevertheless, the Internal Regulations provide for an easier guarantee mechanism, allowing the correspondent to invoke the guarantee of the handling Bureau instead of 'forcing' it to turn to the foreign guaranteeing Bureau.[36] Thanks to this guarantee mechanism, the correspondent can, in case they do not obtain proper reimbursement from the foreign insurer, turn to the Bureau of the country where they are established. That would be the Bureau that had initially approved the correspondent concerned, in accordance with Article 4 of the Internal Regulations, and with which the said correspondent should normally have some kind of contractual relationship, based on the Correspondents' Charter or any other contractual document.

36. It may seem a little bit inappropriate here to speak about a handling Bureau. The real handling entity is in fact the correspondent that has compensated the injured party. Nevertheless, the term handling Bureau allows distinguishing between the Bureau in the country of the accident and the Bureau of the country the insured vehicle originates from (the guaranteeing Bureau).

This guarantee, provided by the handling Bureau in favour of the correspondent, is described in Article 4(8) of the Internal Regulations. The said guarantee is, however, subject to a number of conditions that have been strengthened in 2013 and that will be examined in the following paragraphs.

For many correspondents (either insurers, claims handling offices or other parties), the representation of foreign insurers as a Green Card correspondent is considered to be a commercial activity, offering an income in the form of handling fees. In normal business, no commercial activity exists without any form of entrepreneurial risk; so, in order to limit that risk, correspondents should be selective in deciding which foreign insurance undertakings to represent. They should either avoid insurers that are not respecting their reimbursement obligations or they should only enter into a business relationship with such insurers with heightened caution. Therefore, the challenge facing Article 4(8) of the Internal Regulations is to strike the right balance between guaranteeing the timely and correct compensation of the injured party on the one hand and a fair distribution of entrepreneurial risk between the correspondent and the handling Bureau on the other.

> When Article 4(8) of the Internal Regulations was modified in 2013 in order to strengthen the conditions for invoking the handling Bureau's guarantee, a number of Bureaux were confronted with an increasing amount of reimbursement demands based on this Article. Such demands were very often accrued by correspondents into a 'bundle' of reimbursements that suddenly had to be guaranteed by the handling Bureau. The reason behind such line of action was that correspondents were often reluctant to invoke Article 4(8) at an early stage. This was seen as a breach of confidence in the commercial relationship between insurer and correspondents and, for that reason, the latter tended to wait as long as possible to invoke the Article. Correspondents initially tried to solve the reimbursement problem themselves; and, only when the situation became too problematic, they suddenly presented a 'package' of claims on the basis of Article 4(8) of the Internal Regulations to the handling Bureau. This practice resulted in Bureaux being confronted with a sudden influx in work (claims had to be examined and, if they were not finalised yet, the claims handling activity had to be taken over) and an increase in financial exposure (a whole set of compensation payments suddenly had to be guaranteed). In order to avoid such practices, the conditions for invoking Article 4(8) were therefore tightened.

Today, a correspondent can rely on the handling Bureau's guarantee 'only' under the following conditions:

a. The correspondent must inform the handling Bureau about its inability to receive reimbursement; it can request to be reimbursed by the latter during a period spanning a minimum of six months and a maximum of nine months from the date on which it had initially sent the demand for reimbursement to the foreign insurer.

   i. The minimum period of six months is intended to ensure that the correspondent makes sufficient efforts with the insurer concerned to obtain reimbursement and avoids an immediate transfer of its financial risk on to the handling Bureau;
   ii. The maximum period of nine months, on the other hand, envisages avoiding situations as described above where correspondents wait too long before invoking Article 4(8) until they have accrued a number of unpaid debts and suddenly transfer these on to the handling Bureau.

b. The correspondent must attach a number of supporting documents to his request based on Article 4(8) of the Internal Regulations:
   i. Material proof that the said correspondent had, prior to sending the demand for reimbursement to the insurer, actually compensated the injured party. This is obviously intended to safeguard the respect for the principle that the compensation to the injured party must precede the reimbursement demand. This measure thus tries to protect the interests of injured parties;
   ii. Any document establishing the correspondent's right to handle the claim on behalf of the insurer concerned. This requirement ensures that the correspondent is working under a correct mandate. Therefore, the insurer's confirmation of cover for the vehicle in question is necessary and should be added to the documents presented by the correspondent to the handling Bureau;
   iii. A copy of the demand for reimbursement sent by the correspondent to the insurer. This will allow the handling Bureau to verify whether the date when the demand for reimbursement was sent out falls within the minimum and maximum period of six and nine months mentioned previously. At the same time, the document will also verify whether the injured party had been compensated prior to the despatch of the demand for reimbursement;
   iv. A copy of at least one reminder sent by the correspondent to the insurer; this reminder must have been sent at least one month before the correspondent submits a request to the handling Bureau based on Article 4(8). This requirement ensures that the correspondent has already sought to obtain reimbursement before presenting his request to the handling Bureau.

Once these conditions have been fulfilled, the correspondent can rely on the guarantee of the handling Bureau to be reimbursed for the outlays that remained unpaid by the insurer. The handling Bureau will reimburse the sums paid as compensation to injured parties (as mentioned in Article 5(1), point (1) of the Internal Regulations) as well as the costs for external services (experts, attorneys etc.) in the claims handling process (as mentioned in Article 5(1), point (2) of the Internal Regulations). However, the correspondent will not be compensated for their handling fees and the late payment interest due on the basis of their contract with the insurer. These are considered to be part of the entrepreneurial risk that is to be borne by the correspondent and are therefore not guaranteed by the Green Card system.

The handling Bureau will, in turn, attempt to recover the disbursement it has made. The fact that Article 4(8) of the Internal Regulations was invoked reveals that an insurer in a certain market is not respecting its payment obligations under the Green Card system. This is viewed as a potential threat to the financial stability of the Green Card system. Therefore, the reimbursement sought by the handling Bureau will be done on the basis of a guarantee call issued to the guaranteeing Bureau. As will be explained in more detail in paragraph 3.8.7, the number of guarantee calls addressed to a certain market is an important indicator of the financial discipline within that market. If the number of guarantee calls based on Article 4(8) and related to a specific insurer grows too high, the Bureau of the market in question or the Council of Bureaux will intervene to take appropriate measures.

3.8.6 *The recovery between the handling Bureau and the guaranteeing Bureau*

In paragraphs 3.8.2 and 3.8.3, we described the recovery procedure in the relationship between a handling Bureau or an agent on the one hand and an insurer on the other. In the vast majority of cases, the liable vehicle will be validly insured and the handling entity (handling Bureau or agent) will send a demand for reimbursement directly to the insurer in accordance with Article 5 of the Internal Regulations. In case the claim was handled by a correspondent, the modalities of reimbursement will be governed by its contractual provisions with the insurer concerned.

But there are exceptional circumstances where the handling Bureau or the agent will be unable to address a demand for reimbursement to the insurer of the liable vehicle. For example, such circumstances could be the following:

- A Green Card was presented after the accident happened but it turned out to be invalid;
- The vehicle is not validly insured but normally based in the guaranteeing Bureau's territory and both the handling and guaranteeing Bureaux are signatories of the Multilateral Agreement.

Another scenario that can result in a direct relationship between the handling Bureau (or the agent) and the guaranteeing Bureau is when the vehicle was validly insured but its insurer is insolvent and, hence, unable to meet its reimbursement obligations. The cooperation between Bureaux, in case of an insolvent insurer, is rather particular and will therefore be handled separately in paragraph 3.8.8.

In the situations described above, the handling Bureau or the agent will submit the demand for reimbursement directly to the guaranteeing Bureau. All the provisions and conditions of Article 5 of the Internal Regulations will apply to the reimbursement demand and the guaranteeing Bureau will have to make the necessary payment within a time period of two months, as stipulated in Article 5(2) of the Internal Regulations. In case the guaranteeing Bureau does not respect the reimbursement obligation within the stipulated timeframe, a so-called 'pro-forma' guarantee call will be issued by the handling Bureau or the agent to the guaranteeing Bureau (see further para 3.8.7.3).

3.8.7 The guarantee call

Once an insurer does not respect, for whatever reason, their obligations when confronted with a reimbursement demand, the handling Bureau will rely on the guarantees offered by the Green Card system and will formally invoke the guaranteeing obligation of the guaranteeing Bureau. To that end, the handling Bureau will address a formal guarantee call to the guaranteeing Bureau.
Three different types of guarantee call have to be distinguished and will be examined in this section.

3.8.7.1 The guarantee call based on Article 6(1) of the Internal Regulations (the insurer does not reimburse the handling Bureau or agent on time)

Article 6(1) of the Internal Regulations envisages a handling Bureau or an agent that, having settled a claim, are not reimbursed in time by the insurer of the liable vehicle. In that case, the handling Bureau or the agent will transfer the reimbursement demand to the guaranteeing Bureau.

Since invoking a Bureau's guarantee is an important indicator of possible financial problems, the Internal Regulations specify a number of formalities that have to be fulfilled when issuing a guarantee call (as was also the case for the demand for reimbursement in accordance with Article 5 as explained in paragraph 3.8.2).

Time limit for issuing a guarantee call: as already explained in paragraph 3.8.2.4, an insurer has two months to settle a demand for reimbursement. Once that period has elapsed without any payment being made, the agent or handling Bureau can issue a guarantee call. Article 6(1) of the Internal Regulations stipulates that a guarantee call shall be made "within a period of twelve months after the date of despatch of the demand for reimbursement under Article 5." That period is relevant for the calculation of interest on the demand for reimbursement but does not, in itself, invalidate any guarantee call made after the one-year timeframe. If the guarantee call is made more than one year after the despatch of the demand for reimbursement, then the late payment interest will stop running; nevertheless, a guarantee call can still be issued. The definite and final deadline for the guarantee call to be issued is two years after the despatch of the demand for reimbursement. Indeed, the last paragraph of Article 6(1) reads:

> "no guarantee call shall be admissible if made more than two years after the despatch of the demand for reimbursement."

Timeframe within which a guarantee gall must be settled by the guaranteeing Bureau: once issued, the guaranteeing Bureau has one month to settle a guarantee call. Article 6(1), third paragraph, of the Internal Regulations specifies:

> "the Bureau standing as guarantor shall make the payment (...) within a period of one month."

Interest: We already explained earlier that an insurer must settle a demand for reimbursement within a period of two months from the date of such demand and that, on expiry of that period, late payment interest at 12% per annum shall apply automatically (Article 5(2) of the Internal Regulations). In case the insurer does not pay and a guarantee call is issued against the guaranteeing Bureau, then the interest will stop accruing from the date of the guarantee call. The guaranteeing Bureau is required to settle the guarantee call within one month, failing which interest (again at 12% per annum) shall resume, this time from the date of the guarantee call until the receipt of full payment. This new interest shall apply on the full amount due at the time of the issuance of the guarantee call, *i.e.* the amount of the demand for reimbursement, increased with the late interest accrued according to Article 5(2) of the Internal Regulations. In other words, this generates an 'interest on interest'.

However, the handling Bureau may not wait indefinitely to issue a guarantee call; hence, the Internal Regulations specify that the interest shall stop running if the guarantee call is not made within a period of twelve months from the date of the initial demand for reimbursement. The fourth paragraph of Article 6(1) of the Internal Regulations states:

> "The guarantee call shall be made (...) within a period of twelve months after the date of despatch of the demand for reimbursement under Article 5. On expiry of that period and without prejudice to any late interest for which it may be liable, the liability of the Bureau standing as guarantor shall be limited to the amount claimed from its member plus a 12 months interest calculated at 12% per annum."

Form to be respected when issuing a guarantee call: the number of guarantee calls issued against a national Bureau is an important indicator of the financial discipline of a market in respecting their payment obligations under the Green Card system. Therefore, the number of guarantee calls and the amounts of money for which such guarantee calls are issued are monitored permanently by the Council of Bureaux (and more particularly the Monitoring Committee of the Council of Bureaux) in order to determine whether any measures are to be taken.

In order to have a clear overview on the number of guarantee calls and the amounts of money they represent, any guarantee call must be issued via an online guarantee call platform managed by the Council of Bureaux. This is the only valid and mandatory system to issue guarantee calls; the system provides Bureaux with the possibility to upload supporting documents, such as the initial demand for reimbursement.

Example

Let us return to the earlier example of the Italian Bureau, handling a claim resulting from an accident caused by a French vehicle in Italy. The Italian Bureau presents a demand for reimbursement to the French insurer, amounting to € 1,925.

The Italian handling Bureau sends the demand for reimbursement to the French insurer on 1 January 2017. In accordance with Article 5(2) of the Internal Regulations, the French insurer has two months to settle the demand for reimbursement. If the insurer doesn't pay within that period, the Italian Bureau can issue a guarantee call to the French Bureau as of 1 March 2017. Let us suppose that the Italian Bureau issues a guarantee call on 1 April 2017. This means that the Italian Bureau may claim interest at 12% per annum for the period running from the initial date of the demand for reimbursement (1 January 2017) until the date of the guarantee call (1 April 2017). The French Bureau now has one month to pay the guarantee call, together with the interest that runs from 1 January 2017 until 31 March 2017.

If the French Bureau does not respect the one-month payment deadline and only pays the guarantee call on 1 June 2017, it will have to pay additional interest calculated from the despatch of the demand for reimbursement (1 January 2017) until the actual payment of the guarantee call (1 June 2017).

Therefore, the amount payable by the French Bureau will be composed of:

i. the amount of the demand for reimbursement, increased with 12% interest for the period of 1 January 2017 until 1 April 2017;
ii. additional 12% interest calculated on the full amount mentioned under *i.* for the period of 1 April 2017 until 1 June 2017.

> If the Italian Bureau were to wait for a much longer period before issuing their guarantee call, the interest calculation will become more complicated. Let us suppose that the Italian Bureau only issues a guarantee call on 1 April 2018 (more than one year after the despatch of the demand for reimbursement). In that case, the interest claimable under *i.* above will be limited to twelve months calculated at 12% per annum.
> The interest will however continue to accrue on the amount referred to under *ii.* above.

3.8.7.2 *The guarantee call based on Article 6(2) of the Internal Regulations (the correspondent is not reimbursed on time by the insurer)*

In this scenario, the claim of the injured party has not been compensated by a handling Bureau or an agent, but by the correspondent appointed by the insurer and approved by the handling Bureau.

In paragraph 3.8.5, we have seen that a correspondent, when not being reimbursed by the foreign insurer, can request reimbursement from the handling Bureau under the conditions of Article 4(8) of the Internal Regulations. Provided that the conditions of the Article are met, the handling Bureau will ensure that the correspondent is reimbursed for the compensation advanced to the injured party and for the sums disbursed for external services (such as technical and legal experts). As explained, the handling Bureau's guarantee will however not extend to late payment interests nor to handling fees.

When a correspondent invokes Article 4(8) of the Internal Regulations, that consequently has to result in a guarantee call being issued by the handling Bureau to the guaranteeing Bureau on the basis of Article 6(2) of the Internal Regulations. The handling Bureau will not send an 'ordinary' demand for reimbursement to the guaranteeing Bureau before issuing the guarantee call. Since the application of Article 4(8) necessarily implies that an insurer is not respecting its reimbursement obligations under the Green Card system and since that may be an indication of decreased financial discipline, this warning signal should be translated into a guarantee call issued via the aforementioned online platform of the Council of Bureaux. In turn, if a substantial number of such guarantee calls is issued, the Monitoring Committee will detect this signal and determine whether corrective measures are necessary in respect of the market concerned.

The handling Bureau must issue their guarantee call, based on Article 6(2) of the Internal Regulations, within a period of twelve months from the date when the correspondent initially sent the demand for reimbursement to the insurer. In practice, this results in a relatively short time period for the handling Bureau to issue the guarantee call. Indeed, as already explained when clarifying Article 4(8) of the Internal Regulations, the correspondent can only request reimbursement from the handling Bureau after a minimum period of six months but before a maximum period of nine months has elapsed from the date when the correspondent sent the demand for reimbursement to the insurer. This means that the handling Bureau will only have between three and six months (depending on when the correspondent invoked Article 4(8) of the Internal Regulations) to issue a guarantee call to the guaranteeing Bureau.

Example
An Italian correspondent, Itacor, operates in Italy on behalf of a French insurer, Frins. Itacor settles the claim of an Italian injured party following an accident caused in Italy by a French vehicle, insured by Frins.
Itacor sends a demand for reimbursement to Frins on 1st January 2017 and, despite several reminders, is not reimbursed by Frins. In accordance with Article 4(8) of the Internal Regulations, Itacor can request reimbursement from the Italian (handling) Bureau at the earliest on 1 July 2017 and at the latest on 30 September 2017. Having reimbursed the Italian correspondent Itacor, the Italian Bureau must issue a guarantee call, based on Article 6(2) of the Internal Regulations, to the French Bureau by not later than 31 December 2017.

The guarantee call, based on Article 6(2) of the Internal Regulations, envisages that all the conditions of applicability of Article 4(8) were duly fulfilled.

The other formalities related to Article 6(2) are identical to those relating to a guarantee call based on Article 6(1) of the Internal Regulations: the guarantee call must be issued via the online platform provided by the Council of Bureaux, the same delays for payment apply as well as the rules on interest calculation.

3.8.7.3 The 'pro forma' guarantee call in case of late payment by the guaranteeing Bureau

As we have seen in paragraph 3.8.6, there are possibilities where the demand for reimbursement cannot be sent to an insurer but needs to be addressed directly to the guaranteeing Bureau. This can occur when, for instance, an invalid or falsified Green Card was presented, when the liable vehicle was not validly insured or when the insurer of the vehicle is insolvent.

In such circumstances, the guaranteeing Bureau has the same two-month timeframe, as envisaged in Article 5(2) of the Internal Regulations, to settle the demand for reimbursement.

If the guaranteeing Bureau does not respect the said timeframe, it is obviously difficult to invoke its own guarantee; and this because the guaranteeing Bureau is itself the debtor and, legally, it cannot be the guarantor of its own obligations.

The fact that a Bureau fails to respect its obligations under the Green Card system sends a number of 'warning signals'; this could be a serious indicator of possible problems in a certain market, a possible lack of organisation within the Bureau itself, a decrease in the financial discipline of the Bureau or even a lack of sufficient financial means within the Bureau. Therefore, such late payments should be integrated in the statistics of the online guarantee calls that are regularly examined by the Council of Bureaux.
In order to ensure that such deficiencies are reflected in the statistics, a so-called 'pro forma guarantee call' is issued by a handling Bureau to the guaranteeing Bureau that failed to reimburse it.

All the conditions and formal requirements of a 'standard' guarantee call (as per Article 6(1) of the Internal Regulations) are applicable to such pro forma guarantee calls.

3.8.7.4 Qualified reasons to reject a guarantee call

A guarantee call is issued by a handling Bureau to a guaranteeing Bureau. The latter has to respect its guaranteeing obligations and settle the guarantee call within the prescribed time limit. But it is of course possible that the guaranteeing Bureau disputes the guarantee to be given and wishes to reject the guarantee call. Basing itself on a long history of dealing with guarantee calls and settling disputes between Bureaux, the Council of Bureaux has, in 2011, drafted an exhaustive *list of 'qualified reasons to reject a guarantee call'* that can be invoked by a Bureau in order to dispute a guarantee call. This list is limited and the several reasons it specifies are the only ones that can be invoked to put into question a guarantee call. The list of qualified reasons to reject a guarantee call is incorporated in the Explanatory Memorandum to the Internal Regulations.

If the guaranteeing Bureau invokes one of the qualified reasons within one month from the date of the guarantee call, this is considered as rejected. If the handling Bureau disagrees with the rejection, the formal ways of *dispute resolution* between Bureaux are available. These are either mediation or arbitration between the Bureaux involved.

Dispute settlement within the Council of Bureaux

Article 19 of the Internal Regulations governs the 'resolution of disputes between Bureaux' in the following way:

> "Any dispute arising out of these Internal Regulations or related to them shall be resolved by mediation or by arbitration.
> The rules of the mediation and the arbitration are dealt with in a separate regulation approved by the General Assembly of the Council of Bureaux."

In practice, Bureaux first try to resolve their disputes on a bilateral and amicable basis. Sometimes, the Secretariat of the Council of Bureaux is requested to intervene in the dispute as a kind of mediator or to give advice on the interpretation of certain rules of the Green Card system.
If no amicable settlement can be reached in this way, the Bureaux have to rely on mediation or arbitration. Mediation is compulsory in a number of cases and optional in others. The Council of Bureaux has adopted a set of rules for both the procedure of mediation and that of arbitration. The rules on arbitration are, to a certain extent, based on the arbitration rules of UNCITRAL (United Nations Commission on International Trade Law).

3.8.8 The guarantee between Bureaux in case of insolvency of the insurer

The guarantees offered by the Green Card system do not cease in case an insurer is insolvent. The compensation of a victim of a car accident caused by a foreign motorist must not be dependent on the solvency of the tortfeasor in case the insurer concerned cannot meet its payment obligations because of a bankruptcy. Therefore, the guaranteeing Bureau will guarantee all the liabilities of a member insurer for the consequences of accidents caused in other Green Card territories.

In case of the insolvency of an insurer, the Bureau of which that insurer is a member shall inform the Council of Bureaux. The latter will immediately inform all the other Bureaux of the Green Card system. Demands for reimbursement are no longer to be sent to the insolvent insurer but must be despatched directly to the guaranteeing Bureau. The Bureaux shall inform the latter of all the pending demands for reimbursement that had already been addressed to the insolvent insurer as well as about all the cases that are being handled. Correspondents, acting on behalf of the insolvent insurer, can invoke Article 4(8) of the Internal Regulations in order to be reimbursed by the handling Bureau. In practice, however, a correspondent of an insolvent insurer will end its contractual relationship with the insurer concerned and withdraw from its role as correspondent as quickly as possible.

It is worth mentioning that not in all countries do injured parties benefit from a guarantee scheme in case of accidents caused by vehicles insured by an insolvent insurer (see further para 4.3.6). Sometimes, such protection mechanisms only provide partial compensation; or there may be no protection in place at all. In such circumstances, the injured party in an accident caused by a foreign vehicle can actually be in a better compensatory position than the injured party in a purely domestic accident with a liable party insured with an insolvent insurer.

3.8.9 *The 'second instance recovery'*

At the end of this section dealing with the recovery rights of entities which have compensated an injured party, we cannot overlook the recourse (or subrogation) rights 'in second instance' of such entities whereby they will try to recover their disbursement from the tortfeasor concerned.

A wide variety of scenarios can be listed where a guaranteeing Bureau would prefer not to be the final debtor of the reimbursement paid but would wish to recover its outlays from a third entity or person; these are some examples:

- The guaranteeing Bureau had to guarantee a false Green Card. This can either be a genuine Green Card that was illegally altered (recourse against the person having manipulated the Green Card) or a counterfeited Green Card (recourse against the counterfeiter);
- The guaranteeing Bureau had to guarantee a valid Green Card but the underlying insurance policy was not or no longer valid (recourse against the policyholder in case of fraud);
- The guaranteeing Bureau had to reimburse the compensation paid for an accident caused by an uninsured vehicle normally based in the Bureau's territory of competence where both the handling and guaranteeing Bureaux are signatories to the Multilateral Agreement (recourse against the uninsured driver, keeper or owner of the vehicle);
- The guaranteeing Bureau had to guarantee the reimbursement of compensation paid to the injured party because the insurer did not reimburse on time (recourse against the insurer);
- The guaranteeing Bureau had to guarantee the reimbursement of compensation paid to the injured party because the insurer concerned was insolvent (possible recourse against the liquidator of the insolvent insurer and/or against the Guarantee Fund if the latter has the obligation to intervene in cases of insolvency).

A special case of recourse 'in second instance' by a guaranteeing Bureau is foreseen in a specific Agreement concluded between a number of Green Card Bureaux in the framework of the Council of Bureaux.

As will be described in chapter 7, insurers in the European Economic Area have the possibility to transact insurance business in other Member States, based on the concept of freedom to provide services (FoS) or freedom of establishment (FoE). In that case, the financial control over the insurance activities will be exercised in the insurers' 'home'

Member State (where the insurer received their initial authorisation) by the respective supervisory authority.

Example
Let us consider the following example. insurer A has received their initial authorisation to operate MTPL insurance in Member State A and offers insurance products by way of Freedom to Provide Services in Member State B. A vehicle registered in Member State B can therefore be covered for MTPL insurance by insurer A. If that vehicle, normally based in Member State B, travels to a third Member State C and causes an accident in that Member State, the national Bureau of Member State C will be the handling Bureau and will be reimbursed by the guaranteeing Bureau of Member State B. If in the interim insurer A becomes insolvent, the financial burden of the accident will remain with the national Bureau B, whereas the financial control over the insurer concerned was situat-ed in Member State A.

In the light of the foregoing, a number of Green Card Bureaux have concluded an agreement allowing a Green Card Bureau to recover any outlays – necessarily made for insolvent insurers operating in their territory of competence under Freedom to Provide Services – from the Bureau of the home Member State of the insolvent insurer. In the example described above, the guaranteeing Bureau of Member State B could, under the terms of this Agreement, recover any outlays resulting from accidents caused by vehicles insured by insurer A from the Green Card Bureau of Member State A.
In 2018, the scope of the agreement mentioned above, which was limited to situations of Freedom to Provide Services, has been extended to situations of Freedom of Establishment.

The foregoing was only a non-exhaustive list of examples where a Bureau would like to exercise their right of 'recourse in second instance'.

It is to be emphasised that the Green Card system is a scheme of international cooperation guaranteeing the proper compensation of an injured party in case of an accident caused by a foreign vehicle. The Green Card system does not govern any of the recourse rights described above. Such recourse rights 'in second instance' are entirely subject to national legislation and cannot be based on the Internal Regulations or any other set of rules adopted by the Green Card system or the Council of Bureaux. A Bureau, wishing to recover any outlays from a third party, should therefore refer to and rely on their national law in order to pursue this recourse right.
That such recourse rights have to observe, at least in the European Union, certain fundamental rights of procedural guarantees (such as the right to be heard) is illus-

trated by the decision of the Court of Justice of the European Union in the case *Dockevičius*.[37]

3.9 Financial discipline and financial stability in the Green Card system

The Green Card system being essentially a guarantee system, the compensation of the victim is the first priority while the reimbursement of the handling entity by a guaranteeing entity must be safeguarded at all times. This means that the financial capacity of the guaranteeing entity is to be monitored in order to safeguard the continuity of the system.

The Green Card system is a cooperation scheme in which 51 different countries are participating and where more than 1,300 MTPL insurers are active. Each year, more than 400,000 claims are handled relating to cross-border road traffic accidents; this means that more than 1,000 cases are handled each day. In these activities, multiple stakeholders are involved:

- MTPL insurers, providing cover for MTPL-related risks for motor vehicles. Additionally, insurers also often operate as correspondents in the framework of the Green Card system;
- Claims handling offices operating as correspondents and/or as agents;
- 47 National Motor Insurers' Bureaux, operating either as a handling entity providing compensation to injured parties or as a guaranteeing entity for the reimbursement of the compensation paid.

Naturally, the day-to-day functioning of the system results in constant cash flows between the stakeholders listed above.

The stakeholders operate in distinct markets which differ substantially one from the other. The 51 participating countries differ not only in terms of geographical size and number of inhabitants, but also in the size of their respective vehicle fleet. Not taking into consideration countries like Andorra, Liechtenstein, Monaco, San Marino and Vatican City, the countries with the smallest vehicle fleet account for approximately 200,000 vehicles; whereas the country with the largest vehicle fleet, Germany, accounts for not less than 60 million motor vehicles. It goes without saying that the total premium generated for MTPL insurance also differs substantially from one country to another.

37. CJEU, Judgment of 15 June 2017, *Dockevičius*, C-587/15, EU:C:2017:463.

Example

Let's take the example of a hypothetical country called Motoria, participating in the Green Card system. Motoria has a population of approximately 350,000 people and a total vehicle fleet of 150,000 units. The average annual MTPL premium for a motor vehicle, including Green Card cover for all countries participating in the Green Card system, is € 85 (net premium for the insurer, excluding taxes). This results in a total annual premium of € 12,750,000 for the entire insurance market of Motoria.

This premium income must not only cover the general operational costs of the different MTPL insurers active in the Motoria market (personnel costs, commissions paid to insurance intermediaries, buildings, ...) and the costs of claims for accidents occurring in the territory of Motoria; it should also allow reimbursing any damage caused by vehicles of Motoria in other countries of the Green Card system.

Taking into consideration the fact that the largest personal injury claims in countries of the Green Card system can easily amount to several millions of euros (claims exceeding ten million euro are not exceptional), it is clear that such large claims can present a threat of an existential nature to the MTPL insurance market of Motoria.

The relatively small market of Motoria may therefore opt to cope with such high risks via a reinsurance contract.

Apart from premium income, the countries participating in the Green Card system also differ in the way they 'import' or 'export' Green Card accidents and claims related to such accidents. There are countries which, by their central geographical location or due to their touristic attraction, tend to be a destination country and therefore 'import' more Green Card accidents and claims, caused by foreign vehicles, than they 'export'. On the other hand, there are countries which are 'net exporters' of Green Card accidents. Countries which are net importers of accidents must make sure to constantly have sufficient liquidity available to make advance payments to claimants; whereas net exporting countries must make sure that their national premium income allows the coverage of all reimbursement payments to be made in other countries.

This diversification shows the necessity of constantly watching over the ability of markets to meet their reimbursement obligations. A specific Monitoring Committee has therefore been created within the Council of Bureaux to perform this task.

The Monitoring Committee relies on a number of information sources to have a fair idea about the financial health of the system as a whole as well as of the individual markets cooperating in the Green Card mechanism:

- An annual enquiry on Green Card statistics, presenting the different claims reported in the participating countries as well as the country of origin of the vehicles involved in the accidents resulting in the claims;
- An annual financial stability questionnaire, addressed to the Bureaux eliciting information about a range of financial and other aspects;
- The number of guarantee calls issued by handling Bureaux against guaranteeing Bureaux as well as their financial quantum. The concept of guarantee calls was explained in more detail in paragraph 3.8.7. Guarantee calls are an important indicator that financial obligations are not being respected and that closer attention should be devoted by the Monitoring Committee to the market concerned;
- A periodic survey on the amount of uninsured vehicles circulating in each market;
- In exceptional cases, information provided by supervisory authorities. These are operating in each country within the Green Card system; they monitor, *inter alia*, the solvency criteria which are to be observed and fulfilled by insurers;
- Other external sources providing information about individual markets and/or individual insurers.

In order to safeguard the financial stability of the overall system, financial guarantee requirements exist to make sure that reimbursements are guaranteed at all times:

- A bank guarantee or cash deposit: Bureaux can be required to provide a bank guarantee, concluded with a bank responding to certain criteria. The level of the bank guarantee or cash deposit is dependent on the number of registered motor vehicles within the market in question and on the priority that is applicable in the 'Excess of Loss' reinsurance treaty (see the next bullet point);
- An 'Excess of Loss' reinsurance treaty to be concluded by the Bureau with one or more reputable reinsurance undertakings, guaranteeing that the highest risks of the Bureau are covered by a reinsurance contract. The wording of the contract is subject to the approval by the Monitoring Committee.

The two aforementioned financial guarantee requirements are applicable to all new member Bureaux in the Green Card system. A Bureau that starts participating in the Green Card system will remain a transitional member for a period of ten years during which it will have to provide the said guarantees in support of its transitional membership. Moreover, the Council of Bureaux can, upon a recommendation of the Monitoring Committee, decide to place a (non-transitional member) Bureau under monitoring; this would result in the same, or comparable, financial guarantee requirements being applicable to the Bureau in question.

Apart from the financial guarantee requirements, the Council of Bureaux can impose other measures or sanctions on member Bureaux that are in default of their obligations or where the market situation presents an imminent threat to the financial stability of the Green Card system. Such measures or sanctions can consist of one or more of the following non-exhaustive list:

- An obligation for the Bureau in question to report regularly to the Monitoring Committee;
- The mandatory participation of the Bureau in a training programme run by the Council of Bureaux;
- The submission of the Bureau in question to audits or inspections;
- The withdrawal of the Bureau's right to participate in certain decision-making fora of the Council of Bureaux;
- The imposition of financial penalties;
- The temporary suspension of the Bureau's membership in the Council of Bureaux, resulting in the suspension of participation in the Green Card system;
- The termination of the Bureau's membership in the Council of Bureaux, resulting in the impossibility for the Bureau to participate in the Green Card system.

4 Guarantee Funds

4.1 Introduction

In paragraphs 2.4 and 3.5, we already explained that, from the 1970s, the European Union started getting involved in (cross-border) MTPL insurance with the adoption of the First Motor Insurance Directive and the introduction of the system of deemed insurance cover.[1] By replacing the checks on the existence of a Green Card by the presumption that all vehicles normally based in one of the Member States are validly insured, the European legislator intended to come closer to a harmonised internal market in which the free movement of goods, persons, services and capital is ensured.

Ten years later, the European Union (at that moment, the European Economic Community, already consisting of ten Member States) adopted the 2nd Motor Insurance Directive (2nd MID).[2] With this new Directive, the European legislator wanted to bring more harmonisation in the insurance cover provided by compulsory MTPL insurance and attempted to ensure that victims benefit from a comparable protection, no matter where the accident occurred. In support of that aim, the new Motor Insurance Directive required the individual Member States, amongst others, to create Guarantee Funds, granting protection to victims of *accidents caused by uninsured or unidentified vehicles*.

In most of the Member States, a Guarantee Fund or comparable institution was already in place to offer protection to victims who would otherwise be uncertain as to their compensation of damage caused by uninsured or unidentified vehicles. With the adoption of the 2nd MID, the conditions for and remits of the Guarantee Funds were more harmonised. Because many Member States already had Guaran-

1. At that moment, the European Union in fact did not yet exist. The name European Union was only introduced with the Treaty of Maastricht of 1992. At the moment the first Motor Insurance Directives were adopted, the name was in fact European Economic Community or EEC.
2. Second Council Directive of 30 December 1983 on the approximation of the laws of the Member States relating to insurance against civil liability in respect of the use of motor vehicles (84/5/EEC), OJ L 8, 11.1.1984, p. 17.

tee Funds, the wording of Article 1 of the 2nd MID required the Member States 'to set up or authorise a body':

> "Each Member State shall set up or authorise a body with the task of providing compensation, at least up to the limits of the insurance obligation for damage to property or personal injuries caused by an unidentified vehicle or a vehicle for which the insurance obligation provided for in paragraph 1 has not been satisfied."

Today, the provision on the Guarantee Funds is incorporated in the codified Motor Insurance Directive.[3] The text can be found in Article 10 under the title *'Body responsible for compensation'*.

> This title is unfortunate in that it may cause confusion with another body, the Compensation Body, created by the 4th Motor Insurance Directive and having other tasks and competences in the field of cross-border motor road traffic accidents (see chapter 5: The protection of visitors). This leads to the potentially misleading use of two comparable terms in the codified Directive: 'Body responsible for compensation' in Article 10 and 'Compensation Bodies' in Article 24. Despite their similar name and the fact that their role is performed by the same entity in a number of Member States, their mission and operations are clearly separate. The confusion can be traced to other language versions of the codified MID, where the title of the Articles 10 and 24 are extremely similar. In one language version the title of both Articles is even exactly the same, although referring to two separate institutions (in Dutch, the title of both Article 10 and 24 reads *'schadevergoedingsorgaan'*, which translates in English as *'compensation body'*). Since in many Member States, the body referred to in Article 10 is called 'Guarantee Fund', the latter would have been a more appropriate name. But since the name 'fund' is, in a number Slavic languages, rather reserved for 'funds of money' and difficult to use for an institute, another name has been chosen.

Surprisingly, Solvency II applies the term 'national Guarantee Fund' for the body referred to in Article 10 of the Motor Insurance Directive.[4]
For clarity's sake and in order to avoid any confusion in this book, we will use the term 'Guarantee Fund(s)' whenever speaking about the body referred to in Article 10 of the codified MID and reserve the term 'Compensation Body' for the entity of Article 24 and 25 of the Directive.

---

3. Directive 2009/103/EC of the European Parliament and of the Council of 16 September 2009 relating to insurance against civil liability in respect of the use of motor vehicles, and the enforcement of the obligation to insure against such liability (codified version), OJ L 263, 7.10.2009, p. 11. See para 3.5.1. In this book, the document is referred to as the codified Motor Insurance Directive, the codified MID or, even shorter, the MID or the Directive.
4. Directive 2009/138/EC of the European Parliament and of the Council of 25 November 2009 on the taking-up and pursuit of the business of Insurance and Reinsurance (Solvency II) (recast), OJ L 335, 17.12.2009, p. 1.

The current Article 10 of the codified MID is not exactly the same as the original text of the 2nd MID since the tasks of the Guarantee Funds were modified and extended with the adoption of the 3rd and the 5th Motor Insurance Directives in 1990 and 2005.

Unlike the 1st MID, the aim of which was mainly to focus on cross-border road traffic and accidents caused by foreign vehicles, the scope of applicability of the 2nd MID and the Guarantee Funds created by that document is not limited to accidents with a cross-border element. In principle, the Guarantee Fund will be competent for accidents occurred on its own territory and caused by the use of vehicles normally based in that same territory. In a limited number of cases, the Guarantee Fund will also act for accidents caused by foreign vehicles for which the Green Card Bureau cannot operate, e.g. if the Green Card issued for the foreign vehicle is not (or no longer) valid for the vehicle in question or if, in case of deemed insurance cover, the registration plate of the vehicle does not or no longer corresponds to the vehicle.

Although the topic of this book is 'insurance aspects of *cross-border* road traffic accidents', the responsibilities of the Guarantee Funds in domestic accidents still merit discussion, for the following reasons.

- One of the aims of this book is to describe how the European legislator has gradually harmonised the landscape of compulsory MTPL insurance throughout the Member States and how this harmonisation attempts to offer a higher level of protection to injured parties, suffering damage from a road traffic accident. Since the Guarantee Funds' interventions were partly harmonised with the adoption of the 2nd MID, this book cannot remain silent about this important instrument of victims' protection. Other important initiatives in order to harmonise the Member States' legislation on MTPL insurance will be described under chapter 6 (The protection of the policyholder, liable and injured party under the Directive);
- Although certainly not limited to the protection of foreign victims, the intervention mechanisms offered by the Guarantee Funds can also be to the benefit of injured parties who suffer an accident caused by an uninsured or unidentified vehicle outside their country of residence;
- When foreign vehicles causing an accident in a visited country and the Green Card system cannot be applied (e.g. because there is no Green Card available for the foreign vehicle or the vehicle, although bearing a foreign registration plate, is no longer normally based in another Member State), the injured party suffering damage from the accident may have to address a claim to the Guarantee Fund of the country of the accident.

In some Member States the Guarantee Fund's remit goes beyond the requirements of the Motor Insurance Directive, e.g. if it is obliged to intervene when an accident results from 'force majeure' and the driver bears no liability. As there are too many such variations in the different national schemes to examine here, this chapter does not attempt to cover them.

4.2 Territorial scope

The existence of a Guarantee Fund or equivalent body to intervene in case of accidents caused by – at least – uninsured vehicles, is a relevant factor taken into account by the Council of Bureaux when considering a country's eligibility to participate in the Green Card system. The remits of the European Economic Area countries' Guarantee Funds will be harmonised at least partly under the codified Motor Insurance Directive.

That will not however be the case for countries outside the European Economic Area, which are not bound by the European Directives and can freely determine the intervention mechanisms of the Guarantee Fund. For these countries, it is necessary to consult the national legislation in order to know the exact scope of the Fund's competences. It is for instance possible that in certain countries the intervention of the Guarantee Fund is limited to personal injuries, excluding any compensation for material damage.

4.3 Cases of intervention

4.3.1 Introduction

Under this heading, we will examine the different situations where an injured party can seek compensation from the Guarantee Fund for certain damage suffered. We will only list the different scenarios of intervention provided by the Directive, without any details on the way it is applied. Indeed, the Motor Insurance Directive only requires Guarantee Funds to cover certain kinds of damage without however entirely harmonising the extent of the compensation to be provided. These limitations will be explained in paragraph 4.4.
Article 10 of the codified Motor Insurance Directive starts with the following provision:

> "Each Member State shall set up or authorise a body with the task of providing compensation, at least up to the limits of the insurance obligation for damage to property or personal injuries caused by an unidentified vehicle or a vehicle for which the insurance obligation provided for in Article 3 has not been satisfied."

We will therefore start this section with the two main cases of intervention provided for in the Motor Insurance Directive: damage caused by an uninsured vehicle (para 4.3.2) and damage caused by an unidentified vehicle (para 4.3.3). A third scheme is foreseen in the MID: compensation for damage caused by vehicles stolen or obtained by violence. The MID does not always impose this third task on the Guarantee Fund but only makes it obligatory if national legislation allows insurers not to provide cover in case of damage caused by a stolen vehicle or one obtained by the use of violence. This intervention, provided for in Article 13(2) of the MID will be described in paragraph 4.3.4. In the next paragraph 4.3.5, we will list the scenarios where, in a cross-border context, the Guarantee Fund may have to intervene because there is no obligation for the Green Card Bureau to do so (e.g. because no identified Green Card can be submitted for the vehicle having caused the accident). Finally, in paragraph 4.3.6, we will give some examples of national legislation imposing additional tasks on the Guarantee Fund that are not foreseen in the Motor Insurance Directive. Such is for instance the case when the insurer of the vehicle that caused the accident is in a state of insolvency.

4.3.2 *Uninsured vehicles*

It is clear that the establishment of Guarantee Funds was motivated by the intention to give a sufficient level of protection to victims of road traffic accidents.[5] Victims should not suffer a second time by the fact that the owner, keeper or driver of the vehicle having caused the accident did not respect the obligation to insure the vehicle against MTPL. Indeed, according to rules of liability, the victim may have a claim against the person liable for the accident or against the owner or the keeper of the vehicle in question, but that makes the success of the victim's claim subject to the solvency of those persons. In order to avoid the victim first having to engage in possibly endless discussions with the driver and/or the person responsible for the uninsured vehicle, a claim can be addressed directly to the Guarantee Fund. Moreover, the MID explicitly states that the victim should not have to establish that the person liable for the accident is either unwilling or unable to pay compensation. Article 10(1), last sentence of the first paragraph of the codified MID reads as follows:

> "Member States may not allow the body to make the payment of compensation conditional on the victim establishing in any way that the person liable is unable or refuses to pay."

The general obligation to have all vehicles insured can be found in Article 3 of the codified MID. This provision requires that

5. Most of the time, we will use the name 'victim' in this chapter. As will be described later in paragraph 6.2.12.1, the term 'victim' is stricter than the term 'injured party'. The notion 'injured party' covers a broader circle of persons that can claim for compensation, including subrogated parties. Since subrogated parties will not always benefit from access to the Guarantee Fund, we use the stricter term 'victim' in this chapter.

"each Member State shall (...) take all appropriate measures to ensure that civil liability in respect of the use of vehicles normally based in its territory is covered by insurance."

The question what is to be understood under 'the use of vehicles' has been the subject of much discussion and has resulted in a number of decisions of the Court of Justice of the European Union in recent years. This point, together with the main jurisprudence of the Court of Justice, will be discussed more in detail in paragraph 6.2.4.

The Motor Insurance Directive does not prescribe *who* shall be responsible for insuring the vehicle against MTPL: the owner, the keeper or the driver of the vehicle or any other person. This is left to the Member States' national law.

A very interesting analysis on the kind of risks to be covered by MTPL insurance as well as on the consequences of absence of insurance can be found in the opinion of Advocate General Bobek in case C-80/17 as well as in the decision of the European Court of Justice of 4 September 2018.[6] The Court decided, amongst others, the following:

"(...) it must be held that a vehicle which is registered and therefore has not been officially withdrawn from use, and which is capable of being driven, corresponds to the concept of 'vehicle' within the meaning of Article 1 (1) of the First Directive and, consequently, does not cease to be subject to the insurance obligation laid down in Article 3 (1) of that directive, on the sole ground that its owner no longer intends to drive it and immobilises it on private land."[7]

Subject to national rules of liability and compensation of damage, the Guarantee Fund will provide compensation for both material damage and personal injury.

As will be demonstrated in paragraph 6.2.6, Article 5(2) of the codified Directive allows Member States to derogate from the compulsory MTPL insurance in respect of certain types of vehicle or certain vehicles having a special plate. In such cases, Article 5(2) of the codified MID requires Member States to

"ensure that such vehicles are treated in the same way as vehicles for which the insurance obligation has not been satisfied."

This allows the victim of an accident caused by such an 'exempted vehicle' to address a claim to the Guarantee Fund of the Member State where the accident

6. CJEU, Opinion of Advocate General Bobek of 26 April 2018, *Juliana*, C-80/17, EU:C:2018:290 and CJEU, Judgment of 4 September 2018, *Juliana*, C-80/17, EU:C:2018:661.
7. Para 42 of the Court's Judgment. References to the Articles in the First Directive correspond to the Articles 1(1) and 3 of the codified Motor Insurance Directive.

occurred. If the 'exempted vehicle' is normally based in another Member State than the Member State where the accident occurred, the codified MID specifies that the Guarantee Fund of the country where the accident occurred has a claim against the Guarantee Fund in the Member State where the vehicle is normally based. Strangely enough, the codified MID refers in this provision to the term 'Guarantee Fund', whereas it is to be recalled that the title of Article 10 of the MID reads 'body responsible for compensation' and does not use the name 'Guarantee Fund' (see *supra* para 4.1).

The codified Directive is silent on how the Guarantee Funds are financed in order to be able to meet the obligations imposed on them by the Directive; this is left to individual Member States. Only from Article 150(1) Solvency II is it apparent that the insurance industry should normally finance the operations of the Guarantee Funds.[8] And indeed, in all Member States contributions of motor insurance providers are if not the only, then at least the most important means of financing the Guarantee Funds. Contributions are most often calculated and levied based on the premium income of each insurer in the MTPL branch or, alternatively, related to the number of vehicles insured This means that, albeit in an indirect way, the compensations paid for accidents caused by uninsured vehicles are financed by insurance premiums paid for MTPL insurance. In other words, the financial burden for the consequences of persons not insuring their vehicles is put on the shoulders of those who are so honest to respect the obligation to insure against MTPL and pay premium for it. In order to minimise that financial burden, the Guarantee Fund will of course attempt to recover any outlays from the driver, owner or keeper of the uninsured vehicle, but success will clearly depend on the solvency of the uninsured person. For that reason, Member States, police authorities, Guarantee Funds and the insurance sector should cooperate and do everything possible to combat the phenomenon of uninsured driving. Bringing a vehicle into traffic without insurance is a form of dangerous and anti-social behaviour that is to be fought against. Despite the fact that the need for fighting uninsured driving is felt in all Member States, important differences between Member States in respect of the level of uninsured vehicles compared to the total vehicle fleet of the Member State in question can still be observed.

The annual expenditure of the Guarantee Funds for the consequences of accidents caused by uninsured vehicles can be estimated around one billion euro.

8. Directive 2009/138/EC of the European Parliament and of the Council of 25 November 2009 on the taking-up and pursuit of the business of Insurance and Reinsurance (Solvency II) (recast), OJ L 335, 17 December 2009, p. 1.

It may be clear that the proper protection of victims depends to a large extent on the way in which compliance with compulsory MTPL insurance can be controlled and enforced. Theoretically the continuity of the system of deemed insurance cover can even be dependent on the extent to which Member States are able to limit the rate of uninsured driving on their territory. In this context, the current Article 4 of the codified Motor Insurance Directive is considered a hindrance to the successful fight against uninsured driving. Article 4 is worded as follows:

> *"Member States shall refrain from making checks on insurance against civil liability in respect of vehicles normally based in the territory of another Member State and in respect of vehicles normally based in the territory of a third country entering their territory from the territory of another Member State. However, they may carry out non-systematic checks on insurance provided that those checks are not discriminatory and are carried out as part of a control which is not aimed exclusively at insurance verification."*

This provision fits perfectly in the goal of facilitating cross-border road traffic and the abolishment of time-consuming border checks, pursued by the European Union. It is true that the achievements of the system of deemed insurance cover would be eroded if foreign vehicles were stopped systematically for insurance status checks. Nevertheless, Article 4 is quite radical in its aim of avoiding any possible insurance checks. Especially taking into consideration the development of modern, electronic instruments of control on insurance cover (via technology such as automatic number plate recognition), the current wording of Article 4 may be put into question.

It is in this context that the European Commission suggests a modification of Article 4 in its proposal for a new Motor Insurance Directive, published on 24 May 2018.[9] In the preamble of the proposal for a new MID, the Commission justifies the amendment of Article 4 as follows:

> *"New technological developments allow for checking insurance of vehicles without stopping them and thus without interfering with the free movement of persons. It is therefore appropriate [to] allow those checks of insurance on vehicles, only if they are non-discriminatory, necessary and proportionate, form part of a general system of checks on the national territory and do not require stopping of the vehicle."*

4.3.3 *Unidentified vehicles*

Contrary to the situation where an accident is caused by an uninsured vehicle with an identified driver, the victim of an accident caused by a vehicle that remains unidentified cannot even try to claim against the person liable for the accident.

9. See the Commission's proposal for a new MID, briefly described in para 3.5.1. (COM(2018) 336 final).

Therefore, the Motor Insurance Directive requires Member States to provide for procedures allowing the victim of an accident caused by an unidentified vehicle to claim compensation directly from the Guarantee Fund. In that way, the Guarantee Fund operates as a safety net in a second important category of cases where the victim would otherwise run the risk of remaining without protection.

In the case of accidents caused by vehicles that remain unidentified, it is possible that the driver who caused the damage did not feel any impact or become aware of the accident. This is not unthinkable in case of large trucks, especially when the contact was made only with the trailer. But in the large majority of accidents with unidentified vehicles the driver is less innocent and will be committing a hit-and-run offence, leaving the place of the accident without identifying themselves or giving the insurance data of the vehicle. In that way the liable driver tries to escape any responsibility, administrative actions or possible financial consequences, such as the application of an excess or a higher insurance premium as a result of the increased insurance claims history. But a hit-and-run case often also hides a more important problem. In many cases, a hit-and-run offence is an attempt of the liable driver to escape the consequences of aggravating circumstances, such as road traffic offences, the use of alcohol or other drugs in traffic or uninsured driving. Just like uninsured driving, committing a hit-and-run offence is a form of anti-social behaviour, the impact of which can be extremely hard for the victim. Too many reprehensible examples exist where drivers (often in a state of alcohol intoxication) hit cyclists or pedestrians and leave them for dead in order to escape their own responsibility.

In order to protect victims of such hit-and-run cases, Guarantee Funds have the task to provide compensation for damage caused by unidentified vehicles. Again subject to national rules of liability and compensation of damage, the Guarantee Fund will provide compensation for both material damage and personal injury. Damage to property however can be excluded from compensation by the Guarantee Fund. That will be described more in detail in paragraph 4.4.3.

> Based on an agreement between the Finnish Motor Insurers' Centre (FMIC, fulfilling the function of Guarantee Fund in Finland) and the Finnish insurance undertakings, the FMIC compensates damage caused by vehicles (identified or not) to reindeer. In Finland, all reindeer are privately owned and when they are hit by a vehicle, even while walking freely and outside of an enclosure, the owner will be compensated by the FMIC.

4.3.4 *Vehicles stolen or obtained by violence*

Article 10 of the codified Motor Insurance Directive only requires the Guarantee Funds to compensate victims of accidents caused by uninsured or unidentified vehicles. There is however a third mandatory case of intervention provided for in the Motor Insurance Directive, but this third compulsory task for the Guarantee Funds is only conditional. If the national legislation of a Member State excludes cover for vehicles stolen or obtained by violence or allows insurers to provide for such exclusion in their MTPL policies, the Guarantee Fund of that Member State must respond to claims addressed by victims of accidents caused by such vehicles.[10]

In accordance with Article 13 of the codified MID, insurers may not exclude from insurance cover, in respect of claims addressed by third parties who have been victims of an accident, *the use or driving of vehicles by persons who do not have express or implied authorisation to do so*. This provision is again clearly a protection for victims, ensuring that they do not find themselves without compensation if the accident has been caused by a stolen vehicle or any other vehicle used by a driver without authorisation to do so.

Nevertheless, Article 13(2) of the codified Directive makes an exception to this rule, allowing Member States to adopt legislation where insurers may invoke the exclusion of cover if a vehicle is stolen or obtained by violence, but only on the condition that the Guarantee Fund then intervenes. Article 13(2) is worded as follows:

> "In the case of vehicles stolen or obtained by violence, Member States may provide that the body specified in Article 10 (1) is to pay compensation instead of the insurer under the conditions set out in paragraph 1 of this Article. Where the vehicle is normally based in another Member State, that body can make no claim against any body in that Member State.
> Member States which, in the case of vehicles stolen or obtained by violence, provide that the body referred to in Article 10 (1) is to pay compensation may fix in respect of damage to property an excess of not more than € 250 to be borne by the victim."

In other words, for those Member States that have used the possibility (it is a possibility, not an obligation) provided for in Article 13 under which insurers may exclude cover for any damage caused by vehicles obtained by theft or violence, the intervention of the Guarantee Funds will be obligatory. For those Member States, this will be the third category of compulsory interventions of the Guarantee Fund.

In order to keep the right balance between Member States which have used this possibility and those who have not, Article 13 provides that the Guarantee Fund of Member State A, having compensated the victim of an accident caused by a stolen vehicle normally based in Member State B, cannot recover the outlays from the

10. The Directive seems to make a subtle distinction between 'victims' and 'injured parties'. See for an analysis of this difference para 6.2.12.1.

Green Card Bureau or from the Guarantee Fund of Member State B. This of course leaves intact the recourse right of the Guarantee Fund of Member State A against the person who stole the vehicle or obtained it by violence.

If the Guarantee Fund has to compensate any damage caused by a vehicle obtained by theft or violence, the Fund may apply an excess to the compensation to be paid, but this excess is subject to two limitations:
- It may only be applied to damage to property (in other words only for material damage and not for personal injury);
- It may not exceed € 250.

Example
Mr X is the victim of an accident in Malta caused by the use of a vehicle insured with the Maltese insurance undertaking Maltins. It turns out however that at the time of the accident, the vehicle was driven by a thief who had stolen the vehicle a few hours before the accident took place. Since the insurer Maltins could prove that the vehicle was driven by the thief at the time of the accident, Maltins is, based on Maltese legislation on MTPL insurance, allowed to refuse cover for the damage caused.
As a result, the victim, Mr X, can address a claim for compensation to the Maltese Guarantee Fund. If Mr X only suffers material damage, an excess of € 233 will apply to the compensation paid, in accordance with Maltese law.
If the vehicle that caused the accident is not normally based in Malta but in Italy, the victim may try, in the first place, to address a claim to the Maltese Green Card Bureau but the latter will also be allowed to invoke the exclusion of cover for vehicles stolen or obtained by violence. Again, Mr X will be allowed to present a claim to the Maltese Guarantee Fund. In this case, the Maltese Guarantee Fund will have no possibility of recovering the compensation from an insurer or other body either in Malta or Italy.
The Guarantee Fund may however attempt to recover the outlays from the thief of the vehicle.

Finally, it is necessary to refer to one additional provision in Article 13(1) of the MID, which states that the exclusion of MTPL insurance cover may be invoked

> "against persons who voluntarily entered the vehicle which caused the damage or injury, when the insurer can prove that they knew the vehicle was stolen."[11]

Our first observation is that the wording of Article 13(1) seems to imply that national legislators have no option but to allow insurers to invoke this exclusion. We are however of the opinion, that national law may deny insurers that option.

11. See also para 6.2.12.4.

Furthermore the provision seems to imply that only the insurer can invoke this exclusion. Do we have to understand that the Guarantee Fund, when compensating victims of accidents caused by vehicles obtained by theft or violence, may also invoke this provision and exclude from compensation any person who voluntarily entered the vehicle when the Guarantee Fund can prove that the person knew the vehicle was stolen? We are inclined to answer this question in the affirmative, since Article 13(2) of the MID states that the Guarantee Fund is to pay compensation instead of the insurer under the conditions set out in paragraph 1 of this Article. If the Guarantee Fund must pay under the same conditions as an insurer, then the Guarantee Fund should also be able to rely on the exclusion of passengers of the vehicle if they knew that the vehicle had been stolen. It is to be underlined however that Article 13(1) only refers to passengers who knew the vehicle had been stolen, but does not speak about the knowledge that a vehicle had been obtained by violence. In our opinion it would however only be consistent that passengers knowing that the vehicle was obtained by violence, may also be excluded from cover by the Guarantee Fund. Usually violence precedes theft and as such is also an aggravating element.

4.3.5 *Cases of intervention in a cross-border context*

In chapter 3 (The Green Card system) we have examined under what conditions a victim can invoke the guarantees provided by the Green Card system in order to obtain compensation of damage caused by foreign vehicles. In a number of cases however, the necessary conditions will not be fulfilled and the national Green Card Bureau will not be competent or able to intervene for the damage suffered, even if it is clear that the accident has been caused by a vehicle that does not originate from the country of the accident. In such cases, the victim will not be able to claim compensation from the Green Card Bureau but can fall back on the Guarantee Fund to obtain indemnity.

What kind of circumstances can be imagined where the Green Card Bureau can deny cover and refuse to compensate the victim based on the Green Card system? The following examples have to be taken into account, without this however being an exhaustive list of scenarios where the victim will rather address a claim to the Guarantee Fund than to the Green Card bureau:

- No Green Card is available for the foreign vehicle that caused the accident and the vehicle is not normally based in a country that signed the Multilateral Agreement. If the accident occurred in the European Economic Area (where the Motor Insurance Directive is applicable) and the vehicle having caused the accident originates from a country participating in the Green Card system on the basis of Section II of the Internal Regulations (based on the existence of a Green Card), the absence of an identified Green Card will result in the national motor insurers' Bureau not being competent to intervene. In that case, the injured party will have to turn to the Guarantee Fund of the country where the accident occurred;

- There is a Green Card for the vehicle that caused the accident, but the date of the accident falls outside the term of validity indicated on the Green Card;
- Another possibility is that the Green Card is not valid for the country where the accident occurred since the country of the accident was crossed out in box 8 (territorial validity) of the Green Card;
- The Green Card presented for the vehicle having caused the accident turns out to be false and the vehicle is registered in a country different from the country of the Green Card Bureau under the authority of which the Green Card is purported to be issued. In that case, Article 9(2) of the Internal Regulations will apply and the purported guaranteeing Bureau will be able to deny guarantee since "the false Green Card relates to a vehicle which is not legally registered in that Bureau's country";
- Section III of the Internal Regulations (deemed insurance cover) applies but the vehicle that caused the accident is not or is no longer normally based in another Member State. The registration plate may have been falsified, suspended, expired or deregistered from the registration database. In that case, Article 11(2) of the Internal Regulations or Article 1(4), point (d) of the codified MID will apply and the vehicle will be normally based in the state in which the accident took place. That results in the Green Card Bureau not being competent to answer the claim of the injured party;
- It is clear that the vehicle having caused the accident bears a foreign registration plate but it is not possible to identify the plate entirely (e.g. because it was indicated wrongly or in an unclear way on the accident statement). In that case, the Bureaux involved should cooperate to identify the registration plate and the insurer but if these attempts remain unsuccessful, the vehicle will be considered as unidentified;
- The (foreign) vehicle is exempted from compulsory MTPL insurance on the basis of Article 5(2) of the codified MID (see *supra* para 4.3.2 and *infra* 6.2.6).

In all these situations (and possible other scenarios), the claim will not be handled by the Green Card Bureau but may be submitted to the Guarantee Fund. The latter will however not handle the claim as if it were a Green Card claim (in accordance with the rules of the Internal Regulations) but will apply the national legislation applicable to the Guarantee Fund (as harmonised on the basis of the Motor Insurance Directive). This may include certain limitations as will be discussed in paragraph 4.4.

In many countries, there will hardly be any difference between a case being handled by the Green Card Bureau or by the Guarantee Fund and the victim may not even know which entity is handling the claim. Indeed, in a number of countries the functions of Green Card Bureau and Guarantee Fund are performed by exactly the same body, operating under one and the same legal personality. In other countries, the Green Card Bureau and the Guarantee Fund are two distinct organisations with a different legal personality, but they share the same building and even management and are closely linked to each other. In those cases, the Bureau will often forward the claim, on its own initiative, to the Guarantee Fund in order to be handled by the latter body. But in a number of countries, the Green Card Bureau and the Guarantee Fund are two entirely separate organisations. One example is Italy, where the Bureau (UCI or *Ufficio Centrale Italiano*) and the Guarantee Fund (CONSAP *or Concessionaria Servizi Assicurativi Pubblici S.p.A.*) are based in Milano and Rome respectively and where it is even legally impossible to forward a claim from one body to the other.

4.3.6 *Cases of intervention not imposed by the MID*

As seen in the previous paragraphs, the European Motor Insurance Directive requests Member States to provide for the intervention of Guarantee Funds in at least two and under certain conditions three situations:

- In the case of an accident caused by an uninsured vehicle ("a vehicle for which the insurance obligation provided for in Article 3 [of the codified MID] has not been satisfied");
- In the case of an accident caused by an unidentified vehicle;
- If the national law of the Member State in question allows insurers to refuse cover for accidents caused by vehicles stolen or obtained by violence.

Apart from these mandatory intervention schemes, the MID does not impose any further obligations on Guarantee Funds. Member States are therefore free to provide for additional situations where they consider the Guarantee Fund's intervention appropriate. Examples of complementary tasks imposed by national legislation on Guarantee Funds are the following:

- damage caused by the use of a vehicle, when the driver cannot be held liable as a result of *force majeure*;
- damage which has been caused intentionally;
- damage caused in traffic by a person who is not the driver of a motor vehicle (e.g. a pedestrian or a cyclist) and who is uninsured;
- damage caused by animals the keeper/owner of which is unknown or uninsured.

Certain Guarantee Funds have also been entrusted with other tasks, which are outside the scope of MTPL insurance, such as the intervention for damage caused by terrorist attacks or by hunting accidents.

These types of intervention have not been created by the Motor Insurance Directive and are therefore not governed by the MID provisions on the Guarantee Funds.

A special situation to be examined is the intervention, imposed on many Guarantee Funds but not foreseen in the Motor Insurance Directive, *in the case of an insurance undertaking in state of insolvency.*

Although the intervention of Guarantee Funds for cases of insolvency of MTPL insurers is not explicitly foreseen in the Motor Insurance Directive, the Court of Justice of the European Union has been invited to decide on this possible competence and confirmed that the Motor Insurance Directive does not require Guarantee Funds to cover cases of insolvency of insurance undertakings.[12]

> MÁV Általános Biztosító Egyesület (MAV) was a Hungarian MTPL insurer, declared insolvent in 2008. The claimants in the case before the Court of Justice of the European Union (CJEU) had been insured with MAV and had caused damage to third parties as a result of road traffic accidents. Since their insurer MAV was, following the insolvency, unable to honour its insurance obligations towards third parties, the persons insured with MAV and having caused the accidents had been compelled to compensate the injured parties for their damage. The claimants in the Court case (i.e. the MAV policyholders), after having indemnified the injured parties, claimed reimbursement from the Hungarian State, arguing that the State, by not providing any intervention in case of insolvency of an insurer, had not correctly transposed the Motor Insurance Directive into Hungarian law.
> The CJEU held that the different provisions of the Motor Insurance Directive must be interpreted as not including the obligation of establishing a body
>
> > "to ensure that compensation is provided to victims of road accidents in situations where, although the persons responsible for the damage had taken out insurance covering their civil liability in respect of the use of motor vehicles, the insurer has become insolvent."

In order to support policyholders and victims in case of insolvent insurers, many Member States have adopted national legislation providing for compensation of damage caused by vehicles insured with an insolvent insurer. In that way, a double goal is pursued:

- On the one hand, the legislation ensures that a victim of a road traffic accident has recourse to compensation if the insurer of the vehicle that caused the accident is insolvent (after all, since we are speaking about third party liability insurance, the victim could not influence the choice of insurer for the vehicle that caused the accident);

12. CJEU, Judgment of 11 July 2013, *Csonka and others*, C-409/11, EU:C:2013:512.

- On the other hand, the legislation also exonerates the person who caused the accident having to pay the entire compensation even though they were legally insured and had paid premium for the third party liability insurance cover.

Nevertheless, the scope and application of the intervention schemes adopted in several Member States differ in significant ways:
- There is no uniform way of determining as of when the insurer is to be considered insolvent and as of when the Guarantee Funds should start their action (e.g. as of the date of withdrawal of the insurance authorisation; the date of declaration of bankruptcy; the date of winding-up; or any other trigger);
- Different bodies have been entrusted with the task of compensating victims of accidents caused by vehicles insured with an insolvent MTPL insurer: it can be either the Guarantee Fund (in the meaning of Article 10 of the codified MID) or another national body or organisation;
- The conditions and formalities to be fulfilled by the victim or claimant may differ from one Member State to another;
- There are differences in compensation practice, which may include the application of an excess and/or maximum amounts for which compensation is paid;
- Some intervention schemes only provide compensation to third parties who have suffered damage from an accident, whereas other schemes may also grant reimbursement of the premium paid where insurance cover no longer exists;
- The intervention scheme may also be activated if an insurance undertaking's authorisation has been withdrawn for reasons other than insolvency.

It can be concluded that no harmonisation exists within the European Economic Area as regards the protection of the MTPL insured and/or the injured party following an accident caused by the use of a vehicle insured with an insolvent MTPL insurer.

> The lack of harmonisation and the need for more clarity may be illustrated by the legal uncertainty that was created following the insolvency of the Maltese insurer Setanta, operating under Freedom to Provide Services in Ireland (for the possibility of insurers to operate under Freedom to Provide Services: see chapter 7).
> Setanta was declared insolvent in 2014. Irish legislation could theoretically lead to two different bodies having to intervene for the consequences of Setanta's insolvency: either the Insurance Compensation Fund or the Motor Insurers' Bureau of Ireland (MIBI) operating in the capacity of Guarantee Fund for Ireland. The decision on which of the two bodies had to intervene was not without practical importance since the Insurance Compensation Fund's intervention was limited to 65% of the damage caused with a maximum of € 825,000, whereas MIBI's intervention was not subject to any specific limitations.

Both bodies disputed their obligation to intervene. In some respects the litigation concentrated on the wording of the MIBI (Guarantee Fund) Agreement and a number of specific clauses within that Agreement. The Law Society of Ireland was of the view that MIBI should compensate the claimants and made an application to the High Court to have the point litigated. The High Court permitted their application and thus began a three year legal argument. When finally the Irish Supreme Court rendered a decision in May 2017 and the victims of accidents caused by vehicles insured with Setanta could be compensated for 65% of their damage (and a maximum of € 825,000), three years had elapsed between the declaration of insolvency and the final verdict. Victims had to wait all these years to finally receive their compensation.
Subsequent to the finalisation of the litigation, legislation has been introduced which now provides that in the instances of future insolvencies claimants will be compensated 100% and, separately, Setanta claimants will now receive the balance of 35% of their claim.

Finally, attention may be drawn to the fact that the victim of an accident that falls into the scope of the Green Card system may be better off than the victim of a 'purely national or domestic' accident caused by the use of a vehicle insured with an insolvent MTPL insurer. Whereas on the national level the compensation of the victim will depend on the national legislation and the protection mechanisms for cases of insolvency, the Green Card system provides for the guarantee of the Bureaux including where the (foreign) MTPL insurer is in a state of insolvency (cf. para 3.8.8: the guarantee between Bureaux in case of insolvency of the insurer). In that way, the victim will be compensated by the Green Card Bureau of the country of the accident. The latter will be reimbursed by the Green Card Bureau of the country of origin of the vehicle, in accordance with the rules of the Green Card system.

The proposal for a new Motor Insurance Directive, published by the European Commission on 24 May 2018 (see *supra* para 3.5.1), requires the Member States to set up or authorise a body (not necessarily the Guarantee Fund) to compensate injured parties habitually residing within their territory for personal injuries or material damage, caused by a vehicle insured by an insurance undertaking which is subject to bankruptcy proceedings or winding up procedure, or in case the victim does not receive a reply in time.

4.4 Limitations to the intervention of the Guarantee Fund

4.4.1 *Introduction*

The codified Motor Insurance Directive aims at establishing a certain degree of harmonisation at the European level. Nevertheless, it allows certain limitations to the intervention mechanism, leaving it to the individual Member States to decide whether or not to incorporate them into their national legislation. The options left to the Member States are possibilities, not an obligation. This again shows the nature of the legal instrument chosen by the European Union: a Directive that defines a minimum level of harmonisation while leaving to Member States the choice of form and methods to obtain the desired result. This principle can also be found in recital 14 of the MID's preamble:

> "However, Member States should be given the possibility of applying certain limited exclusions as regards the payment of compensation by that body and of providing that compensation for damage to property caused by an unidentified vehicle may be limited or excluded in view of the danger of fraud."

The limitations allowed by the MID and examined in the following sections are:

- *Subsidiarity:* the right of Member States to regard compensation by the Guarantee Fund as subsidiary or non-subsidiary (Article 10(1), second paragraph of the codified MID and examined in paragraph 4.4.2);
- *Unidentified vehicles and material damage:* the right of Member States to limit or exclude the payment of compensation in the event of damage to property by an unidentified vehicle (Article 10(3) of the codified MID and examined in paragraph 4.4.3);
- *Passengers of uninsured vehicles:* the right of Member States to exclude the payment of compensation by the Guarantee Fund in respect of persons who voluntarily entered the vehicle when they knew it was uninsured (Article 10(2), second paragraph of the codified MID and examined in paragraph 4.4.4; cf also para 6.2.12.2);
- *Vehicles stolen or obtained by violence:* the choice left to the Member States to give insurers the possibility to exclude from MTPL insurance cover any damage caused by the use of vehicles obtained by theft or violence on the condition that Guarantee Funds will compensate such damage (Article 13(2) of the codified MID and examined in paragraphs 4.3.4 and 4.4.5);
- *The application of certain excesses:* the two situations in which Member States are allowed to provide for an excess to be applied by the Guarantee Fund (Article 10(3) and Article 13(2) of the MID, examined in paragraph 4.4.6).

4.4.2 Subsidiarity

Article 10(1), second paragraph of the codified MID reads as follows:

> "The first subparagraph shall be without prejudice to the right of the Member States to regard compensation by the body as subsidiary or non-subsidiary (…)."

The MID does not specify (in the preamble or in the provision cited above) what is exactly to be understood under the term 'subsidiary or non-subsidiary'.

The aim of the provision is to allow Member States to limit the Guarantee Fund's intervention to those cases where the victim is not able to obtain compensation from any other source, such as an insurer or other body. Not only social security bodies are being considered but also private insurers such as those offering comprehensive (casco) insurance or insurers of other vehicles involved in the accident that could potentially be held severally liable. In such circumstances, the victim will first have to obtain compensation from such bodies or insurers and the same bodies or insurers will, after compensating the victim, be deprived from any recourse right against the Guarantee Fund. Only the damage that remains uncompensated by other bodies or insurers can be claimed from the Guarantee Fund.

In those Member States where this possibility offered by the MID has been applied and the Guarantee Fund's intervention is regarded as subsidiary, the Guarantee Fund functions as a kind of safety net, only offering compensation if the victim would otherwise be left without any indemnity.

In France, the combination of the Guarantee Fund's subsidiarity with the specific road traffic liability rules introduced by the Badinter Law leads to a significant limitation of the Guarantee Fund's outlays. The French *Loi Badinter* or Badinter Law of 1985 introduced a complete new way of thinking on the compensation of damage caused by road traffic accidents and lead to a substantial improvement of the victim's protection in road traffic.[13] In case of a road traffic accident in which a motor vehicle is involved, every person suffering damage is in the first place given a right to full compensation of the damage suffered. This right to compensation can only be lowered or even be reduced to zero insofar as a fault of the victim can be proven. Certain particularly vulnerable road users are given a wider protection, leading to only a limited possibility to reduce their right to compensation or even to the exclusion of this reduction. Contrary to the classical fault-based liability, the compensation rules of the Badinter Law are, in other words, reversed. In order to receive compensation, a victim does not have to prove the fault of a tortfeasor but starts with a full right to compensation and this right can only be reduced to the extent that a fault of the victim can be proven. In that way, rules on compensation of damage in motor road traffic accidents are based on the notion of 'a motor vehicle being involved in an accident' (the French notion of *'impliqué'*), rather than on fault. Moreover, the obligation to compensate all victims whose right to compensation cannot be reduced or excluded rests on the shoulders of (the insurers) of all the vehicles involved in the acci-

13. *Loi n° 85-677 du 5 juillet 1985 tendant à l'amélioration de la situation des victimes d'accidents de la circulation et à l'accélération des procédures d'indemnisation, JORF, 6 July 1985, p. 7584.* The text has been amended afterwards and a consolidated version can be found on: www.legifrance.gouv.fr.

dent. This results in all the involved vehicles being held jointly and severally liable towards the injured party or parties.
The combination of the notion of involvement with the joint and several liability of all vehicles involved in the accidents implies that the French Guarantee Fund will only have to intervene insofar as no other insurer must intervene on the basis of involvement.

Example

Vehicles A and B are waiting in front of a red traffic light at a crossroad on French territory. Vehicle A is the first in line, followed by vehicle B. Vehicle C approaches the traffic lights and is unable to stop in time, hitting vehicle B in the rear and pushing it forwards to hit vehicle A. Nobody suffers bodily injury as a result of the accident, but vehicle A is damaged at the rear and vehicle B is impacted both at the rear and at the front. Also vehicle C is damaged at the front.
The owner of vehicle C will see his/her right to compensation being reduced to zero as a result of the driver's at-fault behaviour, which was the sole cause of the accident and the damage suffered.
It turns out that vehicle C is uninsured.
The owners of vehicles A and B, who cannot be blamed for any negligence or at-fault behaviour have the right to full compensation for their damage and can demand this compensation from the insurer of each vehicle involved in the accident (joint and several liability). If they seek compensation from the Guarantee Fund, the latter will invoke the Fund's subsidiarity and state that the insurers of the other vehicles involved in the accident will have to compensate the damage.
This will result in the MTPL or casco insurers of vehicles A and B having to compensate all the damage caused to the vehicles A and B and the Guarantee Fund will not have to cover the damage caused by the uninsured vehicle C.
The casco insurers of vehicles A and B may however execute their recourse right against the driver of vehicle C.

Not all Member States have made use of the possibility to regard the Guarantee Fund's intervention as subsidiary.

The possibility for Guarantee Funds to act on the basis of subsidiarity is inserted in the MID under Article 10 and it is relevant to refer again to the wording of that provision:

> "The first subparagraph shall be without prejudice to the right of the Member States to regard compensation by the body as subsidiary or non-subsidiary (…)."

The first subparagraph of Article 10(1) relates to the Guarantee Fund's intervention for damage caused by unidentified or uninsured vehicles. As explained in paragraph 4.3.4, a Guarantee Fund will also have to cover damage caused by a vehicle obtained by theft or violence if the national legislation allows the insurer to exclude cover in such circumstances. That obligation is to be found in Article 13 of the codified MID and not in Article 10. May a Guarantee Fund then invoke rules of subsidiarity in case of damage caused by vehicles obtained by theft or violence? The fact that the possibility of subsidiarity is written into Article 10(1) and only refers to the Guarantee Funds' role in case of damage caused by uninsured or unidentified vehicles, may lead to the conclusion that the subsidiarity may not be invoked in case of damage caused by vehicles obtained by theft or violence. It can also however be argued (and we share this point of view) that if an insurer may invoke the exclusion of cover for vehicles obtained by theft or violence, the vehicle is to be considered as uninsured. As a result, the Guarantee Fund will act as safety net for damage caused by uninsured vehicles, in which case the Guarantee Fund can invoke the subsidiarity of Article 10 MID.

4.4.3 *Unidentified vehicles and material damage*

Article 10(3), first paragraph of the codified MID:

> "Member States may limit or exclude the payment of compensation by the body in the event of damage to property by an unidentified vehicle."

The intervention of the Guarantee Fund in the case of an accident caused by an unidentified vehicle is without any doubt an important improvement in respect of victims' protection against the consequences of hit-and-run cases. The Guarantee Fund's mission to compensate damage caused by unidentified vehicles may however also lead to undesired consequences such as fraud. Indeed, the protection scheme for damage caused by unidentified vehicles may bring owners of vehicles, who have suffered damage to their car as a result of their own carelessness, into temptation and lead them to declare falsely that the damage was caused by the involvement of an unidentified vehicle.

Example

Mr X is the owner of a beautiful vehicle of which he is very proud and in which he has invested his last penny. The purchase price of the car had been so high that Mr X can in fact only afford MTPL insurance for the vehicle in question and has not enough means to take comprehensive insurance cover for the car.

Although always driving the car with utmost prudence, Mr X once suffered from a sudden moment of reduced attention and hit a lamp post next to the road.

When realising that the absence of comprehensive insurance would leave him without compensation for the damage, Mr X found out that he simply had to declare that the accident had not been caused by his own negligence but that he had to make a manoeuvre to avoid a collision with an unidentified vehicle coming from the opposite direction and that suddenly deviated from the road, causing Mr X to hit the lamp post. This declaration would help him to obtain compensation from the Guarantee Fund, although it is of course a fraudulent declaration.

In order to reduce this risk of fraud, the MID allows the Member States (again it is a possibility, not an obligation) to either limit or entirely exclude the Guarantee Fund's intervention for *material* damage (the MID uses the term 'damage to property') caused by unidentified vehicles.

With the introduction of the 5th Motor Insurance Directive in 2005, this possibility has been reduced. The following two paragraphs have been added to the provisions on the Guarantee Funds:

> "However, where the body has paid compensation for significant personal injuries to any victim of the same accident in which damage to property was caused by an unidentified vehicle, Member States may not exclude the payment of compensation for damage to property on the basis that the vehicle is unidentified. Nevertheless, Member States may provide for an excess of not more than € 500 to be borne by the victim of such damage to property.
> The conditions in which personal injuries are to be regarded as significant shall be determined in accordance with the legislation or administrative provisions of the Member State in which the accident takes place. In this regard, Member States may take into account, inter alia, whether the injury required hospital care."

The reasoning behind the introduction of these new provisions is that in case of significant personal injury, there will be public services (medical emergency services and/or police officers) present at the place of the accident, reducing the possibilities of fraudulent declarations. From the moment the Guarantee Fund had to pay compensation for significant personal injury caused by an unidentified vehicle, the material damage occurred will also be compensated by the Guarantee Fund. The latter may however, if foreseen by national legislation, apply an excess of maximum € 500 to the compensation of the material damage. It is to be understood that the possible application of an excess will only lead to the reduction of the compensation for material damage and not for personal injury.

It is to be emphasised that it is sufficient that only one of the victims was compensated for significant personal injuries. If the material damage was suffered by a victim different from the one who suffered the significant personal injuries, the material damage will still be compensated.

The term 'significant personal injuries' is not defined in the Directive, but it is left to the legislation or administrative provisions of the Member States to determine what is to be regarded as significant personal injuries.

> As an example, the Belgian legislation on MTPL insurance provides that personal injuries are regarded as significant if the accident resulted in one or more of the following consequences:
> - The decease of the victim;
> - A permanent disability of 15% or more;
> - A temporary disability of one month or more;
> - Hospital care of seven days or more.
>
> The Belgian legislation specifies that an implementing decision can further define the conditions under which personal injuries are to be regarded as significant or that it can complete the list of conditions.
>
> The Netherlands are an example of a Member State where the Guarantee Fund also intervenes for material damage caused by an unidentified vehicle, even in the absence of significant personal injuries. The only limitation is that the Dutch Guarantee Fund will apply an excess of € 250 with respect to material damage.

4.4.4 *Passengers of uninsured vehicles*

Article 10(2), second paragraph of the codified MID:

> "Member States may, however, exclude the payment of compensation by that body in respect of persons who voluntarily entered the vehicle which caused the damage or injury when the body can prove that they knew it was uninsured."

A passenger of an uninsured vehicle will in principle also benefit from the Guarantee Fund's obligation to compensate certain damage suffered. Here again however, the Directive offers the possibility to exclude the Guarantee Fund's intervention if the passenger voluntarily entered the vehicle and knew that the vehicle was not lawfully insured against MTPL. One can think about, for instance, the owner or keeper of the vehicle, whose responsibility it is to have the vehicle insured. It would be unfair that this person could claim compensation from the Guarantee Fund for the personal injury that they suffered, as a passenger in their own car, whereas it is that person's own responsibility to have the vehicle validly insured. But persons other than the owner or keeper of the vehicle can also be excluded from the Guarantee Fund's intervention if their national legislation allows for this exclusion and the Guarantee Fund can prove that they knew the vehicle was uninsured. It may, in practice, not be so easy for the Guarantee Fund to provide this proof unless the passenger was the owner or the keeper of the vehicle, responsible for having it insured. It should not be forgotten that the Guarantee Fund has to prove that the passenger had voluntarily entered the vehicle and *knew* that the vehicle was uninsured; the Directive does not allow any exclusion if the passenger ought to have known that the vehicle was uninsured.

4.4.5 *Vehicles stolen or obtained by violence*

It is to be remembered that Article 13(2) of the codified MID offers Member States the possibility to allow insurers to exclude from MTPL cover any damage caused by vehicles stolen or obtained by violence, on the condition that the Guarantee Fund pays compensation for damage caused by such vehicles (see para 4.3.4).

For this type of intervention by the Guarantee Fund, the Directive provides for two limitations:

- National legislation may provide for an excess of maximum € 250 if the Guarantee Fund intervenes for material damage (not personal injury!) caused by a vehicle stolen or obtained by violence (Article 13(2), second paragraph of the codified MID);
- We are of the opinion that national legislation may also allow a Guarantee Fund to exclude any compensation of damage suffered by persons who voluntarily entered the vehicle which caused the damage or injury, when the Guarantee Fund can prove that they knew the vehicle was stolen. Article 13(1) offers this possibility only to the insurer. Since Article 13(2) states however that the Guarantee Fund is to pay compensation instead of the insurer under the conditions set out in paragraph 1 of Article 13, we are of the opinion that the Guarantee Fund may also invoke this exclusion and may refuse cover for damage suffered by persons who voluntarily entered the vehicle while they knew it was stolen. The latter is of course only possible in so far as it is allowed by national legislation. See also para 6.2.12.4.

4.4.6 *The application of certain excesses*

In the previous paragraphs, we have described two possible situations where Member States are allowed to provide for an excess to be applied by the Guarantee Fund:

- Article 10(3) of the MID allows Member States to provide for an excess of maximum € 500 in case the Guarantee Fund has to compensate material damage as

a result of an accident caused by the use of an unidentified vehicle whereby significant personal injuries are also to be compensated;
- Where national legislation allows insurance cover to be excluded in case of accidents caused by the use of a vehicle obtained by theft or violence, the Guarantee Fund is to pay compensation in accordance with Article 13(2) of the MID. In such cases, national legislation may allow the application of an excess of maximum € 250.

These seem to be the only two situations in which the Motor Insurance Directive allows a Guarantee Fund to reduce the compensation with an excess.
It is therefore strange that the preamble of the Motor Insurance Directive, recital 16, seems to announce other rules:

> "In order to alleviate the financial burden on that body, Member States may make provision for the application of certain excesses where the body provides compensation for damage to property caused by *uninsured* vehicles or, as the case may be, vehicles stolen or obtained by violence."[Italics by the authors].

To our opinion, this must be a technical mistake in the formulation of the Motor Insurance Directive.

4.5 Modalities of intervention

4.5.1 *The victim's direct access to the Guarantee Fund*

Article 10(2) of the codified MID offers the victim the possibility to apply directly to the Guarantee Fund.

It is not entirely clear what the European legislator wishes to understand under the term 'apply directly'. Recital 14 of the Directive's preamble specifies that the Guarantee Fund should be a first point of contact:

> "It is important to provide that the victim of such an accident should be able to apply directly to that body as a first point of contact."

Victims would hardly benefit from a Guarantee Fund if they could not engage it in law. Victims should therefore always be able to pursue their rights against the Guarantee Fund in law and to issue court proceedings against the Fund.

4.5.2 *No proof required that the liable person is unable or unwilling to pay*

We already explained (see para 4.3.2) that the victim should not have to establish that the person liable for the accident is either unwilling or unable to pay compensation. See Article 10(1), last sentence of the first paragraph of the codified MID:

> "Member States may not allow the body to make the payment of compensation conditional on the victim establishing in any way that the person liable is unable or refuses to pay."

The MID's preamble (recital 18) further specifies that this rule is adopted because the Guarantee Fund should be better placed to obtain compensation or reimbursement from the person liable for the accident:

> "In the case of an accident caused by an uninsured vehicle, the body which compensates victims of accidents caused by uninsured or unidentified vehicles is better placed than the victim to bring an action against the party liable. Therefore, it should be provided that that body cannot require that victim, if he is to be compensated, to establish that the party liable is unable or refuses to pay."

4.5.3 *Reasoned reply*

Article 10(2), first paragraph of the codified MID:

> "The victim may in any event apply directly to the body which, on the basis of information provided at its request by the victim, shall be obliged to give him a reasoned reply regarding the payment of any compensation."

When a victim has addressed a claim to the Guarantee Fund, the latter is obliged to formulate a reasoned reply. The Directive does not specify what constitutes a reasoned reply, nor within what time period the Guarantee Fund should provide this reply. In the absence of a deadline, the Directive clearly cannot stipulate any sanctions for late replies.

As will be explained more in detail in paragraph 6.3.3, Article 22 of the codified Directive establishes a detailed compensation procedure in order to guarantee to the injured party a smooth settlement of damages. This procedure not only applies to insurers and claims representatives (see para 5.3), but also to national insurers' Bureaux on the basis of Article 19 of the MID. Article 22 requires them to formulate either a reasoned offer for compensation or a reasoned reply to the points made in the claim within a period of three months as of the date when the injured party presented a claim for compensation. Moreover, the Directive requires that this duty is backed by appropriate, effective and systematic financial or equivalent administrative penalties.

The same obligations imposed by Article 22 on insurers, claims representatives and national insurers' Bureaux seem not to be applicable to Guarantee Funds. They only have to provide "a reasoned reply regarding the payment of any compensation."

For the exact understanding of the term reasoned reply, cf paragraph 6.3.3.

Finally, it is to be emphasised that Article 10(2) also imposes a certain obligation on the victim seeking compensation, since the latter can be required, based on the wording of the Article, to provide information at the request of the Guarantee Fund. This provision ensures that the Guarantee Fund does not merely have to act on the basis of any claim without any supporting documentation, but may require the claimant to submit information that enables the Guarantee Fund to handle the claim in an appropriate way.

4.5.4 *Applicable laws, regulations and administrative provisions*

Article 10(4) of the codified MID:

> "Each Member State shall apply its laws, regulations and administrative provisions to the payment of compensation by the body, without prejudice to any other practice which is more favourable to the victim."

Guarantee Funds will, in principle and insofar as national legislation does not impose wider obligations on them also to act in the case of accidents in other territories, only operate for accidents that have occurred on the territory of the State for which the Guarantee Fund is competent. As a logical consequence, the Guarantee Fund will act in accordance with the laws, regulations and administrative provisions applicable to their operations. If however, certain practices may be more favourable to the victim, these can take precedence.

4.6 Recourse rights

In general terms, Guarantee Funds play an important role in the protection of victims of road traffic accidents. Moreover, the efficiency of the protection measure is enhanced by the rule that the victim does not first have to establish that the person liable is unable or unwilling to pay.

In paragraph 4.5.2 we already referred to recital 18 of the Directive's preamble, which states that the Guarantee Fund is better placed than the victim to bring an action against the person liable.

It is evident that the Guarantee Fund, which operates as a safety net to offer victims a form of adequate protection, will not wish to remain the final source of the outlays made in accordance with the provisions of the MID but will attempt to recover these outlays.
For that reason, the second paragraph of Article 10(1) states:

> "The first subparagraph shall be without prejudice to the right of the Member States to (...) make provision for the settlement of claims between the body and the person or persons responsible for the accident and other insurers or social security bodies required to compensate the victim in respect of the same accident."

It is remarkable that this provision only refers to *the settlement of claims between the body and the person(s) responsible for the accident*. In the case of accidents caused by uninsured vehicles, the Guarantee Fund's recourse rights should not be limited to the person responsible for the accident but should also extend to the person responsible for insuring the vehicle.

In an opinion delivered in the *Juliana* case, the Advocate General at the Court of Justice treats this question about the persons against whom a subrogation right should exist.[14] He starts with emphasising that the MID does not impose the subrogation right to be foreseen in national law but only offers the possibility for Member States to do so.[15] In a next step, he examines what is to be understood under the notion 'person responsible for the accident'. Should this term be limited to the liability for the accident itself or can it also include liability based on failure to insure the vehicle?[16] Knowing that Member States are free to determine the rules of civil liability applicable to road accidents and that the interpretation of the notion 'persons responsible for the accident' belongs to the rules of national law, the Advocate General is of the opinion that the Member States are free to determine the scope of persons against whom a subrogation right may exist.[17] This means that national law may, according to his opinion, also provide for the Guarantee Fund's subrogation right against the person who failed to insure the vehicle:

> "To the extent that the referring court asks whether Article 1 (4) of the Second Directive must be interpreted as meaning that the Fund has a right of subrogation against a person liable for fail-

14. CJEU, Opinion of Advocate General Bobek of 26 April 2018, *Juliana*, C-80/17, EU:C:2018:290.
15. Idem, para 121.
16. Idem, para 122.
17. CJEU, Judgment of 23 October 2012, *Marques Almeida*, C-300/10, EU:C:2012:656, para 29.

ure to insure a vehicle, the answer is no. Again such a possibility is simply not referred to under Article 1 (4) of the Second Directive and no such rule can therefore be inferred from that provision. However, that does not mean that the Member States would be prevented from providing for a right of subrogation under other circumstances, including against the person who failed to comply with the obligation to insure imposed by national law transposing Article 3 (1) of the First Directive. That is again a matter for the national law."

This point of view is confirmed by the Court of Justice of the European Union in their *Juliana* decision of 4 September 2018[18]:

"55. While the EU legislature sought to preserve the right of the Member States to make provision for the settlement of the claims of the Compensation Body referred to in Article 1 (4) of the Second Directive, in particular, against 'the person or persons responsible for the accident', it did not however harmonise the various matters relating to the actions brought by such a body, in particular the determination of the other persons against whom such actions might be brought, so that, as the Commission pointed out, those matters fall within the scope of the national law of each Member State.
56. Accordingly, national legislation may provide that, when the owner of the vehicle involved in the accident has failed to comply with his or her obligation to insure that vehicle, as in the present case, under national law, that Compensation Body can bring an action, in addition to an action against the person or persons responsible for the accident, against that owner, irrespective of the civil liability of the latter in the occurrence of the accident."

In case of unidentified vehicles, the exercise of a recourse right will clearly be difficult if not impossible. If the injured party or police authorities have been unable to identify the person who caused the accident and who drove away immediately afterwards, it is hard to imagine that the Guarantee Fund will be more successful unless new information becomes available. But the Guarantee Fund will of course attempt to recover the outlays from the person who, contrary to the rules, did not legally insure the vehicle against MTPL.

Depending on national rules of recourse, the Guarantee Fund will have a recourse action against the driver, the owner or the keeper of the vehicle or against more than one of the categories of persons mentioned. If the Guarantee Fund intervenes for damage caused by vehicles stolen or obtained by violence it may, depending on national legislation, have a recourse right against the thief and/or the driver if the latter was aware that the vehicle had been stolen. Again in these cases, the success of the recourse right will naturally depend on the solvency of the uninsured person or of the person who obtained the vehicle by theft or violence.

18. CJEU, Judgment of 4 September 2018, *Juliana*, C-80/17, EU:C:2018:661, para 55 and 56.

In paragraph 3.8.9, we explained that Green Card Bureaux may have a recourse right 'in second instance' against counterfeiters of Green Cards, against uninsured drivers, keepers or owners of vehicles or against any other persons or instances. As in the case of Green Card Bureaux, the recourse right of the Guarantee Fund against any persons, bodies or entities is not governed by the provisions of the Motor Insurance Directive. Whether a recourse right exists, against whom and in what ways the right can be exercised, should again be subject to the national law of individual Member States. The Motor Insurance Directive, Article 10(1), second paragraph, goes no further than leaving it to the Member States

> "to make provision for the settlement of claims between the [Guarantee Fund] and the person or persons responsible for the accident and other insurers or social security bodies required to compensate the victim in respect of the same accident."

Finally, the question can be raised whether a Guarantee Fund can recover any outlays it had to make, based on national legislation, as a result of the insolvency of an insurer. In most cases, the Guarantee Fund will not have any other recourse possibility than to submit a reimbursement claim to the liquidator(s) of the insolvent insurance undertaking. The chances of success of such recourse will depend on the funds that are still available in the insolvent estate. Moreover, they will be subject to rules and limitations of insolvency or bankruptcy law as applicable in the Member State in question.

A special recourse right for Guarantee Funds in cases of insolvency is provided for in a specific agreement concluded between a number of Guarantee Funds in the framework of, initially, the *Comité Européen des Assurances* (CEA, currently named *Insurance Europe*, the European insurance and reinsurance federation) and, later, of the Council of Bureaux.[19]

As will be described in chapter 7, insurers in the European Economic Area have the possibility to operate insurance business in other Member States, based on the Freedom to Provide Services or the Freedom of Establishment. In that case, the financial control over the insurance activities will be exercised by the supervisory authority of the home Member State of the insurers (where the insurer received their initial authorisation).

If an insurer, having received their original authorisation to operate MTPL insurance in one Member State (the 'home Member State') offers MTPL insurance by way of Freedom to Provide Services or Freedom of Establishment in a second Member State (the 'host Member State'), the financial control over the insurance activities will remain the responsibility of the supervisory authority in the home Member State (the principle of 'home country control'). If this insurance undertaking is declared insolvent and the legislation of

19. The agreement was initially concluded in the framework of the *Comité Européen des Assurances*. The secretarial services for the coordination of the agreement were later transferred to the Council of Bureaux.

> the host Member State provides for the intervention of the Guarantee Fund in such cases, the Guarantee Fund of the host Member State may have to bear an important financial burden as a result of the insolvency. Since the financial control over the insurer's activities is however situated in the home Member State, a number of Guarantee Funds have concluded a special agreement, allowing the Guarantee Fund of the host Member State to be reimbursed by the Guarantee Fund of the home Member State. If both Guarantee Funds have signed the agreement, the financial burden of the insolvency will be transferred from the host Member State to the home Member State, that is to say to the Member State where the supervisory authority exercised financial control over the insolvent insurance undertaking.
> See for the Agreement para 7.4.5.

In paragraph 4.3.6, we already explained that the European Commission intends to amend the Motor Insurance Directive to require Member States to set up or authorise a body for the provision of compensation in cases where the MTPL insurer of the liable party is insolvent.[20] Under the proposals, a right to claim reimbursement will be offered to the body in the Member State where the injured party habitually resides from the body in the Member State where the insurer of the vehicle is established.

It is however unfortunate that this right only allows claims for reimbursement against the insurer's home Member State in the case of insurers operating by way of Freedom to Provide Services. If the insurer is operating by way of Freedom of Establishment, the 'Member State where the insurer is established' is not the same as the home Member State, where the insurer received the initial authorisation. This must probably be seen as a deficient formulation in the Commission's proposal, to be corrected in the further legislative process.

4.7 Article 11 MID: disputes between Guarantee Fund and insurer

We have so far analysed the different provisions of the Motor Insurance Directive relating to the Guarantee Fund in rather clear-cut situations: a vehicle is insured or uninsured, identified or unidentified, stolen or not.

In reality, unfortunately, in many situations the exact status of the vehicle is not so evident. In practice, a lot of discussion can exist with the (potential) insurer whether the latter is to provide cover for the vehicle in question or not. This will happen in case of contractual deficiencies related to the MTPL insurance contract subscribed by the driver, keeper or owner of the vehicle. There can be a lack of

20. See the European Commission's proposal for a new Motor Insurance Directive, as also discussed in para 3.5.1 and 4.3.6.

clarity about the exact identity of the vehicle, its make and type, confusion over (or even possible misrepresentation of) the exact risk to be covered; these and many other discussions can be imagined, bringing the insurer to contest the validity of the insurance cover for the vehicle in question. But there can also be discussion over the insurer's responsibility for providing cover where the vehicle is alleged to have been stolen. Such arguments can lead to lengthy conflicts between the potential insurer and the Guarantee Fund over their respective responsibilities.

The risk is that the victim of the accident then suffers further as compensation is delayed pending resolution of a dispute between insurer and Guarantee Fund, which may go as far as the national courts. In order to avoid this, the European legislator has inserted a specific provision in Article 11 of the Motor Insurance Directive:

> "In the event of a dispute between the body referred to in Article 10 (1) and the civil liability insurer as to which must compensate the victim, the Member States shall take the appropriate measures so that one of those parties is designated to be responsible in the first instance for paying compensation to the victim without delay.
> If it is ultimately decided that the other party should have paid all or part of the compensation, that other party shall reimburse accordingly the party which has paid."

Member States must determine in their national law whether the Guarantee Fund or the (alleged) MTPL insurer is to compensate the victim in the first place in order not to leave the latter without compensation. If upon final settlement of the dispute the party that compensated the victim is found not to have been responsible for the payment, a reimbursement is to be made. Cf. para 6.3.4.

5 The Protection of Visitors

5.1 Introduction and historic development

5.1.1 Introduction

Whenever we have examined, up until now, the situation of a victim suffering an accident in a cross-border context, we have always taken as a starting point the victim in their own country of residence. The road traffic victim either suffered, in their own country, an accident caused by a foreign vehicle (chapter 3, The Green Card system) or suffered an accident in their own country, caused by an uninsured or unidentified vehicle (chapter 4, Guarantee Funds).

Up until now, we haven't considered 'the mirror image' of the Green Card system, that is to say the situation where a person, visiting a foreign country, is involved as an injured party in an accident in that foreign country and wishes to obtain compensation for the damage suffered in the country visited.

To a certain extent it is understandable that the protection of the 'visiting victim' was not the first preoccupation of either the United Nations Economic Commission for Europe or the European Union. Their goal was to facilitate cross-border road traffic without reducing the level of protection offered to the victims of road traffic accidents. A person suffering damage – in their own country of residence – as a result of an accident caused by a foreign vehicle must be assured to receive the correct compensation of that damage. In light of that aim, the Green Card system was developed and, later on, further elaborated by the European legislator. As regards the situation of the visiting victim, travelling on their own initiative to a third country and suffering an accident in that visited country, the idea was that it was the visitor's own free choice to visit that country. Such a visitor could take precautions such as travel insurance or a comprehensive insurance; after an accident the victim should then have to find a route to compensation, even if that meant that the victim had to communicate with a foreign insurance undertaking in a language other than their mother tongue.

It is clear that such a philosophy was no longer tenable in an ever more globalised world and certainly not at the European level, where the aim continues to be the creation of an ever closer union among the peoples of Europe (Article 1 of the Treaty on European Union).
The European Union, in the process of establishing an internal market in which the free movement of goods, persons, services and capital is ensured, realised that the protection of visiting victims contributes to the creation of such an internal market. If a victim is not adequately protected against the consequences of a road traffic accident in another Member State, this may preclude a European citizen from easily travelling to other Member States and constitutes, as such, a hindrance to the efficient functioning of the internal market.

This was behind the initiatives in the 1990s to meet the needs of visiting victims who suffered an accident outside their country of residence and experienced problems in obtaining compensation for the damage caused.

Example
When explaining the Green Card system in chapter 3, we several times used the example of a French resident, travelling by car to Italy and causing an accident in that country, resulting in an Italian resident suffering damage.
In this chapter, we will mainly concentrate on the comparable situation, where a French resident travels to Italy (either by car, train, airplane or any other means of transport) and is involved in an accident in that country, caused by the use of a motor vehicle.
For the protection of visitors system to apply, it is not necessary that the French resident is an occupant of a motor vehicle at the time of the accident (either as a driver or as a passenger). He or she might be the victim of a road traffic accident as a cyclist, pedestrian or in any other capacity when the accident occurs. The only condition is that the damage be caused by the use of a motor vehicle.

5.1.2 *Historical development*

In the 1990s, both the Council of Bureaux and the European Union started reflecting on possibilities to offer a better protection to the visiting victim.

The Green Card Bureaux, operating jointly within the Council of Bureaux, discussed and developed a draft agreement, establishing cooperation between national motor insurers' Bureaux in order to support the visiting victim in seeking compensation. This first 'Protection of visitors Agreement' was mainly characterised by a voluntary cooperation mechanism between Bureaux and did not contain many enforceable protection measures.

The Council of Bureaux left the initiative unfinished when it became clear that the European Union was determined to elaborate a separate protection mechanism, containing compulsory and enforceable provisions and establishing a whole new network of bodies involved in the protection of the visiting victim.
Steered by the German Member of the European Parliament, Willi Rothley, the European legislator adopted on 16 May 2000 the Fourth Motor Insurance Directive (4th MID)[1], leaving the Member States until 20 July 2002 to implement the Directive into national legislation and requiring the system to become applicable at the latest on 20 January 2003.

Today, the provisions of the 4th MID are incorporated in the codified Motor Insurance Directive of 2009.[2] The specific protection mechanism for visiting victims is however so much associated with the adoption of the 4th MID in 2000 that still today it is very often referred to as 'the 4th Directive protection' and claims addressed by visiting victims are often called '4th Directive claims'. In this book, we will speak mostly of 'protection of visitors mechanism' and 'claims of visiting victims', but we may also refer from time to time to the 4th MID, even if that legislative text has been repealed with the adoption of the codified Motor Insurance Directive.

After the implementation of the 4th MID in the national legislation of the Member States and after several years of experience with the new protection scheme, the Council of Bureaux has, in the second decade of the 21st century, resumed consideration of offering protection to visiting victims even beyond the borders of the European Economic Area (EEA). The initial 'Protection of visitors Agreement' was dug up and re-arranged to be used for accidents to which the 4th MID did not apply. This renewed and voluntary agreement will be discussed in paragraph 5.8.

5.2 General principles

5.2.1 *Functioning of the protection mechanism introduced by 4th MID*

The main objective of the protection for visiting victims as introduced by the 4th MID, is to allow the injured party to return to the Member State of residence and to address a claim to an entity established there and able to communicate with the injured party in the official language or languages of that Member State and according to procedures which are familiar to the injured party.

---

1. Directive 2000/26 of the European Parliament and of the Council of 16 May 2000 on the approximation of the laws of the Member States relating to insurance against civil liability in respect of the use of motor vehicles and amending Council Directives 73/239/EEC and 88/357/EEC, OJ L 181, 20.7.2000, p. 65.
2. Directive 2009/103/EC of the European Parliament and of the Council of 16 September 2009 relating to insurance against civil liability in respect of the use of motor vehicles, and the enforcement of the obligation to insure against such liability (codified version), OJ L 263, 7.10.2009, p. 11.

To that end, the protection mechanism requires each MTPL insurer, authorised to offer MTPL insurance in the EEA, to appoint a *claims representative* in each and every other Member State than the one where the insurer received the official authorisation to take up the business of insurance. The role and function of a claims representative will be described in detail in paragraph 5.3. At this stage however, it can already be revealed that the claims representative should, in accordance with recital 37 of the codified Directive's preamble, in relation to injured parties be capable of

> "collecting all necessary information in relation to claims (...) and take appropriate action to settle the claims on behalf and for the account of the insurance undertaking, including the payment of compensation'. Claims representatives should 'have sufficient powers to represent the insurance undertaking."

Being able to communicate with the claims representative in a language and according to procedures that are familiar to them, offers injured parties a better protection and is certainly an important step forward in comparison to the old situation where they had no other choice than to address a claim to an insurer in a foreign country and often in a different language. But it is important to keep in mind that the system introduced by the 4th MID, according to recital 35 of the codified Directive's preamble

> "affects neither the substantive law to be applied in each individual case nor the matter of jurisdiction."

Rules of private international law will determine the law applicable to the accident as well as the competent courts that can judge on such claims in case no amicable settlement can be obtained. These rules of private international law will be examined in detail in chapter 8 but in a large majority of cases, the consequences of an accident will be considered in accordance with the law applicable in the country of the accident. This is not changed by the fact that an injured party can address a claim to a claims representative. The claims representative will, in most cases, have to apply the rules applicable in the country where the accident occurred in order to determine the liability and the compensation to be provided for the damage caused.

In certain circumstances, the system of claims representatives will not offer a satisfactory protection to the injured party. In spite of the obligation, an insurance undertaking may not have appointed a claims representative, or the insurer and/or the claims representative might be late in responding to the claim. Furthermore, if the vehicle that caused the accident turns out to be uninsured or unidentified, the injured party will clearly be unable to address a claim to any claims representative. For these gaps, the protection system provides for a safety net. Member States are required to establish or approve a *Compensation Body* to which the injured party can turn to if the system of claims representatives is unable to offer sufficient protection. The conditions under which a Compensation Body can intervene as well as the modalities of intervention will be described in paragraph 5.4.

Example

Let us return to the example of a French resident, on holiday in Italy and suffering damage as a result of a road traffic accident, caused by the use of a motor vehicle. Let us suppose that the vehicle having caused the accident is normally based in Italy and insured with the Italian insurer Italins.

The protection of visitors system introduced by the 4th Motor Insurance Directive allows the French victim after return to his/her home country to present a claim there. Based on the obligations of the MID, the Italian insurer Italins appointed a claims representative in France, Francerep.

The French victim can formulate and present a claim for compensation in the French language to Francerep and Francerep will settle the claim on behalf and for the account of Italins. Once an agreement is reached on the compensation, Francerep will pay this compensation to the French victim.

When dealing with the claim, Francerep will however apply Italian law on liability (determining who is liable for the accident) and on compensation of damage (deciding on the exact nature and amount of compensation to be provided).

If the Italian vehicle that caused the accident is not insured, the French victim can present the claim, in French, to the French Compensation Body, which will handle and settle the claim in French but according to Italian law. The same will be true if the Italian vehicle cannot be identified or if Italins has not appointed a claims representative in France. Finally, the French victim can also present a claim to the French Compensation Body if they do not receive a reasoned reply within three months from Italins or Francerep.

The protection mechanism brought to life by the 4th Motor Insurance Directive aims at improving the situation of the visiting victim but by no means constitutes an obligation for the latter to follow this route as the only possible solution. The protection of visitors is rather to be considered as a supplementary remedy and does not deprive the victim or the injured party from preferring other means of protection offered by tort or insurance law. This is explicitly stated in Article 21(4) of the codified Directive:

> "The requirement of appointing a claims representative shall not preclude the right of the injured party or his insurance undertaking to institute proceedings directly against the person who caused the accident or his insurance undertaking."

For this reason, an insurer may not simply redirect an injured person, resident in another Member State, to the insurer's claims representative. The injured person has the right to present a claim directly to the insurer, leaving the claims representative in their country of residence out of the picture.

5.2.2 *Conditions for application and geographical scope*

The protection of visitors mechanism established by the 4th MID is not applicable to each and every kind of (cross-border) motor road traffic accident. Introduced as a protection scheme for the European internal market, it will in the first place be applicable in the countries participating in the European Economic Area. Only if certain specific conditions are fulfilled may it also apply to accidents in third countries.

For the protection of visitors mechanism to apply, the following conditions must be fulfilled:

- The injured party must be resident in a Member State, which means that their residence should be in one of the countries participating in the EEA (for the countries participating in the EEA: see para 3.2.2);
- The accident must have occurred in another Member State (Article 20 of the Directive refers to 'a Member State other than the Member State of residence of the injured party');
- The accident must have been caused by the use of vehicles insured and normally based in a Member State. If the accident was caused by the use of a vehicle insured and normally based in a third country that participates in the Green Card system, the injured party will not be able to rely on the protection of the 4th MID but will have to invoke the protection offered by the Green Card system. In that case, however, the injured party will have to present a claim to the Green Card Bureau in the country of the accident and will not be able to present a claim to any entity in their own country of residence.
  If the vehicle is uninsured the 4th MID protection scheme may still apply, but the injured party will not be able to present a claim to any claims representative; therefore, the safety net of the Compensation Body will be available.
- The injured party's country of residence must be different from the Member State of establishment of the insurance undertaking;
- The injured party's country of residence must be different from the Member State where the vehicle having caused the accident is normally based.

These last two conditions may require some more clarification:
- The first condition is related to the possibility for insurers in the internal market to offer insurance in other Member States by way of Freedom to Provide Services. This regime will be explained more in detail in chapter 7, but in principle it means that an insurer, established in Member State A, has the possibility to offer insurance products in any other Member State of the EEA based on the rules of the Freedom to provide Services.[3]

Example

Let us suppose that person A, residing in Member State A, suffers a road traffic accident in Member State B, caused by a vehicle B, normally based in Member State B. The vehicle B is however insured by an insurer A, established in Member State A and offering insurance in Member State B by way of freedom to provide services. Although for injured party A this accident may at first sight fall under the conditions to apply the protection system offered by the 4th MID, there will not be a need to apply that protection scheme since the insurer A of the vehicle B is established in the same Member State as where the injured party A is resident. Therefore, injured party A can perfectly present a claim (drafted in their own language) to the establishment of insurer A in their own country, even if the accident occurred in a different Member State.

- With the second condition (the injured party's country of residence must be different from the Member State where the vehicle having caused the accident is normally based), the 4th MID envisages accidents whereby two persons, resident in the same Member State, have an accident in a different Member State. If a person A, resident in Member State A suffers an accident in Member State B, caused by a vehicle A, normally based in Member State A, then the injured party A does not need the special protection offered by the 4th MID because the injured party A can simply present a claim to the insurer of the vehicle in the own Member State. This claim can either be presented directly or, if the vehicle is insured with an insurance undertaking active in Member State A under the Freedom to provide Services, through the insurer's representative.

Although mainly designed for accidents occurring in the territory of the EEA, the 4th MID's protection of visitors system can exceptionally also apply to accidents in a third country. This will be the case if all of the following conditions are fulfilled:
- The injured party is resident in a Member State of the EEA;

3. As will be explained in chapter 7, an establishment of an insurance undertaking can either be the insurer's head office (where the insurer will have received the authorisation) or any of the insurer's branches. An insurance undertaking with head office in Member State A can operate through a branch in Member State B via the system of Freedom of Establishment.

- The accident occurred in a third country participating in the Green Card system (for a list of countries participating in the Green Card system: see Annex 1);
- The accident is caused by the use of a vehicle insured and normally based in a Member State of the EEA other than the injured party's country of residence.

Again in the case of accidents in third countries, it must be remembered that the application of the 4th MID protection scheme will not influence the applicable law or the rules on jurisdiction.

Moreover, as regards accidents occurring in third countries, it is interesting to refer to recital 9 in the preamble of the 4th Directive as it was originally adopted in 2000:

> "The application of this Directive to accidents occurring in third countries covered by the green card system, affecting injured parties resident in the Community and involving vehicles insured and normally based in a Member State does not imply an extension of the compulsory territorial coverage of motor insurance as provided for in Article 3 (2) of Directive 72/166/EEC."

Strangely enough, this provision is not integrated in the preamble of the codified Motor Insurance Directive of 2009. We assume that this is an unintended omission and that insurers in the Member States are not obliged to provide cover in all the non-EEA Member States adhering to the Green Card system if not compelled to do so under their national legislation.

Example

The conditions for application are of a certain complexity and show a broad range of possible situations, in such a way that it may again be interesting to illustrate the different possibilities by way of some examples:

We will start with the least complex case whereby a resident of one Member State suffers an accident in another Member State, caused by a vehicle insured and normally based in that same Member State, visited by the injured party.

Let us come back to the earlier example of a French citizen, resident in France and travelling to Italy for holidays. They could have travelled to Italy by car and be hit by another vehicle, normally based in Italy. But they could as well have travelled to Italy by train, airplane or by any other means of transport and suffer an accident in Italy as a pedestrian, as a cyclist, as a driver of a rented vehicle normally based in Italy or another Member State or as a passenger in an Italian taxi or any other vehicle. Many more possibilities can be imagined but they all have in common that the French resident is involved in a road traffic accident in a Member State outside their country of residence. Contrary to the example used in chapter 3, the French resident is this time

not the person liable for the accident but suffers damage as a result of the accident occurred in Italy and caused by the use of a motor vehicle in Italy.
The French resident can, after the accident occurred, return to their home country and invoke the protection scheme offered by the 4th MID in order to claim compensation for the damage suffered in Italy. They can present a claim to the claims representative of the Italian insurer in France and ask for compensation in the French language and according to procedures that are familiar to them. Since the accident occurred in Italy, the claims representative will however be compelled to apply the law determined by rules of private international law. In this example, the applicable law will in most circumstances be Italian law. If the Italian vehicle turns out to be uninsured or if the accident was caused by an unidentified vehicle, the French injured party can present a claim to the Compensation Body in France. Again, the French Compensation Body will give the French resident the possibility to communicate in French but will, in most circumstances, have to apply Italian law on liability and compensation of damage.
The possibilities offered by the 4th MID are not the only way for the French person to obtain compensation and are not an obligation to turn to the claims representative. The injured party can choose to address a claim directly to the insurer of the Italian vehicle and the latter insurer will be obliged to formulate a reasoned reply to the claim. The insurer may not redirect the injured party to the claims representative (Article 21(4), second subparagraph of the codified MID). But the Italian insurer may of course require that any communication with the injured party be done in Italian.
Many more scenarios can be elaborated and not all will be covered by the protection of visitors system. We have incorporated most of the possible scenarios in table 1.

Table 1 describes a series of scenarios, many of which are rather unusual and may perhaps hardly ever occur in practice. However they usually are the source of complicated debates in the actual handling of claims.

Common to the situations described is that the injured party is always resident in France. The accident either occurs in Italy (an EEA Member State) or in Tunisia (a third country, the Bureau of which participates in the Green Card system). The vehicle causing the accident can either be normally based in the country visited by the French visitor (Italy or Tunisia) and can be insured or uninsured. If the vehicle is insured (the vast majority of the cases), the insurer can either be established in the same Member State as where the vehicle is normally based or it can be active in the Member State where the vehicle is normally based by way of freedom to provide services. In all of these cases, we will try to indicate whether the 4th MID protection measures can be applied or not and, if applicable, to which entity the French injured party can turn to in order to claim for compensation. In the last column with entities to which the injured party can present a claim, we will in principle only deal with those entities foreseen in the 4th MID. Based on normal rules of liability, the injured party will certainly have other ways of obtaining compensation. Normally, they will have the possibility to present a claim directly to the liable party or to the insurer of the vehicle. Or it may be that in certain scenarios the protection offered by the Green Card system will be open to the injured party (more particularly when the vehicle that caused the accident is normally based outside the country where the accident occurred). We leave these possibilities however untouched in the last column.

Table 1 Possible scenario's

injured party's residence	country of the accident	vehicle normally based in	vehicle insured Y/N	insurer established in[1]	4th MID applicable Y/N	4th MID entity to which a claim can be presented
F	I	I	Y	I	Y	CR
F	I	I	N		Y	CB
F	I	I	Y	F	N	injured party can go to French insurer
F	I	I	Y	SLO	Y	CR
F	I	unknown because unidentified	unknown	N/A	Y	CB
F	I	F	Y	F	N	injured party can go to French insurer
F	I	F	Y	NL	N	injured party can go to representative[2] of Dutch insurer in France
F	I	F	N	N/A	N	Not applicable; however injured party can present claim to I Green Card Bureau
F	I	SLO	Y	SLO	Y	CR
F	I	SLO	N	N/A	Y	CB
F	I	SLO	Y	F	N	Not applicable; however injured party can go to French insurer
F	I	SLO	Y	NL	Y	CR
F	I	TN	Y	TN	N	Green Card system can be relied on[3]
F	I	TN	N	N/A	Y	CB; see Article 25(1), point (c) MID[4]
F	TN	TN			N	
F	TN	TR			N	Green Card system can be relied on
F	TN	F	Y	F	N	injured party can go to French insurer

injured party's residence	**country of the accident**	**vehicle normally based in**	**vehicle insured Y/N**	**insurer established in[1]**	**4th MID applicable Y/N**	**4th MID entity to which a claim can be presented**
F	TN	F	N	N/A	N	Not applicable; however injured party can turn to TN Green Card Bureau
F	TN	F	Y	NL	N	injured party can go to representative[5] of Dutch insurer in France
F	TN	SLO	Y	SLO	Y	CR
F	TN	SLO	Y	F	N	injured party can go to French insurer
F	TN	SLO	Y	NL	Y	CR
F	TN	SLO	N	N/A	N	Not applicable; however injured party can turn to TN Green Card Bureau

Legend: F = France; I = Italy; SLO = Slovenia; NL = The Netherlands; TN = Tunisia; TR = Turkey; CR = claims representative; CB = Compensation Body; N/A = Not applicable.

Notes:

[1] *This means that the insurer either has its head office in the Member State mentioned (and also received authorisation for the taking-up of insurance business in that Member State) or operates in that Member State through the system of Freedom of Establishment (see chapter 7).*

[2] *In accordance with Article 152 Solvency II (2009/138/EC), every insurer operating by way of Freedom to Provide Services in other Member States must appoint a 'representative' in the 'host' Member State where the insurance products are offered by way of Freedom to Provide Services. This system will be explained more in detail in chapter 7 (Freedom of Establishment and Freedom to Provide Services). The term 'representative' should not be confused with the term 'claims representative'.*

[3] *In that case however, the injured party can only present a claim to the Italian Green Card Bureau. No possibility is available to present a claim in France.*

[4] *Article 20(1) states that Article 20-26 are (only) applicable if the accident occurs in a Member State other than the Member State of residence of the injured party and the vehicle that caused the accident is normally based (and normally based) in a Member State. However, Article 25(1), point (c) provides the Compensation Body with a right of recourse against the Guarantee Fund of the Member State of the accident if the liable vehicle was uninsured and originating from a third country. This latter provision only makes sense if the injured party has a claim under the 4th MID against the Compensation Body in the Member State of their residence.*

[5] *Again, this is the representative, appointed in the 'host' Member State by the insurer operating in that 'host' Member State under the Freedom to Provide Services.*

5.2.3 *Difference with the Green Card system*

As explained, the main aim of the protection mechanism created by the 4th Motor Insurance Directive is to improve the situation of the visiting victim wishing to obtain compensation for damage suffered in a different Member State. The injured party is offered the possibility to communicate in their own language and according to procedures which are familiar to them. The claims representative will try to settle the claim with the injured party, while respecting the instructions given by the insurer. The Compensation Body will attempt to streamline the claims handling process and search for possibilities to get the claims management by the insurer or claims representative back on the right track in case the claims representative is not diligent enough in handling the claim. But all these attempts depend on the goodwill of the stakeholders involved and are not characterised by the same guarantees and constraints existing in the Green Card system. The 4th Directive has established a valuable and generally well-functioning, albeit complex system but it does not contain the same guarantees as exist in the cooperation scheme between motor insurers' Bureaux of the Green Card system.

In contrast to the Green Card system, where the handling entity (correspondent, agent or handling Bureau) most often applies their own national law and is therefore given handling autonomy, the claims representative in the 4th MID system will in most cases be confronted with a claim to be settled according to foreign rules on liability and damage compensation. For that reason, the claims representative is less free to decide on questions of liability and/or the quantum of damages to be paid and does not benefit from the handling autonomy as it exists in the Green Card system. It is true that the codified Directive requires the claims representative to "possess sufficient powers to represent the insurance undertaking and to meet claims in full", which suggests that the claims representative can decide autonomously on the compensation of the claim. Such an autonomous decision could however easily cause the claims representative difficulties when claiming reimbursement from the insurance undertaking; they will therefore, in practice, await and follow the instructions of the mandating insurer under the provisions of the applicable law. Such practice is in our opinion not in conflict with the Directive.

Since the claims representative is not backed by the same guarantees as those applicable in the Green Card system, they will be less motivated to advance payments to the injured party (which is an absolute requisite for correspondents, agents and handling Bureaux operating in the Green Card system). If the insurer does not reimburse any sums advanced by the claims representative, the latter cannot rely on any provision such as Article 4(8) of the Internal Regulations, applicable in the Green Card system (see para 3.8.5), which enshrines the right to invoke the guarantee of the handling Bureau. The claims representative cannot turn to the

Compensation Body to obtain payment of any sums advanced to the injured party and not reimbursed by the insurer. Therefore, they will often await payment by the mandating insurer before forwarding those sums to the injured party. Many claims representatives however, particularly when they have a well-established relationship with the insurer based on trust, will even in 4th MID cases advance the compensation to the injured party.

There are however arguments in support of the thesis that the claims representative should make advance payments to the injured party, before being reimbursed by the insurer. Recital 37 of the codified MID's preamble states the following:

> "(…) claims representatives (…) to take appropriate action to settle the claims on behalf and for the account of the insurance undertaking, including the payment of compensation."

Article 21(5) of the codified Directive prescribes that

> "Claims representatives shall possess sufficient powers to represent the insurance undertaking in relation to injured parties (…) and to meet their claims in full."

It can be argued that 'meeting the claims in full' should include making payments to the injured party before receiving the necessary funds from the insurer.

Although the protection mechanisms of the Green Card system and the 4th MID are designed to offer protection in two different road traffic accident scenarios, they can exceptionally be applicable simultaneously to one and the same accident.

Example
In the example described above where a French resident suffered an accident in Italy, both the 4th MID protection system and the Green Card system would be applicable if the accident was caused by the use of a vehicle normally based in a different Member State from Italy and France. If the liable vehicle is insured and normally based in Slovenia, the French injured party can present a claim to the claims representative of the Slovenian insurer in France. But the injured party can also opt for the protection of the Green Card system and present a claim to the Green Card Bureau in Italy. In case the Slovenian insurer is represented by a (Green Card) correspondent in Italy, the claim would be forwarded to that correspondent in Italy. If the injured party opts for this choice, they must however accept that the handling entity in Italy cannot be compelled to communicate with the injured party in French.

This and other examples, where both the Green Card system and the 4th MID protection mechanism can apply simultaneously will be described in paragraph 5.7.

5.2.4 *Who can invoke the protection mechanism for the visiting victim?*

The codified Motor Insurance Directive (including the specific provisions on the protection of visitors as introduced by the 4th MID) uses two terms: victims and injured parties. In paragraph 6.2.12.1, the difference between the two terms will be examined and described in detail. At this point, we can already state that 'injured party' is a wider concept than 'victim'. Under injured party, not only the direct victim of the accident is to be understood, but also parties subrogated in the rights of the direct victim including relatives, employers, social security bodies and private insurers such as comprehensive (casco) insurers and bodily injury insurers.

The Articles 20 to 25 in the codified MID dealing with the protection of visiting victims always use the term 'injured party' and do not mention the term 'victim'.

It may therefore be assumed that the European legislator's intention was to create a special protection mechanism, not only aimed at protecting the direct victim but also intended to be beneficial to the parties subrogated in the victim's rights. This results in direct victims as well as subrogated parties (together referred to as injured parties) being able to present their claim to an entity (claims representative or Compensation Body) in the Member State of their residence. The rights of certain subrogated parties (e.g. private and social insurers) may however be limited, based on rules of subsidiarity (see paragraphs 5.4.4.1 and 5.4.4.2).

In the following pages, we will examine in more detail the different entities to which the injured party can present a claim for compensation. In normal circumstances, this will in the first place be the claims representative (para 5.3). In certain cases, where the claims representative does not offer sufficient protection to the injured party, the latter will be able to present a claim to the Compensation Body (para 5.4), operating as a kind of safety net for the injured party.

The Motor Insurance Directive has also taken the necessary measures to support the claimant (injured party) in finding the right entity to turn to. This has been done by requiring the Member States to establish or approve an Information Centre (para 5.5). In line with its name, this entity will provide the injured party with information regarding the insurance status of a vehicle and the claims representative appointed by European insurers.
Just as in the Green Card system, compensation paid in the framework of the 4th MID protection scheme has to be reimbursed. These reimbursements will be dealt with in paragraph 5.6.

In paragraph 5.7, we will again focus on the possible simultaneous application of the Green Card system and the 4th MID protection mechanism.
The Council of Bureaux also wishes to extend the 4th MID protection system to third countries; this initiative will be described in paragraph 5.8.
Finally, paragraph 5.9 will focus on the protection of visitors if the MTPL insurer is in a state of insolvency.

5.3 The claims representative

5.3.1 *Introduction: the capacity of claims representative*

Each insurer, authorised in the European Economic Area to offer motor third party liability insurance, is bound to appoint a *claims representative* in each Member State other than where the official authorisation was granted (Article 21 codified MID).[4] Moreover, the appointment of a claims representative in each Member State is one of the conditions precedent in order to obtain authorisation for MTPL insurance (recital 39 of the codified MID's preamble and Article 18(1), point (h) Solvency II.[5])

The European legislator has explicitly chosen not to restrict the function of claims representative to a limited number of service providers with a specific recognition or authorisation. The claims representative must be able to perform certain tasks and to meet certain expectations (see the conditions to be fulfilled in paragraph 5.3.3), but there is no prior control or examination whether the person or entity appointed in reality fulfils these requirements. Article 21(2) of the codified Directive states that

> "the choice of its claims representative shall be at the discretion of the insurance undertaking. The Member States may not restrict this freedom of choice."

Stipulated in that way, any natural or legal person, resident or established in the Member State where the appointment is to be made, can be selected by an insurer

4. This requirement is formulated in Article 21 of the codified MID as follows: "Each member State shall take all measures necessary to ensure that all insurance undertakings covering the risks classified in class 10 of point A of the Annex to Directive 73/239/EEC, other than carrier's liability, appoint a claims representative in each Member State other than that in which they have received their official authorisation". Directive 73/239/EEC in the meantime being repealed, the Annex referred to is now to be found as Annex 1 to Solvency II (Directive 2009/138/EC of the European Parliament and of the Council of 25 November 2009 on the taking-up and pursuit of the business of Insurance and Reinsurance (Solvency II) (recast), OJ L 335, 17.12.2009, p. 1). Class 10 of Point A of that Directive is titled motor vehicle liability and described as 'all liability arising out of the use of motor vehicles operating on the land (including carrier's liability)'.
5. Directive 2009/138/EC of the European Parliament and of the Council of 25 November 2009 on the taking-up and pursuit of the business of Insurance and Reinsurance (Solvency II) (recast), OJ L 335, 17.12.2009, p. 1.

to act as claims representative. Claims representatives can be insurance undertakings operating for other insurance undertakings. They can also be claims handling offices, specialised in managing claims resulting from (national and/or cross-border) road traffic accidents. But also loss adjusters, lawyers or any other legal or natural person can be appointed.

A claims representative can simultaneously operate for several foreign MTPL insurers. The role of claims representative can also be combined with other functions such as a Green Card correspondent (see *supra* para 3.7.4). In practice, it happens very often that MTPL insurers and claims handling offices operate for a foreign insurance undertaking as Green Card correspondent and as claims representative at the same time.

5.3.2 *Difference between the claims representative and the representative under article 152 Solvency II directive*

The function of a claims representative is to be distinguished from the representative, operating for a foreign insurer, active in the representative's Member State by way of Freedom to Provide Services.

As will be explained more in detail in chapter 7, insurers authorised in the EEA to operate MTPL insurance business have the right to offer such insurance products in other Member States by way of Freedom to Provide Services. This means that their authorisation in the 'home Member State' allows them, provided that certain conditions are met, to be active in other Member States without establishing a new insurance company in that 'host Member State' and without having to request a new authorisation from the competent authorities in the 'host Member State'. In order to avoid victims of road traffic accidents, caused by the use of a vehicle and insured with a foreign insurer operating by way of Freedom to Provide Services, having to present a claim to a foreign insurer in the home Member State of the insurer, the insurer must appoint a representative in the host Member State to which victims can present their claims. It is therefore important not to confuse the role of representative with that of claims representative.

The obligation to appoint a representative and the role and function of that representative is described in Article 152 Solvency II.[6]

6. Directive 2009/138/EC of the European Parliament and of the Council of 25 November 2009 on the taking-up and pursuit of the business of Insurance and Reinsurance (Solvency II) (recast), OJ L 335, 17.12.2009, p. 1.

Example
A Polish insurer Polins, authorised in the home Member State Poland to conduct MTPL insurance, also offers MTPL insurance products in the host Member State Latvia. This means that vehicles normally based in Latvia can be insured with Polins. If such a Latvian vehicle causes an accident in Latvia and a Latvian injured party suffers damage from that accident, the injured party cannot be compelled to present a claim to Polins in Poland. Therefore, Polins must appoint a representative in Latvia, ensuring in that way that Latvian injured parties can present a claim for compensation in Latvian language and according to Latvian rules to the Latvian representative of Polins in Latvia.
This function of representative is not the same as the one of claims representative as described in paragraph 5.3.1 and which is intended for dealing with cross-border road traffic accidents. The difference lies in that the representative in Freedom to Provide Services deals with accidents in his/her domestic Member State and therefore primarily domestic accidents, whereas the claims representative is responsible for handling and settling claims which occurred in another Member State.

5.3.3 *Conditions to be fulfilled by claims representatives*

Article 21(1) of the codified Directive requires the claims representative to be *responsible for handling and settling claims arising from accidents* occurring in a Member State other than the Member State of residence of the injured party.

In order to be able to execute this function, the claims representative must be able to meet the following expectations or fulfil the following requirements:
- The claims representative shall be resident or established in the Member State where he is appointed (Article 21(1), third paragraph MID). This guarantees to the injured party that they can communicate and settle the claim with an entity established in their own Member State;
- The claims representative shall collect all information necessary in connection with the settlement of the claims and shall take the measures necessary to negotiate a settlement of claims (Article 21(4), first paragraph MID). To perform this task successfully, the claims representative will have to collect information both from the claimant and from the foreign insurer represented. Information from the claimant will include *inter alia* the accident statement, together with all information necessary to document or support the claim made: information about the circumstances of the accident, expert reports, any kind of proof relating to the damage suffered. Information from the insurer, on the other hand, will rather relate to the applicable rules for the evaluation of the liability and quantification of the compensation to be provided. Since the

compensation will be determined on the basis of the applicable law and this law will, most often, differ from the legislation in the Member State of residence of the injured party, the claims representative will have to apply foreign law and can therefore better rely on information and instructions provided by the foreign insurer. Once all the information is available, the claims representative should be in a position to negotiate a settlement with the claimant. To that end, the claims representative must observe the general rules for compensation procedure as stipulated in Article 22 of the MID (see para 6.3.3). This provision imposes certain obligations to be respected during the claims negotiation, handling and settlement process;

- The claims representative shall possess sufficient powers to represent the insurance undertaking in relation to injured parties and to meet their claims in full (Article 21(5), first paragraph MID). This provision again requires the claims representative to act as the first point of contact for the injured party in their country of residence. The claims representative must be experienced in claims handling in order to be able to receive and collect all the information necessary for the claim to be assessed and settled. The claims representative must act as an intermediary between the claimant and the foreign insurer. Since the provision also requires the claims representative "to meet the claims of the injured parties in full", the claims representative should not only "negotiate a settlement of claims" but also make the payment. As we suggested in paragraph 5.2.3, this provision may arguably imply that the claims representative should be able to advance the compensation payment to the injured parties, without waiting for the funds to be transferred first by the insurer to the claims representative.

  The Court of Justice of the European Union further describes the exact task of the claims representative in a judgment of 15 December 2016[7]:

> "26. (...) in the non-judicial phase of that compensation scheme, the claims representative does not in any way act as a substitute for the undertaking it represents and merely acts as an intermediary, which is necessarily more limited in scope. (...)."

- The claims representative must be capable of examining cases in the official language(s) of the Member State of residence of the injured party (Article 21(5), second paragraph MID). This is one of the major achievements of the protection scheme for visiting victims as introduced by the 4th Motor Insurance Directive. It marks an important difference with the difficulties injured parties had to cope with in earlier times when attempting to receive compensation for the damage suffered in a Member State outside their country of residence. Before the adoption of the 4th MID, victims had to address a claim to a foreign insurer

7. CJEU, Judgment of 15 December 2016, *Vieira de Azevedo*, C-558/15, EU:C:2016:957.

and communicate with this insurer in what was most often a foreign language for the victim. Taking into account the quite technical character of terminology frequently used in questions of liability and compensation of damage, it needs no further explanation to understand that these communications were often not easy for a victim unexperienced in these matters. It is important to emphasise that the Directive requires the claims representative to be able to communicate in all the official languages of the Member State where it is active. This is particularly important for those Member States where more than one official language exists. For example, a claims representative operating in Finland, must be able to communicate both in Finnish and in Swedish. For a country like Luxembourg, a claims representative must be able to communicate with injured parties resident in Luxembourg in French, German and Luxembourgish.

The English language version of the MID may suggest that it is sufficient for the claims representative to *examine* cases in the official language(s) of the injured party's Member State of residence. This could be interpreted as if it were sufficient that the claims representative can receive and understand documents drafted in one of these languages but that the claims representative would not be required to be able to communicate actively with the claimant in any of the official languages. This interpretation, which is to our opinion not in line with the spirit and aim of the Directive, can also be based on other language versions such as French, Italian and Spanish. But in other languages of the Directive, the objective of providing the injured party with a point of contact able to communicate in the injured party's language, is more clearly present. This is for instance the case in the Dutch, German and Swedish language versions (*'de zaak te behandelen'*, *'den Fall zu bearbeiten'* or *'De måste kunna behandla ärendet'*), which go more in the direction of 'to handle a case'. An interpretation somewhere in between can be found in the Romanian language version, which seems to suggest that the claims representative must be able to 'analyse' the case in the official language(s) of the injured party's Member State

"Acesta trebuie să fie în măsură să analizeze cererea în limba sau în limbile oficiale ale statului membru de reședință al persoanei vătămate."

As explained earlier in paragraph 5.3.1, the expectations described above are incorporated in the Motor Insurance Directive but they do not constitute conditions, the fulfilment of which will be verified prior to the appointment of a claims representative. Insurers only have to nominate claims representatives and notify the name and address of these claims representatives to the Information Centres in all the Member States (see para 5.5). There is no entity controlling the correct functioning of the claims representatives in the different Member States. The only way in which the inappropriate functioning of a claims representative can be revealed seems to be by analysing the complaints presented to the Compensation Body.

5.3.4 *Legal proceedings against the claims representative?*

As stipulated in Article 21(5) of the MID and as described above, the claims representative

> "shall possess sufficient powers to represent the insurance undertaking in relation to injured parties (...) and to meet their claims in full."

For a long time, it has been unclear how far these 'sufficient powers to represent' should reach. The claims representative being an intermediary between the foreign insurer and the injured party, the question was raised whether the injured party could issue legal proceedings against the claims representative before the courts of the injured party's Member State of residence. This question came before the Court of Justice of the European Union.

In a first case, the German company *Spedition Welter* was the owner of a lorry that was damaged in a car accident on the outskirts of Paris in France.[8] The vehicle that caused the accident was normally based in France and insured by the French insurer Avanssur. In their search for damage compensation, Spedition Welter started proceedings in Germany against the French insurer Avanssur and, to that end, served notice of proceedings against AXA Versicherungs AG, the claims representative of Avanssur in Germany. In other words, the subject of the case was not the question whether proceedings could be initiated against the claims representative, but merely whether judicial documents necessary for proceedings could validly be served on the claims representative. The Court's answer to the preliminary question was that Article 21(5) of the codified Motor Insurance Directive is to be interpreted as:

> "meaning that the claims representative's sufficient powers must include authority validly to accept service of judicial documents necessary for proceedings for settlement of a claim to be brought before the court having jurisdiction."

With that case, however, the question about the claims representative's 'passive legitimisation' (*'légitimation passive'* or *'Passivlegitimation'*) or capability to be sued was not answered yet. The question of the claims representative's capacity to be a defendant in legal proceedings was the subject of a later preliminary question, sub-

8. CJEU, Judgment of 10 October 2013, *Spedition Welter*, C-306/12, EU:C:2013:650.

mitted to the Court of Justice of the European Union, in case C-558/15 (*Vieira de Azevedo*).[9]

In that judgment, the Court did not follow the opinion of the Advocate General, who expressed the view that

> "one of the 'sufficient powers' which claims representatives must possess is the capacity to be sued, as defendant, in legal actions."[10]

The Court took a different view and considered that the provisions in the MID do not

> "of themselves, entail that (the claims) representative may be sued in national courts instead of the insurance undertaking it represents."[11]

The Court continued by arguing that the EU legislature, by the provisions of the MID

> "merely set out the claims representative's tasks in the context of a negotiated settlement of claims, without referring to possible judicial proceedings."[12]

The Court tried to establish the limits of the claims representative's function by making a distinction between the non-judicial phase, where the claims representative acts as an intermediary and the judicial phase, where they do not act as a substitute for the insurer:

> "It must therefore be noted that, in the non-judicial phase of that compensation scheme, the claims representative does not in any way act as a substitute for the undertaking it represents and merely acts as an intermediary, which is necessarily more limited in scope."[13]

The Court continued in recitals 35 and 36 as follows:

> "35. On the other hand, it is apparent neither from the drafting history nor from the recitals in the preamble to Directive 2000/26 that the intention of the EU legislature was to extend those powers to allow injured parties to bring proceedings against that undertaking's representative, in order to seek compensation from the insurance undertaking of the responsible party, before the national court of their place of residence.

9. CJEU, Judgment of 15 December 2016, *Vieira de Azevedo*, C-558/15, EU:C:2016:957.
10. CJEU, Opinion of Advocate General Mengozzi of 19 October 2016, *Vieira de Azevedo*, C-558/15, EU:C:2016:785, conclusion.
11. CJEU, Judgment of 15 December 2016, *Vieira de Azevedo*, C-558/15, EU:C:2016:957, para 20.
12. Idem, para 21.
13. Idem, para 26.

> 36. Since injured parties may notify judicial documents to the representative of the insurance undertaking, it does not appear that the objective of Directive 2000/26, whose purpose is to make the steps to be taken by those persons easier, is not therefore achieved and requires proceedings to be able to be brought against the representative itself before the national court."

The conclusion of the Court is therefore that Article 4 of the 4th MID or today Article 21 of the codified MID must be interpreted

> "as not requiring Member States to provide that the claims representative appointed pursuant to that article may itself be sued, instead of the insurance undertaking which it represents, in the national court before which an action for damages was brought by an injured party falling within the scope of Article 1 of Directive 2000/26, as amended by Directive 2005/14."[14]

Bringing the relevant provision of the codified MID together with the two decisions of the Court of Justice, we may conclude the following about the role and the function of the claims representative:
- in the non-judicial phase, the claims representative acts as an intermediary, capable of collecting information, negotiating a settlement and meeting the claims in full (Article 21 of the MID);
- in the judicial phase, on the other hand, the claims representative may be expected to accept service of judicial documents (*Spedition Welter*) but not to be sued as a defendant (*Vieira Azevedo*).

5.4 The Compensation Body

5.4.1 Introduction

In the vast majority of cases, the obligation for insurers to appoint claims representatives will provide satisfactory protection for the injured party who has suffered damage as a result of an accident that occurred in a Member State other than the injured party's country of residence. When developing this protection of visitors system, the European legislator was aware however that the requirement for claims representatives would not provide an infallible solution and would leave certain victims without protection in specific circumstances. Right from the beginning, the 4th Motor Insurance Directive has therefore provided for a fall-back, offering the injured party the possibility to present a claim to a *Compensation Body* in their own country of residence in those cases where no claim to the claims representative was possible.

14. Idem, para 39 and the dictum of the Judgment.

The following four situations are envisaged, where the network of claims representatives would not offer a sufficient level of protection:

a. *No reasoned reply*: The MTPL insurer of the vehicle which caused the accident or the claims representative of that insurer does not provide a reasoned reply to the injured party within three months from the date when the injured party presented a claim for compensation (Article 24(1), point (a) of the codified MID; examined in para 5.4.2.1);
b. *No claims representative*: Contrary to the Directive's obligation, the MTPL insurer of the vehicle which caused the accident was at the time of the accident not represented by a claims representative in the injured party's country of residence (Article 24(1), point (b) of the codified MID; examined in para 5.4.2.2);
c. *Unidentified vehicle*: it is impossible to identify the vehicle, the use of which caused the accident (Article 25(1) of the codified MID; examined in para 5.4.3.1);
d. *Unidentified insurer* (which in most cases will reveal that the vehicle is uninsured): it is impossible to identify the insurance undertaking of the vehicle, the use of which caused the accident (Article 25(1) of the codified MID; examined in para 5.4.3.2).

In these four circumstances, it is clear that the injured party will not have the possibility to address a claim to a claims representative, either because there is no claims representative (cases b and d), because the claims representative is unknown (case c) or because the claims representative does not provide the necessary protection envisaged by the Directive (case a). In those cases, the injured party has an alternative entity at their disposal in their own country of residence, protecting the injured party's interests: the Compensation Body, operating as a safety net for the injured party suffering damage from a road traffic accident occurred in a Member State other than their country of residence.

5.4.2 *The Compensation Body's tasks based on Article 24 MID*

5.4.2.1 *No reasoned reply*

However innovative the system of claims representatives may have been, it remains of course useless if the injured party does not receive any reaction from the claims representative appointed by the MTPL insurer. As will be described more in detail in paragraph 6.3.3, Article 22 of the MID requires insurers and claims representatives to provide either a reasoned offer of compensation or a reasoned reply to the points made in the claim within three months from the date when the injured party presented a claim for compensation. It is surprising that Article 22 refers both to reasoned offer of compensation and reasoned reply, whereas Article 24 only provides for the Compensation Body's intervention if no reasoned reply has been provided. Theoretically, if the claims representative informed the injured party in a reasoned way that liability was not disputed and that compensation would be provided, but afterwards refrained from making a concrete offer of compensation, the injured party would not have any possibility to present a claim to the Compensation Body. In practice one hopes that if, in such circumstances, the injured party contacts the Compensation Body the latter will contact the claims representative and try to motivate them to formulate an offer of compensation.

In order to assess whether it is competent, the Compensation Body will have to establish whether or not a reasoned reply has been provided. Inevitably, the question thus arises what is to be understood by reasoned reply. The term 'reasoned' implies that the insurer or claims representative should not limit the communication to simply taking a position on acceptance of liability or payment of compensation. Arguments should be provided to justify the position. But how far should that argumentation be elaborated? And what if arguments are delivered but are totally irrelevant or manifestly wrong? To turn it into a caricature: may the following statement of an insurer or claims representative be regarded as a reasoned reply: "We are unable to compensate the damage since liability of the vehicle insured cannot be accepted as a result of the accident having taken place on a Sunday"? It cannot be denied that a reply has been provided and a reason given. But is the argumentation also reasoned in the meaning of the Directive, let alone reasonable?

Confronted with questions of this kind, Compensation Bodies have formulated recommendations, enabling a more harmonised way of evaluating whether or not a reasoned reply has been formulated. The recommendations accept that an insurer or claims representative may explain, in a reasoned reply, why a final response cannot be provided, e.g. because no police report is available (yet) or because no final position can be taken in the absence of an expert or medical report. They further state that a reply must be argued and justified. The recommendations serve as a support tool for Compensation Bodies but have no binding force.

Ultimately, the interpretation of the term 'reasoned reply' lies in the hands of the Court of Justice of the European Union. See para 6.3.3.

5.4.2.2 *No claims representative appointed*

The second reason for a Compensation Body's intervention leaves far less possibilities for interpretation. A claims representative has either been appointed by the MTPL insurance undertaking or not. Article 21 of the MID requires every insurer covering MTPL risks to appoint a claims representative in each and every Member State of the EEA, other than the Member State where the insurer in question received the official authorisation (see para 5.3.1).

Despite this obligation, which had to be complied with in 2003, it still exceptionally happens that insurers have omitted to appoint a claims representative in one or more Member States or that the tenure of a claims representative has been brought to an end without a replacement being appointed.

Although the answer to the question whether there is a claims representative seems to be a binary one (either there is, or there is not a claims representative), in practice it can lead to more confusing situations. The Directive does not provide a clear answer to the question at what exact time a claims representative must have been appointed.

- If an insurance undertaking has no claims representative at the moment of the accident, nor at the time a claim is made, the injured party will contact the Compensation Body. If the Compensation Body subsequently contacts the insurer and urges this insurance undertaking to appoint a claims representative, the latter will most probably be willing to deal with the claim, even if the claims representative was not yet formally appointed as claims representative at the time of the accident;
- The situation becomes more complex when the relation between the insurance undertaking and the claims representative is ended. Can the claims representative still handle claims relating to an accident that occurred at a moment when the claims representative was still in office? And what happens with pending files in which a claims representative has already operated, if the mandate is ended while the case is still in process?

The Directive is silent on these matters and in practice it is sometimes difficult to determine whether a claims representative is still authorised to operate (independently of whether the claims representative is still willing to take action on a file if they know that the relationship has been ended).

5.4.2.3 The Compensation Body's role in the cases described in Article 24 MID

The first two reasons for the intervention of a Compensation Body, both described in Article 24 of the Directive, relate to deficiencies in the protection of visitors mechanism that can still be remedied by the insurance undertaking and/or the claims representative involved. If the insurer or claims representative have not provided a reasoned reply within three months, nothing should withhold them from still doing so after being urged by an external entity. And if the insurer has not appointed a claims representative in a certain Member State there is still possibility to do so, even after an accident occurred, enabling a claim to go forward.

Therefore, the Compensation Body's task in the situations envisaged in Article 24 will in the first place be to try to put the claims handling process back on track. This might be called the 'lubricant' function of the Compensation Body.

Article 24 requires the Compensation Body immediately to inform (a) the insurer or the claims representative of the vehicle, (b) the Compensation Body in the Member State in which the insurance undertaking is established and (c) the person who caused the accident if that person is known. This exchange of information should allow the insurer to be 'alarmed' about the claimant having turned to the Compensation Body and should be an incentive for the insurer or claims representative to rectify the deficiency in the claims handling process. The insurer or claims representative can urgently provide the claimant with a reasoned reply; if there is no claims representative the insurer can still rapidly appoint one and they can handle the claim in the injured party's country of residence.

This lubricant function of the Compensation Body is illustrated by the wording of the 6th sub-paragraph of Article 24(1) of the MID:

> "The compensation body shall take action within two months of the date when the injured party presents a claim for compensation to it but shall terminate its action if the insurance undertaking, or its claims representative, subsequently makes a reasoned reply to the claim."

From this provision it is clear that the Compensation Body has two months to invite and motivate the insurer and/or claims representative to remedy the flaw in the claims handling process. Should that be the Compensation Body's sole responsibility during the period of two months? Or can the Compensation Body already start claims handling activities such as mandating technical or medical experts? Can the Compensation Body already take a position regarding liability for the accident? The Directive does not clarify what is to be understood under the term 'take action'.

Since the Directive requires the Compensation Body to terminate any action if the insurance undertaking makes a reasoned reply, the most prudent approach would seem to be to delay starting to handle the claim for two months. The Directive appears to suggest that the two month period should be used to urge the insurer or claims representative to take action; only if that is unsuccessful should the Compensation Body initiate any handling and settlement activities.

But even then, when the Compensation Body starts handling the claim and takes position regarding liability and damage compensation, the Directive still allows the insurer or claims representative to intervene and make a reasoned reply. This may even take place after the two month period ('it shall terminate its action if the insurance undertaking, or its claims representative, *subsequently* makes a reasoned reply to the claim' [Italics by the authors]). The Directive is unclear as to what happens if the Compensation Body has taken decisive positions in the file (e.g. regarding the liability and/or the amount of compensation) and these positions are subsequently contradicted by the insurer or claims representative. Moreover, it is unclear what will happen if the insurer formulates a reasoned reply after the Compensation Body has taken action, the claims handling process is passed back to the insurer and, subsequently, the insurer is again deficient in giving a reply on time to additional questions or sub-claims in the compensation process. Is the claimant then allowed to address the claim to the Compensation Body again?

We are of the opinion that a strict application of the provision mentioned above is not workable in practice and seriously weakens the position of the injured party. It is unacceptable that the injured party is sent from pillar to post. Once the Compensation Body had to intervene and take action after the two-month period, the claims handling process should remain in the hands of the Compensation Body. After all, the injured party will already have waited at least three months before approaching the Compensation Body (Article 24(1), point (a)) and on top of that the insurer or claims representative will have had two months to remedy the situation (Article 24(1), sixth paragraph).

We are of the opinion that Article 24 is to be interpreted as meaning that the Compensation Body must continue to act once the five-month period (3+2) is over. This is also confirmed in Clause 3.2, second paragraph of the 2002 Agreement:[15]

> "Once this two-month period has expired, the competent compensation body shall proceed to handle the injured party's claim, notwithstanding any subsequent reply given by the insurance undertaking or its representative."

5.4.3 *The Compensation Body's tasks based on Article 25 MID*

5.4.3.1 *Unidentified vehicle*

The first intervention task of a Compensation Body described in Article 25 of the codified MID relates to unidentified vehicles and is identical to one of the two intervention tasks of the Guarantee Fund, described in Article 10 of the MID. Cf. para 4.3.3 (unidentified vehicles and the consequences of *hit and run* cases).

In dealing with claims resulting from accidents caused by the use of an unidentified vehicle, the Compensation Body may therefore also be compelled to limit or exclude any material damage caused by unidentified vehicles if no compensation is to be paid for significant personal injuries (see Article 10(3) of the codified MID and para 4.4.3). In that regard, the Compensation Body in the injured party's country of residence will have to seek information on the legislation applicable in the

15. Agreement between Compensation Bodies and Guarantee Funds, concluded in Brussels on 23 April 2002. See para 5.6.3.

country of the accident in order to know whether the compensation of material damage caused by unidentified vehicles is limited or excluded in the country of the accident.

5.4.3.2 Unidentified insurer

Article 25 also gives the Compensation Body a role to play if it is impossible to identify the insurance undertaking of the vehicle within two months of the date of the accident.

If, within two months of the date of the accident, it is impossible to identify the insurance undertaking, this will in most cases be tantamount to the vehicle being uninsured. But it is of course possible that the vehicle is in reality insured but certain circumstances make it so difficult to identify the insurer that this cannot be done within two months. In such cases, the injured party still has the possibility to address a claim to the Compensation Body.

The formulation of Article 25 is a little unfortunate because it gives the injured party the possibility to apply for compensation from the Compensation Body if the insurer cannot be identified within two months *of the date of the accident*. This does not require the injured party to make any attempt to identify the insurer or engage in other activity. It would be more balanced to let the two-month period run from the first attempts that were made to identify the insurer. Contacting the Information Centre in order to identify the insurer could be required as a condition (see para 5.5).

5.4.3.3 The Compensation Body's role in the cases described in Article 25 MID

In paragraph 5.4.2.3, we explained that the Compensation Body will in the first place try to put the claims handling process back on the right track (lubricant function) before taking over the handling activity and compensating the injured party. In the situations covered by Article 24 of the MID, the insurer and/or claims representative will be allowed to remedy the situation.

In the two cases foreseen in Article 25 (uninsured and unidentified vehicles), there will be no insurer or claims representative available who can be invited to take action. Therefore, the Motor Insurance Directive immediately invites the Compensation Body to initiate claims handling activities and to compensate the injured party if that is justified in accordance with the rules of the applicable law (which will most often be the law of the country of the accident).

Since the two intervention cases of Article 25 are so closely related to the two mandatory intervention scenarios of Guarantee Funds described in Article 10 of the Directive, Article 25 also refers to the provisions of that Article 10 as regards the compensation to be provided. At the same time, reference is also made to Article 9, where the minimum amounts of insurance cover are imposed.

The Compensation Body shall therefore operate in a comparable (or even identical) way to a Guarantee Fund. It is however important to emphasise in this context that the Compensation Body must act in accordance with the rules applicable to the intervention of the Guarantee Fund in the country of the accident. It is the rules of the country where the accident occurred that will determine whether and to what extent the injured party can be compensated for the damage suffered. The Compensation Body in the injured party's country of residence is therefore strongly advised to contact the Guarantee Fund in the country of the accident in order to know the exact modalities of the intervention, imposed by the national law of the country of the accident.

Example

In case of an accident, caused by an unidentified vehicle in the Netherlands, the Dutch Guarantee Fund compensates material damage, even in the absence of significant personal injuries (subject to an excess of € 250). If a resident of the Netherlands suffers an accident in Belgium and the driver of the vehicle that caused the accident leaves the place of the accident without identifying themselves, the victim will have the possibility to present a claim to the Dutch Compensation Body. Despite the rules applicable in the Netherlands for accidents caused by unidentified vehicles, the Dutch Compensation Body will however not be able to compensate the victim for any material damage if there is no significant personal injury. Based on Article 10(3) of the codified Motor Insurance Directive, Belgian rules on compensation of damage caused by unidentified vehicles exclude the compensation of material damage if no significant personal injury has to be compensated.

Conversely if a resident of Belgium suffers a similar accident in the Netherlands, caused by an unidentified vehicle and only resulting in material damage, the victim will be compensated by the Belgian Compensation Body for the material damage, reduced only by an excess of € 250.

5.4.4 *Limitations to the intervention of the Compensation Body*

5.4.4.1 *Who can present a claim to the Compensation Body?*

We have earlier (see para 5.2.4 and 6.2.12.1) made reference to the difference between a victim and an injured party as well as the relevance of that difference to determine who can rely on the provisions of the Motor Insurance Directive to obtain damage compensation. Based on the language used in the Directive, we take the position that the term 'victim' is reserved for the party who has directly suffered damage from a road traffic accident, whereas the term 'injured party' should be considered wider and also covers subrogated parties.

In that regard, the question arises whether access to the Compensation Body can be limited to the party suffering direct damage (the victim) or should be open to the victim as well as to subrogated parties (the injured party).

When analysing this question, the text of the Directive is unfortunately not crystal clear. Based on the text of the preamble (recital 49), the European legislator's intention seemed to go in the direction of limiting the access to the Compensation Body exclusively to direct victims:

> "Legal persons who are subrogated by law to the injured party in his claims against the person responsible for the accident or the latter's insurance undertaking (such as, for example, other insurance undertakings or social security bodies) should not be entitled to present the corresponding claim to the compensation body."

The reason for this recital seems to be that subrogated parties may be presumed to be sufficiently professional and experienced to find their way directly to the insurer or to the Guarantee Fund in the country of the accident.
Moreover the word 'should' could be interpreted as an instruction to national legislators that access to the Compensation Body is not to be provided for.
But the language used in the legal provisions of the Directive seems to go exactly in the opposite direction. The Articles 24 and 25 systematically apply the term 'injured party', which gives the impression that the European legislator wished to open the safety net of the Compensation Bodies to direct victims and to subrogated parties simultaneously.[16]

> In fact, the lack of clarity even goes a step further in such a way that the wording of the preamble's recital 49 excludes access to legal persons who are subrogated by law to the injured party. In other words, subrogated parties to the victim are not excluded but subrogated parties to the injured party are. Should this be interpreted thus that only subrogated parties in a second degree should be excluded? Or is this just to be explained by an unfortunate use of language in the text of the Directive?

In view of this lack of clarity, it must be presumed that the national legislator in the different Member States is free to allow subrogated parties to access the Compensation Bodies or not. In the end, the interpretation of the Directive and the question whether subrogated parties can be excluded from access to Compensation Bodies lies in the hands of the Court of Justice of the European Union in Luxembourg.

16. See for an analysis of the words 'injured party' and 'victim' para 6.2.12.1.

5.4.4.2 *Subsidiarity*

When describing the role and function of Guarantee Funds, the possibility for Member States to make the Guarantee Fund's intervention subsidiary was explained in paragraph 4.4.2. Subsidiarity gives Member States the possibility to limit the Guarantee Fund's intervention to those cases where the victim is not able to obtain compensation from any other source, such as another insurer. As explained in the same paragraph, not only bodies of social security are considered but also private insurance undertakings such as insurers offering comprehensive (casco) insurance or insurers of other vehicles involved in the accident that could potentially be held severally liable.

The MID also leaves the Member States free to decide whether the Compensation Body's intervention should be subsidiary or not. The subsidiarity of Compensation Bodies is formulated in two different ways in the Articles 24 and 25 of the Directive.

Article 24 copies the identical wording as used for Guarantee Funds in Article 10:

> "This provision shall be without prejudice to the right of the Member States to regard compensation by that body as subsidiary or non-subsidiary (...)."

Article 25, on the other hand, states that the compensation for damage caused by uninsured or unidentified vehicles shall be

> "provided in accordance with the provisions of Articles 9 and 10."

Both wordings lead to the same result, since Article 10 contains the same provision, offering Member States the freedom to regard the Guarantee Fund's intervention as subsidiary or not.

The next question is to decide which Compensation Body's subsidiarity is to be taken into account. Is it the Compensation Body in the injured party's country of residence or are the rules on subsidiarity in the country of the accident to be taken into account?

Looking at the wording of Article 24, it should be understood that the Directive takes into consideration the subsidiarity of the Compensation Body in the injured party's country of residence. The wording is to be found at the end of Article 24(1) and refers to 'compensation by that body'. Since in the earlier text of Article 24(1), only the Compensation Body in the injured party's country of residence is referred to, that can be the only Body that is to be understood as 'that body'. The wording of Article 24 should thus lead to the conclusion that only the Compensation Body in the injured party's country of residence may invoke rules of subsidiarity.

Article 25, on the other hand, states that the Compensation Body in the injured party's country of residence should provide compensation "in accordance with the provisions of Article 10." Article 10 of the Directive should however be understood as referring to the subsidiarity of the Guarantee Fund in the country of the accident.

As a conclusion, Article 24 seems to take into consideration rules on subsidiarity in the injured party's country of residence, whereas Article 25 refers instead to rules of subsidiarity in the Member State where the accident occurred. It is very doubtful whether that was the real intention of the European legislator when drafting the 4th Directive.

In reality, there is reason to fear that the injured party will be confronted with the rules on subsidiarity in both their country of residence and the country where the accident occurred. This will particularly be the case in the situations described in Article 25. If an injured party presents a claim to the Compensation Body in their own country of residence, that Body will most probably not intervene if it is subject to subsidiarity rules, even if no subsidiarity exists in the country where the accident occurred. At the same time, when the Compensation Body in the injured party's country of residence is not subject to subsidiarity rules but such rules limit the compensation in the country where the accident occurred, the Compensation Body in the injured party's country of residence will not dare to compensate the injured party entirely, for fear of not being fully reimbursed by the Compensation Body or Guarantee Fund of the country where the accident occurred if the latter entity invokes the subsidiarity rules.

As in the case of the Guarantee Fund, the injured party cannot be required first to present a claim to the person liable for the accident or to establish that the latter is unable or unwilling to compensate the damage. Recital 51 of the preamble reads as follows:

> "Even though Member States may provide that the claim against the compensation body is to be subsidiary, the injured person should not be obliged to present his claim to the person responsible for the accident before presenting it to the compensation body. In such a case the injured party should be in at least the same position as in the case of a claim against the guarantee fund."

Article 24(1), last paragraph of the MID:

> "(...) However, Member States may not allow the body to make the payment of compensation subject to any conditions other than those laid down in this Directive, in particular the injured party's establishing in any way that the person liable is unable or refuses to pay."

5.4.4.3 *Limitations comparable to those that apply to Guarantee Funds*

As also examined in paragraph 4.4, the intervention of Guarantee Funds is subject to other limitations than just the possibility of subsidiarity. Since Article 25 of the MID prescribes the compensation provided by a Compensation Body to be in accordance with the provisions of Article 10, the same limitations as those applicable under that article should be taken into account. That includes the following:

- Unidentified vehicles and material damage (see para 4.4.3): in order to avoid fraudulent claims, the Motor Insurance Directive allows Member States to limit or exclude any material damage caused by unidentified vehicles if no compensation is to be paid for significant personal injuries. This limitation or exclusion, applicable to the intervention of Guarantee Funds, must also be taken into account by a Compensation Body when receiving a claim from an injured party of an accident caused by an unidentified vehicle in a Member State other than the injured party's country of residence;
- Passengers of uninsured vehicles (see para 4.4.4): In accordance with Article 10(2) of the MID, Member States may exclude the payment of compensation by the Guarantee Fund in respect of persons who voluntarily entered a vehicle when the Compensation Body can prove that those persons knew the vehicle was uninsured. This same possible exclusion must be taken into account when a Compensation Body is invited to intervene in the case of an accident caused by the use of an uninsured vehicle.

It is to be reminded that, for the applicability of these limitations, the law of the country of the accident must be taken into consideration.

5.4.4.4 *Vehicles stolen or obtained by violence*

As also explained in paragraphs 4.3.4 and 4.4.5, Article 13(2) of the MID allows Member States to provide for the Guarantee Fund to pay compensation instead of the insurer in the case of vehicles stolen or obtained by violence. Some Member States have made use of this possibility, others have not.

Let us consider a hypothetical Member State A, having made use of this possibility. When a road traffic accident in Member State A is caused by the use of a vehicle obtained by theft or violence, the injured party is to obtain compensation from the Guarantee Fund and not from the insurer of the vehicle. If this injured party is not resident in Member State A but in another Member State, will that injured party then be protected by the protection of visitors mechanism created by the 4th Motor Insurance Directive?

We are of the opinion that the vehicle in this situation is to be considered as an uninsured vehicle. That opens the possibility for the injured party to invoke Article 25 of the MID (impossible to identify the insurance undertaking within two months of the date of the accident) and present a claim to the Compensation Body in their country of residence.

5.4.4.5 *Legal action directly taken against the insurance undertaking*

For the two intervention scenarios described in Article 24, the Directive again underlines the 'lubricant' function of the Compensation Body by excluding the Body's intervention if the injured party has taken legal action directly against the insurance undertaking.

The Directive seems to consider that any lubricant function or any attempt to rectify the claims handling process is useless or inefficient once a national court or tribunal has been invited to judge on the injured party's claim against the insurance undertaking.

5.4.4.6 *Legal proceedings against the Compensation Body?*

One of the points on which the protection of visitors mechanism created by the Motor Insurance Directive is less clear relates to the precise legal status of the Compensation Body and the latter's 'passive legitimisation' or capability to be sued. Should it be possible for an injured party to issue legal proceedings against the Compensation Body in the injured party's country of residence?

This issue was the subject of a preliminary question submitted to the Court of Justice of the European Union in the case *Grilc*.[17] The Court considered the question to be far less opaque than expected and decided to rule by way of an 'order', which is a possibility open to questions that leave no room for reasonable doubt.[18]

The Court decided that court proceedings can be initiated against Compensation Bodies on the condition that a claim has first been addressed to the Body (giving the latter the possibility to come to an out-of-court settlement of the case).

5.5 The Information Centre

As already stated, the introduction of the 4th Motor Insurance Directive constituted a substantial improvement for the protection of road traffic victims in the European Economic Area and, more particularly, for the protection of visiting victims. But at the same time, the 4th MID also increased the complexity of claims handling processes. Apart from the existing motor insurers' Bureaux, agents and correspondents in the Green Card system and the Guarantee Funds operating in the Member States, two more entities were added to the landscape of operators, active

17. CJEU, Order of 17 January 2013, *Grilc*, C-541/11, EU:C:2013:19.
18. An unfortunate result of this procedure is that the text of the order is only available in Slovenian (the language of the procedure in the case *Grilc*) and in French.

in the field of cross-border motor claims handling: claims representatives and Compensation Bodies. Green Card Bureaux must have an overview of correspondents active in the country for which they are competent. But since the 4th MID protection scheme was developed independently from the existing Green Card system, there was no central entity which would play the same role with regard to the claims representatives.

For that reason, the European legislator also required all Member States to establish or approve an Information Centre, with the task of collecting and providing information to injured parties of road traffic accidents in a Member State other than their country of residence.

The establishment of a network of Information Centres throughout the EEA allows visiting victims or injured parties to obtain information about the MTPL insurer covering the vehicle involved in an accident, together with the name of the claims representative, appointed by that insurer in the injured party's Member State. Insurers are obliged to notify to the Information Centres of all Member States the name and address of the claims representatives appointed by them (Article 23(2) MID). In that way, the injured party can easily be referred to the claims representative to which they can present a claim.

Relatively soon after the 4th Directive was implemented by Member States, it became clear that the network of Information Centres could in fact not only be of benefit to visiting victims but also substantially improve the situation of any injured party in a road traffic accident in the EEA. Therefore, in 2005 the 5th Directive extended the scope of applicability of Information Centres to any motor vehicle accident in the EEA, be it a Green Card accident, a 4th MID case or just a national accident without any cross-border element.
Given the fact that the scope of Information Centres now extends to any kind of accidents, their functioning and the kind of data they have to collect will not be described more in detail here but will be treated more extensively in paragraph 6.3.6.

5.6 The recovery of outlays in the framework of the 4th MID

5.6.1 *Introduction*

The protection of visitors mechanism has improved protection for victims of accidents in a Member State other than their country of residence. The claims representative or Compensation Body acts as an intermediary in the claims handling process, offering the injured party a possibility to claim compensation in their own language from an entity established in their country of residence. But it is obvious that this intermediary (claims representative or Compensation Body) will not be the final source of payment and will wish to recover their outlays from a foreign insurer or – in the case of payments made by the Compensation Body – from another foreign body.

In the vast majority of cases, the claims representative will either advance the compensation to the injured party or pay compensation after receiving the necessary funds from the insurer they represent. This will be done in accordance with the contractual terms between the insurer and the claims representative and will be examined in paragraph 5.6.2.

In a minority of cases, the system of claims representatives does not offer sufficient protection to the visiting victim. The four Compensation Body intervention scenarios provided for in the Motor Insurance Directive are designed to remedy any deficiencies in the claims handling process, either because the insurer has not respected the obligations of the Directive or because the owner, keeper or driver of the vehicle disregarded their duties. The Compensation Body, having compensated the injured party, should then be able to recover its outlays from the place where the deficiency originated.

To that end, the MID foresees two steps of recourse. In the first instance, the Compensation Body can seek reimbursement from the Compensation Body or Guarantee Fund in the country where the deficiency originated (the Member State where the insurance undertaking is established or the Member State where the vehicle originates from). Thereafter, that 'reimbursing' Compensation Body or Guarantee Fund may attempt to recover the outlays either from the deficient insurer or the owner, keeper or driver of the uninsured or unidentified vehicle.

In paragraph 5.6.3, we will describe how the Compensation Body can recover the compensation paid to the victim from a foreign Compensation Body in the situations described in Article 24 of the MID.
In paragraph 5.6.4, we will describe how the Compensation Body can recover the compensation paid to the victim from a foreign Guarantee Fund in the situations described in Article 25 of the MID.
In paragraph 5.6.5 finally, we will briefly touch upon the question of 'second instance recourse' between either the 'reimbursing' Compensation Body or Guarantee Fund on the one hand and the insurer, owner or driver of the vehicle the use of which caused the accident on the other.

5.6.2 *The recovery between the claims representative and the insurer*

The Motor Insurance Directive describes the duties of the claims representative towards the injured party, but is silent on the rights and obligations that should characterise the relationship between the claims representative and the mandating insurer.

This silence illustrates the contractual freedom given to insurers and claims representatives to organise and determine their mutual obligations. They are entirely free to agree on the information and documentation that should be exchanged before payments can be made, on the proof of payment that is required, on the delays within which advance payments or reimbursements are to be made and on the handling fees that the claims representative may charge.

It should not be assumed that the relationship between claims representative and insurer is identical to that between a Green Card correspondent and a mandating insurer. In paragraph 5.2.3, we explained that the claims representative does not benefit from the same handling autonomy as the correspondent operating in the framework of the Green Card system, nor can they rely on the same guarantee as that offered to a Green Card correspondent by Article 4(8) of the Internal Regulations. In the absence of this guarantee, it is more difficult to require a claims representative to make advance payments to the injured party. If the insurer does not reimburse the advanced sums of money, the claims representative can only fall back on their contract with the insurer. Nevertheless, it often happens that claims representatives, having a long-standing relationship of trust with the insurer they represent, will make advance payments to injured parties, trusting on being promptly and fully reimbursed by the foreign insurer. Moreover, as was also argued in paragraph 5.2.3, there are arguments to be found in the Motor Insurance Directive for an obligation for claims representatives to make advance payments, even in the absence of any guarantee as existing in the Green Card system (recital 37 of the preamble and Article 21(5) of the MID).

5.6.3 *The recovery between Compensation Bodies mutually*

In the cases described in Article 24 of the MID (no reasoned reply was provided on time or no claims representative was appointed), the text of the Directive prescribes a reimbursement procedure whereby the Compensation Body in the injured party's country of residence (the 'handling Compensation Body') can recover the compensation paid from the Compensation Body of the Member State where the MTPL insurer of the vehicle in question is established (the 'reimbursing Compensation Body'). Article 24(2), first paragraph of the MID reads as follows:

> "The compensation body which has compensated the injured party in his Member State of residence shall be entitled to claim reimbursement of the sum paid by way of compensation from the compensation body in the Member State in which the insurance undertaking which issued the policy is established."

The Motor Insurance Directive does not limit itself to simply mentioning the possibility of recovering compensation paid, but also stipulates that this should be done by way of an agreement to be concluded between Compensation Bodies. Article 24(3) of the MID:

> "This Article shall take effect:
> a. after an agreement has been concluded between the compensation bodies established or approved by the Member States relating to their functions and obligations and the procedures for reimbursement;
> b. from the date fixed by the Commission upon its having ascertained in close cooperation with the Member States that such an agreement has been concluded."

This Agreement, required by the Motor Insurance Directive, was concluded in Brussels on 29 April 2002, that is to say prior to the date on which the provisions of the 4th Motor Insurance Directive became applicable (20 January 2003). The 'Agreement between Compensation Bodies and Guarantee Funds' was initially concluded between the Compensation Bodies and Guarantee Funds of the – at that moment – 18 countries participating in the European Economic Area. It was prepared by and signed in the framework of the CEA (*Comité Européen des Assurances*, the European insurance and re-insurance federation, today called *Insurance Europe*). The secretarial services for the Agreement were later transferred from the CEA to the Council of Bureaux. With the accession of new Member States to the European Union, the Agreement was also extended to the Compensation Bodies and Guarantee Funds of these new Member States. It is worth noting that the Agreement was not only signed by Compensation Bodies, but also by Guarantee Funds, thus covering not only reimbursements in the framework of Article 24 of the MID but also those in accordance with Article 25 of the MID (see para 5.6.4).

The Agreement is not limited to provisions regarding reimbursements to be made, but also contains rules on the way in which Compensation Bodies are expected to handle claims. Depending on the exact situation of the accident and the claims made, Compensation Bodies are required to inform insurers, foreign Compensation Bodies, the person liable for the accident and, in certain situations, even a foreign Green Card Bureau. Rules on reimbursement ensure that the handling Compensation Body is not only reimbursed for the amounts paid as compensation to the injured party but also for sums paid for external services (e.g. technical, medical or legal experts). Moreover, a handling fee is awarded to the handling Compensation Body, covering all other costs related to the claims handling activity. The fee is set at the same level as the handling fees applicable between national insurers' Bureaux in the framework of the Green Card system (see para 3.8.2.2 as well as Article 5(1), point (3) of the Internal Regulations).

It is noteworthy that Article 24(2) of the Motor Insurance Directive provides for the compensation to be reimbursed by the Compensation Body of the Member State in which the insurance undertaking which issued the policy is established. This will not always be the 'home Member State' of the insurance undertaking in question; it will differ, depending on whether the insurer is mainly operating:

i. from the Member State where the head office is established;
ii. under the Freedom to Provide Services, or
iii. under the Freedom of Establishment.

As will be demonstrated more in detail in chapter 7, insurers in the EEA can operate in different capacities:

- They can be solely active in their own Member State of origin (= the Member State where they received their prior authorisation) without any insurance activities in any other Member State;
- They can operate in one or more other Member States (the 'host Member State(s)'), without creating any new legal personality in those other Member States, under the formula of Freedom of Establishment. Making use of the Freedom of Establishment, the insurance undertaking will create a branch (without legal personality) in the host Member State and offer insurance products via this branch;
- They can also operate in one or more other Member States (again host Member State(s)) making use of the Freedom to Provide Services. Under the system of Freedom to Provide Services, an insurance undertaking will offer insurance products in the host Member State without establishing any subsidiary or branch.

In case the insurance undertaking operates under the Freedom to Provide Services, the Member State of establishment of the entity having issued the policy for a specific vehicle will be the home Member State of the insurance undertaking, which is the Member State where it received the prior authorisation. When an insurance policy is however issued by the branch of an insurance undertaking (operating via the Freedom of Establishment), the Member State of Establishment will be the host Member State, where the branch is situated.

In other words, the 'reimbursing Compensation Body' will be different depending on whether the insurance undertaking having issued the insurance policy is operating under the Freedom to Provide Services or under the Freedom of Establishment.

Example

A French resident suffers an accident in Italy, caused by a vehicle normally based in Italy. The French victim, wishing to be compensated for the damage caused, returns to France and finds out that the insurance undertaking, having issued the insurance policy covering the Italian vehicle, has not appointed a claims representative in France. The French victim presents a claim to the French Compensation Body and since the situation is not rectified in time, the French Compensation Body pays compensation for the damage suffered. Depending on the capacity under which the insurer of the Italian vehicle operates, the French Compensation Body may be reimbursed by another body:

- If the insurer received the prior insurance authorisation in Italy, the Member State of establishment of the insurer is Italy and the French Compensation Body will be able to ask reimbursement from the Italian Compensation Body;
- If the insurer received prior insurance authorisation in Slovenia and offered insurance policies in Italy under the Freedom of Establishment, the Member State of establishment is again Italy and the French Compensation Body will be able to ask reimbursement from the Italian Compensation Body;
- If the insurer received prior insurance authorisation in Slovenia and offered insurance policies in Italy under the Freedom to Provide Services, the Member State of establishment is Slovenia and the French Compensation Body will be able to seek reimbursement not from the Italian Compensation Body but from the Slovenian one.

5.6.4 *The recovery between the Compensation Body and the Guarantee Fund*

In case of accidents caused by uninsured or unidentified vehicles, the handling Compensation Body will not have any right of recourse from a Compensation Body, but the compensation paid will have to be recovered from a Guarantee Fund. Article 25 of the Motor Insurance Directive defines the route to reimbursement in the following way:

> "The compensation body shall then have a claim, on the conditions laid down in Article 24 (2):
>
> a. where the insurance undertaking cannot be identified: against the guarantee fund in the Member State where the vehicle is normally based;
> b. in the case of an unidentified vehicle: against the guarantee fund in the Member State in which the accident took place;
> c. in the case of a third-country vehicle: against the guarantee fund in the Member State in which the accident took place."

Strangely enough, the Directive does not require any specific agreement to be concluded for the application of the reimbursement procedures in the framework of

Article 25. Fortunately, the Compensation Bodies and the Guarantee Funds of the European Economic Area have always taken a holistic view and also involved the Guarantee Funds in the Agreement concluded on 29 April 2002. The Agreement thus consists of two separate parts, whereby the 'First Part' covers the reimbursement procedures between Compensation Bodies referred to in Article 24 of the MID and the 'Second Part' deals with the reimbursement procedures between Compensation Bodies and Guarantee Funds envisaged in Article 25. The two parts are very similar and require Compensation Bodies and Guarantee Funds to exchange information, regarding not only the claim received but also the content of the law applicable to the accident. The Agreement provides for sanctions if essential information is not provided (resulting in a reduction of the reimbursements to be made). The Agreement not only requires the compensation paid to the injured party to be reimbursed, but also the costs related to external services (e.g. technical, medical and legal experts). Moreover the Compensation Body that dealt with the claim will be granted a handling fee.

5.6.5 *The 'second instance recovery'*

Article 24 of the Motor Insurance Directive offers the handling Compensation Body a right to be reimbursed by the Compensation Body of the Member State in which the insurer is established. It is however not the aim of the Motor Insurance Directive that this latter 'reimbursing' Compensation Body be the final source of the compensation paid to the injured party. As explained earlier, the intervention of the handling Compensation Body in the framework of Article 24 finds its origin in a deficiency of the insurance undertaking, either by not having provided a reasoned reply in time or by not having appointed a claims representative in one or more Member States. In that regard, it is logical and legitimate that the reimbursing Compensation Body, in the insurer's Member State of establishment, will ask reimbursement from the 'deficient' insurer. After all, the insurer received premium for covering the risk of the vehicle involved in the accident and would have paid the compensation if they had respected their obligations under the Motor Insurance Directive.

The Compensation Body's right to be reimbursed by the insurer can also be deduced from recital 50 in the Directive's preamble: "This body [the Compensation Body in the insurer's Member State of establishment] is the best placed to institute proceedings for recourse against the insurance undertaking." It is indeed true that the Compensation Body in the insurer's Member State of establishment has better means to claim reimbursement from the 'deficient' insurer. How and under which modalities this right to be reimbursed should be exercised should be subject to rules of national law and is not governed by the provisions of the Motor Insurance Directive.

It is however surprising that Article 24(2) of the Directive also allows Member States to provide for subrogation of the Compensation Body in the injured party's rights against the person who caused the accident. It is difficult to imagine why the person liable should be faced with a reimbursement claim from the Compensation Body if that person had a valid policy of insurance. Such a right of recourse could in our opinion only be justified if there was a deficiency in the insurance contract, imputable to the policyholder.

In the cases envisaged in *Article 25* (unidentified vehicles and impossibility to identify the insurer within two months after the accident), the Guarantee Fund must in the first instance reimburse the Compensation Body in the injured party's Member State of residence. But the intention here is also not that the Guarantee Fund should be the final source of the compensation paid to the injured party. If the vehicle in question was not insured, the Guarantee Fund will attempt to recover the outlays from the owner, keeper and/or driver of the vehicle. If the vehicle was insured but the insurer could only be identified more than two months after the accident, recourse should be possible against the insurer. Finally, in the case of an unidentified vehicle, the possibilities of recourse will be extremely limited. Common to all these possibilities of recourse is however again that they are subject to rules of national law and are not governed by EU law. Since Article 25 states that "compensation shall be provided in accordance with the provisions of Articles 9 and 10", this should include the recourse right foreseen in Article 10. In this regard, reference is made to what is written earlier in paragraph 4.6.

5.7 Concurrent application of the Green Card system and the 4th MID

In paragraph 5.2.3 we set out that, although the Green Card system and the 4th MID protection scheme aim at two different accident scenarios, they can apply simultaneously to one and the same accident under certain circumstances.

The following situations can be envisaged:

- An accident occurs in a Member State other than the injured party's country of residence and the vehicle liable for the accident is normally based in a third Member State. The injured party can present a claim to the Green Card Bureau or correspondent of the insurer in the country of the accident since the liable vehicle originates from a different country (application of the Green Card system). But the injured party can of course also return home and invoke the protection measures offered by the 4th MID and present a claim to the insurer's claims representative in the injured party's country of residence;

Example
In the example described earlier, where a French resident suffered an accident in Italy, both the 4th MID protection system and the Green Card system could be applicable if the accident was caused by the use of a vehicle normally based in a Member State other than Italy or France. If the liable vehicle is normally based and insured in Slovenia, the injured party can present a claim to the claims representative of the Slovenian insurer in France. But they can alternatively opt for the protection of the Green Card system and present a claim to the Green Card Bureau in Italy. If the Slovenian insurer is represented by a (Green Card) correspondent in Italy, the claim would be forwarded to that correspondent in Italy. If the injured party opts for this choice, they must realise however that the handling entity in Italy cannot be compelled to communicate with the injured party in French.

- An accident occurs in Member State A, involving the driver of a vehicle normally based in Member State A and the driver of a vehicle normally based in Member State B. If the parties cannot agree on liability for the accident, the driver of the vehicle normally based in Member State A will consider the accident as a Green Card case whereas the driver of the vehicle normally based in Member State B may choose to return home and present a claim to the claims representative in Member State B of the insurer covering the vehicle normally based in Member State A. If the liability is determined as a shared liability, both parties can demand compensation for part of the damage in accordance with the relevant proportion of liability. To that end, the driver of the vehicle normally based in Member State A will probably claim compensation based on the Green Card system whereas the driver of the vehicle normally based in Member State B is likely to invoke the protection scheme created by the 4th MID;

Example
In the same accident occurred in Italy, involving an Italian and a French vehicle, both drivers may be of the opinion that the other is liable for the accident. The driver of the Italian vehicle will consider the accident to be a Green Card case and will present a claim to the Italian Green Card Bureau or to the Green Card correspondent of the French vehicle's insurer in Italy. The driver of the French vehicle, on the other hand, finding that the accident constitutes a 4th MID case is most likely to present a claim to the claims representative of the Italian vehicle's insurer in France. In that way, both systems can apply to the same accident until the liability is finally decided upon. And once the liability is determined (either based on an amicable settlement or after a court decision) and it turns out that both drivers have partly contributed to the accident

(shared liability), each claimant could invoke a different protection scheme to obtain compensation for their damage in proportion to the other party's share in the liability.

- An accident occurs in a third country, the Bureau of which participates in the Green Card system and both vehicles involved in the accident are normally based in a Member State of the EEA and benefit of cover in that third country under their MTPL policies. The injured party can either present a claim to the Green Card Bureau in the country of the accident (or to the insurer's correspondent in that country) or return home and invoke the 4th MID protection mechanism in order to present a claim to the insurer's claims representative in their country of residence.

Example
This third situation may be illustrated by way of the example of a French resident suffering an accident in Tunisia caused by a vehicle normally based in Italy. As a first possibility, the injured party can present a claim to the Tunisian Bureau. If the insurer of the Italian vehicle is represented by a Green Card correspondent in Tunisia, the Tunisian Bureau will forward the claim to that correspondent. But the injured party might also return to France and present a claim to the claims representative of the Italian vehicle's insurer. The precondition is that the Italian insurance policy gives cover in Tunisia.

The concurrent application of both protection mechanisms should not pose a problem but requires good communication and cooperation between all the entities involved in the claims handling process. The possibility for an injured party to choose between the two mechanisms makes it possible to invoke both protection mechanisms and see what claims handling entity is the more diligent in reacting and settling the claim. In the worst case, this may lead to double payments and this kind of situations must be avoided by establishing good ways of communication. Normally, the insurer of the liable vehicle should be informed of the accident, both by the claims representative and by the Green Card Bureau or correspondent. It is then the insurer's task to make sure that the instructions are such that double payments are avoided.

For the same reason, the 2002 Agreement between Compensation Bodies and Guarantee Funds (see para 5.6) provides for information exchange if the accident was caused by a vehicle normally based in a country other than that in which the accident occurred:

> "The compensation body which has received a claim for compensation [resulting from the absence of a reasoned reply or from the absence of an appointed claims representative] must immediately inform (...) the national insurers' Bureau of the place of the accident if the accident was caused by a vehicle normally based in a country other than that in which the accident occurred."

The information given to the Green Card Bureau should help to avoid double handling activities and double payments.

Example
A French resident suffers an accident in Italy caused by the use of a vehicle normally based in Slovenia. If neither the insurer nor the claims representative provides a reasoned reply within three months or the insurer of the Slovenian vehicle has not nominated a claims representative in France, the injured party can present a claim to the French Compensation Body. The latter will then, based on the 2002 Agreement, inform the insurer of the Slovenian vehicle, the Slovenian Compensation Body, the person who caused the accident (if known) as well as the Green Card Bureau of Italy. The information given to the Italian Bureau allows finding out whether the French injured party has also presented a claim to the Green Card Bureau, in which case the handling and settlement of the claim must be fine-tuned between the handling entities involved.

5.8 Protection of the visiting victim outside the European Economic Area

5.8.1 *Introduction*

As explained in paragraph 5.2.2, the protection of visitors system is, from a geographical point of view, mainly limited to the territory of the European Economic Area or EEA. Only in exceptional circumstances, the protection mechanism as established by the 4th MID can be applicable in third countries.

Taking into consideration the many compulsory rules and protection mechanisms introduced by the 4th Motor Insurance Directive (compulsory appointment of a claims representative, establishment of Information Centres and Compensation Bodies, reasoned reply procedure, sanctions, etc.), the extension of the protection of visitors' system beyond the borders of the EEA would be difficult to establish on a voluntary basis. And obviously the European legislator has no power to 'export' their rules to third countries.

Nevertheless, the Green Card Bureaux cooperating in the framework of the Council of Bureaux have attempted to install a comparable system, offering a level of protection to visiting victims based on a voluntary Agreement to be concluded between Bureaux wishing to offer this additional protection (para 5.8.2). Moreover, for damage caused by uninsured or unidentified vehicles, a second voluntary Agreement has been elaborated, providing for cooperation between Guarantee Funds of countries participating in the Green Card system (para 5.8.3).

5.8.2 Agreement between Bureaux on the protection of visitors

The aim of the first Agreement is to assist visitors who suffered damage as a result of a road traffic accident outside their state of residence but in a non-EEA state participating in the Green Card system.

The Agreement contains two separate parts, whereby Bureaux are free either to limit the scope of the Agreement to the first part (a Basic Agreement, characterised by the cooperation between Bureaux) or to apply the second, optional part as well. This second part will allow insurers (without any obligation) to nominate claims representatives.

- The purpose of the *Basic Agreement* is mainly to assist injured parties in the identification of the insurer. Moreover, the cooperation between Bureaux should enable the injured party to obtain basic information and documentation regarding the road traffic accident in question;
- If Bureaux also choose to sign the *second, optional part* of the Agreement, they agree to hand over the claims handling process to a claims representative. Any insurer whose national motor insurers' Bureau adheres to the optional Agreement has the possibility (not the obligation!) of appointing a claims representative in the other state. The claims representative will have a role comparable to the claims representatives as established by the 4th Motor Insurance Directive. In appointing a claims representative, the insurer authorises them to represent the insurer in relation to injured parties and to meet claims in full. The claims representative will handle claims subject to the instructions of the mandating insurer and in accordance with the applicable law. Contrary to the system of the 4th MID, the insurer may however revoke the claims representative's authority to handle a specific claim at any time. Moreover, having regard to the voluntary character of the Agreement, no coercive provisions or sanctions are applicable and the Compensation Body has no role to play in the protection scheme.

  If the insurer has not made use of the possibility to appoint a claims representative, this role may, subject to the insurer's approval, be assumed by the national insurers' Bureau of the injured party's country of residence or be entrusted to an agent.

5.8.3 *Agreement between Guarantee Funds on the protection of visitors*

The second Agreement attempts to provide protection to visiting victims suffering damage as a result of a road traffic accident caused by an uninsured or unidentified vehicle and occurring in a non-EEA state participating in the Green Card system. Again the Agreement consists of two parts, whereby Guarantee Funds are free to sign either just the first or both parts.

- The first part or *basic level* again limits the support given to the visiting victim to exchanges of information and documentation. This information and documentation relates to the accident caused but will also contain particulars regarding the applicable law and the intervention modalities of the Guarantee Fund;
- If the second part or *optional level* is also signed, the Guarantee Fund in the victim's country of residence has the right to initiate claims handling activities such as assessing the extent of damage and to negotiate a settlement with the victim, based on instructions from the Guarantee Fund in the country of the accident. The compensation is however paid to the victim by the Guarantee Fund in the country of the accident and not by the Guarantee Fund in the victim's country of residence.

5.9 The application of the 4TH MID in case of insolvency of the insurer

In paragraph 4.3.6, we already explained that the codified Motor Insurance Directive of 2009 does not provide for any protection of injured parties suffering damage as a result of a road traffic accident caused by the use of a vehicle insured with an insurer in state of insolvency. This scenario does not belong to the mandatory cases of intervention imposed by the Directive on Guarantee Funds.

Since the insolvency of MTPL insurers presents an important risk for both injured parties and policyholders, however, many Member States have by way of national legislation provided for the intervention of the Guarantee Fund or another entity in the case of insolvency of an MTPL insurer. As we have explained in paragraph 4.3.6, these national protection mechanisms can vary widely both in terms of conditions for intervention and in terms of amounts covered.
Since the Motor Insurance Directive does not provide for the intervention of Guarantee Funds in the case of insolvency of an MTPL insurer, *a fortiori* nothing is foreseen in case of insolvency in a cross-border context.

Given that national legislation often makes Guarantee Funds competent to intervene for cases of insolvency, the Council of Bureaux has supported the conclusion of a specific agreement between Compensation Bodies and Guarantee Funds in order to offer a certain form of protection. This is however again a voluntary agreement, in which only those Compensation Bodies and Guarantee Funds able and willing to offer this additional protection to road traffic victims participate.

On 6 November 2008, the Compensation Bodies and Guarantee Funds of 22 different Member States signed in Rome the *Agreement between Compensation Bodies and Guarantee Funds in the event of the insolvency of an insurance undertaking providing civil liability motor insurance in the single market*. The Compensation Body and Guarantee Fund of a 23rd Member State joined two years later in 2010.

The Agreement more or less transposes the protection of visitors system set up by the 4th Directive to cases of insolvency. When a victim suffers damage as a result of a road traffic accident in a Member State other than their country of residence and caused by the use of a vehicle insured with an MTPL insurer in a state of insolvency, the injured party will be able to address a claim to the Compensation Body in their own country of residence. That Compensation Body will inform the Guarantee Fund in the Member State where the accident occurred and will ask for claims handling instructions based on the rules applicable in the country of the accident. After having compensated the injured party, the Compensation Body will be reimbursed by the Guarantee Fund of the Member State in which the accident occurred. The scope of the Agreement is however limited to accidents caused by the use of vehicles that are normally based in the Member State where the accident occurred. When an injured party, resident in Member State A, is injured as a result of an accident in Member State B, caused by the use of a vehicle insured with an insolvent insurer, the injured party will only have access to compensation in Member State A if (*i*) both the Compensation Bodies and Guarantee Funds of Member States A and B are signatories to the Agreement and (*ii*) the vehicle the use of which caused the accident is normally based in Member State B.

Moreover, the Agreement operates on a reciprocal basis, which means that Compensation Bodies and Guarantee Funds signing the Agreement must be willing to operate both in the capacity of Compensation Body, providing support to injured parties, and in the capacity of (debtor) Guarantee Fund responsible for cases of insolvency and reimbursing the Compensation Body that has indemnified an injured party.

As set out in paragraph 4.3.6, the European Commission's proposal for a new Motor Insurance Directive (see also para 3.5.1) provides for an obligation on all Member States to set up or authorise a body (the Guarantee Fund or another entity) to compensate injured parties for damage caused by a vehicle insured with an insurance undertaking which is subject to bankruptcy or winding up proceedings. In that way, a protection mechanism will exist in each Member State to safeguard the compensation of injured parties in case of damage caused by the use of a vehicle insured with an insolvent insurer. Moreover, the body will be competent to provide compensation, whether the vehicle in question is normally based in the body's Member State or in any other Member State. In case of cross-border elements, the proposal provides for a reimbursement mechanism. If the Commission's proposal is adopted as a new Directive by the Council of the European Union and the European Parliament, the Agreement signed between Compensation Bodies and Guarantee Funds in 2008 will in its present form most probably become redundant and may be terminated. This will however depend on the exact provisions as they will finally appear once the new Directive is adopted. One may moreover presume that a new Agreement, containing operational rules for the exercise of the reimbursement procedure between the respective bodies, is to be concluded.

6 The protection of the policyholder, liable and injured party under the Directive

6.1 Introduction

The previous chapters described the structures which have been developed to facilitate the settlement of cross-border road traffic accidents: Green Card Bureaux, nominated correspondents, Guarantee Funds, Compensation Bodies and claims representatives. In chapter 2, dealing with the historical development of the protection of cross-border road traffic victims, we already explained that as early as 1972, MTPL insurance became compulsory in the then six Member States of the European Economic Community, without however harmonising the content of the compulsory insurance policy. Since 1972, more specifically since the 2nd Directive of 1983, the European legislator has increasingly expanded his influence on the content of the cover under the insurance policy and of the protection provided by specifically the Guarantee Funds.

In this chapter we will discuss the mandatory cover of the MTPL policy under the Directive. We will also describe the differences between the cover under a policy of insurance and the protection provided by the Bureaux and Guarantee Funds.

An important remark has to be made directly at the beginning of this chapter: the Directive provides for *minimum harmonisation*. That implies that reading the Directive will not automatically lead to understanding the various national legal systems on compulsory motor insurance: national legislators are permitted to provide for more protection than guaranteed by the Directive – and they more often than not use that room for manoeuvring. This can be most clearly demonstrated by looking at the amounts of cover: many Member States provide for higher amounts, even unlimited cover, than prescribed by the Directive. The same can be said with regard to the protection of the Guarantee Funds, which may be given a subsidiary role – as a sort of safety net of last resort – whereas in a number of countries their responsibility is much wider, providing more protection to the victims of road accidents. In the various paragraphs of this chapter we will go into further detail.

The structure of this part of the book is as follows: in paragraph 6.2 we will deal with the (minimum) content of the cover under the insurance policy. Paragraph 6.3 will be devoted to aspects of procedure: which rules have to be followed by the various parties – insurance undertakings, Bureaux, claims representatives, Guarantee Funds and Compensation Bodies – when handling and settling claims from victims and injured parties. Although not strictly a matter of procedure, the Information Centre will also be discussed in paragraph 6.3. In paragraph 6.4 we will then describe the differences between the protection offered under the policy and by the Bureaux respectively the Guarantee Funds. Where appropriate we will also discuss the various proposals for a new Directive presented by the European Commission in its document COM(2018) 336 final, published on 24 May 2018 and the amendments proposed by European Parliament on the Commission Proposal.[1,2]

6.2 Cover under the motor third party liability policy

6.2.1 General remarks

In this paragraph we will discuss the content of the compulsory MTPL policy as regulated by the Directive: the types of risk to be covered; in which countries the policy must be valid; the types of damage that the insurer must compensate for, and to which persons; the amounts to be insured; and the legal and policy restrictions and exclusions that the insurance company can rely on in their relationship with insured or third parties.

As mentioned before the Directive provides for minimal harmonisation: national legislation may therefore deviate from the Directive, provided the parties protected by the Directive (insured persons and victims/injured parties) have at least the protection guaranteed by the Directive. In this paragraph several examples of such deviation will be described.

1. Proposal for a Directive of the European Parliament and the Council amending Directive 2009/103/EC of the European Parliament and the Council of 16 September 2009 relating to insurance against civil liability in respect of the use of motor vehicles, and the enforcement of the obligation to ensure against such liability.
2. Amendments adopted by the European Parliament on 13 February 2019 on the proposal for a directive of the European Parliament and of the Council amending Directive 2009/103/EC of the European Parliament and the Council of 16 September 2009 relating to insurance against civil liability in respect of the use of motor vehicles, and the enforcement of the obligation to ensure against such liability (COM(2018)0336 – C8-0211/2018 – 2018/0168(COD)).

6.2.2 *The goals of the Directive*

Before discussing the details of the Directive it is useful to describe its goals. Two of the recitals of the Directive's preamble are worth quoting in this context:

> "(2) Insurance against civil liability in respect of the use of motor vehicles (motor insurance) is of special importance for European citizens, whether they are policyholders or victims of an accident. It is also a major concern for insurance undertakings as it constitutes an important part of non-life insurance business in the Community. Motor insurance also has an impact on the free movement of persons and vehicles. It should therefore be a key objective of Community action in the field of financial services to reinforce and consolidate the internal market in motor insurance."

> "(20) Motor vehicle accident victims should be guaranteed comparable treatment irrespective of where in the Community accidents occur."

A dual purpose therefore: facilitating free movement of persons and goods and the guarantee of a 'comparable treatment' of victims of accidents irrespective of the Member State of accident. The free movement of persons and goods follows directly from the EU Treaties. It is one of the elements of the Single Market.

The second goal, the equal treatment of victims, is frequently used by the Court of Justice of the European Union (CJEU) as part of the motivation of their decisions.

CJEU, Judgment of 28 March 1996, *Ruiz Bernáldez*, C-129/94, EU:C:1996:143, para 13; EFTA Court, Advisory Opinion of 17 November 1999, *Storebrand Skadeforsikring*, E-01/99, para 32; CJEU, Judgment of 14 September 2000, *Mendes Ferreira and Delgado Correia Ferreira*, C-348/98, EU:C:2000:442, para 24; EFTA Court, Judgment of 14 June 2001, *Halla Helgadóttir*, E-07/00, para 31; CJEU, Judgment of 30 June 2005, *Candolin a.o.*, C-537/03, EU:C:2005:417, para 17; EFTA Court, Judgment of 20 June 2008, *Nguyen*, E-08/07, para 23; CJEU, Judgment of 17 March 2011, *Carvalho Ferreira Santos*, C-484/09, EU:C:2011:158, para 24; CJEU, Judgment of 9 June 2011, *Ambrósio Lavrador and Olival Ferreira Bonifácio*, C-409/09, EU:C:2011:371, para 23; CJEU, Judgment of 1 December 2011, *Churchill Insurance Company and Evans*, C-442/10, EU:C:2011:799, para 27; CJEU, Judgment of 23 October 2012, *Marques Almeida*, C-300/10, EU:C:2012:656, para 26; CJEU, Judgment of 21 March 2013, *Freitas a.o.*, C-96/12, EU:C:2013:199, para 23; CJEU, Judgment of 21 March 2013, *Gomes Oliveira*, C-362/11, EU:C:2013:184, para 17; CJEU, Judgment of 21 March 2013, *Rodrigues Esteves*, C-486/11, EU:C:2013:188, para 21; CJEU, Judgment of 21 March 2013, *Pendão Lapa Costa Ferreira and Pendão Lapa Ferreira*, C-229/10, EU:C:2013:179, para 25; CJEU, Judgment of 24 October 2013, *Haasová*, C-22/12, EU:C:2013:692, para 37; CJEU, Judgment of 23 January 2014, *Petillo*, C-371/12, EU:C:2014:26, para 26; CJEU, Judgment of 4 September 2014, *Vnuk*, C-162/13, EU:C:2014:2146, para 50; CJEU, Judgment of 20 July

2017, *Fidelidade-Companhia de Seguros*, C-287/16, EU:C:2017:575, para 22; CJEU, Judgment of 7 September 2017, *Neto de Sousa*, C-506/16, EU:C:2017:642, para 26; CJEU, Judgment of 14 September 2017, *Delgado Mendes*, C-503/16, EU:C:2017:681, para 35; CJEU, Judgment of 28 November 2017, *Rodrigues de Andrade*, C-514/16, EU:C:2017:908, para 35; CJEU, Judgment of 20 December 2017, *Núñez Torreiro*, C-334/16, EU:C:2017:1007, para 25.

'Comparable treatment' however is to a large extent an illusion, since the European Union is not competent in the field of law on liability and damage compensation. Moreover, the large disparities in terms of economic development in the EU, and as a consequence, the differences in compensation paid to injured parties also contribute to the diversification.[3]

6.2.3 *The concept of 'motor vehicle'; trailers*

The Directive is only applicable to motor vehicles, which are defined in Article 1 as "any motor vehicle intended for travel on land and propelled by mechanical power, but not running on rails, and any trailer, whether or not coupled."

This definition raises a number of questions, the first of which is whether a vehicle must be intended for transport of persons or goods. Examples of motorised equipment with other purposes are motorised lawn mowers and some types of construction machinery, such as pile drivers.

Then there is the question of vehicles with an auxiliary engine, such as some electric bicycles with an engine that only works as long as the cyclist moves the pedals. In our opinion this type of vehicle is a motor vehicle too, since the additional energy of the electric motor gives (or can give) the bicycle speed. This interpretation is apparently shared by the Dutch legislator, having explicitly exempted such bicycles ('e-bikes') from compulsory insurance under Article 5(1) of the Directive, an exemption that wouldn't make much sense if an e-bike is not a motor vehicle.

In their proposal for a new Directive the European Commission aims to codify recent jurisprudence of the European Court. This jurisprudence will be discussed in detail in the following paragraph when dealing with the question whether a vehicle should be used in traffic in order to fall within the scope of the Directive, The proposed new Article 1(1), point (1a) would read as follows:

3. In two EFTA cases the Court of the European Free Trade Association seems however to open the possibility to harmonise liability law as well as the law on MTPL insurance. In *Storebrand Skadeforsikring* and in *Halla Helgadóttir* the Court accepted the possibility that certain provisions in liability law might be incompatible with the Directive. See further para 6.2.13.12.

> "'use of a vehicle' means any use of such vehicle, *intended normally to serve as a means of transport*, that is consistent with the normal function of that vehicle, irrespective of the vehicle's characteristics and irrespective of the terrain on which the motor vehicle is used and of *whether it is stationary or in motion* [italics inserted by the authors]."

In this paragraph we will focus on the words in italics.[4] These words seem to confirm that the function as a means of transport is part of the concept of 'motor vehicle' in the context of the Directive. It is however not an essential element that the vehicle is in motion; a stationary vehicle which is intended to function as a means of transport is still a motor vehicle.[5]

The European Parliament showed itself not content with this modification, as is demonstrated by the following amendment:

> "'use of a vehicle' means any use of a vehicle in traffic that is consistent with the vehicle's function as a means of transport *at the time of the accident* [italics by the authors], irrespective of the vehicle's characteristics and irrespective of the terrain on which the motor vehicle is used and of whether it is stationary or in motion."

Whereas in the European Commission's definition a vehicle which is intended to serve as a means of transport will still be a motor vehicle when it is used for other purposes, in the approach of the European Parliament the use of the vehicle as a means of transport at the time of the accident is an essential part of the definition. A movable crane or a dragline lifting objects or dragging soil will according to the Commission still fall within the scope of the Directive, whereas in the view of Parliament it would not.

The definition of the European Parliament seems to be a more accurate codification of the case law of the European Court, more specifically the *Rodrigues de Andrade* decision.[6] In that decision the decisive factor was whether a (motor) vehicle was *at the time of the accident* used as a machine to carry out work.

---

4. Other elements of the proposed new wording will be discussed in paragraph 6.2.4, which deals with the question whether a vehicle should have to be used in traffic or not.
5. See also the decision of the European Court of Justice in the Linea Directa Aseguradora case (CJEU, Judgment of 20 June 2019, (*Linea Directa Aseguradora*), C-100/18, EU:C:2019:517). In this case the issue is whether damage caused by a vehicle that spontaneously caught fire when stationed for more than 24 hours in a private garage, falls within the scope of the MID. The Court, following the opinion of the Advocate-General, ruled that the codified Motor Insurance Directive "must be interpreted as meaning that a situation such as that at issue in the main proceedings, in which a vehicle parked in a private garage of a building, used in accordance with its function as a means of transport, has caught fire, giving rise to a fire which originated in the electrical circuit of that vehicle and caused damage to that building, even though that vehicle has not been moved for more than 24 hours before the fire occurred, falls within the concept of 'use of vehicles' referred to in that provision."
6. CJEU, Judgment of 28 November 2017, *Rodrigues de Andrade*, C-514/16, EU:C:2017:908; see para 6.2.4.

European Parliament proposes to amend the Proposal for a Directive modifying the codified Directive by excluding from the scope of the Directive vehicles that do not require EU type-approval. The line of thought is that vehicles that are not subject to type-approval do not have the potential to cause significant damage in a cross-border situation. The amendment especially has in mind electric bikes and Segways since such vehicles

> "are smaller and are therefore less likely to cause significant damage to persons or property than others. It would be disproportionate and not future proof to include them in the scope of Directive 2009/103/EC, as it would impose an obligation to have an expensive and excessive insurance cover for these vehicles."[7]

This seems to us a debatable statement. We fail to see why an electric bicycle, which easily reaches speeds up to 25 km/h, is likely to cause less damage than a moped or a small scooter. The same can be said of Segways, which in addition are frequently used in pedestrian areas. The argument that bringing such vehicles under the scope of the Directive would discourage innovation is questionable: should victim protection really be sacrificed to innovation? A strange argument in the context of a Directive the aim of which is victim protection. And if it would be true that a certain type of vehicle is less 'dangerous' than others and therefore less likely to cause serious damage, then the MTPL premium will reflect such lower amounts of damage and the policy would as a consequence not be 'expensive and excessive'.

In a rather curious Recital 3b the Report suggests that Member States may require such vehicles to be mandatorily covered by MTPL insurance:

> "However, it is important to allow Member States to decide at national level the appropriate level of protection of parties potentially injured by vehicles other than those subject to EU type-approval. Therefore, it is important that Member States are allowed to maintain or introduce new mandatory provisions covering the protection of users of these other types of vehicles in order to protect potential injured parties from a traffic accident. Where a Member State choses to require such insurance coverage in the form of compulsory insurance, it should take into account the likelihood that a vehicle might be used in a cross-border situation and the need for protection of potential injured parties in another Member State."

It remains unclear how in the proposal victims of cross-border accidents can be adequately protected. Moreover it seems to us that the proposal regarding light vehicles is completely superfluous: Article 5(2) of the codified Directive already offers the possibility to exclude vehicles from the scope of the Directive and also protects cross-border victims. See para 6.2.6.

7. Proposal for a new Recital 3a.

The most important (and perhaps in some Member States most controversial) aspect however is the question of cover for trailers. In our opinion and based on the wording of the Directive, it goes without saying that trailers have to be covered by compulsory insurance, whether they are coupled to a towing vehicle or not. Although various different solutions are imaginable, varying from separate cover for the trailer to cover under the policy of the towing vehicle, a separate policy for the trailer seems to be the most obvious and practical solution. The cover must after all also be provided if the trailer is not or no longer attached to a towing vehicle and it will not always be possible to identify the last towing vehicle of an abandoned trailer. Moreover in most jurisdictions trailers, specifically over a certain weight, have a separate registration number, attached to the rear of the vehicle. It frequently happens that at the time of an accident only the registration number of the trailer is taken down in the accident statement or the police report. It is an open question whether such a combination of towing vehicle and trailer, if the trailer is not covered under a specific policy, is then to be regarded as uninsured or – in view of the unknown identity of the last towing vehicle – as unidentified.

The approach of a separate MTPL policy for trailers is not however shared by all countries. Neither the Netherlands nor the UK require the owner of a trailer to hold a separate policy for the vehicle, nor does EEA State Norway. This leads to various problems in the context of cross-border claims handling.

European Parliament, in an amendment to the Proposal for a new Directive by the European Commission, introduces a new Article 15a, reading as follows:

> "Liability in case of an accident involving a trailer towed by a powered vehicle.
> In case of an accident caused by a set of vehicles consisting of a trailer towed by a powered vehicle, the injured party shall be compensated by the undertaking that insured the trailer, where:
> - separate third party liabilities were taken out; and
> - the trailer can be identified, but the powered vehicle that towed it cannot be identified.
>
> The undertaking compensating the injured party in this case shall have a right of recourse to the undertaking that insured the towing vehicle if this is provided for under national law."

The lack of precision in this proposal is obvious. Apart from the fact that the condition for the compensation by the insurer of the trailer seems to be that the powered vehicle cannot be identified and that it is incomprehensible how in that case the insurer of the trailer can take recourse against the insurer of the powered vehicle, there is a fundamental mix-up of the concepts of liability and insurance. One of the main problems in the context of trailers is the fact that in some jurisdictions trailers do not have to be separately insured and that problem will not be resolved by the amendment.

6.2.4 *Use of the vehicle in traffic?*

A question which for a long time has escaped attention is the following: is the policy required to cover liability only when the vehicle is used in traffic, or also in other situations, such as the use as a machine? And if not, does 'traffic' also include the use of the vehicle on private property or on terrain that does not qualify as a (private or public) road? Only in recent years have these questions been the subject of case law by the Court of Justice of the European Union (CJEU).

The issue is complicated by the fact that various language versions of the Directive seem to differ. The title of the Directive reads differently in the equally authentic language versions of the Directive and that also has relevance for the question what is to be understood by the 'use of the vehicle'. In the French text reference is made to the vehicle in use in traffic (*'circulation'*). This is also the case in the Dutch, the Italian, the Spanish and the Portuguese languages, which can be regarded as derived from the original French wording. The English text does not refer to the notion of traffic, nor does the German text, which does not even refer to *the use* of the vehicle.[8] This obviously raises questions with respect to accidents where a vehicle is not used as a means of transport, or when a vehicle is operated in an area where traffic is not allowed or where the public is not admitted.

In a sense it is surprising that it took the legal practice so long to bring the question of cover in case of accidents outside classic traffic situations before the courts but it was not until 2013 that a Slovenian case, involving Mr Vnuk, reached the European Court of Justice.[9]

> Bales of hay were being stored in the loft of a barn. A tractor to which a trailer was attached was reversing in the courtyard of the farm in order to position the trailer in that barn, and it struck the ladder on which Mr Vnuk had climbed, causing his fall with bodily injuries as a consequence.

---

8. The fact that the EU recognises as many as 24 languages spoken in the Member States as official languages and that all official texts such as directives and regulations will have to be translated into each of these languages, is a complicating factor in the legislative process. Obviously the various language versions will be based on two or three 'ground texts'. Minor or even not so minor differences may easily develop and in the process of the further translation into the remaining official languages even be enlarged. The Court then argues that all languages are equally authentic. Examples of this method of argumentation can be found in the *Vnuk* decision, and – in the context of Regulation 44/2001 – in CJEU, Judgment of 13 December 2007, *FBTO Schadeverzekeringen*, C-463/06, EU:C:2007:792. The fact that English was not an official language of the then EEC when the 1st Directive was written and that the difference with other language versions may simply have been a wrong translation, apparently played no role in the analysis of the Court in the *Vnuk* case, which will be discussed below.
9. CJEU, Judgment of 4 September 2014, *Vnuk*, C-162/13, EU:C:2014:2146.

The questions to which this case may give cause can be related to the fact that 1) the manoeuvre of the tractor was not a normal traffic operation and 2) the barn was not a public road but private property. The latter question was however already decided by the relevant Slovenian case law, but the first question was put before the European Court. In the process the Court also gave an opinion as to the second question. This decision of the Court raised much concern in the motor insurance world.

The Court held that

> "Article 3 (1) of Council Directive 72/166/EEC of 24 April 1972 on the approximation of the laws of Member States relating to insurance against civil liability in respect of the use of motor vehicles, and to the enforcement of the obligation to insure against such liability must be interpreted as meaning that the concept of 'use of vehicles' in that article covers any use of a vehicle that is consistent with the normal function of that vehicle. That concept may therefore cover the manoeuvre of a tractor in the courtyard of a farm in order to bring the trailer attached to that tractor into a barn, as in the case in the main proceedings, which is a matter for the referring court to determine."

The decision raised questions on the consequences of the scope of motor insurance policies. The motor vehicles category covers a range of very different machines, from electric bicycles to heavy construction machinery, the principal purpose of which is not to move from A to B, but to build, dig or lift. Any of these operations may cause damage (sometimes substantial) and can be regarded as *'use of a vehicle that is consistent with the normal function of that vehicle'*. But in many countries these activities and the consequent damage is covered not under the MTPL policy but under a commercial liability policy of the owner or user, or under a construction-all-risk policy (CAR policy). The *Vnuk* decision seemed to shift the cover from that type of policy to the MTPL market.

Other concerns related to the opinion of the Court that accidents on private property also fall within the scope of the comprehensive MTPL cover and – a particular concern for the UK – that activities such as racing competitions would also have to be covered.

A decision of the Court in 2017 brought further clarification. In *Rodrigues de Andrade* the Court in one respect backtracked on its *Vnuk* judgment. The facts were as follows:

> Mrs Alves, an employee in the vineyard of Mr and Mrs Rodrigues de Andrade, was applying herbicide to the vines in their vineyard on land that was on a slope and terraced.

> The herbicide was inside a drum with a spraying device mounted on the back part of an agricultural tractor and suspended therefrom. The tractor in question was stationary, on a flat track, but with the engine running to drive the herbicide spray pump. The weight of the tractor, the vibrations produced by the engine and by the spray pump and the movement, including by Mrs Alves, of the herbicide hose leading from the drum, together with the heavy rainfall that day, caused a landslip which carried the tractor away. The tractor in question fell down the terraces and overturned, reaching the four workers who were applying herbicide to the vines below. Mrs Alves was hit and crushed by the tractor in question, and died as a result.

The Court held that

> "Article 3 (1) of Council Directive 72/166/EEC of 24 April 1972 on the approximation of the laws of the Member States relating to insurance against civil liability in respect of the use of motor vehicles, and to the enforcement of the obligation to insure against such liability, must be interpreted as meaning that the concept of 'use of vehicles', referred to in that provision, does not cover a situation in which an agricultural tractor has been involved in an accident when its principal function, at the time of that accident, was not to serve as a means of transport but to generate, as a machine for carrying out work, the motive power necessary to drive the pump of a herbicide sprayer."[10]

More particularly, the difference between the use of a vehicle 'as a means of transport' and 'as a machine for carrying out work' is important: the difference implies that the scope of MTPL insurance should be limited to that which it is conceived for. Moreover, the words 'at the time of the accident' invites consideration of the real factual circumstances of the machine as it was used at the very moment when it caused damage.

In another decision in 2017, in the *Núñez Torreiro* case, the Court shed some light on the question of the use of a motor vehicle on terrain that is not meant for traffic.[11] The facts were as follows:

> Mr Núñez Torreiro, an officer in the Spanish army, was taking part in night-time military manoeuvres at a military exercise area in Chinchilla (Spain), when the all-terrain military vehicle fitted with 'Anibal' wheels, in which he was a passenger, a vehicle for which compulsory insurance cover was provided by AIG, overturned, causing him various injuries. The vehicle was travelling not in an area for wheeled vehicles, but in an area for tracked vehicles.

10. CJEU, Judgment of 28 November 2017, *Rodrigues de Andrade*, C-514/16, EU:C:2017:908.
11. CJEU, Judgment of 20 December 2017, *Núñez Torreiro*, C-334/16, EU:C:2017:1007.

The Court held that

> "(t)he first paragraph of Article 3 of Directive 2009/103/EC of the European Parliament and of the Council of 16 September 2009 relating to insurance against civil liability in respect of the use of motor vehicles, and the enforcement of the obligation to insure against such liability, must be interpreted as precluding national legislation, such as that at issue in the main proceedings, which makes it possible to exclude from compulsory insurance cover injuries and damage that result from the driving of motor vehicles on roads or terrain that are not 'suitable for use by motor vehicles', with the exception of roads or terrain which, although not suitable for that purpose, are nonetheless 'ordinarily so used'."

Would these decisions mean that *Vnuk* has been overruled entirely? Not in our opinion. It can after all be debated whether the tractor in the *Vnuk* case was used as a means of transport or not, since it was used to reposition a trailer and it was moving. The decision that cover would also have to be provided for accidents on private property, such as in the *Vnuk* case, has also been upheld. And in *Núñez Torreiro* the Court decided that the cover under the policy cannot be limited to roads or terrain suitable for use by motor vehicles. On the other hand, the concern that the use of a motor vehicle as a means of carrying out work, was to a certain extent taken away by the *Rodrigues de Andrade* decision.

In its *BTA vs BAN* decision the Court further clarified that the opening of a passenger door is consistent with the concept of the 'use of a vehicle as a means of transport'.[12]

In the proposal for a new Directive, amending the codified Directive, the Commission addressed the issues raised by the *Vnuk, Rodrigues de Andrade* and *Núñez Torreiro* case law.[13] The intention of the Commission was to codify the decisions of the Court in the Directive. In our opinion, the Commission has only partly succeeded in translating the three decisions. In the proposal, a new provision 1a is inserted in Article 1 which gives a definition to the notion 'use of a vehicle' and reads as follows:

> "1a. 'use of a vehicle' means any use of such vehicle, intended normally to serve as a means of transport, that is consistent with the normal function of that vehicle, irrespective of the vehicle's characteristics and irrespective of the terrain on which the motor vehicle is used and of whether it is stationary or in motion."

12. CJEU, Judgment of 15 November 2018, *BTA Baltic Insurance Company*, C-648/17, EU:C:2018:917.
13. See also *supra*, para 6.2.3.

As already observed in paragraph 6.2.3 in the context of the definition of 'motor vehicle', this is in our opinion an inadequate codification of the case law of the European Court: in *Rodrigues de Andrade* the decisive factor was whether a (motor) vehicle was *at the time of the accident* used as a machine to carry out work. In the proposal for a Directive the criterion is whether a machine or piece of equipment is *normally intended* to be used as a means of transport (whatever that may mean).

This criticism also seems to be shared by European Parliament in its Report on the proposal for a Directive, since according to their amendment the new wording of Article 1(1), point 1 limits the scope of 'motor vehicle' to the use of the vehicle as a means of transport *at the time of the accident*.
In addition in a new paragraph in Article 3 of the codified Directive, Parliament tries to clarify the situation further:

> "Member States shall ensure that when a vehicle is required to hold insurance pursuant to the first paragraph, the insurance is also valid and covers injured parties in the case of accidents occurring
>
> a. when the vehicle is in traffic and not being used in accordance with its primary function; and
>
> b. outside the use of the vehicle in traffic.
>
> Member States may adopt limitations on insurance coverage in respect of the use outside the use of the vehicle in traffic as referred to in point (b) of the fifth paragraph. This provision shall be used as an exception and only when necessary, where Member States consider that such coverage would go beyond what can be reasonably expected from a motor insurance. This provision may never be used to circumvent the principles and rules set out in this Directive."

Although the new Article is in our opinion rather confusing, it seems to be the intention that all motor vehicles must be insured for accidents whether in traffic or not and – if used in traffic – also when they are not used in accordance with their primary function. One may think of a dragline machine, the primary function of which is to move soil: but when it is moving from A to B – and therefore used in traffic, it must be covered by the insurance policy.
But Member States may limit the cover when a vehicle is used outside traffic, when such coverage "would go beyond what can be reasonably expected from a motor insurance."
Whose expectations have to be taken into consideration (the insurer, the policyholder, the injured party or the public in general) remains unclear and how the cover under the policy can be restricted without circumventing the principles and rules set out in this Directive is also enigmatic.
If read in connection with the proposed recitals (3e) and (3f), the exact meaning of the new paragraph becomes even more obscure:

> "(3e) 'Use of a vehicle in traffic should include the use of a vehicle in circulation on public and private roadways. This could include all driveways, parking lots or any other equivalent areas on private terrain which are accessible by the general public. The use of a vehicle in a closed area, where no access is possible by the general public, should not be considered to be use of a vehicle in traffic. Nonetheless, when a vehicle is used in traffic at any point and is therefore subject to a compulsory insurance requirement, Member States should ensure that the vehicle is covered by an insurance policy that includes potential injured parties, during the period of the contract, regardless of whether the vehicle is used in traffic or not at the time of the accident, except where the vehicle is used in a motorsports event. Member States should be able to limit non-traffic related insurance cover where there is no reasonable expectation of cover, as is the case of a tractor involved in an accident of which the primary function, at that time, was not to serve as a means of transport, but to generate, as a machine for carrying out work, the motive power necessary to function.
> (3f) Use of a vehicle exclusively in non-traffic situations should be excluded from the scope of Directive 2009/103/EC. Moreover, Member States should not require insurance cover for vehicles which are permanently or temporarily de-registered due to their inability to be used as a means of transport, because, for example, they are in a museum, they are undergoing restoration or they have not been used for an extended period of time for another reason, such as seasonal use."

What is to be understood by 'use in traffic'? The concept is obviously wider than the use in public roads, since accidents on private roads, as well as driveways and parking lots should also be covered. The essential element seems to be the accessibility of the terrain by 'the general public'.

Our first observation is that the area should be *inaccessible* to the general public. It seems not to be sufficient that access is merely not allowed. That limits the effect of this apparent restriction of the scope of the Directive, since few areas are so thoroughly closed off that the public cannot have access. We venture to conclude that most private property thus falls within the scope of the proposed wording of the Directive, including commercial and industrial areas.

The last sentence of the Recital (3e) refers to the case law of the European Court, more specifically *Rodrigues de Andrade*.

Whatever the intentions of Parliament may have been, their amendments to the recitals of the MID are difficult to bring in line with the proposal for a new Article 1a:

> "'Use of vehicle' means any use of a vehicle in traffic that is consistent with the vehicle's function as a means of transport at the time of the accident, irrespective of the vehicle's characteristics and irrespective of the terrain on which the motor vehicle is used and of whether it is stationary or in motion."

The amendment by Parliament also addresses the concerns of the motor sports branch. A new paragraph is inserted in Article 2:

> "This Directive shall not apply to vehicles that are intended exclusively for use in the context of participation in a competitive sport activity, or in related sport activities, within a closed area."

It is remarkable that the Directive should not apply to vehicles *exclusively intended* for use in the context of motor sports. That is not entirely consistent with the proposed new wording of Article 1(1), point (1). The criterion in that context is whether the vehicle was used as a means of transport *at the time of the accident*. A racing car used outside the closed area would therefore not have to be covered by insurance.
Also interesting is Recital (3f). Member States "should not require" insurance cover for vehicles which are permanently or temporarily de-registered due to their inability to be used as a means of transport. However the vehicles in the examples are – with the exception perhaps of a vehicle in restoration – not incapable of being used as a means of transport.

Not all questions and concerns that were raised by the *Vnuk* and subsequent decisions, are therefore resolved – neither in the Commission text nor by the amendments by Parliament – and one can only hope that the proposals will be modified to be more practical.

A special case of the use of a vehicle is the subject of an amendment of European Parliament on the Proposals by the European Commission for a new Directive. The amendment proposes to include in the 'cover' by the Guarantee Funds:

> "(...) incidents where a motor vehicle is used as a weapon to commit a violent crime or terrorist act."

We assume that the amendment will only be relevant in those situations where the vehicle is uninsured or – if insured – when cover under the policy of insurance would not be valid or damage caused intentionally can be excluded from cover.

6.2.5 *The obligation to insure, the normally based concept and dispatched vehicles*

6.2.5.1 *General remarks*

Two concepts are relevant in the context of compulsory motor insurance: the Member State in which the risk is situated and the Member State where a vehicle is normally based. Both are usually linked.

According to Article 13(13) Solvency II the risk relating to a vehicle (of any type and therefore also of motor vehicles) is situated in the Member State of its registration.[14] If that Member State imposes an obligation to insure such a vehicle, the contents of such compulsory cover are defined by the legislation of that Member State.

The codified Motor Insurance Directive imposes an obligation on each Member State to take all appropriate measures to ensure that civil liability in respect of the use of vehicles normally based in its territory is covered by insurance and therefore the legislation of that Member State governs the (minimum) content of that cover.

Usually the Member State of the risk and the Member State in whose territory a vehicle is normally based are identical. As we will see however, in specific circumstances each notion may refer to a different Member State.

6.2.5.2 *The 'normally based' concept*

a) The concept of the territory of the Member State where according to the Internal Regulations a vehicle is normally based has already been discussed in paragraph 3.5.5. The Directive in its Article 1(4) gives the following definition:

> "'territory in which the vehicle is normally based' means:
> a. the territory of the State of which the vehicle bears a registration plate, irrespective of whether the plate is permanent or temporary; or
> b. in cases where no registration is required for a type of vehicle but the vehicle bears an insurance plate, or a distinguishing sign analogous to the registration plate, the territory of the State in which the insurance plate or the sign is issued; or
> c. in cases where neither a registration plate nor an insurance plate nor a distinguishing sign is required for certain types of vehicle, the territory of the State in which the person who has custody of the vehicle is permanently resident; or
> d. in cases where the vehicle does not bear any registration plate or bears a registration plate which does not correspond or no longer corresponds to the vehicle and has been involved in an accident, the territory of the State in which the accident took place, for the purpose of settling the claim as provided for in the first indent of Article 2(a) or in Article 10."

It is to be emphasised that the Directive refers to the registration *plate*, rather than to the *registration* as such of the vehicle, as did the 1st Directive. The background of this modification of the definition, which was introduced in the 2nd Directive, was to avoid that a check on the validity of the Green Card would be replaced by a necessary verification of the registration of the vehicle.[15]

b) The Directive concerns not only registered vehicles, but also vehicles which bear insurance or other distinguishing plates or even are not required to bear a

---

14. Directive 2009/138/EC of the European Parliament and of the Council of 25 November 2009 on the taking-up and pursuit of the business of Insurance and Reinsurance (Solvency II) (recast), OJ L 335 of 17.12.2009, p. 1.
15. See CJEU, Judgment of 9 February 1984, *Gambetta*, C-344/82, EU:C:1984:50.

plate at all. In so far, the Motor Insurance Directive contrasts with Solvency II, where the notion 'Member State where the risk is situated' only refers to registered vehicles. The broader concept of the Motor Insurance Directive is logical since the scope of the Directive extends to every kind of motor vehicle and not just registered vehicles.

c) The reference under *a)* of vehicles provided with temporary plates ensures that not only 'normally' registered vehicles fall within the scope of the Directive but also vehicles provided with customs plates, export plates and other registrations with a validity limited in time.
   In the absence of an obligation to provide a vehicle with a registration plate, according to letter *b)* other plates also determine the Member State where the vehicle is normally based: insurance plates are the most common of such distinguishing signs.
   Should a vehicle not be required to bear any plate or distinguishing sign, the territory of the Member State of permanent residence of the custodian of the vehicle determines where the vehicle is normally based. The place of residence of the custodian, not (just) the owner of the vehicle, is relevant – the background possibly being that it is easier to establish who has in fact the custody of the vehicle than who is the legal owner.

6.2.5.3 *The 'normally based' concept according to the Court of Justice of the European Union*

The notion of the 'territory in which a vehicle is normally based' being a concept used in European law brings its interpretation within the competence of the Court of Justice of the European Union. In the 1980s and 1990s, the Court was asked to pronounce itself on the concept as it was defined in the original text of the Directive. Since, however, the definition of the normally based concept has substantially changed with the adoption of the 5th MID in 2005, the importance of this jurisprudence has in fact been mainly reduced to historical relevance.

Nevertheless, it is still interesting to outline the historic evolution briefly to see how the concept is closely related to the registration procedures of a vehicle; this is a domain that still belongs, to a large extent, to the competence of the national legislator, rather than being regulated at European level.

> On 9 February 1984, the Court of Justice of the European Union gave an interpretation to the concept 'territory in which a vehicle is normally based' in two distinct judgments, rendered on the same day.

In the *Gambetta*-judgment, a vehicle bearing an Austrian registration plate had caused an accident in Paris, damaging a parked vehicle belonging to Gambetta Auto.[16] At the time of the accident, the 'authorisation' to use the Austrian vehicle was withdrawn since its insurance had been cancelled. The Court ruled that the vehicle was still to be regarded as normally based in Austria, the territory of the State of which the vehicle bore a properly issued registration plate; and this even if at the time of the accident the 'authorisation' to use the vehicle had been withdrawn. The Court justified this decision as follows:

> "It must be remembered that the directive seeks to abolish checking of the 'green card' at the frontier. For that purpose it is imperative that the State where the vehicle is normally based should be easily identifiable, and this is ensured by the issue of a registration plate. To require that the plate should be currently valid would amount to replacing checking of the 'green card' by systematic checking of registration and would deprive the directive of any useful purpose."[17]

It is to be remembered that the 2nd MID replaced the criterion 'registration of the vehicle' with the criterion 'registration plate' to determine where a vehicle is normally based.
In the other judgment of the same day, the *BCF*-judgment, a French vehicle was damaged in France, after a road traffic accident caused by a vehicle bearing a German registration plate.[18] The registration had, however, been cancelled in Germany since the vehicle had been stolen. The Court ruled that when a vehicle bears a properly issued registration plate, that vehicle must be regarded as being normally based in the territory of the State in which it is registered; and this even if, at the time of the accident, the 'authorisation' to use the vehicle had been withdrawn and irrespective of the fact that such withdrawal renders the registration invalid or entails its revocation.
In the two judgments of 1984, there was clearly a flaw with the registration plate issued to the respective vehicle; but the two judgments had in common that the registration plate had initially been properly issued for each vehicle in question.
In a third judgment, rendered eight years later in the *Fournier* case, the 'registration flaw' of the liable vehicle was even more complicated.[19] The accident took place in France but this time the liable vehicle had been registered in Germany and stolen in the Netherlands. After the theft, it had been deregistered by the German registration authorities. At the time of the accident, false Dutch registration plates were attached to the vehicle. In reality, the false registration plates corresponded to a different Dutch vehicle. The Court ruled that the vehicle in question was to be considered as normally based in the Member State that had issued the registration plates; and this even if those plates were related to a different vehicle.

16. CJEU, Judgment of 9 February 1984, *Gambetta*, C-344/82, EU:C:1984:50.
17. Idem, para 13.
18. CJEU, Judgment of 9 February 1984, *Bureau Central Français*, C-64/83, EU:C:1984:54.
19. CJEU, Judgment of 12 November 1992, *Fournier*, C-73/89, EU:C:1992:431.

6.2.5.4 *The response of the Bureaux on the decisions of the EU Court*

The question of the Member State where a vehicle is normally based if the registration is either absent or imperfect has a long and sometimes confusing history, especially in the relations between Bureaux. As observed earlier, the importance of this evolution has primarily historic relevance, but it also demonstrates that different solutions can be found for the problem of accidents caused by vehicles with deficient registration plates.

Registration plates sometimes expire, vehicles escape the obligation to be insured – especially when they circulate for a prolonged period in other countries than the one of their registration. Already in the 1970s a number of Bureaux (although definitely not all) of the (then) European Economic Community who had signed the predecessor of the Multilateral Agreement (the Supplementary Agreements) came to the realisation that they would be exposed for an indefinite period of time to the risk of having to guarantee vehicles which would not be insured. That was felt to be too heavy a burden and they decided to conclude an agreement limiting that risk: the Luxembourg Protocol. In that Agreement the signatories put a time limit on their obligation to reimburse the Bureau of the Member State of the accident. The criterion was different from one Signatory to another, but usually it was 12 months after a specific date, such as either the termination of the legal registration of the vehicle or the expiry of the (registered) policy of insurance. The concept of normally based was not modified, only the right to reimbursement was limited in time. In the *Demouche* and the *Gambetta* decisions the European Court confirmed the competence of the Bureaux to conclude such Agreements.[20] This competence was later confirmed in the *Fournier* decision.[21] See recital 22 of the *Fournier* judgment:

> "It must be stated in that regard that even though the national court submitted its question with a view to obtaining a ruling on the interpretation of the agreement between national bureaux, the purpose of which is to determine which of the bureaux must, ultimately, bear the cost of paying compensation to the victim, that argument is not relevant since the determination, in that agreement, of the bureau which is to pay the compensation was arrived at in an area not covered by the Directive and the terms used in the agre[e]ment do not therefore necessarily have to have the same meaning as those used in the Directive."

The *Fournier* decision changed the playing field. It implied – in its essence – that the registration plate which was attached to the vehicle when crossing a border determined in which Member State a vehicle is normally based. Even a false plate – as was the case in the *Fournier* situation – would have that effect.

20. CJEU, Judgment of 6 October 1987, *Demouche and others*, C-152/83, EU:C:1987:421. CJEU, Judgment of 9 February 1984, *Gambetta*, C-344/82, EU:C:1984:50.
21. CJEU, Judgment of 12 November 1992, *Fournier*, C-73/89, EU:C:1992:431.

This jurisprudence resulted in a Bureau, in this case the Dutch Bureau, having to bear the final costs of an accident occurring in France and caused by a vehicle that was last registered in Germany and which was only indirectly linked to the Netherlands by the mere fact that false Dutch registration plates had been attached to the vehicle.
The Luxembourg Protocol, which was moreover only signed by a limited number of Bureaux, was felt to bring an inadequate answer to the situation after *Fournier* and was cancelled. The Bureaux of the Signatories of the (then) Multilateral Guarantee Agreement, concluded a new Agreement, the False Plate Agreement. The Bureaux agreed that, as far as it can be determined in which Member State the vehicle in question had last been lawfully registered, the Bureau of that State is to be the final debtor of the accident caused by the vehicle.
However, as was the case with the Luxembourg Protocol, not all Bureaux were prepared or in a legal position to sign this Agreement.

6.2.5.5 Vehicles without or with no longer corresponding plates

The 5th Motor Insurance Directive in 2005 followed yet another path. In that year, a new provision was integrated in the definition of 'territory in which a vehicle is normally based', dealing with flawed registration plates. That provision is now to be found in Article 1(4), point (d) of the codified Directive.

Henceforth, if a registration plate does not correspond or no longer corresponds to the vehicle, the said vehicle will be considered to be normally based in the territory of the Member State in which the accident took place. Vehicles that bear such plates will not be considered to be normally based in the Member State that issued the (flawed) registration plate, nor in the Member State where the vehicle had last been properly registered; rather, it would be considered to be normally based in the Member State where the accident had occurred. Since such vehicles are very often not insured, in many cases this will result in the Guarantee Fund of the Member State where the accident occurred being competent to handle the case, to compensate the injured party and to bear the final costs of the accident (without prejudice to the Guarantee Fund's possibility to recover its outlay from the holder and/or liable driver of the vehicle of course). For the function and situations of intervention of the Guarantee Funds, see chapter 4.

The provision of Article 1(4), point (d) of the Directive immediately gave rise to questions: what is to be understood by 'a plate which does not correspond or no longer corresponds to the vehicle'? The matter was taken up with the services of the European Commission and the answer received was that this notion encompassed a wide range of situations including *inter alia* falsified, suspended or expired plates. Article 1(4) must cover:

> "a broad range of situations in which the vehicle plate may be considered false or illegal is covered by this provision. The terms 'not corresponding' and 'no longer corresponding' should include inter alia falsified, suspended or expired plates. In the case of a vehicle bearing a plate that can be only partly identified, this provision does not necessarily apply unless the plate has been identified as being false or illegal."[22]

And whereas under the *Fournier* decision the Member State where the vehicle is normally based is the Member State which issued the suspended or expired plate or the Member State to which the false plate seems to refer, under the new provision, the risk is for the Member State of the accident. Both situations cannot be regarded as totally satisfactory: under *Fournier* it is the thief of a vehicle who decides which Bureau will have to pay, under the 5th Directive the Guarantee Fund of the coincidental country of the accident will have to bear the risk.[23]

6.2.5.6 *Dispatched vehicles*

a) In normal circumstances the Member State where the vehicle is normally based is identical to the Member State where the risk is situated. That is different when a vehicle is dispatched from one country to another.

> In a single market vehicles can no longer be said to be exported, which is why the Directive introduced the concept of 'dispatched vehicles': vehicles bought in another Member State and sent to the Member State of the buyer.
> The concept was introduced in the 5th Directive to address the problems citizens of the Member States encountered when buying a vehicle – new or second hand – in a Member State other than their country of residence and wishing to insure their new property. The difficulties were that the insurance market in the Member State of dispatch (the Member State of origin) was reluctant to insure the vehicle – or rather its new owner – because they were unfamiliar with the risk. The insurance market in the Member State of destination on the other hand was faced with other difficulties: they would not be authorised to insure vehicles registered in other countries and even if they were, the registration authorities in their Member State would not be able to register a policy of insurance issued for a foreign vehicle.
> The European Commission felt that this was a hindrance to the free movement of goods and tried to remedy these obstacles. The result is Article 15 of the Directive. As we shall see, the Directive created perhaps as many obstacles as it tried to resolve.

22. European Commission, Internal Market and Services DG, Main conclusions of the meeting on 28 September 2006 on the transposition of the 5th Motor Insurance Directive, Brussels, document MARKT/2531/06-EN.
23. Need we say that any attempt by the Guarantee Fund to be reimbursed by the person liable for the accident will in such cases turn out to be extremely difficult or even impossible?

b) The Directive introduces in a fairly compact Article 15, consisting of only two paragraphs, a rather complicated regime. Let us first describe the principles and mechanisms and then analyse their consequences.

In the first place Article 15 modifies, for vehicles dispatched from one Member State to another, the notion of the Member State in which the risk is situated. Whereas this is in principle the country where a vehicle is registered (see *supra* para 6.2.5.2), when a vehicle is dispatched in the meaning of this Article it will be the Member State of destination, even if the vehicle is not yet registered in that Member State (which will be the normal situation). However, the risk will only be 'transferred' to that Member State for a period of 30 days, starting immediately from the acceptance of delivery by the buyer. Should the vehicle not be registered in the Member State of destination within that 30 day timeframe, the risk returns to the Member State of dispatch.

Should the vehicle provoke an accident within the 30 days whilst being uninsured, the Guarantee Fund of the Member State of destination will be responsible for compensating the victim.[24]

c) Article 15 confronts the insurance markets with a series of questions and difficulties. First of all we must observe that the Directive changes the Member State where the risk is situated. That means that the vehicle has to be insured in the insurance market of that Member State.

On the other hand, Article 15 does not change the notion of the Member State in which the vehicle is normally based. Since the vehicle will in all likelihood either bear an export plate or possibly even the original registration plate of the Member State of dispatch, the vehicle will continue to be normally based in that Member State.

For the question which entity can be held liable to handle and settle claims in relation to accidents provoked by a dispatched vehicle, the 'normally based' concept is decisive and not the question in which Member State the risk relating to the vehicle is situated. This leads to confusion and potential problems.
Several possible scenarios can be identified. A few examples:

24. In practice, it often appears difficult to establish with certainty that a vehicle is dispatched from one Member State to another. Green Card Bureaux and Guarantee Funds have agreed on the means of proof that can be relied on to establish a vehicle's dispatched status.

A. ***A vehicle is registered in and dispatched from Member State A to Member State B The vehicle is insured with insurance company INSB, authorised in Member State B An accident occurs within the 30 day period***

a. The accident occurs in Member State A

The victim is a resident of Member State A: since the vehicle is normally based in Member State A (and thus not a visiting vehicle) the victim has no entity to turn to in their own country. The Green Card system is not applicable, nor are the 4th Directive structures. The Guarantee Fund will not be liable since the vehicle is insured.

The victim is a resident of Member State C: the victim can approach either the claims representative of INSB in Member State C or – if the insurer cannot be identified within 2 months – the Compensation Body in Member State C. That Compensation Body will have a right of recourse against the Guarantee Fund of Member State B.

If the fact that the vehicle has been dispatched to Member State B cannot be established within two months, the Compensation Body will address its claim for reimbursement to the Guarantee Fund of Member State A, since that is where the vehicle is normally based.

b. *The accident takes place in Member State B*

The victim is a resident of Member State B: the vehicle is insured with INSB, with an authorisation in Member State B, and the victim can turn directly to this insurance company. But if the driver of the vehicle does not cooperate, the victim will have problems in identifying the insurance company: the registration authorities in Member State B will not be able to register a vehicle with a foreign registration number, nor will the insurance company be able to notify the authorities of the policy.

Since the vehicle is normally based in Member State A the victim can approach the Green Card Bureau of Member State B. That Bureau cannot refuse to handle the claim and will, after compensating the victim, exercise its right to reimbursement against the Bureau of Member State A. Assuming INSB has been identified as the MTPL insurer, Bureau A will in turn seek reimbursement from INSB. This recourse action falls outside the scope of the Green Card Agreements and is therefore not safeguarded by any guarantee from Bureau A. Needless to say that this is a rather complicated procedure.

The victim is a resident of Member State C: the same answers as when the victim is a resident of Member State B, in addition to which the victim can approach the claims representative of INSB in Member State C.

c. *The accident takes place in Member State C*

The victim is a resident of Member State C: the vehicle is insured in Member State B and is to be considered as a vehicle normally based in Member State A. If the identity of the insurer is established in time, the victim can approach the correspondent of INSB in country C. If not, they can address the Bureau of Member

State C which, after compensating the victim, will exercise its right of recourse against the Bureau of Member State A, which in turn will seek reimbursement from INSB. As in scenario *b)* the Green Card system will not guarantee this reimbursement. Again: complicated.

B. ***A vehicle is registered in and dispatched from Member State A to Member State B***
The vehicle is not insured
An accident occurs within the 30 day period

a. *An accident occurs in Member State A*

The victim is a resident of Member State A: the vehicle is normally based in Member State A but the Guarantee Fund of Member State B is responsible for handling and settling the victim's claim. The Directive has no solution for this victim: the Green Card Bureau cannot be held responsible since the vehicle is normally based in the Member State of the accident. The Guarantee Fund of Member State A is not responsible since the risk is situated in Member State B. The visiting victim's protection is not applicable since the victim is a resident of the country of the accident.

The victim is a resident of Member State C: the victim may address the Compensation Body of their country of residence. This is in fact a rather simple situation: the Compensation Body of Member State C has a right to reimbursement by the Guarantee Fund of Member State B, on the basis of Article 15(2) of the Directive.

b. *An accident occurs in Member State B*

The victim is a resident of Member State B: According to the Directive the risk is situated in Member State B and its Guarantee Fund is responsible for compensating the victim. But since the vehicle is normally based in Member State A the victim can also approach the Bureau of Member State B. This option will lie open if the status of the vehicle as a dispatched vehicle is not clarified in time. Needless to say that the recourse process in this scenario will also be extremely complicated.

The victim is a resident of Member State C: the victim can approach the Compensation Body of their country of residence. That will have a right of recourse against the Guarantee Fund of Member State B or – if the status as a dispatched vehicle cannot be established in time – against the Compensation Body in Member State A, since the vehicle is normally based in that Member State.

c. *An accident occurs in Member State C*

The victim is a resident of Member State C: the victim can address the Bureau of their country of residence. On the basis of the Internal Regulations the Bureau of Member State C would have a right of recourse against the Bureau of Member State A, where the vehicle is normally based. That Bureau should then seek reimbursement from the Guarantee Fund in Member State B.

However, it has been suggested that the Directive derogates in this respect to a private contract such as the inter-Bureaux agreement, as a consequence of which the Bureau of Member State C should directly seek reimbursement from the Guarantee Fund of Member State B.

> Whichever way is chosen, the recourse action of either the Bureau of Member State A or of Member State C against the Guarantee Fund of Member State B is not covered by any international Agreement between Bureaux and Guarantee Funds.
> In the absence of any case law a final answer to this question cannot be provided.

d) Many of the complications described above are the result of the separation of the Member State where the risk is situated from the Member State where the vehicle is normally based. Moreover the Directive does not address the issues that may result from the registration authorities being unable to register vehicles with foreign registration numbers, or any related insurance issues. As a result the Information Centres of the Member States are unlikely to be able to provide the necessary information to the victim 'without delay' (as Article 23 of the Directive requires).

e) Our conclusion: Article 15 should be withdrawn as soon as possible or replaced by a solution which takes better account of the complexities of this issue.

> In the European Commission's *Proposal for a Directive of the European Parliament and the Council amending Directive 2009/103/EC of the European Parliament and the Council of 16 September 2009 relating to insurance against civil liability in respect of the use of motor vehicles, and the enforcement of the obligation to ensure against such liability*, the Article on dispatched vehicle remains untouched.[25] The rapporteur on this proposal in European Parliament suggests a limited number of changes to the provision but leaves the separation between the Member State where the risk is situated and the Member State where the vehicle is normally based intact. It remains to be seen what will happen in the final text of the Directive, once adopted.

6.2.6 *Exempted persons and vehicles: article 5(1) and 5(2) of the directive*

Although the starting point of the Directive has always been to encompass all motor vehicles, exceptions on a national level have been a possibility from the beginning. Article 4 of the 1st Directive introduced the possibility of two different derogations, which still exist under Article 5(1) and 5(2) of the codified Directive although the solutions for especially the claims handling issue is somewhat different:

a. Certain *persons* can be exempted from compulsory insurance of their vehicles. The background was the existing practice in a number of countries to derogate (mainly) government vehicles from this obligation in view of the fact that the

25. Document COM(2018) 336 final.

financial strength of public bodies made insurance either unnecessary or – in the case of the State – economically unpractical.

Examples of this derogation are vehicles of the State, military vehicles, vehicles of public transport, exemptions which can be found in many jurisdictions; a rather unique example can however be found in the Dutch legislation: vehicles belonging to persons recognised as conscientious dissenters based on their religious convictions.[26]

b. Certain *vehicles* offer so little risk that compulsory insurance for that reason would be undesirable – at least from the point of view of the owner. The criterion would be the type of vehicle or the type of plate attached to the vehicle. This latter criterion is based on the fact that these vehicles are likely to be easily identifiable through their plate.

A few random examples: self-propelled machinery with engine power of up to 10 KW: wheeled tractors, chain tractors, all kind of self-propelled machinery, all kind of self-propelled agricultural and forest machinery (Bulgaria), vehicles designed to move slowly (Germany), agricultural equipment (Finland), certain motorised bicycles and invalid chairs (Luxembourg) and 'e-bikes' (The Netherlands).

As for the derogation of Article 5(1) – regarding (the vehicles of) certain public or private natural or legal persons – the Member State has to communicate a list of the exempted persons to the Commission. Moreover the Member State has to designate a body responsible for compensation to injured parties. In the absence of such a designated body, the injured party has no entity to turn to and as a result they should have access to the Guarantee Fund.

The solution with regard to the exemption of Article 5(2) – low risk vehicles – is different: vehicles exempted from compulsory insurance under application of Article 5(2) are, according to paragraph (2), treated as uninsured vehicles, as a consequence of which the injured party will be compensated by the Guarantee Fund. The requirement to communicate the list of (types of) vehicles or plates is still existent, but whereas the 1st Directive authorised the Member States to require the visiting owner of such a vehicle to present a valid Green Card, the 5th Directive chose another path: the exemption is recognised by all other Member States and eventual claims will be compensated by the Guarantee Fund of the visited Member State,

26. The Dutch MTPL law allows persons with religious convictions that forbid them to take out any form of insurance to apply for an exemption under the MTPL law. Injured parties can apply to the Guarantee Fund for compensation of their damage. The exempted person will be obliged to contribute to a special fund within the Guarantee Fund from which fund the claims will be paid and to pay an administrative fee to the Guarantee Fund. They are liable to reimburse the Guarantee Fund for the damage they provoked. The total number of (registered and non-registered) vehicles exempted on such religious grounds is approx. 6,300 (2018).

with a right of recourse on the Guarantee Fund of the Member State where the vehicle is normally based.

6.2.7 *Liability regimes; no fault and first party schemes*

The title of the Directive already gives an indication of its contents. It reads in its English version:

> "Directive (...) relating to insurance against civil liability in respect of the use of motor vehicles, and the enforcement of the obligation to insure against such liability."

Other – equally authentic – versions show differences. The French language version reads:

> "Directive (...) concernant l'assurance de la responsabilité civile résultant de la circulation de véhicules automoteurs et le contrôle de l'obligation d'assurer cette responsabilité."

In the German version the Directive is called:

> "Richtlinie (...) über die Kraftfahrzeug-Haftpflichtversicherung und die Kontrolle der entsprechenden Versicherungspflicht."

In paragraph 6.2.4 we have analysed the implications for the scope of the Directive of the fact that the words *'circulation de véhicules automoteurs'* in the French text (and in several other equally official language versions, such as the Dutch, the Italian, Portuguese and Spanish) do not appear in the English nor in the German wording – nor in those language versions which have in the past most probably been based on these two languages, such as the Nordic and the central and eastern European ones – but here we will focus on another aspect: the applicability of the Directive to the insurance against civil liability in respect of (the use of) motor vehicles.

The Directive is not applicable to other types of insurance of motor vehicles, such as full comprehensive cover (casco insurance), legal assistance policies, policies guaranteeing the person insured with a defined sum in case of bodily injury or death after a traffic accident or other insurance covers that are independent of the liability of the person or persons insured. A confirmation of this opinion can be found in the *Bejan*-decision of the European Court of Justice.[27] In this decision the Court held that the Directive does not preclude national legislation which permits an insurance undertaking to exclude from the cover of a non-mandatory insurance policy damage caused while the vehicle is driven by a person under the influence

27. CJEU, Judgment of 28 October 2010, *Bejan*, C-102/10, EU:C:2010:654.

of alcohol. As we shall see in paragraph 6.2.13.4, such clauses are not permitted under the Directive in MTPL policies.

Liability however comes in various forms. An increasing number of countries have abandoned the traditional liability systems based on fault or negligence in favour of schemes of objective or strict liability, often founded on the notion of the inherent danger of the use of motor vehicles: their speed, weight and the fact that even minor mistakes or brief moments of lack of attention by the driver frequently cause serious damage. These factors have motivated legislators to introduce systems where negligence or fault no longer play a role when determining the liability of the user of the vehicle. A fine example of such a regime can be found in France under the *Loi Badinter*, but other countries have a similar solution. Other countries, where strict no fault regimes do not apply, have introduced legislation under which negligence still plays a role but to a lesser extent, often in relation to vulnerable users of the road, or with victims under or above a certain age. Germany and the Netherlands can be called examples of these mixed regimes.

In some cases, these no-fault systems are combined with liability to be 'channelled' to a specific party. An example (albeit from a country outside the EEA) of such a scheme can be found in Switzerland where all liability evolving from the use of motor vehicles rests on the holder of the vehicle, even if the driver of the vehicle in question would, under the 'normal' liability rules, have no right of compensation because they had caused the accident themselves.

And then there are countries which have abandoned the notion of liability completely: Norway, Sweden and Finland no longer apply their traditional liability system and instead settle the consequences of traffic accidents completely through their insurance companies: traffic insurance schemes or first party insurance.

These different ways of compensating (or not) traffic accident victims for their damage raise the question of how the Directive must be applied. Is it also applicable to strict liability systems? And if a legislation has different liability regimes for different types of victims or accident situations, does the Directive then apply to all these regimes? Do the rules also apply to no fault traffic insurance schemes such as can be found in the Nordic countries and if so, how can they be brought into line?

It is useful to observe that the Directive itself gives no indication that its applicability is restricted to certain types of liability. Three decisions of the Court of Justice of the EU confirm this conclusion: in *Mendes Ferreira and Delgado Correia Ferreira* the Court held that

1. "Article 3 of the Second Council Directive (84/5/EEC) of 30 December 1983, on the approximation of the laws of the Member States relating to insurance against civil liability in respect of the use of motor vehicles, requires compulsory insurance against civil liability in respect of the use of motor vehicles to cover personal injuries to passengers who are members of the family of the insured person, of the driver of the vehicle or of any other person who incurs civil liability for an accident and whose liability is covered by compulsory motor-vehicle insurance, where those passengers are carried free of charge, whether or not there is any fault on the part of the driver of the vehicle which caused the accident, only if the domestic law of the Member State concerned requires such cover in respect of personal injuries caused in the same conditions to other third-party passengers.
2. Articles 1 (2) and 5 (3) of Directive 84/5, as amended by Annex I, Part IX F, entitled 'Insurance', of the Act concerning the conditions of accession of the Kingdom of Spain and the Portuguese Republic and the adjustments to the Treaties, preclude domestic laws laying down maximum amounts of compensation that are lower than the minimum amounts of cover laid down by those provisions where, in the absence of fault on the part of the driver of the vehicle which caused the accident, only civil liability for materialisation of risk arises."[28]

In *Messejana Viegas* the Court decided that

"Article 1(2) of the Second Council Directive 84/5/EEC of 30 December 1983 on the approximation of the laws of the Member States relating to insurance against civil liability in respect of the use of motor vehicles precludes national laws which provide for a number of types of civil liability applicable to road-traffic accidents laying down, in respect of one of them, maximum amounts of compensation that are lower than the minimum amounts of cover laid down by that article."[29]

A similar decision can be found in *Drozdovs*, where the Court held that

"Article 3 (1) of Directive 72/166 and Article 1(1) and (2) of Second Directive 84/5 must be interpreted as precluding national provisions, pursuant to which compulsory insurance against civil liability in respect of the use of motor vehicles covers compensation for non-material damage resulting from the death of a person's next of kin in a road traffic accident – payable in accordance with national civil liability law – only to a maximum amount which is lower than the minimum amounts laid down in Article 1(2) of Second Directive 84/5."[30]

On the other hand: the fact that the Directive does not specify the sort of liability that has to be covered under the policy also implies that different schemes of liabil-

28. CJEU, Judgment of 14 September 2000, *Mendes Ferreira and Delgado Correia Ferreira*, C-348/98, EU:C:2000:442.
29. CJEU, Judgment of 12 May 2005, *Messejana Viegas*, C-166/02, EU:C:2003:417.
30. CJEU, Judgment of 24 October 2013, *Drozdovs*, C-277/12, EU:C:2013:685.

ity are permitted. *Ambrósio Lavrador,*[31] *Pendão Lapa Costa Ferreira and Pendão Lapa Ferreira,*[32] *Gomes Oliveira,*[33] *Rodrigues Esteves*[34] and *Freitas a.o.*[35] all essentially contain the same decision, in the English version of the *Ambrósio Lavrador* decision:[36]

> "(the Directives) must be interpreted as not precluding national provisions falling within civil liability law that allow exclusion or limitation of the right of the victim of an accident to claim compensation under the civil liability insurance of the motor vehicle involved in the accident, on the basis of an individual assessment of the exclusive or partial contribution of that victim to his own loss or injury."

In the case leading to the decision the victim, a young cyclist, was riding on the wrong side of the road, in breach of the priority rules.

We can therefore conclude that the Directive is neutral with respect to the national liability regime.

Would that conclusion also imply that the Directive is applicable to other compensation schemes for road traffic victims, such as the Nordic first party schemes? This is a far more complicated question, since there is no explicit case law.
It is a fact that the legislation in Sweden and Finland was in place when these countries joined the European Union on 1 January 1995. The fact that the compensation of traffic victims in both countries was not based on liability insurance was apparently not seen as an obstacle.

That there was some awareness of the potential problems can be demonstrated by the discussions in the Council of Bureaux. In 1976, the Council of Bureaux discussed a related question. In Sweden (as in Norway and Finland) not only persons who are not to blame for an accident have a right to compensation from the traffic insurer, but also persons who have caused the accident themselves, including the driver of the (sole) vehicle involved in the accident. This rule also applies to foreign vehicles and their drivers. The Swedish Bureau acts in these circumstances as if it was the MTPL insurer of the foreign vehicle. The question was whether the Bureau in that capacity has, when it has compensated the faulty driver of the visiting vehicle, a right of recourse against the insurer of that vehicle or against the Bureau of the country where the vehicle is normally based.

31. CJEU, Judgment of 9 June 2011, *Ambrósio Lavrador and Olival Ferreira Bonifácio*, C-409/09, EU:C:2011:371.
32. CJEU, Judgment of 21 March 2013, *Pendão Lapa Costa Ferreira and Pendão Lapa Ferreira*, C-229/10, EU:C:2013:179.
33. CJEU, Judgment of 21 March 2013, *Gomes Oliveira*, C-362/11, EU:C:2013:184.
34. CJEU, Judgment of 21 March 2013, *Rodrigues Esteves*, C-486/11, EU:C:2013:188.
35. CJEU, Judgment of 21 March 2013, *Freitas a.o.*, C-96/12, EU:C:2013:199.
36. The other decisions are currently only available in French and the language of the procedure, Portuguese.

> The Council presented the question to the UNECE and the answer was that the Green Card system is essentially a liability based system and in such a construction there is no room for compensation to persons who have caused the accident themselves. Following that opinion of the UNECE the Council decided that the Swedish Bureau had no right of recourse against the foreign Bureau or insurer.

Strictly speaking the Nordic systems of compensation do not conform to the requirements of the Directive, since they are not based on a liability insurance policy *strictu sensu*. But the compensation to which victims – and even liable parties! – are entitled, fully complies with the rules of the EU, both in amounts insured and conditions as well as exclusions.[37] Therefore, although along a different path, the goals of the Directive can be regarded as met. And since Directives aim at achieving certain results, leaving the way how to implement these results to the Member States, the conclusion can be that first party schemes as an alternative for MTPL policies are acceptable under EU law.

6.2.8 *Geographical aspects of the cover*

6.2.8.1 *Cover in the EEA*

The 1st Directive already introduced a Community wide MTPL policy. According to Article 3 of the current codified Directive all vehicles normally based in a Member State, with an exception for vehicles which are exempted from that obligation under Article 5 of the Directive, have to be covered for damage not only in the territory of their own Member State, but also for damage in the other Member States.

> Article 3(3), point (b) also refers to damage suffered by nationals of Member States during a direct journey between two territories in which the Treaty is in force, if there is no national insurers' Bureau responsible for the territory which is being crossed. This clause referred to the situation of West Berlin. This part of Berlin belonged to the Federal Republic of Germany but could only be reached by road via the territory of the German Democratic Republic, which in 1972 when the 1st Directive came into force, was not a member of the Green Card system. The clause can be regarded as obsolete.

The Community wide cover was (and is) a fundamental prerequisite for the abolition of the frontier checks on a valid Green Card. Only if the entire vehicle fleet of a Member State can be trusted to be insured for the entire Community, can a vehicle

37. In CJEU, Judgment of 30 June 2005, *Candolin a.o.*, C-537/03, EU:C:2005:417, the Court held that a specific clause in the Finnish law, limiting or excluding compensation to passengers of a vehicle with a driver under influence of alcohol, was not compliant with EU legislation. In an indirect way this decision may be seen as an indication that the Court sees no obstacle in first party compensation schemes as an alternative to the MTPL policy as made mandatory by the Directive.

normally based in that State be admitted to another Member State. The financial burden on the Guarantee Funds would otherwise be unsupportable.
The policy must now give cover not only in the entire European Union but also in those Member States of the European Free Trade Association (EFTA) that participate in the European Economic Area, being Iceland, Norway and Liechtenstein, as well as in those countries the Bureau of which is a signatory of the Multilateral Agreement.[38,39] See also paragraph 3.5.4 and – for signatory Bureaux of non-EEA countries – para 6.2.8.3.

6.2.8.2 Single premium

Apparently the clause in the 1st Directive that the policy should provide cover in all the Member States of the Communities wasn't clear enough, since in a number of countries insurers gave such Community-wide cover only after payment of additional premium. This was the fairly common practice in the UK, but also in the Netherlands for mopeds. The 3rd Directive tried to make an end to this practice by introducing the clause that now appears as Article 14 of the 2009 codified Directive. It reads in so far as relevant here:

> "Member States shall take the necessary steps to ensure that all compulsory policies of insurance against civil liability arising out of the use of vehicles:
> a. cover, on the basis of a single premium and during the whole term of the contract, the entire territory of the Community, including for any period in which the vehicle remains in other Member States during the term of the contract; and
> b. (...)"[40]

The words 'including for any period in which the vehicle remains in other Member States during the term of the contract' refers to insured persons who spend time in other Member States for purposes of work or study or who prefer to spend the winter season in a more agreeable climate than the one of their country of residence.

The phrase 'during the whole term of the contract' is somewhat ambivalent. In some countries insurance contracts will be concluded on a yearly basis only. In others the contract runs for an indefinite period of time. In the former the insurer can apply new conditions whereas in the latter they would be bound until the contract

38. The Directive mentions in its heading that it is relevant for the EEA.
39. Switzerland is not a member of the EEA. A complicating factor in the context of the Green Card system is the responsibility that the Swiss Bureau has assumed for accidents under the Green Card system in Liechtenstein and for vehicles from the Fürstentum Liechtenstein in other countries belonging to the Green Card system. As a result, the Swiss Bureau may have to apply different rules, depending on whether the accident occurred in Liechtenstein (part of the EEA) or in Switzerland (outside the EEA).
40. Article 14 point (b) will be discussed in paragraph 6.2.10.4.

expires.[41] Another question arises when the customer replaces their vehicle. New contract or modification of the existing? That being said, the intention of the Directive is clear: to remove as many obstacles to the free movement of persons as possible.

That the Directive apparently is (or was) still not always understood in the way it was meant to be is illustrated by the *Litaksa* decision of the European Court.[42]

> On 24 November 2008, Litaksa concluded two MTPL policies with insurance company BTA, to cover Litaksa's liabilities in respect of the use of two vehicles it owned. The contracts stipulated that the vehicles would be used only within Lithuania. Litaksa was also obliged, if it intended to use the vehicles beyond a 28-day period in another Member State, or to transport persons or goods there, to inform BTA and pay additional premium. In 2009 the two vehicles were involved in road traffic accidents in the United Kingdom and Germany, without Litaksa having previously notified BTA of their intention of using the vehicles in those Member States.
> BTA compensated the victims of those accidents and then tried to obtain reimbursement of 50% of the compensation paid to the victims. The case went to court.
> After losing the procedure in first instance Litaksa appealed and the Court of Appeal submitted the following questions before the Court in Luxembourg:
>
> 1. "Is Article 2 of [the Third Directive] to be interpreted as meaning that the parties to a compulsory motor insurance contract do not have the right to agree on a territorial restriction of the insurance cover for the person insured (to apply a different insurance premium depending on the territory in which the vehicle is used — either in the entire territory of the European Union or only in Lithuania), but in any event without the cover of victims being restricted, that is to say, to define use of the vehicle outside Lithuania in another Member State of the European Union as a factor increasing the insurance risk, in which event a premium supplement has to be paid?
> 2. Are the principle of the free movement of persons and vehicles in the entire territory of the European Union and the general principle of equality (non-discrimination) to be interpreted as being contravened by the aforementioned agreement of the parties to an insurance contract whereby the insurance risk is linked to the territorial use of the vehicle?"

The Court ruled – in our opinion not very surprisingly – that

> "Article 2 of the Third Council Directive 90/232/EEC of 14 May 1990 on the approximation of the laws of the Member States relating to insurance against civil liability in respect of the use of

41. Unless 'the term of the contract' refers to the period for which premium has been paid.
42. CJEU, Judgment of 26 March 2015, *Litaksa*, C-556/13, EU:C:2015:202.

motor vehicles, as amended by Directive 2005/14/EC of the European Parliament and of the Council of 11 May 2005, must be interpreted as meaning that a premium which varies according to whether the insured vehicle is to be used only in the territory of the Member State in which that vehicle is normally based or in the entire territory of the European Union does not fall within the concept of 'single premium', within the meaning of that article."

6.2.8.3 Third countries

Vehicles normally based in third countries are in principle only allowed to enter the territory of the Union if they are covered by an insurance policy which is valid in the entire European Union (or more precisely: the entire EEA) and which conforms to the applicable legislation. See Article 7 of the Directive. Article 8(1) clarifies that third country vehicles have to be provided with either a valid Green Card or a certificate of frontier insurance – which is also accompanied with a Green Card – valid for the entire territory of the EU.

Already the 1st Directive however recognised the necessity of a possibility to widen the geographical scope of the Directive and the system of deemed insurance cover. The existence of Agreements with the effect of abolishing border checks on the Green Card between Germany as a Member State and Austria, Czechoslovakia and Hungary made that inevitable.[43] The same could be said a few years later with regard to similar Agreements between Denmark, soon to become a Member State, and the other Nordic countries.

Whereas vehicles entering the EU from third countries in principle will be checked on their valid Green Card or certificate of a frontier insurance policy (Article 8(1), first sentence), the Directive, in its Article 8(1), second sentence, opens a possibility to abolish this check for vehicles normally based in specific countries:

> "However, vehicles normally based in a third country shall be treated as vehicles normally based in the Community if the national bureaux of all the Member States severally guarantee, each in accordance with the provisions of its own national law on compulsory insurance, settlement of claims in respect of accidents occurring in their territory caused by such vehicles."

The Bureaux of the Member States only provide the guarantee referred to in this clause after the conclusion of an agreement with the Bureau of the third country in question. This agreement is the Multilateral Agreement between Bureaux.[44] Thus the reimbursement by the insurance market of the third country of the outlays of the Bureaux of Member States will be guaranteed.

43. See *supra* para 2.4.
44. See *supra* paragraphs 3.2.2 and 3.5.4.

The consequence of this Agreement is not only that vehicles from certain third countries will be regarded and treated as 'Community vehicles', but also that vehicles normally based in the EU may equally enter the third country in question without (checks on) Green Cards. This results from the reciprocal character of the Multilateral Agreement.

At this moment, Andorra, Serbia and Switzerland are recognised as third countries in the meaning of Article 8 and as a consequence their vehicles are admitted to the EEA territory without any checks on insurance.[45] Vice versa, vehicles normally based in any of the EEA Member States are on a similar footing admitted to these three countries.

See for the question whether Andorra, Serbia and Switzerland are bound by the interpretation of the European Court of Justice regarding the notion of *normally based,* paragraph 3.5.4.

6.2.8.4 Checks on insurance

A few remarks on the Member States' obligation under Article 7 to ensure that incoming vehicles from third countries – other than the three countries referred to above (Andorra, Serbia and Switzerland) – are covered by an insurance policy. The first and most logical measure is a verification at the borders. Incoming vehicles from third countries other than vehicles as referred to in Article 8(2) will have to be checked at the borders of the EU. Once they have entered the territory of one of the Member States, Article 4 of the Directive precludes the Member States from checking their insurance status either at the frontiers between Member States or internally. Article 4 does however allow non-systematic checks on insurance provided that those checks are not discriminatory and are carried out as part of a control which is not aimed exclusively at insurance verification.

> This provision seriously reduces the possibilities of the Member States to combat uninsured driving and has been criticised widely. The issue is addressed In the Proposal for a new Directive already referred to in paragraphs 3.5.1 and 3.5.3. In the new wording:
>
> > "such checks on insurance (may be carried out) provided that those checks are non-discriminatory, necessary and proportionate to achieve the end pursued, *a)* are carried out as part of a control which is not aimed exclusively at insurance verification or *b)* they form part of a general system of checks on the national territory and do not require the vehicle to stop."

45. The Bureau of Bosnia and Herzegovina having signed the Multilateral Agreement in 2019, it is to be expected that the system of deemed insurance cover will soon become applicable in that country. A decision of the European Commission is necessary and may be expected to be adopted in the course of 2019.

In other words: electronic means of checking the vehicle (registration plate recognition techniques) would henceforth be allowed. Definitely an improvement although if stopping the vehicle is not permitted, it will still be unclear how this may work out in practice. Close cooperation between the national authorities will be essential.

6.2.8.5 *National legislation: Germany, Belgium*

The character of the Directive as an instrument of minimum harmonisation allows national legislators to go even further than to oblige insurers to provide cover in the EEA, Andorra, Serbia and Switzerland. Germany for instance has introduced a (truly) European wide cover: accidents occurring in Europe in a geographical sense – although that concept is not overly well defined – have to be covered.
On the one hand this means that accidents in countries not (yet) belonging to the Green Card system must also be covered; on the other hand is the mandatory cover more restricted than the Green Card system: the Russian Federation and Turkey are only partly European, the larger part of their territory being situated in Asia. This would fall outside the scope of the German compulsory cover, but under the rules of the Council of Bureaux insurers who cover these countries will have to extend their cover to the entire territory of the country and not only the European part.

Belgium too has legislation obliging insurers to provide a geographically wider cover than just the EEA, Andorra, Serbia and Switzerland: Belgian MTPL insurers may not exclude from cover Morocco, Tunisia and Turkey.

6.2.9 *Different types of damage*

6.2.9.1 *Property and bodily injury*

According to Article 3(4) the compulsory insurance policy has to cover both damage to property and personal injuries (including fatalities). Paragraph 2 of Article 3(2) states that the extent of the liability covered and the terms and conditions of the cover shall be determined by the national legislation. In our opinion that includes the scope of the notions of 'damage to property' and of 'personal injury'. Because the Directive only provides for minimum harmonisation Member States are free to extend the scope of their compulsory MTPL policies to other types of damage, as will be discussed in the following two paragraphs.

Does this mean that damage has to be compensated in full, *restitutio in integrum*? The *Petillo* decision of the CJEU seems to cast some doubt on this issue:

> "(The MID Directives) must be interpreted as not precluding national legislation such as that at issue in the main proceedings, which lays down a specific compensation scheme for non-material damage resulting from minor physical injuries caused by road traffic accidents, limiting the

> compensation payable for such damage in comparison with the compensation allowed for identical damage arising from causes other than those accidents."[46]

A similar approach follows from the (EFTA) *Halla Helgadóttir* decision of the EFTA Court.[47]

> Helgadóttir argued that under the rigid and standardised rules of the applicable Icelandic Torts Damages Act, she would not be compensated for all the damage to her person or the actual loss caused by the accident and that the Directives contain minimum requirements of how the amount of compensation is to be determined and how the amount is to relate to the actual damage.

The Court didn't follow this line of reasoning and decided that it falls within the competence of the Contracting Party (in this instance Iceland) to establish a standardised system for calculating the losses (in this case: determining the compensation for loss in the absence of adequate indicators regarding earning possibilities in an uncertain future for victims for whom there is no previous record of income from employment, or where such income is lower than would result from full-time employment).

In another decision, by the EFTA Court of Justice, in the *Nguyen* case, the Court on the other hand decided that it is not compatible with the Motor Insurance Directives to except compensation for non-material damage ('pain and suffering') from the cover under the national law.[48] This decision of 2008 is at first sight somewhat difficult to understand in the light of the later decision in the *Haasová* case, discussed in the next paragraph, which seems to open the possibility that national law may exclude non-material damage from the compulsory cover. The relevant difference with the *Nguyen* case however seems to be the position of the 'injured person': in *Nguyen* the victim of the accident itself was the plaintiff, whereas in *Haasová* the question was whether next-of-kin could be excluded from compensation of their pain and suffering

The *Nguyen* decision is confusing in another aspect as well: it is common understanding that the European Union has no competence in the field of the law on liability or the law on compensation. The Court expressed this principle in a number of decisions. *Nguyen* however can hardly be understood other than as a decision on

46. CJEU, Judgment of 23 January 2014, *Petillo*, C-371/12, EU:C:2013:652.
47. EFTA Court, Judgment of 14 June 2001, *Halla Helgadóttir*, E-07/00.
48. EFTA Court, Judgment of 20 June 2008, *Nguyen*, E-08/07. The Court also held that 'excepting redress for non-economic injury ('pain and suffering'), which is a form of civil liability, from compulsory insurance coverage under national law constitutes a sufficiently serious breach of EEA law to be able to entail State liability'.

the law of liability. This issue will be discussed in further detail in paragraph 6.2.13.12.

It is relevant in the context of the question of *restitutio in integrum* that *Nguyen* seems to imply that non-material damage of the victim must be *compensated*, but does not define to what extent the damage should be *covered*.

In another decision, in the *Evans* case, involving a Guarantee Fund, the Court expressed the opinion that the amount of compensation to the victim should take into consideration the period of time between the accident and the actual payment of compensation:

> "The compensation awarded for damage or injuries caused by an unidentified or insufficiently insured vehicle, paid by the body authorised for that purpose, must take account of the effluxion of time until actual payment of the sums awarded in order to guarantee adequate compensation for the victims. It is incumbent on the Member States to lay down the rules to be applied for that purpose."[49]

Whether Member States have seen reasons to lay down such rules remains to be seen.
It seems to us that, although the dispute was between a Guarantee Fund and the victim of an unidentified vehicle, the same principle should also apply to compensation paid by an insurance company. The emphasis in the Advocate-General's opinion on equal treatment of victims would appear to support this point of view.

Our cautious conclusion is therefore that full compensation of damage is not required under the Directive, with a possible exception for the compensation of interest.

6.2.9.2 *Non pecuniary damage*

The *Nguyen* decision of the EFTA Court was discussed in the previous paragraph. Reference was also made to the *Haasová* decision.[50] The Court held that the Directives

> "must be interpreted as meaning that compulsory insurance against civil liability in respect of the use of motor vehicles must cover compensation for non-material damage suffered by the next of kin of the deceased victims of a road traffic accident, in so far as such compensation is

49. CJEU, Judgment of 4 December 2003, *Evans*, C-63/01, EU:C:2003:650; the opinion of the Advocate-General, which gives more details on the proceedings and the various positions of the parties involved than the Court decision as published on the website of the Court, can be found under reference number EU:C:2002:615.
50. CJEU, Judgment of 24 October 2013, *Haasová*, C-22/12, EU:C:2013:692.

provided for as part of the civil liability of the insured party under the national law applicable in the dispute in the main proceedings."

A similar ruling is to be found in *Drozdovs*.[51] The Court adds that national law may not lay down maximum amounts of cover for non-material damage resulting from the death of a person's next of kin in a road traffic accident – payable in accordance with national civil liability law – which are lower than the minimum amounts laid down in the Directive.

In combination with the *Nguyen* decision the Court seems to find that victims – the persons directly involved in the accident – must receive compensation for their non-material damage ('pain and suffering'), but that for other victims (next-of-kin, dependents of a deceased victim) this only applies if and when the applicable law recognises their non-material damage as a head of damage.

6.2.9.3 *Other types of damage: legal costs, late payment interest; costs of preventive measures*

The question of late payment interests has already been discussed in paragraph 6.2.9.1 in the context of the *Evans* decision of the European Court.

As far as the compensation of legal costs which the victim had to make and costs of preventive measures, it seems to us that a logical approach would be that these costs must be covered under the policy if and in so far as they are to be compensated according to the applicable law on liability and compensation. This would be consistent with European case law.[52]

6.2.10 *Amounts of cover*

6.2.10.1 *History*

The issue of the amounts of cover under the policy was addressed for the first time in the 2nd Directive; the 1st Directive intriguingly enough was silent on the subject. Article 1(2) of the 2nd Directive, after having instructed the Member States to encompass both property damage and bodily injury in the compulsory cover under the policy, provides for minimum amounts for both heads of damage:

"2. Without prejudice to any higher guarantees which Member States may lay down, each Member State shall require that the amounts for which such insurance is compulsory are at least:

51. CJEU, Judgment of 24 October 2013, *Drozdovs*, C-277/12, EU:C:2013:685.
52. *Haasová* and *Drozdovs* are examples.

- in the case of personal injury, 350,000 ECU where there is only one victim; where more than one victim is involved in a single claim, this amount shall be multiplied by the number of victims,
- in the case of damage to property 100,000 ECU per claim, whatever the number of victims.

Member States may, in place of the above minimum amounts, provide for a minimum amount of 500,000 ECU for personal injury where more than one victim is involved in a single claim or, in the case of personal injury and damage to property, a minimum overall amount of 600,000 ECU per claim whatever the number of victims or the nature of the damage."[53]

These amounts remained untouched for more than 20 years, despite the sometimes significant inflation in various countries. The general inflation of consumer prices is frequently even exceeded by the rise of the amounts of compensation in practice negotiated between insurers and victims or awarded by the courts.

An important reason behind this 'super-inflation' is the development of the costs of medical treatment, which often grow faster than the general inflation index, due to improved and new treatments and new approaches to the victim's disability (rehabilitation of partly disabled victims). In the sphere of material damage the advancing technology of vehicles plays a role: sensors in the front and rear bumpers of vehicles, airbags, electric mirrors etc. increase the costs of repair in case of an accident. Since the costs of repair of vehicles seldom exceed the minimum sum insured under the 2nd Directive, even in case of a multiple accident, the average amount claimed may increase but will only rarely result in under-compensation of victims due to insufficient insurance cover.

The 2nd Directive offers the Member States a number of alternatives:

For property damage the first option is an amount of 100,000 ECU per accident.
For personal injury the Member States can opt either for an amount of 350,000 ECU for each victim in the accident, or for an amount of 500,000 ECU for all victims in the accident combined. It depends on the number of victims which alternative offers the best protection to the victim.
A third option is to settle for an amount of 600,000 ECU for bodily injury and property damage combined for all victims in the accident.
In the first two alternatives the amounts for bodily injury and property damage are 'earmarked': excessive property damage will not be compensated at the expense of bodily injury claims and vice versa. In the third alternative there is a possibility that victims with bodily injuries will be undercompensated because of excessive material damage. National legislation will have to offer a solution for this dilemma.

53. The ECU – the European Currency Unit – can be seen as the predecessor to the Euro. Its conversion value to national currencies, which was reviewed every four years, was calculated on the basis of a 'basket' of European national currencies. At the introduction of the Euro its conversion rate was fixed at the level of the ECU at that date.

6.2.10.2 5th Directive: two alternative regimes

The 5th Directive recognised the necessity to increase the amounts in the light of more than 20 years of inflation. The Commission calculated the inflation based on the European consumer price index from 1984 until 2002 at approximately 73%.

> It would have implied an increase of the amounts of the 2nd Directive from 100,000 ECU to € 173,000, from 350,000 ECU to € 605,000, from 500,000 ECU to 865,000 and from 600,000 ECU to € 1,038,000.
> In the course of the debates on this issue in European Parliament a range of different alternatives were proposed. In the original proposal of the Commission the possibility of a limit per accident or a cap on the number of bodily injury victims was absent. In Parliament the proposals varied from € 2 Million per accident for bodily injury and property damage combined to two times € 10 Million: one amount for property and another for bodily injury. Parliament in its first reading accepted amounts of € 5 Million per accident for bodily injury and € 2 Million for property. In the Common Position of Parliament and Council the final amounts are € 5 Million per accident for all bodily injury victims together or – alternatively – € 1 Million per victim without a limit to the number of victims; for property damage the amount of cover will be a minimum of € 1 Million.

And these amounts were eventually adopted as the new limits in the Directive. It is useful to emphasise that they are minimum amounts and that, in line with the principle that the Directive offers minimum harmonisation, national legislation may provide for higher cover. And they frequently do. A fairly up-to-date overview of the actual national amounts can be found on www.cobx.org.

The introduction of the new limits is however not completely harmonised. The Member States may opt for a transitional period which was to end at the latest on 11 June 2012, five years after the date of publication of the 5th Directive in the Official Journal of the EU. After two and a half years the minimum amounts should however been brought at a level of at least half of the new sums.

The background of the possibility of a transitional period was the significant difference in the existing national amounts of cover. Not every Member State was felt to be economically in a position to increase these amounts in one stroke to the new elevated levels.
Since the Member States could decide individually on the duration of the transitional period – albeit with 11 June 2012 as the deadline for adapting – the situation regarding the applicable amounts on a national level was for a considerable time rather confusing, not least because of the indexation system discussed in the next paragraph.[54]

6.2.10.3 *Periodic indexation*

In order to prevent future inflation eroding the limits again, a new element of periodic indexation is introduced.
Every five years, starting 11 June 2007, the date by which every Member State should have brought the Directive into force, or on the expiry of any transitional period, the amounts referred to above will be subject to adjustment in line with the European consumer price index, as defined in Regulation (EC) 2494/95, the EICP.

Since the duration of the transitional periods has varied, the dates of first indexation were also different. Was this complexity really necessary?

The amounts are automatically reviewed – not unsurprisingly the Directive only speaks of *increased*, thus neglecting the possibility of deflation – with a percentage corresponding with the development of the EICP in the five years' period immediately preceding the date of review, and are rounded off at a multiple of € 10,000.

The Directive claims the automatic adaptation of the amounts of cover. The new limits are periodically published in the Official Journal. This information has until now always been published rather late. It seems that the Commission itself is not overly happy with the procedure of Article 9(2) of the Directive.

The last review of 1 January 2017 has increased the amounts to € 1,220,000 per bodily injury victim or € 6,070,000 for all bodily injury victims combined and € 1,220,000 for damage to property. Inflation since the previous review amounted to 8,36%.
The next indexation is scheduled for 2022.

54. In their proposal for a new Directive (referred to in para 3.5.1), the European Commission presents a more harmonised way of adapting the amounts of cover to the inflation. This proposal should put an end to the different indexation periods, still applicable in the different Member States. The amounts of € 1 million and € 5 million, adopted with the 5th Directive, are increased in the new proposal to € 1,220,000 and € 6,070,000.

> It seems to us that this indexation scheme does not entirely rule out the desirability of periodic fundamental reviews of the amounts, first of all because inflation levels in the EU may vary – which leads to erosion of the minimum cover in Member States with high inflation – but also because, for reasons explained above, the consumer price index does not in all likelihood reflect the inflation of claimed (and awarded) amounts of compensation. The introduction of such reviews is not however being considered with any urgency.

Due to the fact that different transitional periods as referred to in paragraph 6.2.10.2 apply in different Member States, it can be rather complicated to determine which amounts are applicable in a given Member State.

> Currently 13 Member States are subject to lower minimum amounts than the higher amounts laid down in the Directive. This is due to the fact that the 5th Directive allowed Member States to apply transition periods during which they could delay applying the full minimum amounts. However, due to different reference dates for different Member States for periodically recalculating the minimum amounts, there remains a gap between those 13 Member States and all other Member States. This is because, although the transition periods have meanwhile expired, the respective dates of the end of the transition periods are still used as reference dates for the five-yearly inflation updating. Therefore these minimum amounts are still not the same across all Member States.

In the proposal for a new Directive the indexation date will be identical for all Member States: every five years after the date of entry into force of the amended Directive.

6.2.10.4 Which cover is applicable? Article 14 point (b) of the Directive

Amounts of minimum cover vary from Member State to Member State. A number of countries – not only in the EU, but also non-Members – have introduced unlimited cover for bodily injury damage; one country – Luxembourg – even has unlimited cover for property damage as well.[55] Others demand significantly higher amounts than foreseen in the Directive.

That raised the question which amount would have to be taken into consideration in case of an accident involving a visiting vehicle: the amount of the country of accident, or – alternatively – the legal minimum amount of the country where the vehicle is normally based if the latter is higher? The question was resolved in the 3rd Directive in its Article 2, second indent, now Article 14 point (b) of the codified Directive.

55. Albeit with an exception for damage caused by fire or explosion, which seems to reduce the impact of this unlimited cover for property damage significantly.

The highest of the two amounts has to be applied. Although the wording of the Directive may not be altogether conclusive, we are of the opinion that Article 14 only refers to the *amounts* of cover and not to other elements, such as types of damage, circle of persons insured or protected by the cover or even the liability regime.

This interpretation is supported by the European Court in its *ERGO Insurance* and *Gjensidige Baltic* decisions.[56] In case C-475/14 the referring court asked whether Article 14 of the codified Directive contains a conflict-of-law rule (with the consequence that it would 'overrule' the rules of the *Rome I* and *Rome II Regulations* under Article 23 of *Rome I* and 27 of *Rome II*). The Court held that

> "(Article 14) (...) deals exclusively with the territorial extent and the level of cover that the insurer is required to provide (...). The term 'level of cover' indicates the financial aspect rather than other aspects of the cover."[57]

The Directive clearly states that this cover has to be provided on the basis of the same single premium as referred to in paragraph 6.2.8.2.

6.2.10.5 Amounts per claim or per accident?

An interesting aspect of the wording of the Directive can be observed in the English language version, compared with several others. Whereas for instance the French, the German, the Italian, the Spanish and the Dutch language versions of the Directive refer to the equivalent of the English word 'event', or 'accident', the English text uses the word 'claim'.[58] This is obviously a major difference: any accident may not only lead to more than one victim or injured party, but each injured party may bring more than one claim: for medical costs, loss of earnings, pain and suffering etc. If the principle behind the Directive would be that the minimum amounts of cover would be at the disposal of the injured party for each and every *claim*, the difference between the option for an overall amount per event irrespective off the number of victims and an amount per victim would be negligible.

The difference in wording has in our experience never led to different interpretations: even in the UK the word 'claim' has always been interpreted as referring to the accident.

56. CJEU, Judgment of 21 January 2016, *ERGO Insurance*, C-359/14 and CJEU, Judgment of 21 January 2016, *Gjensidige Baltic*, C-475/14, EU:C:2016:40 (joined cases). See for a further analysis of the decisions para 8.4.5.3.
57. C-359/14 and C-475/14, para 42.
58. Dutch: *'ongeval'*; German: *'Schadensfall'*; French: *'sinistre'*; Italian: *'sinistro'*; Spanish: *'siniestro'*.

In an amendment to the Proposals of the European Commission for a new Directive, European Parliament proposes to replace the word 'claim' in Article 9 by the word 'accident' (and the word 'victim' by the term 'injured party'). See also *infra* para 6.2.12.1.

6.2.11 *Persons insured: the liable party or parties*

6.2.11.1 *The Directive*

The circle of persons whose liability has to be covered under the policy is wider than the driver of the vehicle alone. The subsequent Directives are however silent on the question whose liability is to be covered under the policy. The answer is apparently left to the national legislators.

The 1st Directive is silent on the subject. The only hint is to be found in its title: "Council Directive of 24 April 1972 on the approximation of the laws of the Member States relating to *insurance against civil liability in respect of the use of motor vehicles* [Italics by the authors] and to the enforcement of the obligation to insure against such liability."[59] No indication is given of whose liability has to be covered.

The 2nd Directive however refers to the issue, albeit in a rather indirect way. Article 3 reads: "The members of the family of the insured person, driver *or any other person who is liable under civil law in the event of an accident* [Italics by the authors], and whose liability is covered by the insurance referred to in Article 1 (1) shall not be excluded from insurance in respect of their personal injuries by virtue of that relationship."

Other persons than the driver may be held liable as well. In many jurisdictions liability rests by law on the registered owner or keeper of the vehicle, in addition to the liability of the driver; passengers may be liable for damage caused when inattentively opening the passenger door and injuring a cyclist or they may contribute to the accident by distracting the attention of the driver. All these potentially liable parties will have to be covered under the insurance policy.

In *BTA Baltic Insurance Company* the European Court ruled that the concept of 'use of the vehicle' also covers damage caused by a passenger when opening the passenger door of a vehicle which is parked in a car park and damaging the vehicle parked next to it. Arguments proposed by the MTPL insurer of the vehicle which caused the damage (*i*) that the vehicle was not in motion, (*ii*) that the damage was caused by the passenger and not the

59. The confusion which is the result of the different language variants regarding the phrase 'use of the vehicle – in traffic or not – was already discussed in paragraphs 6.2.3 and 6.2.4. It seems that the German language version of the Directive is even more vague about the issue. The German text simply refers to '*die Angleichung der Rechtsvorschriften der Mitgliedstaaten bezüglich der Kraftfahrzeug-Haftpflichtversicherung und der Kontrolle der entsprechenden Versicherungspflicht*', without any reference to the use – in traffic or otherwise – of the vehicle.

driver were dismissed by the Court. Opening a passenger door is an act which is consistent with the normal function of a vehicle as a means of transport.[60] See also para 6.2.4.

6.2.11.2 National legislation; liability regimes; Switzerland and the Netherlands

Several legislations hold more than one party in the accident accountable, jointly and severally. Others channel liability to certain players: Switzerland for instance channels liability to the registered keeper of the vehicle.

In the Netherlands liability for damage caused or enhanced by the transport of dangerous substances and goods in a vehicle with a maximum mass exceeding 3,500 kg is channelled to the registered keeper of the vehicle whilst at the same time exonerating other potentially responsible parties, such as the driver of the vehicle, from liability.[61]

Although the Directive is silent and there is no European Court of Justice case law, it is in our opinion safe to assume that all persons liable for the consequences of the accident under the applicable national law should be covered under the policy.

6.2.12 Protected parties

6.2.12.1 Victims and persons injured, a relevant distinction?

One of the most difficult aspects of the Directive is its wording, not only because of the variations in the different language versions (an example has already been discussed in paragraphs 6.2.4) but also apparent inconsistencies in the use of expressions. The question therefore occasionally rises of whether or not a different word in a similar or at least comparable context has a different meaning.

The Directive's use of different expressions to indicate persons who are entitled to compensation, whether from insurance undertakings, Bureaux, Guarantee Funds, claims representatives or Compensation Bodies, is perhaps the most confusing. Since some – unexpressed – principle may lie behind the different use of words in the various Articles of the Directive, it is useful to analyse this aspect further.

The problem to begin with is that only one of the expressions used in the Directive has been defined in Article 1 (Definitions): *injured party*:

> "'Injured party' means any person entitled to compensation in respect of any loss or injury caused by vehicles."

---

60. CJEU, Judgment of 15 November 2018, *BTA Baltic Insurance Company*, C-648/17, EU:C:2018:917.
61. This channelled liability is combined with compulsory insurance under the MTPL law, with a wider notion of heads of damage to be compensated and including accidents occurring whilst the vehicle is not participating in traffic.

This expression – the Directive also refers to 'the party injured' – appears in Articles 5, 17, 18, 20 – 25 and 28. The context consistently seems to be that of an insured vehicle, with an exception in Article 25, which deals with claims against the Compensation Body in case of unidentified vehicles or unidentifiable insurance undertakings.
Another expression is however not defined: *victim*. This word is used in the Articles 9, 10, 11, (the title of) 12 (although not in its body), 13 and 26.
Both expressions are used in the recitals of the preamble, in a seemingly not entirely consistent way.

Linguistically it appears that 'victim' refers to the person directly involved in the accident, i.e. the person directly suffering damage, be it to property or bodily injury. The scope of persons (and entities) entitled to compensation under any applicable law is usually wider and includes: next of kin; dependents of an injured or deceased victim; subrogated entities such as private insurers or social security institutions that have compensated the victim. These are covered by the notion of 'injured party'.

The Court of Justice of the European Union, in two decisions in the context of Regulation 44/2001 (now Regulation 1215/12), attached importance to the difference.[62,63,64]

> The first of the two decisions is the *FBTO Schadeverzekeringen* decision of 13 December 2007.[65] The question was whether Mr Odenbreit, a German resident, who was the victim of an accident in the Netherlands caused by a vehicle insured by FBTO Schadeverzekeringen, a Dutch insurance company, could start proceedings against FBTO in his Member State of residence on the basis of Article 11(2) of Regulation 44/2001. The answer of the Court was in the affirmative.
> The second decision is the *Vorarlberger* decision.[66] In this case the social insurer Vorarlberger Gebietskrankenkasse, after having compensated the Austrian victim of a car accident in Germany for which a German motorist was held liable, argued that they in the same way as Mr Odenbreit in the FBTO case, could start proceedings in their Member State of residence, Austria. In this instance however the Court decided negatively, based

62. Council Regulation (EC) No 44/2001 of 22 December 2000 on jurisdiction and the recognition and enforcement of judgments in civil and commercial matters, OJ L 12, 16.1.2001, p. 1, (*Brussels I Regulation*).
63. Regulation EU No 1215/2012 of the European Parliament and the Council of 12 December 2012 on jurisdiction and the recognition and enforcement of judgments in civil and commercial matters (recast), OJL 351, 20.12.2012, p. 1, (*Brussels Ia Regulation*).
64. The two decisions discussed here will be analysed more in detail in para 8.3.6.3.
65. CJEU, Judgment of 13 December 2007, *FBTO Schadeverzekeringen*, C-463/06, EU:C:2007:792. (often also referred to as the 'Odenbreit decision').
66. CJEU, Judgment of 17 September 2009, *Vorarlberger Gebietskrankenkasse*, C-347/08, EU:C:2009:561.

on both a comparison of the various language versions of the Regulation as well as its intentions: the protection of 'weaker' claimants.

Not only persons directly involved in the accident fall under the notion of 'victim', however: dependants may under circumstances also be regarded as such, as the Court observes in *FBTO Schadeverzekeringen*, paragraph 44:

> "In contrast, where the statutory assignee of the rights of the directly injured party may himself be considered to be a weaker party, such an assignee should be able to benefit from special rules on the jurisdiction of courts laid down in those provisions. This is particularly the situation, as the Spanish government states, of the heirs of the person injured in an accident."[67]

It is a general principle that identical phrases and expressions should be interpreted as much as possible in a harmonised way, by reference to the purpose and general scheme of rules, of which that provision forms part. Strictly speaking, 'victim' may be interpreted differently in Regulation 44/2001 (or 1215/12) than in the Directive, since the latter concerns a different set of provisions (a different piece of legislation). In our opinion, however, the narrow relation between the Directive and the Regulation argues for a harmonised interpretation of the word 'victim' in both texts.

Consequently, 'victim' refers to a narrower circle of persons than 'injured party'. It follows that not all 'injured parties' benefit from – for instance – the protection of the Guarantee Fund. This interpretation would also be in keeping with the concept of the subsidiarity of the Guarantee Fund. We admit however that this thesis has not yet been tested before the Court in Luxembourg.

It may be useful to bear in mind that the Directive offers minimum harmonisation and that Member States may provide for higher levels of protection. In the Netherlands for instance, access to the Guarantee Fund is not restricted to victims and their dependants: all persons entitled to compensation in respect of any loss or injury caused by vehicles have a right to claim, including subrogated insurance companies and social security institutions.

67. In another decision the Court held that an employer, having continued to pay his employee's salary after an accident and being subrogated in the victim's rights, can also start legal proceedings against the insurer in the Member State of his residence, providing he has a direct right of action. Apparently the employer is also regarded to be a weaker party. CJEU, Judgment of 20 July 2017, *MMA IARD*, C-340/16, EU:C:2017:576.

The European Parliament, in its amendments to the proposal for a new Directive amending the codified Directive, also addressed the issue of the not always consistent use of the words 'victim' and 'injured party'.[68] The solution resembles the approach of Alexander the Great when faced with the Gordian knot: it is simply proposed to replace the word 'victim' throughout the Directive by the phrase 'injured party'. Whereas this may seem the simplest solution, it may have serious consequences. One consequence will be that the minimum amount of cover to be provided under an insurance policy in those jurisdictions which have chosen for the variant of an amount per victim, now will have to provide this same amount not only for the person directly involved and injured in the accident but also for other injured parties – such as next of kin of the injured of deceased victim and for his or her subrogated insurers. Also Guarantee Funds and Compensation Bodies, in those jurisdictions where other injured parties than the victim are deprived of access to those bodies, may be confronted with a larger circle of claimants. It is to be hoped that the effects of this amendment will be analysed thoroughly before adopting it in the final text of the Directive.

6.2.12.2 Passengers

a) The 1st Directive was silent on the question of cover for passengers, as was the 2nd. The 3rd Directive addressed the issue, now codified in Article 12(2) point (1):

> "Without prejudice to the second subparagraph of Article 13 (1), the insurance referred to in Article 3 shall cover liability for personal injuries to all passengers, other than the driver, arising out of the use of a vehicle."[69]

The European Court clarified Article 13(1) in quite a series of cases. They deal with different aspects of cover of or damage to passengers.

In *Mendes Ferreira* the Court decided on the question of equal treatment of passengers who are members of the family of the insured and other third-party passengers.[70] Family members cannot be exempted from cover for their personal injuries if other third-party passengers would receive compensation in the same circumstances.

b) The protection of passengers of drunken drivers came before the Court in *Storebrand Skadeforsikring* and *Candolin*.[71,72] In *Storebrand*, the (EFTA) Court delivered an advisory opinion regarding a passenger's right to compensation if that passenger knew or must have known that the driver of the motor vehicle was under the influ-

68. Document COM (2018) 336.
69. The matter of Article 13(1) of the codified Directive will be discussed in para 6.2.13.3.
70. CJEU, Judgment of 14 September 2000, *Mendes Ferreira*, C-348/98, EU:C:2000:442.
71. EFTA Court, Advisory Opinion of 17 November 1999, *Storebrand Skadeforsikring*, E-01/99.
72. CJEU, Judgment of 30 June 2005, *Candolin a.o.*, C-537/03,EU:C:2005:417.

ence of alcohol at the time of the accident and there was a causal link between the influence of alcohol and the injury. The Court held it to be incompatible with EEA law for such a passenger to be denied compensation unless there are special grounds for doing so.

In *Candolin*, the Court of Justice of the European Union had to pronounce on legislation permitting refusal or disproportionate reduction of compensation to passengers on the basis of their contribution to the injury or loss. In the case that led to the decision, the driver was under influence of alcohol and the passengers knew about the driver's status. The Court ruled that such legislation was not compatible with the Directive.[73,74]

More or less in parallel to the *Candolin* decision, the 5th Directive, on an initiative of European Parliament, inserted a provision in the Directive in its Article 4, amending the 3rd Directive, now Article 13(3) of the codified Directive, which also deals with the issue:

> "Member States shall take the necessary measures to ensure that any statutory provision or any contractual clause contained in an insurance policy which excludes a passenger from such cover on the basis that he knew or should have known that the driver of the vehicle was under the influence of alcohol or of any other intoxicating agent at the time of an accident, shall be deemed to be void in respect of the claims of such passenger."

There seems to be a minor difference between the *Candolin* decision and the provision in the Directive: whereas the Court also forbids (disproportionate) reductions of cover, the Directive only refers to exclusions. We are however of the opinion that *Candolin* still holds and that (disproportionate) reduction of compensation is also not permitted.

Candolin leaves us with another question: the Court refers to the passenger's own contribution to the injury or loss they have suffered. That raises the question of the admissibility of exclusions or limitations in other contexts, for example passengers

73. See also paragraph 34 of the *Storebrand* opinion: 'Submissions have been made about the possibility of reducing compensation as a consequence of contributory negligence. The Court limits itself to stating that a reduction to compensation due to contributory negligence must be possible in exceptional circumstances. However, the principles set out in the Motor Vehicle Insurance Directive must be respected. A finding that a passenger who passively rode in a car driven by an intoxicated driver is to be denied compensation or that compensation is to be reduced in a way which is disproportionate to the contribution to the injury by the injured party would be incompatible with the Directives.'
74. The Court also ruled that the fact that the (lethally injured) passenger was the owner of the vehicle is not relevant and cannot be used to deny compensation.

not wearing seatbelts or – as a passenger of a moped or motor cycle – crash helmets. This issue has until now not been put before the Court.

c) The question of passengers in a part of a vehicle not designed or construed for the transport of persons was the issue in two decisions, but the outcomes were totally different. In the first case, *Withers*, the Court held that legislation which does not require the policy to cover personal injuries of passengers in such a part of the vehicle was permissible.[75] In the second case, *Farrell I*, the outcome was the opposite: the Directive precludes national legislation whereby compulsory motor vehicle liability insurance does not cover liability in respect of personal injuries to persons travelling in a part of a motor vehicle which has not been designed and constructed with seating accommodation for passengers.[76] Since *Farrell I* is from a later date than *Whithers*, the Court seems to have swung around.[77]

Then there is the question of passengers of uninsured vehicles, especially if their awareness of the uninsured status can be proven. In *Churchill Insurance Company and Evans*, the problem was the specific situation in the UK, where it is technically not the vehicle that is insured, but the driver.[78] In this case the driver was not insured for driving the vehicle, though the injured passenger was and he also had given the driver permission.[79] In *Commission v Ireland*, the Court ruled that an exclusion from the right to compensation by the Guarantee Fund of any person who entered any uninsured vehicle – and not only those who entered an uninsured vehicle which caused the damage or injury – is not compatible with the Directive.[80]

The question of liability for injuries of a passenger in case of a collision between two vehicles, the event not being attributable to the fault of the drivers, was

75. CJEU, Advisory Opinion of 14 October 2002, *Withers*, C-158/01, EU:C:2002:580.
76. CJEU, Judgment of 19 April 2007, *Farrell I*, C-356/05, EU:C:2007:229; another issue that rose from the same accident, the possible direct effect of the Directive against the Irish Guarantee Fund was decided in CJEU, Judgment of 10 October 2017, *Farrell II*, C-413/15, EU:C:2017:745.
77. See also CJEU, Judgment of 7 August 2018, *David Smith v Patrick Meade a.o.*, C-122/17, EU:C:2018:631. National courts cannot, solely on the basis of EU law, disapply national rules of law, or clauses in insurance contracts, incompatible with EU law; private persons may however obtain from the Member State, if justified, compensation for any loss sustained. This relates to the question whether private persons may rely in their mutual relations on EU law if national legislation is incompatible with EU law, the so called 'horizontal effect'. This aspect of EU law will however not be discussed in detail, since it is a matter of generic EU law.
78. CJEU, Judgment of 1 December 2011, *Churchill Insurance Company and Evans*, C-442/10, EU:C:2011:799.
79. It is quite possible that the injured and insured passenger was also the owner of the vehicle. That would not make any difference for his claim under the insurance policy, as *Candolin* demonstrates.
80. CJEU, Judgment of 21 February 2008, *Commission v Ireland*, C-211/07, EU:C:2008:111.

decided in *Marques Almeida*.[81] There is no rule of EU law that precludes civil liability in such a situation to be limited or excluded.

d) The *conclusion* seems to be that Article 13(1) does not require Member States to introduce (a form of) liability for damage to passengers, but if such a liability exists under national law, then it should be covered by the MTPL insurance policy. It is not relevant whether a vehicle (or the driver) is insured or not, nor whether the vehicle (or the part of the vehicle where the passenger is seated) is designed or construed for transport of passengers. The question of passengers of stolen vehicles and of passengers in a vehicle with a driver under influence will also be discussed in paragraphs 6.2.13.3 and 6.2.13.4 respectively, since they are the subject of specific provisions in the Directive.

6.2.12.3 Passengers carried free of charge

It follows from *Mendes Ferreira and Delgado Correia Ferreira* that it is irrelevant whether the passenger was transported free of charge or not.[82] Hitchhikers and other non-paying passengers are protected, as are paying passengers, provided other passengers would in similar circumstances be entitled to compensation.

6.2.12.4 Passengers of stolen vehicles

Since the position of passengers of stolen vehicles is closely related to the question of the admissible exclusions, the discussion on this topic will be referred to paragraph 6.2.13.3. The intervention of the Guarantee Fund is furthermore described in paragraphs 4.3.4 and 4.4.5. Let it suffice here to say that any exclusion in respect of claims by third parties who have been victims of an accident caused by – *inter alia* – persons who do not have express or implied authorisation to use the vehicle shall be deemed to be void, according to Article 13(1), first paragraph and (*a*). Obviously a thief will not have authorisation to use the stolen vehicle. However, there is a special provision limiting the protection of passengers of such vehicles. Article 13(1), second paragraph states:

> "However, the provision or clause referred to in point (a) of the first subparagraph may be invoked against persons who voluntarily entered the vehicle which caused the damage or injury, when the insurer can prove that they knew the vehicle was stolen."

Although this sub-paragraph seems to offer no room for another decision by national legislators we are of the opinion that national law may opt not to allow insurers to insert such an exclusion in their policies.

81. CJEU, Judgment of 23 October 2012, *Marques Almeida*, C-300/10, EU:C:2012:656.
82. CJEU, Judgment of 14 September 2000, *Mendes Ferreira and Delgado Correia Ferreira*, C-348/98, EU:C:2000:442.

In a third sub-paragraph the Directive further complicates the regime of protection of victims of amongst others stolen vehicles: Member States have the option of not applying the provision in the first subparagraph (and therefore to apply an exclusion from the cover under the policy) if and in so far as the victim may obtain compensation for the damage suffered from a social security body.

6.2.12.5 *Vulnerable road users*

Sometimes the Directive seems to state the obvious. Article 12(1) is an example of such a seemingly superfluous provision:

> "The insurance referred to in Article 3 shall cover personal injuries and damage to property suffered by pedestrians, cyclists and other non-motorised users of the roads who, as a consequence of an accident in which a motor vehicle is involved, are entitled to compensation in accordance with national civil law."

The Article is the remnant of a lengthy and somewhat confusing discussion between Commission and Parliament when drafting the 5th Directive. The Commission initially proposed a 100 % liability of the vehicle for damage to pedestrians and cyclists, leaving at the same time open the possibility that the pedestrian or cyclist would also be to some extent liable for damage to the motor vehicle. It seems that the Commission confused questions of cover with questions of liability.

This approach went too far for the taste of European Parliament and the provision was rejected. In the following Conciliation procedure between Parliament and the Commission the above text was accepted.

> The provision seems rather unnecessary: we can hardly imagine any MTPL law that would allow an exclusion of cover for pedestrians and cyclists, although that would not necessarily imply full, objective liability. But then, Article 12(3) does not require national law to provide for objective liability. The rapporteur in European Parliament for the Committee for legal affairs and Internal Market, Willy Rothley (D), made a remark during the 3rd European Traffic Law Days in Trier, 2002, concerning the significance of Article 12(3), stating that vulnerable road users are henceforth recognised as a separate category of road victims, thus offering an opening to introduce more focused protection. But we fail to understand why the European legislator would require such a stepping stone to improve the protection of vulnerable road users.

6.2.13 *Statutory and contractual exclusions and restrictions of cover*

6.2.13.1 *General remarks*

Since the 2nd Directive, provisions regarding the admissibility of statutory or policy exclusions and restrictions of cover are in place. Article 13 of the codified Directive is not easy to comprehend since it is construed as a rule, but with (sometimes conditional) exceptions. Moreover the European Court of Justice has expressed itself on the subject in a series of decisions regarding the basic principles and the scope of the Directive. Article 13 will be discussed in paragraphs 6.2.13.3 and 6.2.13.4. Article 17 of the Directive deals with franchises and deductibles. They will be the topic of paragraph 6.2.13.5. The case law of the CJEU will be analysed in paragraph 6.2.13.6. In that paragraph and in paragraph 6.2.13.7 – 11 we will investigate whether policy exclusions not referred to in either the Directive or – until now – case law, such as an exclusion for damage caused with intent or non-payment of premium are admissible under the Directive.

In a final paragraph 6.2.13.12 we will discuss the distinction between cover under the policy and liability, a distinction that sometimes seems to be an increasing source of confusion, that both the European legislator and the CJEU have to cope with.

But first we will discuss the distinction between external and purely internal effects of any exclusion under the policy (para 6.2.13.2).

6.2.13.2 *Internal and external effect*

In a regime without a direct right of action for the injured person, or a stronger regime like a *droit propre,* such a distinction would be meaningless. But since the very beginning of compulsory motor third party liability insurance, legislators have reinforced the victim's rights with – at least – a direct right of action and this has been recognised in the 5th Directive as an indispensable element of the protection of victims of road accidents.[83]

From a pure contractual point of view, there can only be a legal relation between the insurance undertaking and the policyholder. The third party suffering damage from an accident caused by that policyholder would, in that classical contractual framework, only have a claim against the tortfeasor (policyholder).

The construction of a direct right of action is the third party exercising the right of action of the insured against the insurer. In its basic form this means that she/he has to accept the possibility of any limitations of cover – including the absence of cover – in the contractual relationship between insurer and policyholder. This obviously is a significant flaw in the protection of the injured party.

The introduction of a direct right of action was therefore usually accompanied by a limitation of the right of the insurance company to rely on policy conditions limiting their obligations towards the insured, thus giving an even better protection to

83. French jurisprudence introduced a direct right of action for victims of traffic accidents as early as 1918. Other third parties already benefitted from such a right since the late 19th century, such as tenants of property or in case of fire the owners of neighbouring property.

the injured party since they would insofar no longer be dependent on the content of the policy.[84] In its most extreme form, the direct right of action takes the legal shape of a *droit propre*, an independent right of the injured party against the insurance company, indeed independent of any flaws in the underlying contractual relationship between the latter and its insured.

But that does not automatically imply that any limitation of the possibility of an insurance company to restrict its cover in the relationship with the injured party is also inadmissible in the contractual context with the insured. That would be a serious infringement on the freedom of contract, for which there must be compelling reasons. One reason to limit the freedom of contract and to give policy restrictions (only) internal effect might be found in the functioning of the single market, more specifically in the free of movement of persons. We will describe an example in paragraph 6.2.13.9. However, we will have to analyse case by case whether an injunction to limit or exclude the rights of the injured party also implies that the policy should protect the policyholder and the insured.

The direct right of action and the limitation for the insurer to invoke any exclusions or restrictions included in the policy will however not affect the insurer's rights entirely. Based on the contractual clauses, the insurer will most often be entitled to invoke these exclusions and restrictions against the policyholder, after having compensated the third party. This may result in a recourse right of the insurer against the policyholder and/or the driver of the vehicle. Such recourse right is however subject to (national) rules of contract law and will not be further examined here.

6.2.13.3 The exclusions of Article 13(1) of the Directive

Article 13(1) will also be discussed in the context of passengers of motor vehicles in general and of stolen motor vehicles. The provision goes beyond the scope of persons inside the vehicle, however.

It is useful to reproduce the text of Article 13(1) of the Directive in full:

> 1) "Each Member State shall take all appropriate measures to ensure that any statutory provision or any contractual clause contained in an insurance policy issued in accordance with Article 3 shall be deemed to be void in respect of claims by third parties who have been victims of

---

84. It is interesting to note that, whereas usually the right of direct action precedes the restrictions to apply policy conditions against the third party, the 2nd Directive introduced such restrictions before the introduction of a direct right of action in the 5th Directive. One might ask oneself whether a direct right of action implicitly didn't already exist since 1984. After all, in CJEU, Judgment of 28 March 1996, *Ruiz Bernáldez*, C-129/94, EU:C:1996:143 and therefore well before the 5th Directive, the Court held that the third party of an accident provoked by an intoxicated driver should be compensated but the insurer may have a contractual right of recovery against the insured. This recital wouldn't make sense without a direct right of action.

> an accident where that statutory provision or contractual clause excludes from insurance the use or driving of vehicles by:
>
> a. persons who do not have express or implied authorisation to do so;
>
> b. persons who do not hold a licence permitting them to drive the vehicle concerned;
>
> c. persons who are in breach of the statutory technical requirements concerning the condition and safety of the vehicle concerned.
>
> However, the provision or clause referred to in point (a) of the first subparagraph may be invoked against persons who voluntarily entered the vehicle which caused the damage or injury, when the insurer can prove that they knew the vehicle was stolen.
>
> Member States shall have the option — in the case of accidents occurring on their territory — of not applying the provision in the first subparagraph if and in so far as the victim may obtain compensation for the damage suffered from a social security body.
>
> 2) In the case of vehicles stolen or obtained by violence, Member States may provide that the body specified in Article 10 (1) is to pay compensation instead of the insurer under the conditions set out in paragraph 1 of this Article. Where the vehicle is normally based in another Member State, that body can make no claim for reimbursement against any body in that Member State.
>
> Member States which, in the case of vehicles stolen or obtained by violence, provide that the body referred to in Article 10 (1) is to pay compensation may fix in respect of damage to property an excess of not more than € 250 to be borne by the victim."

In short: an insurer may not rely on policy conditions restricting or excluding compensation for accidents caused by

- stolen or 'borrowed' vehicles (joy riding);
- persons without a driving licence or without a licence to drive the vehicle in question;
- vehicles that would fail to pass the periodical technical safety tests.

Member States may introduce rules of subsidiarity in the sense that social security benefits may be deducted from the compensation by the MTPL insurer. And passengers of stolen vehicles may be excluded if the insurer can prove they voluntarily entered the vehicle whilst knowing that the vehicle was stolen.

But Member States may even go further and allow insurers to exclude any compensation in case of vehicles stolen or obtained by violence, on the condition that the Guarantee Fund compensates the injured person (with the possibility of a deductible of no more than € 250); if the stolen vehicle is normally based in another Member State the Guarantee Fund will not be eligible for reimbursement from any body there, including the insurer (see also para 4.3.4 and 4.4.5).

In case of an accident caused by a stolen vehicle, the legislation of the Member State of the accident is applicable, even if the law of the Member State where the stolen vehicle is normally based does not allow a policy or statutory exclusion of cover, as was decided in *Fantozzi*:

> "Article 2 (2) of Council Directive 72/166/EEC must be interpreted as meaning that, with reference to the payment of compensation for damage caused in the territory of one Member State of the EEC by a vehicle normally based in the territory of another Member State of the EEC, if the driver of the vehicle obtained it by theft or duress, the national insurers' bureaux are under an obligation to settle such claims upon the terms laid down by their own national legislation."[85]

The second sub-paragraph only refers to 'stolen vehicles'. That raises the question whether vehicles used for joyriding also are to be regarded as 'stolen' in the meaning of the Directive. The question becomes even more confusing since Article 13(2) in permitting a deductible, not only uses the phrase 'stolen' but also 'obtained by violence'.[86] There is no jurisprudence of the European Court of Justice regarding the concept of 'stolen vehicles' or 'obtained by violence'.

Policy conditions as referred to in Article 13(1) may not be relied upon with respect to the injured third party. But would Article 13(1) also have internal effect, in the relationship between the insurer and the policyholder or the unauthorised user of the vehicle? In our opinion there is no convincing argument why such a policy condition could not be used to take recourse, not only against a thief or joyrider who causes an accident, but also against a driver without a licence or a policyholder who fails to respect the applicable technical requirements regarding the condition or the safety of the vehicle.

6.2.13.4 Alcohol exclusions: Article 13(3) of the Directive

The issue of the use of alcohol by the driver has already been discussed in paragraph 6.2.12.2. In addition to the *Storebrand* and *Candolin* decisions of the Court, the following case law deals with accidents caused under influence of alcohol:

- *Ruiz Bernáldez*, apparently involving a third party not being a passenger:[87]

> "(...) a compulsory insurance contract may not provide that in certain cases, in particular where the driver of the vehicle was intoxicated, the insurer is not obliged to pay compensation for the

85. CJEU, Judgment of 21 June 1984, *Bureau belge des assureurs automobiles/Fantozzi*, C-116/83, EU:C:1984:226.
86. There may be a subtle difference between the two concepts. A vehicle might be obtained by violence for the purpose of joyriding. Under Dutch criminal law for instance joyriding does not qualify as theft.
87. CJEU, Judgment of 28 March 1996, *Ruiz Bernáldez*, C-129/94, EU:C:1996:143.

damage to property and personal injuries caused to third parties by the insured vehicle. It may, on the other hand, provide that in such cases the insurer is to have a right of recovery against the insured."

- *Bejan:*[88]

"national law may allow insurers to exclude from a non-compulsory insurance policy – such as a casco insurance – compensation for damage caused by a driver under influence of alcohol. On the other hand a statutory obligation for insurers to exclude such damages is an infringement of both the Freedom of Establishment and the Freedom to Provide Services, although the competent national court will have to examine whether such a clause may be justified in view of explicit exceptions in the Treaty on the functioning of the EU or of compelling reasons of general interest."[89]

It is however to be emphasised that the *Bejan* decision only relates to non-compulsory insurance products and cannot simply be transposed to compulsory insurance products such as MTPL.

In *Storebrand* the EFTA Court held that an exclusion of cover is not admissible, but that – on the other hand – a proportional reduction of compensation based on the contribution of the victim to his own damage, may be justified.[90]

Ruiz Bernáldez puts beyond any doubt that a right of recourse may be exercised by an insurer who compensates third parties – including any passengers, even if they were aware that the driver was intoxicated; see *Candolin* and *Storebrand*. Article 13(3) therefore only has external and no internal effect.

6.2.13.5 *Deductibles and franchises: Article 17 of the Directive*

Insurance policies often contain clauses that subject the insured to franchises, deductibles or thresholds, having as a consequence that the insurer deducts an

88. CJEU, Judgment of 28 October 2010, *Bejan*, C-102/10, EU:C:2010:654.
89. The decision is not available in English and the above quotation is a free translation made by the authors. The official French text of the decision reads as follows: « *Le système d'assurance obligatoire de la responsabilité civile résultant de la circulation des véhicules automoteurs établi par [les directives] ne s'oppose pas à une législation nationale qui prévoit que l'assureur exclut de la couverture d'un contrat d'assurance facultative d'un véhicule automoteur les dommages causés lorsque ce véhicule est conduit par une personne se trouvant sous l'influence de l'alcool. Une législation nationale qui prévoit que l'assureur exclut de la couverture d'un contrat d'assurance facultative d'un véhicule automoteur les dommages causés lorsque ce véhicule est conduit par une personne se trouvant sous l'influence de l'alcool constitue une restriction tant à la liberté d'établissement qu'à la libre prestation des services. Il incombe à la juridiction de renvoi d'examiner dans quelle mesure cette restriction peut néanmoins être admise au titre des mesures dérogatoires expressément prévues par le traité FUE ou justifiée, conformément à la jurisprudence de la Cour, par des raisons impérieuses d'intérêt général.* »
90. EFTA Court, Advisory Opinion of 17 November 1999, *Storebrand Skadeforsikring*, E-01/99.

amount from the damages. That either means that the insured receives less than their damages (or in case of small damages nothing at all), or that they only are entitled to (full) compensation if the amount of damages exceeds the amount of the contractual threshold.

Article 17 deals with the question of the effect of such a contractual clause for the relationship with the third party: such a clause will not affect the injured party. The reference to the 'party injured' however implies that such a contractual clause may be relied upon by the insurer vis-à-vis the insured. This means in practice that the insurer has a right of recourse for the amount of the excess on his contractual counterpart or the person liable for the accident, if other than the policyholder. Excesses therefore only have internal effect.

6.2.13.6 *The case law of the Court of Justice of the EU: is the list of admissible exclusions limitative?*

In a number of decisions, the Court has interpreted the system of (the admissible exclusions of) Article 13. The question was whether in the system of the Directive, exclusions other than those explicitly mentioned in Article 13 would be permitted. In other words, does Article 13 merely give examples of inadmissible exclusions, others being equally forbidden if not explicitly allowed by the Directive? The Court consistently decided that exclusions other than those explicitly mentioned in the Directive are not permitted.

The Directive allows

- exclusion of cover for persons voluntarily entering a stolen vehicle (Article 13(1), second paragraph);
- exclusion of cover for vehicles stolen or obtained by violence, provided the Guarantee Fund intervenes, with a possibility of an excess of € 250 for property damage (Article 13(2)).

In *Ruiz Bernáldez* the Court ruled:

> 18) "In view of the aim of ensuring protection, stated repeatedly in the directives, Article 3(1) of the First Directive, as developed and supplemented by the Second and Third Directives, must be interpreted as meaning that compulsory motor insurance must enable third-party victims of accidents caused by vehicles to be compensated for all the damage to property and personal injuries sustained by them, up to the amounts fixed in Article 1(2) of the Second Directive.
>
> 19) Any other interpretation would have the effect of allowing Member States to limit payment of compensation to third-party victims of a road-traffic accident to certain types of damage, thus bringing about disparities in the treatment of victims depending on where

the accident occurred, which is precisely what the directives are intended to avoid. Article 3(1) of the First Directive would then be deprived of its effectiveness.

20) That being so, Article 3(1) of the First Directive precludes an insurer from being able to rely on statutory provisions or contractual clauses to refuse to compensate third-party victims of an accident caused by the insured vehicle.

21) In that context the first subparagraph of Article 2(1) of the Second Directive merely recalls that obligation with respect to provisions or clauses in a policy excluding from insurance the use or driving of vehicles in particular cases (persons not authorized to drive the vehicle, persons not holding a driving licence, persons in breach of the statutory technical requirements concerning the condition and safety of the vehicle). However, by way of derogation from that obligation, the second and third subparagraphs of Article 2(1) provide that certain persons may be excluded from compensation by the insurer, having regard to the situation they have themselves brought about (persons entering a vehicle which they know to have been stolen) or to the compensation they can claim elsewhere (victims who may obtain compensation for the damage suffered from a social security body)."

A similar line of argumentation can be found in *Candolin*:

18) "In view of the aim of protecting victims, the Court has held that Article 3(1) of the First Directive precludes an insurer from relying on statutory provisions or contractual clauses in order to refuse to compensate third-party victims of an accident caused by the insured vehicle (Ruiz Bernáldez, paragraph 20).

19) The Court has also held that the first subparagraph of Article 2(1) of the Second Directive simply repeats that obligation with respect to provisions or clauses in a policy excluding from insurance the use or driving of vehicles in particular cases (persons not authorised to drive the vehicle, persons not holding a driving licence, persons in breach of the statutory technical requirements concerning the condition and safety of the vehicle) (Ruiz Bernáldez, paragraph 21).

20) By way of derogation from that obligation, the second subparagraph of Article 2(1) provides that certain persons may be excluded from compensation by the insurer, having regard to the situation they have themselves brought about (persons entering a vehicle which they know to have been stolen) (Ruiz Bernáldez, paragraph 21).

21) However, as it is a provision which establishes a derogation from a general rule, the second subparagraph of Article 2(1) of the Second Directive must be interpreted strictly.

22) As the Advocate General rightly stated, in point 42 of his Opinion, any other interpretation would allow Member States to limit payment of compensation to third-party victims of a road accident to certain circumstances, which is precisely what the directives are intended to avoid."

In *Storebrand*, the EFTA Court – in conformity with these decisions – considered in an Advisory Opinion in an EFTA case[91]:

> "33) That the appellant, supported by the Government of Iceland and the Government of Norway, points out that Article 2 of the Second Motor Vehicle Insurance Directive contains an exception to the principle of compulsory insurance cover for passengers and argues that the provision should not be interpreted as being exhaustive. In the view of the Court, it is sufficient to state that Article 2 is an exception to a general rule and must so be interpreted narrowly (...). Any other conclusion would jeopardize the overall goal of the Motor Vehicle Directives, *viz*, to ensure that all passengers are, as a rule, covered."

We therefore conclude that there is little or no room for national law to facilitate other exclusions or limitations of cover than the ones mentioned above. We will examine the consequences of this approach for some restrictions or limitations that can be found in a number of national jurisdictions in paragraphs 6.2.13.7 – 11.

6.2.13.7 Intentional damage

Damage caused by wilful acts are not insurable. That is a fundamental principle of insurance law. It would be against public policy to cover damage caused intentionally by the insured. Even though the Directive is silent on the issue, this principle holds also for compulsory MTPL insurance.

That raises the question of how the innocent victim of an intentionally provoked accident will be compensated. Several solutions can be found in different jurisdictions.

In France the wilful act to cause damage renders the policy invalid *ex tunc*. The victim has a claim on the Guarantee Fund.[92] Since there is no longer any policy, it cannot be said that this is an exclusion and the question whether the clause is opposable to the injured third party under (the interpretation of the Court of) Article 13 of the Directive is irrelevant. The policy is – in retrospect – deemed never to have existed.

The Dutch MTPL law shows a different approach. The law is silent on the subject and the accepted interpretation of the law is that the insurer cannot refuse to compensate the injured third party. This is however not regarded to be against public policy, since – from the point of view of the insured – the damage is not insured, because the insurer has a claim on the insured. Under Dutch law the issue of wilfully provoked damage is purely relevant in the contractual relationship between the insurer and the insured.

91. EFTA Court, Advisory Opinion of 17 November 1999, *Storebrand Skadeforsikring*, E-01/99.
92. Albeit with a strong element of subsidiarity. See for the issue of subsidiarity of the Guarantee Funds *supra* para 4.4.2.

In an Amendment to the Commission Proposal for a new Directive the European Parliament proposes a new provision, bringing under the protection of the Guarantee Fund "*incidents where a motor vehicle is used as a weapon to commit a violent crime or terrorist act.*"

6.2.13.8 *Non-payment of premium and expiry of cover*

Non-payment of premium as such is not a valid reason to refuse compensation to third parties. It may of course be a reason to cancel the policy. And the insurer having compensated a victim in case of an accident that occurred after the date when premium was due but before the cancellation or suspension of the policy has external effect, will have a right to receive the premium and perhaps a right to be reimbursed for the compensation paid to the injured third parties.

6.2.13.9 *Contractual geographical limitations of cover*

Article 14 of the Directive states that the policy must provide cover, at a single premium, in the entire Community. Third parties in Member States other than that in which the vehicle is normally based therefore always have a claim against the Bureau of the Member State of the accident, which – unless the vehicle is not insured at all – will always have a right of recourse against an insurance company.

But does Article 14 also preclude a condition in the policy that the insured vehicle may not be used abroad and that the insurer has a right of recourse in case of accidents in other Member States? The *Litaksa* decision of the CJEU makes clear that such a clause is in conflict with Article 14.[93] In the first place since Article 14 refers to a 'single premium', which would make no sense if the insurer would have the right to be reimbursed by the insured. There is also a more fundamental argument: one of the goals of the Directive is to remove any obstacles to the free movement of persons. Absence of cover for traffic accidents can be regarded as a significant deterrent to this freedom of movement and hence would be in conflict with the fundamentals of the Directive (and European law as such).
Article 14 has therefore not only external effect but also internal.

6.2.13.10 *Restrictions to the use of a vehicle on certain days or hours*

Sometimes it is better for road safety reasons for motorists not to drive their vehicle at certain times of the day or the week. Elderly people may have problems seeing in the dark. Other drivers may have a habit of drinking on Friday or Saturday night. Sometimes insurers add a condition to their policy dealing with this type of problem.

Such a clause clearly cannot affect the rights of third parties, since Article 13 of the Directive doesn't allow it. But is it also forbidden in the internal relationship with

93. CJEU, Judgment of 26 March 2015, *Litaksa*, C-556/13, EU:C:2015:202. See also para 6.2.8.2.

the insured? In our opinion it is not and insurers may either provide for a deductible or exercise a right to recover any outlays from the driver who acted in breach of such a contractual obligation.

6.2.13.11 Misrepresentation

In the case that led to the *Fidelidade* decision of the Court, the policyholder had misled the insurer as to the identity of the owner and of the usual driver of the vehicle or as to the fact that the person for whom or on whose behalf that insurance contract was concluded had no economic interest in the conclusion of that contract.[94] The question was whether the nullity of the contract can affect the rights of third parties. The Court decided that the Directive precludes national legislation making it possible to invoke such a clause against third party victims. Obviously a clause to this effect can be invoked against the policyholder.

6.2.13.12 Distinction between cover and liability; case law of the Court of Justice of the EU

In deciding on the admissibility of certain statutory or contractual clauses which exclude or restrict the cover under an MTPL policy, the Court occasionally borders on the distinction between questions of cover and of liability. The Court is clearly authorised to decide on matters regarding the cover under the insurance contract in so far as it is the subject of the Directive. On the other hand, it is debatable whether the Court has jurisdiction in liability matters, since the (national) law on liability and compensation of damage are not within the competence of the EU.[95] But CJEU case law shows that there is a narrow line between the two areas.

The classic approach in liability insurance has always been that the policy follows the law on liability and that the existence of a policy of liability insurance as such does not create liability.[96] That approach is, in the jurisprudence on the Directive, no longer completely valid.

In two EFTA cases, the Court paid attention to the distinction between liability and cover, in one case deciding that the liability regime in question was not compatible with the (purposes of the) Directive, whereas in the other case the applicable rules were considered not to be conflicting.

94. CJEU, Judgment of 20 July 2017, *Fidelidade-Companhia de Seguros*, C-287/16, EU:C:2017:575.

95. It has to be borne in mind that the EU is only competent within the principles of conferral, subsidiarity and proportionality. Questions of liability and compensation have not been attributed to the EU.

96. Although the existence of a liability policy or the obligation to conclude such a policy can in some jurisdictions be a factor when deciding on the liability issue.

In *Storebrand* the Court held that the Directives preclude a statutory rule in Norwegian law, according to which, in case of an accident involving a drunken driver, passengers who voluntarily and knowingly entered the vehicle and sustained injury were not entitled to compensation unless there were special grounds.[97] In its paragraph 29 the Court addresses the distinction between insurance cover and liability questions:

> "29) Even if the main text of the First Motor Vehicle Insurance Directive focuses on insurance coverage, that Motor Vehicle Insurance Directive has been supplemented by the Second and Third Motor Vehicle Insurance Directives in such a way that the three Motor Vehicle Insurance Directives, taken as a whole, provide for limits on the extent to which insurers may rely on contractual clauses or national statutory provisions on liability for compensation to exclude certain situations from coverage altogether. Consequently, the distinction between provisions on personal liability and insurance cover is not decisive in the case at hand. (...)."

In the *Halla Helgadóttir* decision, again in an EFTA case, the applicable Icelandic law was upheld:

> "31) Although the basic aim of the three Directives is to harmonise the insurance coverage in case of motor vehicle accidents, the Directives, taken as a whole, may have some effect on the liability regimes of the Contracting Parties. From this it follows that it cannot be excluded that certain liability rules could be seen as conflicting with the aims of the Directives to harmonise the rules relating to insurance coverage, and to guarantee comparable treatment of victims of road accidents in the EEA States. This has been held to be the case when national provisions on liability exclude certain situations from insurance coverage altogether (see Case E-1/99, (*Storebrand Skadeforsikring*, cited above). The same might be true if national liability rules were to operate to exclude victims from protection in a manner that would depart significantly from what may be considered as the general standards of the law of civil liability within the EEA in similar situations. However, in the light of the basic aim of the Directives, and having regard to the nexus between considerations of comparable treatment and the rules and practices concerning insurance coverage, the possible effect of the Directives upon the liability regimes will be exceptional and limited, and the contracting parties have a wide margin of appreciation."[98]

In the *Halla Helgadóttir* case the question was whether a standardised system for calculating compensation for loss of future income from employment for victims with low income, or no income at all, would be compatible with the Directives and the answer of the Court was affirmative. A significant factor in this instance was that the provision was not intended to exclude, nor had it the intention to exclude, any group of victims from compensation of insurance cover.

97. EFTA Court, Advisory Opinion of 17 November 1999, *Storebrand Skadeforsikring*, E-01/99.
98. EFTA Court, Judgment of 14 June 2001, *Halla Helgadóttir*, E-07/00.

In *Halla Helgadóttir*, paragraph 32, the Court puts emphasis on the goal of the Directives to ensure comparable treatment of victims irrespectively of where in the European Economic Area the accident occurs and in that context the Court notes

> "that in most of the Contracting Parties a passenger is fully covered by insurance even if the driver is intoxicated."

Fully covered? Without even a reduction of the compensation in view of the passenger's own contribution to the accident or his damage? That seems doubtful. But even so, the decision gives no indication as to which of the (then) 18 states of the EEA the Court has examined. Nor does it provide any clue what is to be understood by "general standards of the law of civil liability within the EEA." This may be a source of future jurisprudence, given the disparities in the law on liability and compensation in the now 31 states participating in the EEA.

The Court suggests that the principle that the Directives go beyond the classical 'cover area' could already be read in *Ruiz Bernáldez*.[99]

6.3 Aspects of procedure; the Information Centre

6.3.1 General remarks

The Directive protects the injured party – and the insured – by giving rules for the content of the cover under the policy, but also gives rules on aspects of procedure: the injured party has a direct right of action; they are entitled to a reasoned reply on all aspects of their demand for reimbursement within three months; and in the case of a dispute between insurance company and Guarantee Fund, national law must provide a procedure to establish which of the two should compensate the victim. The Directive also instructs Member States to establish or approve an entity called *Information Centre* to provide injured parties with the information necessary to present their claims.

All these elements were introduced in later stages. The direct right of action was introduced in the 4th Directive with a limited scope, covering only 'visiting victims' in the meaning of that Directive. The scope was extended by the 5th Directive to include all injured parties with a claim on an insurance company or Bureau. The reasoned reply procedure and Information Centres were also introduced by the 4th Directive, albeit again with a limited scope, and also later broadened in the 5th Directive. The 'dispute procedure' was on the other hand introduced as early as the 3rd Directive.

99. CJEU, Judgment of 28 March 1996, *Ruiz Bernáldez*, C-129/94, EU:C:1996:143.

The Directive also instructs the Member States to create a central facility with the task of providing interested parties with the basic data necessary for the settlements of their claims.
These elements of the Directive form the subject of this part of chapter 6.

6.3.2 *Direct right of action or 'droit propre'?*

The 4th Directive introduced the direct right of action for the victim of an accident in a Member State other than their country of residence and caused by a vehicle normally based and insured in a Member State other than the victim's country of residence. Victims of purely domestic accidents and accidents caused by visiting vehicles (Green Card accidents) did not initially benefit from this reinforcement of victim protection. That 'flaw' was remedied in the 5th Directive and the direct right of action can now be found in Article 18 of the Directive:

> "Member States shall ensure that any party injured as a result of an accident caused by a vehicle covered by insurance as referred to in Article 3 enjoys a direct right of action against the insurance undertaking covering the person responsible against civil liability."

A direct right of action is the legal instrument which gives the injured party the power to exercise the insured's right to claim that derives from the insurance contract.

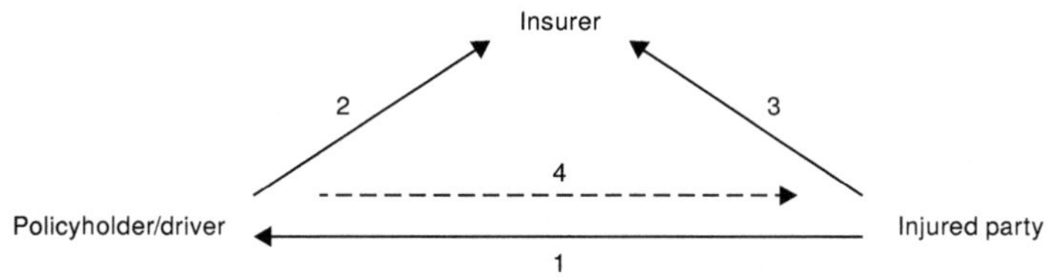

1. represents the claim of the injured party on the liable driver;
2. is the claim of the liable party against the insurer of the vehicle based on the insurance contract covering the insured's liability;
3. is the third party exercising the claim of the insured against the insurer. The right to claim shifts from the insured to the injured third party;
4. represents the transfer of the right to claim from the policyholder/driver to the injured party.

In its basic form, the injured party exercising a direct right of action cannot claim more than the insured could have claimed and the insurer can invoke against the third party the same exceptions and defences that could be invoked against the policyholder and the insured.

The Directive restricts this possibility, however, as explained in paragraph 6.2.13: the insurer may have a contractual right to refuse or limit cover in his relationship with the policyholder and the insured. He cannot however oppose any of these policy limitations to the injured third party, with an exception for the few options offered in Article 13: passengers willingly entering the vehicle which caused the damage or injury when they knew it was uninsured or stolen, damage caused by vehicles stolen or obtained by violence provided the Guarantee Fund compensates the injured party and damage to third parties caused by stolen vehicles in so far as their damage is covered by social security.

In view of these strong limitations of the insurer's right to invoke policy exceptions and limitations against the injured third party, the direct right of action might also be classified as a *'droit propre'* of the injured third party against the insurer, a right (to a large extent) independent of the (content of the) insurance contract.

> It is important to emphasise the use of the term 'injured party'. Not only the direct victim but also dependents, subrogated parties such as private insurers and social security institutions, employers having continued to pay the victim's salaries, in short, anybody who under the applicable law on liability has a claim against the liable party, benefits from the direct right of action against the MTPL insurer.[100]

Article 18 refers to 'vehicles covered by insurance'. What is the position of an injured party with respect to the Green Card Bureau or the Guarantee Fund? Can they exercise a direct right of action? For an answer to that question, we have to consider the legal construction of the direct right of action. It means that the injured party exercises the right to claim which belongs to the insured. And therefore is a direct right of action on Bureau or Guarantee Fund a legal impossibility, since the liable motorist does not have any claim on the Bureau, nor the uninsured motorist on the Guarantee Fund.

The right of an injured party to claim on the Bureau or the Guarantee Fund must therefore have another legal basis. In the case of the Guarantee Fund this basis can be found in Article 10(2) of the Directive:

> "2. The victim may in any event apply directly to the body which, on the basis of information provided at its request by the victim, shall be obliged to give him a reasoned reply regarding the payment of any compensation."

A clear provision concerning the rights of the injured party against the Green Card Bureau cannot be found in the Directive. The only Article that gives an indication

100. *Cf.* CJEU, Judgment of 20 July 2017, *MMA-IARD*, C-340/16, EU:C:2017:576.

about the responsibilities of the Bureau are Articles 2 and 6. Article 2 point (a) merely states that the Bureaux of the Member States are obliged to conclude an Agreement in which they undertake to guarantee the settlement of claims caused by vehicles normally based in another Member State. How this guarantee should be legally shaped and executed, remains unclear. Article 6 only relates to the exchange of information concerning the liable vehicle and the data that can be found on a Green Card. Nothing about the settlement of claims.

6.3.3 *Reasoned reply procedure*

The 4th Directive introduced the obligation for the insurance undertaking or the claims representative to make either a reasoned offer of compensation in cases where liability is not contested and the damages have been quantified, or to provide a reasoned reply to the points made in the claim in cases where liability is denied or has not been clearly determined or the damages have not been fully quantified. This duty was limited to 4th Directive situations. The 5th Directive expanded the three months reasoned reply procedure to all accidents covered by insurance as well as covered under the Green Card system.

The obligation to provide the claimant either with an offer or a reasoned reply must be backed with appropriate, effective and systematic financial or equivalent administrative penalties. Moreover, Member States must ensure that where the offer is not made within the three months' time limit, interest shall be payable on the amount of compensation offered by the insurance undertaking or awarded by the court to the injured party.

It is interesting to note that the three-month period does not apply to claims against the Guarantee Fund. Article 10 of the Directive only states that

> "the victim may in any event apply directly to the body which, on the basis of information provided at its request by the victim, shall be obliged to give him a reasoned reply regarding the payment of any compensation."

Moreover, the question is whether the 'reasoned reply' in Article 10 has to comply with the same criteria as the reply of Article 22. We assume that this is the case since the wording is virtually identical, even though the provision of Article 10 goes back to the 2nd Directive.

The obligation to provide the claimant with an offer for compensation or with a reasoned reply should be backed by 'appropriate, effective and systematic financial or equivalent administrative penalties'. Recital (40) of the Directive's preamble sheds some light on the ideas of the European legislator in this respect:

> "In addition to ensuring that the insurance undertaking has a representative in the State where the injured party resides, it is appropriate to guarantee the specific right of the injured party to have the claim settled promptly. It is therefore necessary to include in national law appropriate effective and systematic financial or equivalent administrative penalties — such as injunctions combined with administrative fines, reporting to supervisory authorities on a regular basis, on-the-spot checks, publications in the national official journal and in the press, suspension of the activities of the company (prohibition on the conclusion of new contracts for a certain period), designation of a special representative of the supervisory authorities responsible for verifying that the business is run in line with insurance laws, withdrawal of the authorisation for this business line, sanctions to be imposed on directors and management staff — in the event that the insurance undertaking or its representative fails to fulfil its obligation to make an offer of compensation within a reasonable period of time. This should not prejudice the application of any other measure, especially under the law applicable to supervisory matters, which may be considered appropriate. However, it is a condition that liability and the damage and injury sustained should not be in dispute, so that the insurance undertaking is able to make a reasoned offer within the prescribed period of time. The reasoned offer of compensation should be in writing and should contain the grounds on the basis of which liability and damages have been assessed."

Quite some catalogue!

It is not exactly clear what constitutes a reasoned reply. The sanction on failure to provide such a reply to the victim is not only the above-mentioned threat of financial and administrative sanctions, but also the possibility for the claimant to approach the Compensation Body in case of a 4th Directive claim. The Compensation Bodies and Guarantee Funds have therefore developed 'recommendations' to assert whether they have a role to play in a particular case. It is useful to point out that these 'recommendations' are simply a tool to facilitate a harmonised approach by the Compensation Bodies in the Member States and that they cannot bind third parties such as injured persons. In the end it is up to the national courts to decide whether in a particular case a given reply can be regarded as 'reasoned' and to the Court in Luxembourg to clarify the concept of 'reasoned reply'.

The obligation to pay interest if the offer is not presented and payment not made within three months can be implemented by reference to existing national rules regarding late-payment interest, according to the last sentence of recital (41). That is a useful addition, since otherwise it would be debatable whether the 'late payment interest' of Article 22 should be paid in addition to the normal late payment interest, as a sort of extra penalty or incentive.[101]

---

101. See for late payment and the obligation to pay interest by a guarantee fund also CJEU, Judgment of 4 December 2003, *Evans*, C-63/01, EU:C:2003:650.

6.3.4 *Disputes between insurer and Guarantee Fund*

The third Directive addressed the situation of disputes regarding which of the two – an insurance company or the Guarantee Fund – is required to compensate the injured party: Member States are required to designate a party responsible for compensating the victim in first instance.[102]

> The Directive refers to the victim, but we assume that injured parties other than the victim also benefit from this procedure. We fail to see why they should not enjoy the same protection, providing they have a claim on the Guarantee Fund in the first place, which is not always the case due to the subsidiary position of many Guarantee Funds.[103]

The Member States are free to decide on a procedure and as a consequence different solutions can be found. A few examples:

- Austria, Belgium, Germany, Hungary, Portugal and Sweden have all designated the Guarantee Fund to be responsible in the first instance for paying compensation;
- France: the insurance company settles the claim with the claimant;
- The Netherlands and Slovenia: the party which is first addressed by the injured party settles the claim, with a right of recourse against the ultimate liable party.

The entity which compensated the injured party in accordance with the national procedures has a right of recourse on the other party for its share in the liability, according to the second sub-paragraph of Article 11.[104]

6.3.5 *The central body*

Article 26 of the codified Directive instructs the Member States to set up a central entity, dubbed *'Central Body'* with the task of providing victims, their insurers or their legal representatives with basic data necessary for the settlement of their claims. The provision is not completely new, pre-dated as it is by an apparently comparable Article in the 3rd Directive. That provision however had a different category of data in mind: data necessary for the identification of the insurance company. When the 5th Directive introduced the *Information Centres*, that function of the *Central Body* became obsolete.

102. This aspect of the Directive has also been discussed in para 4.7.
103. If this interpretation is correct, then it is another example of the sometimes inaccurate wording of the Directive.
104. The right of recourse of an insurance company which has initially compensated the injured party is of course also dependent on the eventual subsidiarity of the Guarantee Fund.

The preamble gives no indication as to what sort of information the *Central Body* is required to provide, but we are inclined to think of police reports.

The Directive states that the required data shall, where appropriate, be made available in electronic form in a central repository in each Member State, and be accessible by parties involved in the case at their express request.

> In a number of Member States such bodies have existed for decades:
> In France, *Trans PV*, receives all police reports of road traffic accidents in France and distributes them to the insurance companies involved in the accident.
> In the Netherlands, *Stichting Processen Verbaal*, associated with the Dutch association of insurers, also receives all police reports relating to traffic accidents but only sends them to insurance companies and other interested parties at their request.
> In a new Article 18a, the European Parliament, in an amendment to the Proposal for a new Directive by the European Commission, suggests to give more detailed 'instructions' to the Central Body: the copy of the accident report must be provided in a timely manner and if national law prevents the Body to release the report in full, a redacted version – the redactions being limited to strictly those necessary and required under national law – should be provided until the full version becomes available.

6.3.6 *The Information Centre*

6.3.6.1 *Introduction*

Any form of protection of victims and injured parties will fail to serve its purpose if they are not in a position to identify the vehicle which caused the accident, the liable party (owner, holder, driver), and the insurer who provided cover. Most countries will have a vehicle register in place which contains the details of vehicles registered in the country. Many countries also operate a central database of insurance data pertaining to these vehicles.

> Article 5 of the 3rd Directive, Article 1(1) already contained the following provision:
>
> > "Member States shall adopt the necessary measures to ensure that the parties involved in a road traffic accident are able to ascertain promptly the identity of the insurance undertaking covering the liability arising out of the use of any motor vehicle involved in the accident."
>
> The way this information was collected and made available differed widely from one Member State to another. Some Member States had (and have) central databases in place, others had, before the entry into force of the 4th and 5th Directive, other methods. An example is France, where no central database was available and where in case of a request by an injured or otherwise interested party, an enquiry was made to all insurers to establish whether they provided cover for the vehicle in question.

But even if such a central database exists, it does not necessarily follow that parties injured and other interested parties have easy access to these data, a conclusion that may be even more applicable to persons resident in the country. And without these and other data, any scheme of protection of the parties injured in a traffic accident will be by and large ineffective.

The 4th Directive introduced the concept of the *Information Centre*, initially only with the task of providing visiting victims (in the meaning of Article 20 of that Directive) with the necessary data. With the 5th Directive, the scope of the Information Centres was enlarged to include not only 4th Directive accidents but also domestic accidents and Green Card situations. The Information Centre is now to be found in Article 23 of the codified Directive.

The Information Centre is to be welcomed as a useful, perhaps even indispensable instrument to assist injured parties in identifying those with whom they can negotiate their compensation claims. Article 23 is however not easy to read or understand.

6.3.6.2 The information to be collected

Article 23 compels the Member States to establish or approve an entity – dubbed Information Centre – responsible for either keeping a register containing a defined set of information or for coordinating the compilation and dissemination of that information.

Many Member States already had an entity in place at the time of the 4th Directive and could simply approve that entity. Others had to 'build' one. In all circumstances however their national legislation would need to be modified to comply with the new rules. Moreover, the Directive requires the Information Centres of the Member States to cooperate and even if Member States already had an 'Information Centre' in place, cooperation would be scant.

Importantly, the Directive does not compel the Member States to hold all data in one database. A solution may involve one entity, existing or newly established, collecting the data required by the parties involved in a traffic accident from different sources. This complies with the requirements of the Directive, providing the person asking for the information only has to contact one access point, the 'Information Centre'.

The Information Centre has to provide the following data:

i. the registration numbers of motor vehicles normally based in the territory of the State in question;

ii. The MTPL insurance policy numbers and – if applicable – the date of expiry of the policy;
iii. The insurance undertakings authorised to transact MTPL insurance as well as their claims representatives in the other Member States, whose names have to be notified to the Information Centres by the insurance companies;
iv. The list of vehicles derogated from the obligation to be insured under Article 5(1) and 5(2) of the Directive;
v. The names of the bodies or entities responsible for handling claims and compensating injured parties as meant in Article 5(1) and 5(2).

The information referred to in *i, ii and iii* has to be preserved for seven years after the termination of the registration of the vehicle or the termination of the insurance contract. It is not quite certain what this obligation implies, especially with regard to the termination of the registration of the vehicle. In several Member States, the registration of the vehicle changes when the registered owner sells the vehicle to another person, either because the registration number is linked to the person in question or to his place of residence; a logical interpretation of the obligation would be that the seven-years period starts from the date of re-registration. In other Member States, however, the same registration number sticks with the vehicle, irrespective of who owns it, until it is scrapped or exported.[105] It is unclear when the seven-year period starts or ends in such cases. We would defend the interpretation that the decisive date is that on which the vehicle is registered in the name of a new owner. That would be consistent with the interpretation given above for those countries which link the registration either to a specific person or to his place of residence.

Items *iv* and *v* refer to vehicles owned by persons or entities which are exempted from the obligation to insure their vehicles. In many Member States, vehicles owned by the State or other public bodies benefit from such an exemption, but other examples exist as well. See *supra*, para 6.2.6.

6.3.6.3 The information to be provided

Article 23(3) and (4) detail the information the injured party is entitled to receive:
a. the name and address of the insurance undertaking;
b. the number of the insurance policy; and
c. the name and address of the insurance undertaking's claims representative in the State of residence of the injured party.

This information has to be provided 'without delay'. Of course everything is dependent on the availability of the information. Member States should therefore

105. Or 'dispatched' to another Member State.

ensure that their data are accurate and up-to-date. But in certain circumstances the information should be gathered in other Member States and delays cannot be excluded, notwithstanding that the Directive rather bluntly states that the Information Centres 'shall cooperate with each other'.

In certain circumstances the injured party has a legitimate interest in obtaining the name and address of the owner or usual driver or registered keeper of the vehicle. This may *i.a.* be the case when the vehicle is uninsured (see Recital (45)), when the damage exceeds the cover under the policy or if the claim against the insurance undertaking is barred by statute.

In order to collect the required information, the Information Centre will contact the insurance undertaking and the vehicle registration authorities.

With respect to vehicles which benefit from an exemption from the compulsory insurance, the Information Centre will provide the injured party with the identity of the body responsible for handling claims relating to these vehicles, either in the Member State where the accident occurs (Article 5(1)) or in the Member State where the vehicle is normally based (Article 5(2)). This provision merits some comment.

In the situation of the exemption of Article 5(1) – exempted vehicles belonging to legal or natural persons – the Directive states that the Member State

> "shall take the appropriate measures to ensure that compensation is paid in respect of any loss or injury caused in its territory and in the territory of other Member States by vehicles belonging to such persons.
> It shall in particular designate an authority or body in the country where the loss or injury occurs responsible for compensating injured parties in accordance with the laws of that State in cases where Article 2(a) is not applicable."[106]

Strictly speaking, the nomination of such an entity or body is therefore not compulsory in the Member State where the vehicle is normally based, but only in the other Member States, since Article 2 point (a) refers only to accidents in other Member States. Most Member States will however have designated an entity to deal with claims in their own country, that being either the registered owner of the vehicle itself or another body such as the Guarantee Fund. That is not the case with the nomination of entities in the other Member States, dealing with 'Green Card claims'.

106. Article 23(1), point (a) refers incorrectly to the procedure of Article 2(2), point (a). That should be Article 2, point (a).

In such a situation the injured party has access to the Bureau if an accident occurs with a visiting vehicle that is exempted from compulsory insurance under Article 5(1) when the Member State where the vehicle is normally based has not designated an entity responsible for claims handling in the Member State of accident. It seems to us that hardly any Member State has appointed such entities, if at all.
See para 6.2.6 for the situation of domestic accidents.

In the situation of the exemption of Article 5(2) – certain types of vehicle or certain vehicles having a special plate – the Information Centre has to collect and provide 'the name of the body covering the vehicle in the Member State where it is normally based'. That is remarkable, because in the system of the Directive the injured party has access to the Guarantee Fund. Why this oblique wording?

In a final paragraph 6 of Article 23, reference is made to data protection rules.

> "The processing of personal data resulting from paragraphs 1 to 5 must be carried out in accordance with national measures taken pursuant to Directive 95/46/EC."[107]

Although this only seems logical – why would the exchange of information in the context of traffic accident claims be exempted from the protection by the General Data Protection Regulation? – a certain level of uncertainty seems to exist and sometimes information that has to be provided under the Directive is refused with a reference to the Regulation.

6.3.7 *Claims history statement*

Although strictly not within the realm of this study – not being directly related to (insurance aspects of) cross-border road traffic accidents – some attention has to be paid to Article 16 of the codified Directive if only for the sake of completeness. Article 16 reads as follows:

> "Member States shall ensure that the policyholder has the right to request at any time a statement relating to the third party liability claims involving the vehicle or vehicles covered by the insurance contract at least during the preceding five years of the contractual relationship, or to the absence of such claims.
> The insurance undertaking, or a body which may have been appointed by a Member State to provide compulsory insurance or to supply such statements, shall provide that statement to the policyholder within 15 days of the request."

107. This Directive 95/46/EC has been superseded by Regulation (EU) 2016/679 of the European Parliament and the Council of 27 April 2016 on the protection of natural persons with regard to the processing of personal data and on the free movement of such data, and repealing Directive 95/46/EC (General Data Protection Regulation), OJ L 119, 4.5.2016, p. 1.

One of the major objectives of this provision is to improve the possibilities for the policyholder to insure their vehicle by way of Freedom to Provide Services.

It is an open question whether the provision in this form is really helpful. In the first place the content of the claims history statement is not defined. Since the bonus-malus systems in the Member States tend to vary widely it is hardly to be expected that a claims history statement provided by an insurance undertaking in Member State A will meet the requirements of an insurer in Member State B. As an Example in some markets 5 years of claims history may be sufficient but in other markets that period will be too short. Moreover insurance undertakings not only take into account the history of the potential client in the field of MTPL insurance but they also wish to be informed about any casco claim.
In the proposal for a review of the Directive, published in 2018, the Commission amends Article 16.[108] The content of the claims history statement will be harmonised as far as their format and the information provided, insurance undertakings may not discriminate on the basis of nationality or previous Member State of residence and lastly, they should publish their policies in respect of their use of claims history statements when calculating premiums.
European Parliament proposes to amend Article 16 further by emphasising that insurance undertakings should treat a statement from another Member State as equal to a domestic statement and apply any discounts available to an otherwise identical potential client and those discounts that are required by a Member State's national legislation. The amendment proposed by Parliament however also states that Member States should remain free to adopt national legislation on the 'bonus-malus' systems since such systems are national in nature, without any cross-border element, and therefore, under the principle of subsidiarity, decision-making with regard to those systems should remain with the Member States.
In an amendment to the proposals of the European Commission the European Parliament adds further information that shall be provided in the claims history statement, which would bring even more administrative burden to insurance undertakings. The fact that Parliament proposes that the European Commission shall consult with stakeholders – it may be assumed that *inter alia* insurance organisations are envisaged – is of little comfort, since the text of the proposal by the Commission and Parliament states that the information *shall* be provided in the statement. That seems to leave little room for fruitful discussions.
Again, not all the remaining practical issues seem to be addressed and it remains therefore to be seen whether Article 16 will effectively help policyholders to take out their MTPL insurance by way of Freedom to Provide Services.

108. See document COM(2018) 336 final.

6.4 Cover by the Green Card Bureau and protection by the Guarantee Fund

6.4.1 Cover by the Bureau

The protection by the Bureau of persons injured (victims as well as other injured persons, cf. para 6.2.12.1) is essentially identical to the protection they receive under an insurance policy. The Bureau steps in in place of the – foreign – insurer, which is logical in situations of accidents caused by insured visiting vehicles: the Bureau handles and settles the claim on behalf of the foreign insurer. But even when the visiting vehicle is not insured (and the Bureau settles the claim on the basis of a false Green Card or on deemed insurance cover) the same rules apply to the Bureau as they would apply to a domestic insurer: same amount of cover (with an exception however if the minimum amount of cover in the home country of the vehicle is higher, see below); same circle of persons covered; same circle of persons injured; same restrictions to the use of exemptions and exclusions.

In one respect, the protection by the Bureau is even better than the cover under a domestic insurance policy. Under Article 14, point (b) of the codified Directive the insurer has to provide the highest of two covers: the amount insured according to the law of the Member State of the accident or – if higher – that of the Member State in the territory of which the visiting vehicle is normally based.[109]

It is useful to add that the Bureau not only has to observe the minimum level of protection of the Directive but eventually also the higher or better protection on the basis of the applicable national MTPL law. After all the Directive only gives a minimum level of harmonisation. Cf. para 6.2.1.

The Directive is silent on the legal basis for a claim from the injured party against the Bureau. Article 2 merely refers to a guarantee by the Bureaux of the Member States to settle claims relating to vehicles normally based in other Member States. Article 8 only refers to a valid Green Card for vehicles normally based in third countries. It seems therefore that the question of the legal basis of a claim on the Bureau is left to national legislation.

In most – if not all – Member States, the Bureau has passive legitimisation: the courts can hear a case against the Bureau based on either the deemed insurance

109. See *supra*, para 6.2.10.4. The Green Card system provides for a comparable rule if the vehicle benefits from a higher sum insured under the insurance contract: the handling Bureau will consult the insurance company and try to receive authorisation to handle and settle the claim up to the higher contractual amount of cover. Cf. para 3.7.2. This procedure however is not based on the Directive and also has to be applied when the accident has no relation with the EU.

concept or a valid Green Card. The legal construction might be different but the result is the same.

The defendant in legal proceedings relating to claims out of Green Card accidents will usually be the Bureau. The correspondent does in the majority of the member countries of the Green Card system not possess passive legitimisation.[110] In practice the Bureau will leave the actual handling of the procedure to the correspondent.

6.4.2 *Protection by the Guarantee Fund*

The position and the responsibilities and tasks of the Guarantee Fund have already been exhaustively discussed in chapter 4 and we can be succinct in this paragraph.

> Contrary to the Bureaux, the Guarantee Funds cannot be said to be on the same footing as an insurance company, active in its country. That is mainly the consequence of their character as a means of protection of last resort, as a 'safety net'. In the system of the Directive there is no necessary role for the Guarantee Funds if the victim is or can be compensated through other means or must for other reasons assume responsibility for the expense. Deductibles are also permitted in certain circumstances. However, it has to be emphasised that the Directive provides for minimum protection and national law may – and in a number of Member States does – provide for wider protection.

One remark should however be made. In our opinion there is a difference between the question of access to the Guarantee Fund – which may be restricted, for example to victims as opposed to injured parties or through the mechanism of subsidiarity – and the question of the material cover to be provided.
If a victim has a right to compensation by the Guarantee Fund, the compensation they are entitled to should be identical to that which an insurance company would have to pay. The Directive gives some justification for this opinion in the opening paragraph of Article 10:

> "Each Member State shall set up or authorise a body with the task of providing compensation, *at least up to the limits of the insurance obligation* [Italics by the authors] for damage to property or personal injuries caused by an unidentified vehicle or a vehicle for which the insurance obligation provided for in Article 3 has not been satisfied."

We are aware of the difference between the amount of cover and the compensation to which the victim is entitled, but see no justification in the Directive to allow Guarantee Funds to reduce the compensation they pay as compared to that which

110. An exception seems to be Spain.

an insurance company would pay in similar circumstances. An exception must of course be made for the deductibles which are allowed in case of accidents caused by stolen vehicles (€ 500) or in case of hit-and-run accidents without or with only minor bodily injury (€ 250).

A few words about the legal position of the Guarantee Fund, especially in legal proceedings. The Directive is silent, leaving open to interpretation the grounds on which the Guarantee Fund might be brought before the courts.

Article 10(1) of the Directive merely states that

> "the body (has) the task of providing compensation, at least up to the limits of the insurance obligation for damage to property or personal injuries caused by an unidentified vehicle or a vehicle for which the insurance obligation provided for in Article 3 has not been satisfied."

Paragraph (2) gives the victim the right to apply directly to the body which, on the basis of information provided at its request by the victim, shall be obliged to give him a reasoned reply regarding the payment of any compensation. Nothing about passive legitimisation. But it seems undoubtable that the Guarantee Fund can be summoned in court as a defendant by the victim. It has an obligation to compensate the victim, is therefore a debtor and just as is the case with any other debtor, the courts are competent to hear a case. How could the victim effectuate his claim in case of a dispute, if not in court?

7 Providing Motor Insurance in the European Internal Market

7.1 Introduction

In previous chapters, the usual starting point for our examination was the occurrence of a road traffic accident with a cross-border element and an injured party's quest for compensation for the damage suffered. In this chapter, we will not only concentrate on claims handling activities after the occurrence of an accident, but we will also examine the pre-contractual and contractual phase of the conclusion of an insurance contract.

One of the main objectives of European integration was and still is the creation of an internal market, comprising an area without internal frontiers in which the free movement of goods, persons, services and capital is ensured.[1] As insurance activities are considered a service, they can equally benefit from this internal market and the related free movement of services. Consequently, European insurance undertakings will be able to offer insurance products across the entire internal market with a minimum of formalities to be observed.

Whilst the principles of the internal market and subsequent freedoms are also applicable to insurance products, the rights of policyholders, insured persons and injured parties may not be jeopardised. Since insurance products are financial instruments entailing a range of specific risks for European consumers, the insurance market is more regulated than other markets for consumer products in the European Union.

The regulation of the insurance market in the European Economic Area is subject to the provisions of Solvency II.[2] In the following pages, we will examine how the European legislator has attempted to reconcile the principles of the internal market

1. Article 3 of the Treaty on European Union and Article 26 of the Treaty on the Functioning of the European Union.
2. Directive 2009/138/EC of the European Parliament and of the Council of 25 November 2009 on the taking-up and pursuit of the business of insurance and reinsurance (Solvency II) (recast), OJ L 335, 17.12.2009, p. 1, hereinafter referred to as 'Solvency II'.

with the interests of European consumers: policyholders, insured persons and citizens suffering damage resulting from a road traffic accident.

In this chapter, we will explain that becoming an insurance provider on the internal market is subject to prior authorisation, enabling the insurance undertaking to be active in other Member States by way of the Freedom of Establishment or the Freedom to Provide Services (para 7.2). Once authorised, insurance activities will be subject to supervision in the insurer's 'home' Member State (para 7.3). The consequences of insurers being active under the Freedom of Establishment or the Freedom to provide Services for MTPL insurance will be described in paragraph 7.4.

7.2 Single authorisation

7.2.1 *Introduction*

Insurance activities cannot simply be undertaken freely in the European Economic Area, but require certain formalities to be respected. Article 14 Solvency II requires European undertakings that wish to take up the business of direct insurance or reinsurance to obtain *prior authorisation*. Article 18 describes the conditions that are to be fulfilled before an authorisation can be granted. The aim of these conditions is to secure the financial stability and overall soundness of insurance undertakings, resulting in a higher level of security for the European consumer. The conditions include the submission of a scheme of operations, requiring the insurance provider to make a fair and realistic estimation of the risks they intend to cover. Moreover, the insurance undertaking is required to hold sufficient own funds to cover a *Solvency Capital Requirement* as well as a *Minimum Capital Requirement*, thus safeguarding the financial health of the company. In chapter 5, we described the European protection of visitors mechanism as introduced by the 4th Motor Insurance Directive. As already explained in paragraph 5.3.1, one of the conditions precedent for obtaining the authorisation to offer MTPL insurance products is the appointment of a claims representative in each Member State other than the Member State in which the authorisation is sought (Article 18(1), point (h) Solvency II).

Prior authorisation is to be sought from the supervisory authorities of the Member State in which the head office of the insurance undertaking in question is situated (the 'home Member State'). The supervisory authorities are the national authority or authorities empowered by law or regulation to supervise insurance or reinsurance undertakings (Article 13(10) Solvency II). In accordance with Article 20 Solvency II, insurance undertakings have to ensure that their head office is situated in the same Member State as their registered office.

Prior authorisation is granted for one or more classes or branches of insurance, as specified in Annexes I and II to Solvency II. Regarding the specificities related to motor insurance and particularly taking into consideration the interests of victims of motor road traffic accidents, taking up MTPL insurance activities is subject to a number of other, more specific requirements. These will be examined in more detail in paragraph 7.4.

Once authorisation is granted in the insurer's home Member State by the supervisory authorities of that home Member State, this authorisation will enable the insurance undertaking to be active in the entire territory of the European Economic Area (Article 15 Solvency II). The authorisation will serve as a kind of 'European passport', a single authorisation or single license allowing the insurer to offer insurance products in other Member States without having to obtain a separate authorisation in those other Member States (the 'host Member State(s)').

Activities in other Member States can either be pursued by way of the Freedom of Establishment (FoE) or the Freedom to Provide Services (Freedom of Services or FoS). Strangely enough, an insurance undertaking that has obtained authorisation in a specific Member State is not obliged to offer insurance products in that home Member State. Although the system of FoE and FoS was initially not designed for this kind of situation, there are insurance undertakings that seek and obtain authorisation in one Member State for one or more insurance classes and subsequently do not offer any insurance products in that home Member State, instead only focussing on insurance markets in other Member States (the host Member States). The home Member State will then only serve as the place where the insurance undertaking obtained their authorisation and where the head office is situated, whereas the insurance activities are pursued in other host Member States by way of FoE and/or FoS.

Based on an assessment of the conditions to be fulfilled, the supervisory authorities of the home Member State can refuse to grant the authorisation required. Such a decision must state in full the reasons for the refusal and is to be notified to the undertaking concerned. The latter can challenge the decision before the courts of the Member State in question.[3]

Should the conditions for the authorisation no longer be fulfilled, the authorisation can be withdrawn. This procedure is laid out in Article 144 Solvency II. Since the supervisory authorities of the home Member State are the only body to grant authorisations, it is logical that the competence to withdraw the authorisation equally lies in the hands of those supervisory authorities. A distinction is made

3. Article 25 Solvency II.

between situations where the supervisory authorities *may* withdraw the authorisation and those where the withdrawal is mandatory. Cases where the supervisory authorities may withdraw the authorisation are the following (Article 144(1), first paragraph Solvency II):

> "a) the undertaking concerned does not make use of the authorisation within 12 months, expressly renounces it or ceases to pursue business for more than six months, unless the Member State concerned has made provision for authorisation to lapse in such cases;
> b) the undertaking concerned no longer fulfils the conditions for authorisation;
> c) the undertaking concerned fails seriously in its obligations under the regulations to which it is subject."

The withdrawal of the authorisation is mandatory (Article 144(1), last paragraph Solvency II):

> "in the event that the undertaking does not comply with the Minimum Capital Requirement and the supervisory authority considers that the finance scheme submitted is manifestly inadequate or the undertaking concerned fails to comply with the approved scheme within three months from the observation of non-compliance with the Minimum Capital Requirement."

Article 144(2) Solvency II requires the supervisory authorities of the home Member State to inform their counterparts in the host Member State(s) if authorisation is withdrawn. The supervisory authorities of the host Member State are then required to take appropriate measures to prevent the insurance undertaking from commencing new operations within their territories.

7.2.2 Freedom of Establishment (FoE)

The Freedom of Establishment will allow an insurer that has obtained single authorisation in their home Member State to establish a branch in one or more host Member States. Through this branch, the insurance undertaking will provide insurance services to customers in the host Member State.

A branch is to be distinguished from a subsidiary. A subsidiary is characterised by a legal personality of its own, distinct from the legal personality of the holding (parent) insurance undertaking. In this way, international groups of insurance undertakings set up subsidiaries in different Member States, often providing insurance products under the same brand name as the one used by the umbrella insurance undertaking. Given their distinct legal personalities, subsidiary insurance undertakings will need separate authorisation in order to be active in the Member State where they are incorporated. A branch, on the other hand, has no separate legal personality and is merely a physical presence or establishment of the insurer in the host Member State.

An insurance undertaking wishing to operate via a branch in one or more other Member States must declare this intention to the supervisory authorities of the insurer's home Member State. Together with this declaration, the insurer will have to provide information to the supervisory authorities including a scheme of operations setting out, at least, the types of business envisaged and the structural organisation of the branch. The insurer will also have to provide the name of an *authorised agent* who will possess sufficient powers to bind the insurance undertaking in relation to third parties and to represent the insurer in dealings with the authorities and courts of the host Member State.[4]

The supervisory authorities of the home Member State will communicate the insurer's intention, together with the information received, to the supervisory authorities of the host Member State where the insurer intends to establish a branch. This communication must be sent within three months of the moment at which all the information required is received from the insurer. The supervisory authorities shall inform the insurer of the communication sent to the host Member State's supervisory authorities. Upon receipt of the information, the supervisory authorities of the host Member State may inform the home Member State's supervisory authorities of the conditions that apply to the insurance activities the insurer wishes to undertake.

Taking the planned business into account, the supervisory authorities of the home Member State may, however, have doubts about the adequacy of the insurance undertaking's system of governance or about their financial situation or the fit and proper requirements of the authorised agent. In this case, the supervisory authorities may refuse to send the communication as mentioned above to the supervisory authorities of the host Member State and inform the insurance undertaking of this refusal. Together with the refusal, the supervisory authorities shall state the reasons for their decision, resulting in an opportunity for the insurer to challenge this decision.[5]

It is to be stressed that the cooperation between the supervisory authorities of the home Member State and the host Member State, as described in Articles 145 and 146 Solvency II, is designed to safeguard the smooth exchange of information but does not provide any opportunity for the supervisory authorities in the host Member State to preclude any insurance activities through the establishment of a

4. Article 145 Solvency II.
5. Article 146 Solvency II.

branch. The supervisory authorities of the home Member State are the sole body to preclude such activities via the refusal procedure described in Article 146(2) Solvency II.

7.2.3 Freedom to Provide Services (FoS)

The Solvency II-Directive also offers insurers the opportunity to be active in other Member States via the Freedom to Provide Services (Freedom of Services or FoS). Unlike FoE, where the insurer still operates a branch in the host Member State, FoS is characterised by the insurer's lack of any permanent presence in the host Member State. The insurance undertaking will offer insurance products in the host Member State without creating any establishment, rather merely by way of online advertisement, for example.

The formalities to be fulfilled by an insurance undertaking wishing to operate in one or more host Member States by way of FoS are to a large extent comparable to those applying to FoE. They are laid out in Articles 147, 148 and 149 Solvency II. The insurance undertaking has to inform their 'own' supervisory authorities in the home Member State about their intention to operate via FoS in one or more host Member States. The supervisory authorities will subsequently inform their peers in the host Member State(s) of this intention, together with the following information:

- A certificate attesting that the insurance undertaking complies with the Solvency Capital Requirement and Minimum Capital Requirement;
- The classes of insurance that the insurance undertaking has been authorised to offer;
- The nature of the risks or commitments which the insurance undertaking proposes to cover in the host Member State.

The timeframe within which the information exchange between the supervisory authorities has to take place is shorter than the one applicable in FoE cases.

Again, the supervisory authorities of the home Member State have the option of refusing to communicate the insurer's intention to the supervisory authorities of the host Member State(s), provided that they state their reasons for this refusal and that this decision can be challenged before the courts in the home Member State. And, again, the possibility to preclude the insurer from being active in other Member States by way of FoS lies exclusively in the hands of the home Member State's supervisory authorities. The supervisory authorities of the host Member State cannot influence the decision *a priori*. They can only act *a posteriori*, once the insurer has begun their activities in the host Member State. This will be described later in paragraph 7.3, when discussing Article 155 Solvency II.

Insurers can even choose to combine the possibilities of FoE and FoS. An insurer with head office in Member State A can be active in Member State B by way of a branch operating via FoE. But this branch on its turn can offer insurance products in Member State C by way of FoS.

7.3 Home country control

Providing insurance services is a financial business, aiming to cover risks to which policyholders, insured persons and victims of road traffic accidents are exposed. In order to safeguard the insurer's ability to continue providing cover when the risk manifests itself, the insurance business is subject to supervision that aims to protect the interests of these consumers. This objective is addressed in Article 27 Solvency II:

> "Member States shall ensure that the supervisory authorities are provided with the necessary means, and have the relevant expertise, capacity, and mandate to achieve the main objective of supervision, namely the protection of policy holders and beneficiaries."

We have already seen that granting single authorisation to provide insurance services in the internal market is the sole responsibility of the supervisory authorities in the home Member State, albeit in cooperation with the supervisory authorities of the host Member State(s). The same principle will apply to the supervision of insurance undertakings. Financial supervision lies exclusively in the hands of the home Member State, that is to say the Member State in which the head office of the insurance undertaking is situated. This principle is incorporated into Article 30 Solvency II:

> "The financial supervision of insurance and reinsurance undertakings, including that of the business they pursue either through branches or under the freedom to provide services, shall be the sole responsibility of the home Member State."

This principle, which is usually referred to as 'home country control', results in the supervisory authorities of the home Member State not only being responsible for supervising the insurance activities performed in the home Member State but also taking into account the services provided in one or more host Member States where the insurer is active either through branches (FoE) or by way of FoS. As explained earlier, it is possible that an insurance undertaking has their head office in one (home) Member State and merely operates in other, host Member States by way of FoE or FoS, without carrying out any insurance business in the home Member State itself. It is evident that such circumstances render the home Member State's supervisory authorities' task of exercising effective control over the insurer's activities in the host Member State(s) even more difficult. One may even question the motivation of the home Member State's supervisory authorities when it comes to exercising detailed control over insurance activities operated in the host Member State(s) if the insurance undertaking in question does not operate any insurance business in the home Member State at all.

In order to allow this supervision, Article 159 Solvency II requires insurance undertakings to submit information to the supervisory authorities in the home Member State distinguishing between activities carried out in other Member States by way of FoE or FoS. The supervisory authorities of the home Member State are subsequently required to forward this information to their counterparts in the relevant host Member State(s).

However important the principle of home country control may be, the continuity of the internal market and the soundness of the system necessitate good cooperation between the supervisory authorities of the different Member States. Therefore, Article 30(3) Solvency II requires that the supervisory authorities of the home Member State be informed when there is

> "reason to consider that the activities of an insurance or reinsurance undertaking might affect its financial soundness."

But the last paragraph of Article 30 again refers to the basic principle of home country control by laying the ultimate responsibility in the hands of the home Member State's supervisory authorities:

> "The supervisory authorities of the home Member State shall determine whether the undertaking is complying with the prudential principles laid down in this Directive."

Article 30(2) Solvency II further specifies that financial supervision shall include verifying the insurance undertaking's state of solvency, the establishment of technical provisions, the assets and the insurer's own eligible funds. In order to execute this task properly, the supervisory authorities of the home Member State are given the necessary powers in Article 33 Solvency II:

> "Member States shall provide that, where an insurance or reinsurance undertaking authorised in another Member State carries on business through a branch, the supervisory authorities of the home Member State may, after having informed the supervisory authorities of the host Member State concerned, carry out themselves, or through the intermediary of persons appointed for that purpose, on-site verifications of the information necessary to ensure the financial supervision of the undertaking.
> The authorities of the host Member State concerned may participate in those verifications."

Where prior authorisation and supervision lie entirely in the hands of the home Member State's supervisory authorities, the supervisory authorities of the host Member State still have the opportunity to intervene once the authorisation has been granted and insurance activities have begun in the Member State. This procedure of *a posteriori* influence is laid out in Article 155 Solvency II.

In an initial step, the supervisory authorities of the host Member State can require that the insurance undertaking remedy any irregularities if there is a lack of compliance with the legal provisions applicable in the host Member State. If the insurance undertaking fails to take the necessary action, the host Member State's supervisory authorities shall inform their counterparts in the home Member State. These supervisory authorities in the home Member State can subsequently take all appropriate measures to ensure that the insurance undertaking remedies the irregularities. At the same time, they shall inform the host Member State's supervisory authorities of the measures taken. If all of these steps still do not result in a satisfactory situation, the supervisory authorities of the host Member State may, "after informing the supervisory authorities of the home Member State, take appropriate measures to prevent or penalise further irregularities."[6] Insofar as strictly necessary, these measures may include preventing the insurance undertaking "from continuing to conclude new insurance contracts within the territory of the host Member State."

Moreover, Article 155(4) Solvency II makes it clear that Member States retain the power to take emergency measures if the situation requires in order to prevent or penalise irregularities within their territories. The provision specifies that this power includes the possibility of preventing insurance undertakings from continuing to conclude new insurance contracts within their territories.

In the case of a Romanian insurance undertaking active on the Italian insurance market by way of FoS, the Court of Justice of the European Union was required to clarify how far the competences of the supervisory authorities in the host Member State can go.
In a judgment on 27 April 2017, the Court first referred to the two principles of offering insurance services on the internal market:

> "Those principles are, first, the creation of a single authorisation which, once granted, allows insurance undertakings to carry on business throughout the European Union and, secondly, the principle of supervision of insurance undertakings by the home Member State."[7]

6. Article 155(3) Solvency II.
7. CJEU, Judgment of 27 April 2017, *Onix Asigurări*, C-559/15, EU:C:2017:316, para 42.

The Court further sheds more light on the competences of the supervisory authorities in the host Member State if they find irregularities in the insurance undertaking's operations:

The Court of Justice of the European Union interprets the competences of the host Member State's supervisory authorities in such a way that they do not have the possibility to take emergency measures on the mere basis of an assessment as to whether the conditions for the granting of authorisation were fulfilled by the insurance undertaking or not. On the other hand, if those supervisory authorities are of the opinion that the non-fulfilment of one or more of these conditions presents "a real and imminent danger that irregularities will occur to the detriment of the interests of insured persons or other persons who may benefit from the insurance cover", those supervisory authorities may take the emergency measures provided for in Solvency II, including prohibiting the insurance undertaking from concluding new contracts in the host Member State's territory.

7.4 Consequences of FoE and FoS for MTPL insurance

7.4.1 *Introduction*

When describing the principles of FoE and FoS in the previous paragraphs, we did not particularly focus on MTPL insurance and rather described the rules as they are applicable to non-life insurance products in general.

The specificities of motor third party liability insurance – its compulsory nature and its aim to not only protect the policyholder and the insured person but also the injured party – justify certain particular rules for this branch of insurance. These will be described in the following paragraphs. Motor insurance undertakings that have their head office in one Member State and offer MTPL policies in other Member States will have to be a member of the Motor Insurers' Bureau and contribute to the financing of the Guarantee Fund in the host Member State. This requirement will be discussed in paragraph 7.4.2. The fact that an insurance undertaking operates in other Member States may not result in the injured party being compelled to present a claim to the insurer's head office in the home Member State. How this is solved will be described in paragraph 7.4.3. The nomination of correspondents and claims representatives by insurance undertakings operating under FoE and FoS will be the subject of paragraph 7.4.4. In paragraph 7.4.5, we will finally examine the consequences of insurance activities under FoE or FoS if the insurance undertaking becomes insolvent.

7.4.2 *Membership of the Bureau and Guarantee Fund in the host Member State*

Once an insurance undertaking starts operating in a host Member State under FoE or FoS and offers MTPL insurance products in that host market, it must respect the rules and obligations applicable to MTPL insurance in that host Member State. This principle ensures a level playing field for all competitors active on the market, whether they have their head office in that particular Member State or in a different Member State. This includes membership of the Motor Insurers' (Green Card) Bureau as well as contributing to the financing of that Member State's Guarantee Fund.

All market players covering risks related to the use of motor vehicles registered or normally based in a specific Member State must guarantee the continuity of the Green Card system. Consequently, their membership to the Green Card Bureau and the related contribution to the financing of the Bureau is a prerequisite for offering MTPL insurance products.

At the same time, the solidarity of all market players will be required to enable the Guarantee Fund of the Member State in question to observe the tasks imposed on that Guarantee Fund. As was explained in chapter 4, this includes – as a minimum – the Guarantee Fund's role in accidents caused by uninsured or unidentified vehicles. Moreover, national legislation may subject the Guarantee Fund to other, additional cases of intervention, for which financial means will be necessary and to which all insurers will have to contribute.

Therefore, Solvency II requires insurance undertakings wishing to operate in other Member States by way of FoE or FoS to produce a declaration that they have become a member of the host Member State's Motor Insurers' Bureau and of the Guarantee Fund.

For insurance undertakings operating under FoE, this obligation is formulated in Article 145(3) Solvency II:

> "Where a non-life insurance undertaking intends its branch to cover risks in class 10 in Part A of Annex I, not including carrier's liability, it shall produce a declaration that it has become a member of the national bureau and the national guarantee fund of the host Member State."

For insurance undertakings operating under FoS, a similar obligation is to be found in Article 148(2), point (b) Solvency II:

> "Member States within the territory of which a non-life insurance undertaking intends, under the freedom to provide services, to cover risks in class 10 in Part A of Annex I other than carrier's liability may require that insurance undertaking to submit the following:
>
> a. (...);
>
> b. a declaration that it has become a member of the national bureau and national guarantee fund of the host Member State."

For FoS, this obligation is repeated in Article 150(1) Solvency II:

> "Where a non-life insurance undertaking, through an establishment situated in one Member State, covers a risk, other than carrier's liability, classified under class 10 in Part A of Annex I which is situated in another Member State, the host Member State shall require that undertaking to become a member of and participate in the financing of its national bureau and its national guarantee fund."

Although the Articles cited clearly require insurers 'to become a member of the national Guarantee Fund of the host Member State', formal membership of the Guarantee Fund will not be possible in all Member States. The legal status of certain Guarantee Funds does not allow insurance undertakings to become members. Contributing to the financing of the Guarantee Fund may therefore be considered more important and, probably, the main objective of the provisions cited above.

As explained in paragraph 7.2.1, some insurers with a head office in one Member State merely operate their insurance business in one or more host Member States without pursuing any insurance activity on their home Member State's market. In this case, the insurance undertaking in question may not be required to be a member of the Bureau and/or the Guarantee Fund of their home Member State. This will depend on national legislation. If the home Member State's national legislation sets membership of the national Bureau and Guarantee Fund as a condition in order to obtain authorisation in that home Member State, the insurer will have to be a member of both organisations even though they are not active on the home market. But there are Member States where membership of the Bureau and Guarantee Fund is not required as long as no MTPL insurance policies are subscribed in the Member State in question.[8]

8. The difference in practice is modest: in both situations – whether the insurance undertaking is required to become a member or not – it will not financially support the Bureau or the Guarantee Fund since the levy must be either based on the number of policies written or the amount of premiums received on that market. As a consequence, the financial contribution of a company that does not conduct business in that country will be nil.

7.4.3 *Consequences for the injured party of a road traffic accident*

7.4.3.1 *Introduction*

For the injured party suffering damage caused by the use of a motor vehicle, it should not make a difference whether the vehicle in question is insured with an insurer that has their head office in the Member State where the vehicle is registered or whether the insurer operates in that Member State under FoE or FoS. It would be unacceptable if the injured party were required to present a claim for compensation to the insurance undertaking's head office in another Member State.

To avoid such problems, the Solvency II Directive provides for safeguards protecting parties injured in motor vehicle accidents. To understand these, we have to distinguish between situations where the insurer is operating under FoE (para 7.4.3.2) or under FoS (para 7.4.3.3).

For the sake of clarity, it is to be remembered that the insurer operating under the regime of FoE or FoS will not automatically result in the injured party being able to invoke the guarantees of the Green Card system and having access to the Green Card Bureau. This will be illustrated by referring to a similar example as the one that has already been used earlier in this book:

Example

A Slovenian insurer, Slovins, does business in Italy by making use of the Freedom to Provide Services. This means that vehicles registered and normally based in Italy can be insured in MTPL with Slovins.

If an Italian resident suffers damage as a result of an accident caused in Italy by the use of an Italian vehicle insured with Slovins, the Italian injured party will not be able to present a claim for compensation to the Italian Green Card Bureau. Indeed, the Italian Bureau will only be able to act in the case of accidents caused by the use of vehicles that are not registered or not normally based in Italy.

If the Italian vehicle insured with Slovins causes an accident in France, a claim may be presented to the French Green Card Bureau.

7.4.3.2 *FoE: access to the insurer's branch*

When an insurance undertaking operates under the Freedom of Establishment, the insurance undertaking will at least have a permanent presence in the host Member State. This should already be a sufficient safeguard for the injured party to be able to present a claim to that permanent establishment in the host Member State.

In order to make sure that this branch or establishment is able to accept and handle claims for compensation, Article 145(2) Solvency II requires the following:

> "Member States shall require every insurance undertaking that proposes to establish a branch within the territory of another Member State to provide the following information when effecting the notification provided for in paragraph 1:
>
> a. (...);
> b. (...);
> c. the name of a person who possesses sufficient powers to bind, in relation to third parties, the insurance undertaking or, in the case of Lloyd's, the underwriters concerned and to represent it or them in relations with the authorities and courts of the host Member State (the authorised agent);
> d. the address in the host Member State from which documents may be obtained and to which they may be delivered, including all communications to the authorised agent."

7.4.3.3 *FoS: access to the insurer's representative*

If an insurance undertaking operates by way of the Freedom to Provide Services, the insurer has no permanent presence in the host Member State. In this case, an injured party has no branch to turn to in order to claim for compensation for any damage suffered.

Under the heading 'non-discrimination of persons pursuing claims', Article 151 Solvency II describes this situation as inadmissible:

> "The host Member State shall require the non-life insurance undertaking to ensure that persons pursuing claims arising out of events occurring in its territory are not placed in a less favourable situation as a result of the fact that the undertaking is covering a risk, other than carrier's liability, classified under class 10 in Part A of Annex I by way of provision of services rather than through an establishment situated in that State."

Therefore, the insurance undertaking operating by way of FoS must appoint a *representative* in the host Member State to handle claims on behalf of the insurance undertaking. Injured parties suffering damage in the host Member State as a result of an accident caused by the use of a vehicle insured with an insurer operating by way of FoS can present a claim for compensation to this representative. The representative should be sufficiently authorised to represent the insurer and to settle claims, as well as to represent the insurer or to have the insurer represented before the courts of the host Member State.

Article 152 defines the role of the representative as follows:

> "For the purposes referred to in Article 151, the host Member State shall require the non-life insurance undertaking to appoint a representative resident or established in its territory who shall collect all necessary information in relation to claims, and shall possess sufficient powers to represent the undertaking in relation to persons suffering damage who could pursue claims, including the payment of such claims, and to represent it or, where necessary, to have it represented before the courts and authorities of that Member State in relation to those claims."

For the sake of clarity, Article 152(3) specifies that "the appointment of the representative shall not in itself constitute the opening of a branch." Stating the opposite and considering the appointment of a representative as the opening of a branch would mean that, in practice, the Freedom to Provide Services would not exist. Indeed, operating by way of FoS requires the appointment of a representative but, if the appointment of that representative would be considered the opening of a branch, this would automatically transpose the activity into Freedom of Establishment.

The function of a *representative* is to be distinguished from the role of a *claims representative* in the framework of the protection of visitors mechanism as introduced by the 4th Motor Insurance Directive and as described in paragraph 5.3.

In accordance with Article 21 of the codified Motor Insurance Directive, all insurance undertakings offering MTPL insurance are required to appoint claims representatives in each Member State other than the one in which they received their authorisation. This claims representative has to be responsible for handling and settling claims presented by injured parties suffering damage caused by a motor vehicle accident that occurred in a Member State other than the Member State of the injured party's residence. The role and responsibilities of a claims representative (Article 21 of the codified Motor Insurance Directive) and of a representative (Article 152 Solvency II) may be comparable but are not the same. One of the main differences is that a claims representative is authorised to handle claims resulting from accidents that occurred in a Member State other than the one where they are established. A representative, on the other hand, will handle claims resulting from accidents that occurred in the Member State where they are established. As a consequence, claims representatives will most often have to apply rules of law that differ from the rules of the country where the claims representative is established, whereas representatives will usually apply their own national law when handling claims for compensation.

In order to increase the chances of all insurers that operate by way of FoS having a representative, Article 152(4) Solvency II states the following:

> "Where the insurance undertaking has failed to appoint a representative, Member States may give their approval to the claims representative appointed in accordance with Article 4 of Directive 2000/26/EC to assume the function of the representative referred to in paragraph 1 of this Article."

In January 2019, a request for a preliminary ruling of the Court of Justice of the European Union has been lodged to clarify the representative's role in judicial proceedings initiated against the insurance undertaking for which the representative operates. In this *Corporis* case, the Court of Justice will have to answer the question whether the representative's role includes "the receipt of a document which initiates court proceedings for damages in respect of a road traffic accident."[9] At the moment of finalising the manuscript of this book, the case was still pending before the Court. The similarity with the *Spedition Welter* case is apparent. In paragraph 5.3.4 we explained that the Court of Justice decided that a claims representative's role must include authority validly to accept service of judicial documents necessary for proceedings.[10] In the present *Corporis* case, a comparable question is raised, but this time not about the claims representative's role but about the authority of a representative in the framework of the Freedom to Provide Services.

7.4.4 Appointment of correspondents and claims representatives

The creation of the internal market and the opportunities offered to insurance undertakings to be active in other Member States' markets by way of FoE or FoS certainly present a number of advantages to both European consumers and to the insurance business. At the same time, it also makes the landscape of cross-border claims handling more complicated. As such, these complicating factors should not be a problem but it is up to professional partners and organisations involved in the claims handling process to understand the systems and to make the processes understandable to injured parties, so that the latter are not lost when pursuing their claims for compensation.

The Green Card system makes Green Card Bureaux able to handle claims resulting from accidents caused in their territory by foreign vehicles. Foreign insurers covering these vehicles have the right to appoint *correspondents*, who will be responsible for the claims handling process. The protection of visitors system, as introduced by the 4th Motor Insurance Directive, requires insurers to appoint *claims representatives* in all other Member States than the one in which they received their official (single) authorisation. Insurers operating by way of FoE have a *branch* in the host Member State; if they are operating by way of FoS, they are required to appoint a *representa-*

9. CJEU, Request for a preliminary ruling lodged on 15 January 2019, *Corporis*, C-25/19, published in OJ C 164, 13.05.2019, p. 11.
10. CJEU, Judgment of 10 October 2013, *Spedition Welter*, C-306/12, EU:C:2013:650.

tive in the host Member State. This already results in four different potential actors involved in the claims handling process: correspondents, claims representatives, branches and/or representatives. The system can become even more complicated if there is a succession of operations by way of FoE or FoS. Indeed, an insurer with their head office in Member State A (home) can operate in Member State B (host) by way of FoE and establish a branch in Member State B. But this branch, in turn, can operate via FoS in Member State C (also host).

If an insurance undertaking operates in one or more host Member States, it will not only have the opportunity to appoint a (Green Card) correspondent for the insurer's activities in the home Member State, but will also have the possibility of appointing correspondents for MTPL insurance activities pursued by way of FoE or FoS in other Member States. Theoretically, the insurance undertaking could choose to appoint two different correspondents in one and the same country participating in the Green Card system: one correspondent for activities pursued in the home Member State and a different correspondent for activities pursued by way of FoE or FoS in a host Member State. Needless to say, these situations will lead to confusion, especially since the insurance undertaking always operates under the same company name. It may lead to accident files being submitted to the wrong correspondent, therefore delaying the compensation process to the detriment of the injured parties. To avoid such confusion, the Council of Bureaux requires MTPL insurers to appoint only one correspondent, both for activities pursued in the home Member State and for activities pursued in one or more host Member States by way of FoE or FoS. Since Bureaux have to give their approval to the nomination of a correspondent, the Bureaux can control the compliance with this requirement.

Example

A Polish insurer, Polins, is authorised to conduct MTPL insurance in its home Member State of Poland and also offers MTPL insurance products via a branch (making use of the FoE system) in the host Member State of Latvia.

Under the rules of the Green Card system, Polins has the right to appoint correspondents in other countries participating in the Green Card system. Polins decides to appoint a correspondent in Lithuania and chooses Litcor to act as its Green Card correspondent to handle all cases resulting from accidents that were caused by Polish vehicles insured with Polins and that occurred in the territory of Lithuania.

For their activities pursued under FoE in Latvia, Polins could theoretically choose to appoint a different Green Card correspondent in Lithuania. The Latvian branch of Polins could decide that the Lithuanian correspondent Lithuclaims is to act as correspondent for accidents caused in Lithuania by the use of Latvian vehicles insured through the Latvian branch of Polins.

> For injured parties suffering damage in Lithuania, this situation would make it confusing to know which exact correspondent to submit a claim for compensation to. Therefore, the Council of Bureaux requires Polins to appoint only one correspondent in Lithuania (either Litcor or Lithuclaims) to act as correspondent for MTPL insurance activities carried out by Polins, pursued both in the home Member State of Poland and in the host Member State of Latvia.

At first sight, one may be tempted to say that exactly the same situation could occur regarding the appointment of claims representatives in the protection of visitors system as introduced by the 4th Motor Insurance Directive. An MTPL insurer would be able to appoint different claims representatives for their activities pursued in their home Member State and for their activities pursued in other Member States by way of FoE or FoS. It is, however, questionable whether this is legally possible. Article 21 of the codified Motor Insurance Directive requires insurance undertakings to "appoint a claims representative in each Member State other than that in which they have received their official authorisation." Since a branch itself is not granted official authorisation separately from the insurer in the home Member State (principle of single authorisation), Article 21 of the Motor Insurance Directive does not require the branch to appoint claims representatives. As a result, the claims representatives appointed by the insurer should automatically also be competent for that insurer's activities pursued under FoE or FoS.

Nevertheless, the Council of Bureaux has issued a comparable recommendation to insurance undertakings as the one applicable under the Green Card system, asking them to appoint only one claims representative in other Member States, both for insurance activities pursued in their home Member State and for activities pursued in other Member States by way of FoE or FoS.

7.4.5 Insolvency

We already expressed our opinion that the opportunity for insurance undertakings to operate by way of FoE or FoS offers important advantages to both consumers and insurance undertakings in Europe. Although they still do not make use of these possibilities very often, consumers benefit from a wider choice of insurance providers including not only national insurers but also insurance companies originating from other Member States within the internal market. From the perspective of insurance undertakings, they are able to offer insurance products across the entire internal market on the basis of the single authorisation they obtained in their home Member State. At the same time, we also expressed the opinion that the possibilities offered by FoE and FoS substantially increase the level of complexity in the European insurance and claims handling landscape. This complexity will also be manifested in the case of an insurance undertaking's insolvency.

In accordance with the principle of home country control, it will again be the relevant authorities of the home Member State who can decide on reorganisation measures (Article 269 Solvency II) or winding-up proceedings (Article 273 Solvency II) regarding an insurance undertaking. These reorganisation measures or winding-up proceedings will also impact any branches operated by the insurance undertaking in other Member States by way of FoE. Solvency II requires that the authorities responsible for reorganisation measures or for winding-up proceedings in the home Member State inform the supervisory authorities in the host Member State(s) as a matter of urgency. Contrary to reorganisation measures, the mounting of winding-up proceedings will result in the withdrawal of the insurance undertaking's authorisation (Article 279 Solvency II).

Article 160 Solvency II guarantees equal treatment in the case of winding-up proceedings regarding any obligations arising from insurance contracts concluded by an insurer, whether they operate in their home Member State or in a host Member State by way of FoE or FoS:

> "Where an insurance undertaking is wound up, commitments arising out of contracts underwritten through a branch or under the freedom to provide services shall be met in the same way as those arising out of the other insurance contracts of that undertaking, without distinction as to nationality as far as the persons insured and the beneficiaries are concerned."

A study carried out by the Council of Bureaux has shown that MTPL insurance undertaking insolvencies may tend to occur more often when these insurance undertakings not only operate in their home Member State, but also offer insurance products in other Member States by way of FoE or FoS. Moreover, this difference is even more apparent when the insurance undertaking does not operate any MTPL insurance business in their own home Member State but merely operates under FoE or FoS in one or more host Member States. MTPL insurance undertakings only offering insurance products in host Member States without any insurance activity in the Member State where they obtained their authorisation seem to be overrepresented compared to their market presence in the number of insolvencies during the last ten years.

As we have described in paragraph 4.3.6, European Union law as it currently stands does not obligate Member States to provide for a protection scheme in case of the insolvency of an MTPL insurer. Despite this absence of a Europe-wide obligation, the national legislation of many European Member States requires that the

Guarantee Fund or any other organisation plays a role if an MTPL insurer operating on their market becomes insolvent.

As a result, a Guarantee Fund or other body has to act and pay compensation if an insurance undertaking that is active in their market by way of FoE or FoS becomes insolvent. In accordance with the principle of home country control, the supervisory authorities of that (host) market have much more restricted options in the case of irregularities but the host market has to bear the financial consequences of the foreign insurance undertaking's insolvency. Confronted with this situation, the Guarantee Funds of a number of Member States in 1995 concluded a voluntary Agreement enabling the Guarantee Fund of the host Member State to recover their outlays from their counterpart Guarantee Fund in the home Member State.[11] As stated in paragraph 4.6, this Agreement shifts the financial burden resulting from the host Member State's insurance market towards the home Member State's market. In 2004, a comparable voluntary Agreement was also signed by a number of Green Card Bureaux wishing to realise the same transfer of financial burdens, this time relating to accidents falling under the scope of the Green Card system.[12]

The principle behind the voluntary Agreements concluded between Guarantee Funds and between Bureaux can be put into question when considering the ways in which Guarantee Funds are financed in order to meet their (national) obligations to provide compensation in the case of insolvency among insurance undertakings. Indeed, there are many ways to provide Guarantee Funds with the necessary means to safeguard their obligations related to insurers' insolvencies. In broad terms, these can however be divided into the following three groups:

- *Ex ante* financing: insurance undertakings have to pay contributions to the Guarantee Fund of the Member State where they are active (also if they are active in that Member State by way of FoE or FoS) and these contributions are calculated so that they also cover potential insolvencies among insurance undertakings. This results in the Guarantee Fund having substantial financial means at their disposal in case an insurance undertaking goes bankrupt on their market;
- *Ex post* financing: contributions levied by the Guarantee Fund are only calculated to cover the Guarantee Fund's other obligations, excluding cases of insolvency. If an insolvency does occur on the market, the Guarantee Fund will ask for additional contributions from the insurers. The advantage of this system is that it does not withdraw amounts of money from the insurance industry to set

11. Insolvency of a motor liability insurer operating in the Single Market, Convention on recourse between Guarantee Funds, concluded in the framework of the *Comité Européen des Assurances* (CEA, today Insurance Europe) in Paris on 24 July 1995 and as amended afterwards.
12. Agreement between Bureaux within the framework of Freedom of Services in Compulsory Motor Insurance, concluded on 27 May 2004 and amended afterwards.

aside for hypothetical incidents. The inconvenience, however, is that the bankrupt insurer will not have contributed to the consequences of its own insolvency. The other insurance undertakings will have to bear the costs;
- Mixed financing: a combination of (limited) *ex ante* financing whereby additional contributions are levied if the *ex ante* contributions paid turn out to be insufficient to cover the consequences of the insurer's insolvency.

If a Guarantee Fund's financial reserves for insolvency cases are entirely based on *ex ante* financing, the principle of transferring the financial burden of the insolvency to the home Member State's market may result in 'double taxation'. The insolvent insurance undertaking has already paid contributions to the host Member State's Guarantee Fund for cases of insolvency, whereas the home Member State still has to reimburse the financial consequences of the insolvency to the host Member State's Guarantee Fund.[13] In reality, however, the number of Guarantee Funds that are entirely financed on an *ex ante* basis is very limited.

As already explained earlier in paragraphs 4.6 and 5.9, the European Commission's proposal for a new Motor Insurance Directive includes a mechanism to protect injured parties in the case of accidents caused by the use of vehicles insured with an insolvent insurance undertaking. The Commission's proposal also includes a recovery mechanism whereby the competent body (Guarantee Fund or any other body for cases of insolvency) in the host Member State will be reimbursed by their counterpart in the home Member State for any compensation paid as a result of the insolvency of an insurer that received their authorisation in the home Member State. As explained in paragraph 4.6, the Commission's proposal only covers situations where the insolvent insurer was operating in the host Member State by way of FoS and does not cover situations of FoE. The latter is most probably a deficiency in the Commission's proposal that can be corrected during the legislative process of adopting the new Directive.

13. Article 189 Solvency II stipulates that "Host Member States may require non-life insurance undertakings to join and participate, on the same terms as non-life insurance undertakings authorised in their territories, in any scheme designed to guarantee the payment of insurance claims to insured persons and injured third parties."

8 Aspects of Private international law

8.1 Introduction

The topic of this book is the insurance aspects of cross-border road traffic accidents. It would, however, not be complete (nor entirely useful for the day to day handling and settlement of (insurance) claims resulting from such accidents) if we were not to pay at least some attention to a few aspects of private international law, even if private international law is, strictly speaking, not insurance law.

We feel justified in dedicating a chapter of this book to this subject, since it is not possible to handle and settle an international motor insurance claim correctly without having at least some basic knowledge of the *rules on jurisdiction* (which court is or would be competent to hear the case) and of the *law of conflict* (which – national – material law is applicable). The answers to these two questions will greatly define the outcome of discussions between liable party, victim and insurance company, even if a dispute between parties never reaches court and is settled amicably. The question of which law defines the victim's rights gives the negotiating parties clarity concerning liability rules, heads of damage and amounts of compensation that can be successfully claimed. But in order to find the applicable law, one first has to 'find' the relevant jurisdiction, as will be explained in more detail later on.

Jurisdiction and applicable law are only two of the three aspects of private international law. The third – the law on the *recognition and execution of court decisions* – is equally important but will not be discussed in this book. The reason is a practical one: it rarely plays an important role in insurance matters. Insurers, in the overwhelming majority of cases, simply pay after a court decision has become irrevocable.

Unfortunately, private international law is not what its name seems to suggest: *international* law.[1] Private international law is essentially national law. Only insofar

1. Strictly speaking, it is not private law either, as it does not (or at least not exclusively) govern relationships between private persons.

as states have agreed upon harmonisation through conventions or have introduced uniform or harmonised rules through supranational legislation, such as the Regulations of the European Union on jurisdiction and on applicable law, can we observe some more or less generally applicable rules.[2,3] Unfortunately, these harmonised or uniform rules do not cover the entire geographical scope of the Green Card system as will be explained in more detail below. This means that, for a substantial number of cases, pure national law will have to be taken into consideration, especially if the accident involves a country that is not a Member State of the European Union nor bound by a specific convention such as the *Hague Convention.*

That creates a problem: although our aim is to write a book which is equally useful for readers in EU Member States as in non-Member States, it proves impractical or even impossible to describe the legal situation in the field of jurisdiction and the law of conflict for each country participating in the Green Card system, even considering the level of harmonisation in the 28 (after Brexit 27) Member States of the EU. This book would inevitably become rather 'top heavy'.

We will therefore concentrate on the aforementioned international and supranational sets of rules on jurisdiction and applicable law. Although perhaps not entirely satisfactory for all our readers, we flatter ourselves with the hope that the content of this chapter will still provide enough information to be useful. A large proportion of international motor traffic accidents has, after all, an 'EU component'.

In the following paragraphs, we will first (para 8.2) outline the subject and explain the various legal instruments in general, also touching upon their interdependence. In paragraph 8.3, we will focus on Regulation (EU) 1215/12, hereinafter referred to as the *Brussels Ia Regulation* or simply as *Brussels Ia*, and on the *Lugano II Convention*, dealing with matters of jurisdiction. Paragraph 8.4 is dedicated to the law of

2. An example relevant to our subject is the Hague Convention of 4 May 1971 on the Law Applicable to Traffic accidents.
3. Regulation (EC) 593/2008 of the European Parliament and of the Council of 17 June 2008 on the law applicable to contractual obligations (Rome I), OJ L 177, 4.7.2008, p. 6; Regulation (EC) No 864/2007 of the European Parliament and of the Council of 11 July 2007 on the law applicable to non-contractual obligations (Rome II), OJ L 199, 31.7.2007, p. 40; Regulation (EU) No 1215/2012 of the European Parliament and of the Council of 12 December 2012 on jurisdiction and the recognition and enforcement of judgments in civil and commercial matters, OJ L 351, 20.12.2012, p. 1. For the relations between the remaining three Member States of the European Free Trade Association (Iceland, Norway and Switzerland) and for the relations between these three States and the Member States of the EU, there is the Lugano II Convention, originally concluded in 1988 and superseded by its 2007 version. The Lugano II Convention is largely based on the jurisdiction rules of the EU. Note that Liechtenstein is not a party to the Lugano II Convention.

conflict, successively dealing with the *Rome II Regulation*, the *Hague Traffic Law Convention* and the *Rome I Regulation*.

8.2 General remarks

Private international law exists because of the differences between national systems of material law. It comes into effect whenever a choice has to be made between two (or more) national sets of laws.

Example

A German motor vehicle collides with a Portuguese pedestrian in Spain. Which law governs questions of liability and compensation of damage? The Spanish law, since the accident occurred on Spanish territory, the Portuguese law, because that is the country where the victim suffers his damage or the German law, as the law of the country of the (potentially) liable party? And what if the German motorist has concluded an MTPL contract with a Belgian insurer under the Freedom to Provide Services and the Portuguese victim decides to start legal proceedings in Belgium?

Private international law provides the answers to the questions of (a) which court or courts is or are competent to hear the case and (b) which national legal system of material law will that court apply.

Private international law is, as previously observed, national law, even if the source of that national law is an international convention or an EU Regulation. This goes for the law on jurisdiction as well as for the rules on conflict of law. In order to decide which set of material law will be applicable (in the Example Spanish, Portuguese, German or Belgian), the court applies its own national rules on the conflict of law. These rules can differ even between Spain, Portugal, Germany and Belgium, since Germany and Portugal are bound by the rules of the *Rome II Regulation*, whereas Spain and Belgium are party to the *Hague Convention*. And *Rome II* and the *Hague Convention* can lead to a different outcome under certain circumstances.

It follows that the first issue that has to be addressed is the question of the competent (national) court. Fortunately – at least insofar as disputes within the EU are concerned – the rules on international jurisdiction are uniform in the entire EU thanks to the *Brussels Ia Regulation*, which superseded Regulation (EC) 44/2001 (or *Brussels I Regulation*), which in turn was the successor to the 1968 Brussels Convention on the recognition and enforcement of judgments in civil and commercial cases (*Brussels Convention*). The Lugano Convention 1988 (or *Lugano I Convention*) and its successor, the Lugano Convention of 2007 (or *Lugano II Convention*), concluded between Iceland, Norway, Switzerland and the EU, are by and large identical to the subsequent *Brussels Convention* and *Brussels I Regulation*. But, as stated before, if an accident has relevant links with non-EU Member States, the jurisdiction of non-EU courts may come into view as well as the applicability of the material law of a non-Member State.[4] And matters of jurisdiction and applicable law will in all likelihood have to be decided upon by applying the private international law systems of the non-Member States in question.

Since the first task whenever a situation of conflict of law emerges is to decide which national court will be competent, this will be the subject of paragraph 8.3. This will be dedicated to the *Brussels Ia* Regulation and to the *Lugano II Convention*. Logically, the issue of applicable national material law will follow in paragraph 8.4. There, we will deal with three international instruments: the *Rome II Regulation* and the *Hague Convention*, both applicable to non-contractual relations, and the *Rome I Regulation*, which is applicable to disputes resulting from a contractual relationship. Although less important in the context of road traffic accidents, *Rome I* can still be relevant, for instance in the case of an accident involving injured passengers in a touring car, as they will have entered into a contract of carriage.

Before delving deeper into the various regulations and treaties, a few observations relevant for all the instruments may be useful: each private international law instrument has a material, a formal and a temporal scope.
The *material scope* is determined by the type of legal relationship to which the treaty or regulation refers. Thus, the two subsequent *Brussels* Regulations are applicable to civil and commercial matters, irrespective of the nature of the court or tribunal hearing the case. Tax matters, customs matters and administrative cases (Article 1(1)), along with issues of personal rights, bankruptcies, agreements and similar procedures, social security and arbitration disputes are explicitly excluded from its scope.
The *Rome II Regulation* lays down rules for determining the law applicable to non-contractual obligations when it is necessary to choose between different countries' legal systems. The term 'non-contractual obligations' includes not only torts, but unjust enrichment, management of another's affairs (*negotiorum gestio*) and pre-contractual liability (*culpa in contrahendo*). Similarly, certain contractual obligations are, however, excluded from the scope of the Regulation. These include those resulting from family law relationships, the law of matrimonial property, bills of exchange, cheques and promissory notes, from non-contractual obligations arising out of the law of companies, trust relationships, nuclear accidents and violations of privacy. Evidence and matters of procedure also do not fall within its scope.

4. Since *Rome I* and *II* and the *Hague Convention* all have a universal material scope of applicability, the law designated to be applicable may also be the law of a non-Member State or a country that has not signed the Convention.

The *formal scope* of a private international law instrument, an instrument's spatial scope is defined in terms of human and/or territorial criteria. Thus, the two subsequent *Brussels* Regulations will be applicable if the defendant's domicile is in the territory of one of the EU Member States. *Rome II* has a universal formal scope: the law designated by the Regulation shall apply, whether it is the law of a Member State or of a non-Member State. The same applies to the *Rome I Regulation* and the *Hague Convention*.

The final criterion for determining whether an instrument should be applied – and if so, which instrument – in a specific case is the question of *temporal scope*. In essence, this is the question of when the regulation or the treaty entered into force and what must be taken into account as the 'trigger'. This is therefore a question of transitional law. For the *Brussels Ia Regulation*, legal action must be taken on a date after the Regulation became effective, i.e. 10 January 2015. It should be noted that its predecessors, the *Brussels I* Regulation and the *Brussels Convention* 1968, already led to the same outcome in broad terms.
For *Rome II*, the 'trigger' is the date of the event giving rise to the damage. This date must come after its entry into force, i.e. 11 January 2009.[5]

8.3 Jurisdiction under the Brussels Ia Regulation and the Lugano II Convention

8.3.1 *Introductory remarks*

The most important part of this section will be dedicated to the *Brussels Ia Regulation*. We will also cover the *Lugano II Convention*.

The full title of the *Brussels Ia Regulation* is: "Regulation (EU) No 1215/2012 of the European Parliament and of the Council of 12 December 2012 on jurisdiction and the recognition and enforcement of judgments in civil and commercial matters (recast)."
It therefore covers two areas of private international law: jurisdiction and the recognition and enforcement of court rulings. As already stated, we will only discuss the first sub-area in view of the second's lack of sufficient relevance for insurance practice.

The Regulation replaced Regulation (EC) 44/2001. This Regulation was, in turn, the successor to the *Brussels Convention* of 1968.

5. The temporal scope of the *Hague Convention* is more complicated, as will be shown in paragraph 8.4.3.2.

In 1968, the EEC Treaty did not yet provide for the possibility of regulating the matter of private international law. However, Article 220 of the Treaty establishing the European Economic Community opened up the possibility of concluding a parallel treaty. In the French language version (English was not yet an official language of the EEC), the clause reads:

> *"Les États membres engageront entre eux, en tant que de besoin, des négociations en vue d'assurer, en faveur de leurs ressortissants:*
> - *(....)*
> - *la simplification des formalités auxquelles sont subordonnées la reconnaissance et l'exécution réciproques des décisions judiciaires ainsi que des sentences arbitrales."*

In English:

> "The Member States shall, as necessary, negotiate with each other in order to ensure, for their nationals,
> - (...)
> - the simplification of the formalities to which the mutual recognition and enforcement of court decisions and arbitration are subjected."

Because the *Brussels Convention* also included the matter of jurisdiction, it contained, strictly speaking, more than Article 220 EEC of the Treaty asked for. This is logical, however, since it seems a little contrived to regulate the recognition and enforcement of judgments, but not the basic question of which court is competent to decide on the case.

The *Brussels I Regulation* was based on Article 65 of the then applicable EC Treaty, which gave the EC the power to regulate matters of private international law. This opportunity was also used to partially revise the matter.

Initially, Denmark used their 'opt-out' option in the Treaty of Amsterdam in order to not participate in the *Brussels I Regulation*. But the Regulation is also applicable to Denmark from 1 July 2007, as is its successor, the *Brussels I Regulation*.

The *Brussels I Regulation* was evaluated in 2010, which led to a recast in 2012 (which explains the addition of *'recast'* in the title of the Regulation). The changes mainly concern recognition and enforcement as well as the field of jurisdiction. This is important because this means that the case law of the European Court with regard to the *Brussels I Regulation* will also maintain its relevance to the *Brussels Ia Regulation*. This can also be said for the case law on the *Brussels Convention*. In the following, we will base ourselves on the *Brussels Ia Regulation*.

In 1988, a parallel treaty was established between the EC Member States and the European Free Trade Association, which then included Austria, Finland, Iceland, Norway, Sweden and Switzerland.[6] This *Lugano Convention*, regulates the matter of jurisdiction and the recognition and enforcement of court and arbitration statements in a broadly similar way to that of the *Brussels Convention* (and now the Regulation). Since Austria, Finland and Sweden have since joined the EU, the *Lugano Convention* is only relevant to relationships between Iceland, Norway and Switzerland and to their relations with EU Member States. In 2007, the Treaty was adapted to be harmonised with the *Brussels I Regulation*. This *Lugano II Convention* came into force in the EU and in the other three contracting Member States on different dates in 2010/2011 (Iceland being the last Member State to join the Convention). The *Brussels I Regulation* has already been replaced by the *Brussels Ia Regulation*, but this has not yet resulted in adjustments to the *Lugano II Convention*.

8.3.2 *Scope of the Brussels Ia Regulation and the Lugano II Convention*

Paragraph 8.2 already explained that, in order to be applicable, instruments of international private law should always be viewed in the light of three criteria in any specific situation: the material, the formal and the temporal scope of application.

The *Brussels Ia Regulation*'s *material scope of application* includes civil and commercial matters, irrespective of the nature of the court or tribunal (Article 1(1)). This means that (the consequences of) road traffic accidents will fall within the scope of the Regulation.[7] The clarification in this subsection, stating that fiscal, customs and administrative matters, as well as the liability of a state due to an act or omission in exercising public authority, remain outside the scope of the Regulation is of no importance to our subject.[8] The same goes for most of the claims listed in the second paragraph of Article 1: they will not arise in a dispute following a road traffic accident.

6. Liechtenstein has not signed the *Lugano Convention*, nor its successor, the *Lugano II Convention*.
7. From CJEU, Judgment of 14 October 1976, *Eurocontrol – LTU*, C-29/76, EU:C:1976:137 it follows that the notion of civil and commercial matters must be interpreted in an autonomous way, that is to say that "reference must not be made to the law of one of the States concerned but, first, to the objectives and scheme of the Convention and, secondly, to the general principles which vote from the corpus of the national legal Systems." This ruling given under the Brussels Convention 1968 still exists as prevailing law. In traffic matters, the notion of 'civil or commercial matters' will not quickly lead to problems of interpretation. The principle of the autonomous interpretation of concepts in EU Regulations will reappear several times over the following paragraphs.
8. Although doubts could be expressed regarding the exception of acts or omissions by a state, perhaps one should understand the claim against a state following the failure or improper implementation of a directive in national law. But we'll leave this question unanswered for now.

These are disputes arising from

- the state and jurisdiction of natural persons, questions of matrimonial property and the right of property in respect of marriages or similar relationships,
- bankruptcy, judicial arrangements and similar procedures,
- social security,
- maintenance obligations arising from family relationships, kinship, marriage or similar
- wills, legacies and maintenance obligations arising from death.

These areas could be excluded from the scope of the Regulation because other instruments have been created or are expected to be established.

One type of claim referred to in the second paragraph may, however, be relevant under some circumstances: exclusion from the scope of arbitration. This derogation may be of interest if a dispute arises regarding the recognition or enforcement of an arbitration ruling in the context of the Internal Regulations of the Green Card system. The jurisdiction of the arbitrators referred to in the Internal Regulations is comprehensively regulated in the relevant procedure and will not often lead to litigation, but an enforcement dispute does not seem to be unthinkable. The exception in Article 1(2), point (d) implies that the Convention on the recognition and enforcement of foreign arbitral awards of 10 June 1958, better known as the UNCITRAL arbitration rules, will apply in such a case.

The substantive scope of the *Lugano II Convention* is identical to that of the *Brussels Ia Regulation*. See Article 1.

For the *formal scope of application*, the defendant's domicile is the relevant criterion. It is important to note that the defendant is not required to be a national of a Member State. Even if the defendant is a national of a non-Member State, the Regulation applies as long as they are domiciled in a Member State. This is still the case even if they are also a resident of the country of which they are a national. Conversely, a claim against a national of a Member State who is not domiciled in a Member State is not covered by the Regulation. To be clear, the defendant's nationality is of no relevance.
Nor is the domicile or nationality of the plaintiff relevant. Even if the plaintiff is not domiciled in any Member State, the Regulation shall apply if the claim is lodged in a Member State.
The concept of 'domicile' is not an autonomous one. The question of whether the defendant is domiciled in a Member State must be established by the law of that assumed place of residence. Whether the defendant is domiciled in a Member State other than that of the requested court must be determined on the basis of that Member State's law.

Example
Take an accident caused by a Croatian student who is studying in Belgium under the Erasmus Exchange Programme and who is inattentively crossing the street in Luxembourg, as a result of which a German suffers damage. Whether the Croatian student's place of domicile is in Belgium or in Croatia must be decided on the basis of Belgian or, respectively, Croatian law.

In contrast to the concept of domicile regarding natural persons, the place of domicile for legal entities – such as insurance companies – is established autonomously. According to Article 63(1), legal entities have their place of domicile in the EU if their registered office ('statutory seat'), their central administration or their principal place of business is located in a Member State.

For the purposes of Ireland, Cyprus and the United Kingdom, 'statutory seat' means the registered office or, where there is no such office anywhere, the place of incorporation or, where there is no such place anywhere, the place under the law of which the entity was formed. See Article 63(2).

Legal entities can be domiciled in more than one Member State. Insurance undertakings frequently will be.

Contractually, parties may have agreed upon a forum choice clause, designating a competent court or courts in a Member State. Even if both parties do not have their domicile in a Member State, that court will be competent based on Article 25. Because such clauses are very unusual in road traffic accident matters – both the choice of the forum itself and (even more exceptional) the choice of a court or courts of countries with which neither party has any connection – Article 25 will not be discussed.

The *Lugano II Convention* has an identical arrangement regarding the formal scope of competence. See Art. 2 for natural persons and Article 60 for legal entities.

The *Brussels Ia Regulation*'s *temporal scope* is to be found in Article 66:

> "This Regulation shall apply only to legal proceedings instituted, to authentic instruments formally drawn up or registered and to court settlements approved or concluded on or after 10 January 2015."

Regulation 44/2001 has been repealed and references to the repealed Regulation shall be construed as references to the successor Regulation.

However, legal proceedings instituted and court settlements approved or concluded before that date are governed by the *Brussels I Regulation* (unless, of course, the temporal scope of that Regulation means that the *Brussels Convention* would be applicable, which seems highly unlikely considering the time elapsed), as Article 66(2) states explicitly.

The *Lugano II Convention*'s temporal scope is more complicated. This is due to the differing natures of Regulations and treaties. An EU Regulation enters into force on the same date in all Member States, whereas treaties can only enter into force after their ratification by Contracting Parties, and this moment may be different for each of the Parties. Article 63(1) of the *Lugano II Convention* therefore stipulates that

> "this Convention shall apply only to legal proceedings instituted and to documents formally drawn up or Registered as authentic instruments after its entry into force in the State of origin and, where recognition or Enforcement of a judgment or authentic instruments is sought, in the State addressed."

Whether the Convention governs the legal relationship shall therefore have to be assessed separately for each Contracting Party. For legal relations that date from before the *Lugano II Convention* came into force, the second paragraph of Article 63 contains rather complicated rules that we shall not elaborate on because of the exceptional nature of such situations.

8.3.3 Structure of the jurisdiction rules in Brussels Ia and Lugano II

Before entering into the jurisdictional rules of the Regulation and the Convention, it may be helpful to make a few comments on their structure.
The rules of jurisdiction can be found in Chapter II of the *Brussels Ia Regulation*. This chapter is divided into ten Sections, of which Sections 1 to 3 and 9 are the most relevant. Although, section 4 (jurisdiction in cases of contracts concluded by consumers) may also play a role.

> Section 1 (General provisions) contains the basic rules. Section 2 (Special jurisdiction) provides for, inter alia, alternative competent courts in the event of torts and offences. The most important part for our subject is Section 3 (jurisdiction in insurance matters). Here, the jurisdiction is regulated both for claims against and by the insurer, with special rules for liability insurance. Section 4 (jurisdiction over consumers contracts) may be important in the event of package travel in the context of road traffic accidents.
>
> Section 9 (Lis pendens – related actions) is of importance if the same road traffic accident results in several procedures in different Member States between the same or different parties.

Section 7 (prorogation of jurisdiction) is more important in the practice of international trade than in the context of road accidents, because an agreement is required in order to reach a choice of jurisdiction. In the context of tort, such as a road traffic accident, such an agreement is highly unlikely to exist nor to be concluded at a later stage. However, a jurisdiction clause may appear in a contract of carriage (including package travel contracts). The choice of jurisdiction will therefore be discussed in the context of a contract of carriage.

When examining each of these sections, we shall determine whether, and if so in what respect, the *Lugano II Convention* differs from *Regulation Brussels Ia*. It may, however, already be noted that the structure of the *Brussels Ia Regulation* described above is fully reflected in the *Lugano II Convention.*

8.3.4 Section 1 – general provisions

The Regulation's basic rule can be found In Article 4: persons domiciled in a Member State shall, whatever their nationality, be sued in the courts of that Member State.

Persons who are not nationals of the Member State in which they are domiciled shall be governed by the rules of jurisdiction applicable to nationals of that Member State.

These basic rules are, however, not without additions and exceptions. These can be found in Sections 2 to 7. Only by virtue of these Sections can the basic rule be deviated from, according to Article 5. These Sections usually provide for one or more alternative jurisdictions.

Exclusive jurisdiction is only created in the event of a dispute as referred to in Section 6, but this type of dispute is irrelevant to our subject. It concerns disputes over property, legal persons, the validity of registrations in public registers, patents, trademarks etc.

However, one provision in Section 6 may be relevant: for the enforcement of (judicial) decisions, only the courts of the Member State in which the place of enforcement is located are competent. But this aspect of private international law will not be discussed in this book.

It is, of course, also possible that a defendant is not domiciled in the territory of any Member State. In the event of an international road traffic accident, this will often be the case. According to Article 6, jurisdiction is then governed by the (national) legislation of each Member State.

> This implies that the plaintiff will have to verify the possibilities to summon the defendant in their own country – or in another Member State – under the relevant legislations. Consider the accident in the example in paragraph 8.3.2, but now with a Moroccan student rather than Croatian. The German injured party must now determine on the basis of German legislation whether the Moroccan student can be summoned before a German court or before the courts of another Member State.

It should be noted that Articles 4 to 6 speak of 'the courts'. The question of which specific court will be competent in a Member State is therefore determined by the internal law of that Member State. As will be demonstrated below, the following Sections may designate a specific competent court in certain circumstances.

The *Lugano II* convention has an almost identical main rule in Articles 2 to 4.

8.3.5 Section 2 – special jurisdiction

8.3.5.1 General remarks

This Section consists of three articles. In Article 7, an alternative jurisdiction is established for a number of specific legal relationships (alternative meaning in addition to the main rule that the defendant is summoned before the courts of the Member State where they are domiciled). Article 8 regulates competence – also alternatively – for cases of (*1*) plurality of defendants (domiciled in several Member States), (*2*) protection, joinder and third party intervention, (*3*) a counterclaim stemming from the same contract or legal fact which forms the basis of the original claim and (*4*) the combination of a contract with a business claim relating to real estate. Article 9 relates to claims with respect to the liability or exploitation of ships and is not relevant here. We will concentrate on Article 7 and on the first three parts of Article 8.

Not all parts of Article 7 are relevant either. Only the elements (*1*), (*2*) and (*3*) are interesting in our context.

> The various components provide for alternative jurisdictions for disputes concerning (*1*) contractual obligations, (*2*) obligations arising from tort, (*3*) obligations arising from a criminal offence, (*4*) ownership-based claims for the return of cultural property, (*5*) disputes relating to the operation of branch offices, agencies or other establishments, (*6*) disputes concerning trusts and (*7*) disputes relating to salvage and rescue charges.

8.3.5.2 The specific jurisdictions of Article 7

It is noteworthy that the basic rule remains in full force. This clearly follows from the opening words of Article 4(1): the main rule applies 'without prejudice to this Regulation'.

a) First, let us consider the special jurisdiction in the case of a contractual obligation (Article 7(1). This provision may be of interest in the event of a travel agreement (a type of contract of carriage) other than a package travel agreement (an agreement (with a consumer) offering both transport and residence for a single price). Section 4 applies to the latter form of transport agreement.
According to Article 7(1), point (a) the courts of the place of performance of the obligation in question will be competent. The use of the term 'place' – rather than 'Member State' – implies that the Regulation not only determines in which Member State the claim can be made, but even for which specific court.

What should be understood by 'the place of performance of the obligation in question' has to be determined in a multi-stage process: first of all, it is necessary to establish whether the agreement contains a (valid) jurisdiction clause, which will then have precedence. In the absence of such a clause, Article 7(1), point (b) provides a rule for two specific agreements. Only the second indent is important for our subject: in the context of providing services, 'the place of performance of the obligation' is the place in a Member State where the service was or should have been provided according to the agreement.

The question is of where a transport service is or should have been provided according to the agreement. It seems logical that this would be the destination. The purpose of a transport agreement is, after all, the safe arrival of the transported persons or goods.

The above can be summarised in an Example

Example
A bus belonging to a Dutch commercial bus transport company, on its way from Bucharest (Romania) to Hamburg (Germany), has an accident on the motorway near Salzburg (Austria). Unless otherwise agreed in the contract of carriage (which is not unlikely, but this is irrelevant for the example), the German courts – in this case, the court in Hamburg – will be competent for the claim of an injured party who purchased a ticket to Hamburg. German procedural law then determines before which court the claim must be brought.
Based on the basic rule, the injured party may, of course, also bring the claim before the courts of the Member State of the place of domicile of the defendant, the Dutch bus company. In this case, this would mean the Dutch courts, because the company is domiciled in the Netherlands.

A question that may still arise is of the agreement's qualification to transport free of charge, out of sheer benevolence. The 'spontaneous hitchhike agreement' probably poses the most problems. The law of the requested court will then have to determine whether a legal agreement exists and thus whether the agreement falls within the scope of Article 7(1), point (b), second indent. See also para 8.4.3.2, point *a*.

b) Article 7(2) is more important in the context of an international road traffic accident: jurisdiction in the case of an obligation out of tort, delict or quasi-delict. After all, a road traffic accident will usually qualify as tort. The injured party will at least start their claim on that legal basis.[9]

The court of the place where the damage occurred or may arise is the competent court.
The opening words of Article 7 make it clear that this can only affect courts in the Member States. The words 'may arise' can be relevant, for example, in the case of potential environmental damage and will not play a role in traffic practice.[10] Here, again, the Regulation designates the *specific* competent court.

Example
In the above-mentioned accident involving the Dutch bus at Salzburg in Austria, the claim – which qualifies not only as a contractual claim from a transport agreement, but also from an unlawful act – by an injured party may also be brought before the competent court in Salzburg.
In this case, there are already three competent courts for a claim against the Dutch bus company: based on the basic rule of Article 4, the Dutch court, the court in Hamburg on the basis of Article 7(1), point (*b*) and the court in Salzburg on the basis of Article 7(2).

c) Frequently, a road traffic accident will not only qualify as tort but also as a criminal offence: speeding, not giving way and alcohol consumption are unfortunately all too often the cause of road traffic accidents, often with serious outcomes.

If prosecution is indeed carried out *and* the law of the country in which such criminal proceedings are instituted provides for the possibility to do so, the injured

9. The question of whether an unlawful act has been committed can only be answered after the next step in the private international law decision-making process. Only when we know which law is applicable can it be assessed whether an unlawful act has been committed. In the phase of determining jurisdiction, we assume the qualification of the legal basis of their claim on the basis of the claimant's claim.
10. Except in the case of a road traffic accident involving a tank lorry containing dangerous substances that has tilted on or near the border between two Member States and that is likely to leak.

party may lodge a claim for compensation with the criminal court where the criminal proceedings are to be filed. See Article 7(3).
Usually, the criminal case will be served at the courts of the place where a civil claim can also be brought on the basis of tort, so the extra jurisdiction of Article 7(3) seems to add very little. However, it may be of interest to the injured party, potentially because the costs of litigation for a joinder in a criminal case could be lower than for a standalone civil case.

Example
Revisiting the example of the accident with the Dutch bus: assuming that the driver has committed a traffic offence, that he is prosecuted for this offence and that Austrian law provides for the legal concept of joinder in criminal proceedings, the civil claim for damage compensation against the driver can therefore also be brought before the criminal court in Salzburg.
A rich palette of possibilities begins to develop. We will, however, demonstrate that our victim's options are still far from exhausted.

We don't have to go into detail on the *Lugano II Convention*'s rules in the field of Article 7: they are identical. See Article 5 of the *Lugano II Convention.*

8.3.5.3 The regime of Article 8
Until now, the starting point for our line of thinking has been the position of the injured party in the road traffic accident: which courts are competent to hear their case?
For Article 8, however, our perspective is that of the defendant: by which courts can they be summoned? This is, of course, the other side of the same coin, but this approach is well-advised. After all, Article 8 (except for 8(4), which is not relevant to us) concerns cases in which a claim is already pending. The injured party has therefore already made a choice for a specific jurisdiction.

a) Article 8(1) relates to the plurality of defendants. If all defendants are domiciled in different Member States, the basic rule would imply that each of them may be brought before the courts of his or her domicile. This would pose the risk of conflicting rulings.

Providing there is such a close link between the claims that the proper administration of justice would require simultaneous treatment in order to avoid incompatible decisions being made in the various courts, a defendant may be summoned before the court of any defendant's place of residence.

Example
A passenger of a vehicle involved in a two-vehicle accident is uncertain as to which of the two drivers he should address. One thing is certain, however: either one or both of them should compensate him for his or her damages in proportion to their share in the liability.
According to the basic rule, if the defendants are domiciled in two different Member States, they should be summoned before the courts of each of their Member State of residence. This implies the risk that both courts assume full liability on the part of the other motorist, with the result that the injured party is deprived of compensation altogether. According to Article 8(1), the passenger may bring the second driver before the court already hearing the case against the other motorist.

There is a certain connection with the matter of *lis pendens* and related actions (see also para 8.3.8).

b) The case of a defendant impleading a third party is related to the plurality of defendants (Article 8(2)). The same applies to the legal concept of procedural third party intervention.

Example
An injured party decides for reasons of his own to sue the liable party in person (and not the MTPL insurer). It is obvious that the insured party wants to involve the insurer in the proceedings: the liability of the insurer will then be settled, should the insured be held liable.[11] This is possible by calling the insurer into the proceedings. Of course, it goes without saying that the insurer has an interest in a favourable decision for the insured as well and may therefore intervene in proceedings, even if the insured party hasn't called them in for purposes of indemnification.

In this case, the insurer may be summoned to the court where the injured party's original claim against the insured party is pending, or may intervene in the proceedings.

c) Article 8(3) relates to claims arising from the same legal facts as the original claim.

11. Possible defects in the insurance policy cover not taken into consideration.

Example
Imagine an international road traffic accident in which both parties suffer damage and mutually believe the liability to rest with the other party. The claim of one party will inevitably be answered with a counterclaim from the other. If both parties are domiciled in different Member States, it would then be desirable to ensure that both claims are assessed by the same court. This means that a party may be summoned before a different court than the one which would be competent under Article 4 or 7.

Article 8(3) opens up this possibility. The precondition is that both claims evolve from the same legal fact. If the original defendant still has a bone to pick with their counterpart because of a previous accident, for example, Article 8(3) will not be applicable.

Article 6 of the *Lugano II Convention* is in its content identical to Article 8 of *Brussels Ia*.

8.3.6 Section 3 – jurisdiction in matters relating to insurance

8.3.6.1 General remarks

So far, we have discussed the general rules of jurisdiction and the special rules of jurisdiction that apply to all citizens. However, Section 3 contains special rules for insurance cases. These are justified on the one hand by the special position of insurers in social and economic life and, on the other hand, by the fact that they are – especially in comparison with consumers – entities with great expertise. They need less protection than the 'common man', and so the jurisdictional rules that can be invoked against insurers are broader. In other words, the 'weaker' citizen deserves more protection against the 'big' insurer. See recital (18) in the preamble of *Brussels Ia*, which, *inter alia* in relation to insurance cases, considers that the weaker party should be protected by rules of jurisdiction that are more favourable to their particular interests than the general rules.

These special rules of competence in insurance cases distinguish between claims instituted against the insurer and claims that the insurer sets against their own insured party or contractual counterpart, the policyholder. There are also separate rules for liability insurance within the specific rules in matters of insurance. The situation looks complex, particularly because of Article 13(2), which initially confusingly also makes Articles 10, 11 and 12 applicable to the claim under a direct right of action of the injured party against the insurer.

An important preliminary observation is the following: the rules of Section 3 are exclusive, according to Article 10. Only Section 3 governs the claim against and by the insurer. The other rules of competence are thus not applicable (with the exception of the provisions of Article 6 – which is irrelevant to us – and Article 7(5) – which concerns disputes relating to the operation of a branch office, an agency or any other establishment, and does not need to be discussed). The exclusive character of Section 3 sounds more dramatic than it is: the general rules of Articles 4 and 5 and the special jurisdiction rules of Section 2 are 'repeated' in Section 3. But it also results in the rules of Section 3 requiring autonomous interpretation, in order to ensure that they are interpreted in the same way throughout the whole of the EU.[12]

8.3.6.2 Action against the insurer; general rules

a) The main rule regarding the claim brought against the insurer is the same as that in Article 4: the insurer is summoned before the courts of the Member State of their domicile. See Article 11(1), point (a).

But the first derogation immediately follows in 11(1), point (b): the policyholder, insured or beneficiary may also summon the insurer before the court of the claimant's place of residence.

Because co-insurance is less common here, Article 11(1), point (c) is less relevant for motor insurance. In any such case, the action against the insurer may also be brought before the court of the Member State where the claim was brought against the first insurer.

b) Also, insurers not domiciled in the territory of a Member State – where residence is understood as the place of the insurer's registered office, the place of its main administration or of its head office – but that have a branch office, an agency or any other establishment in a Member State may be called to appear in the courts in that Member State if the dispute relates to the exploitation of that branch office, agency or other establishment. See Article 11(2).

Example

An American insurer has a branch office in the Netherlands and sells MTPL policies through that branch office. The Dutch courts are then competent for claims relating to those insurance policies.

12. See CJEU, Judgment of 17 September 2009, *Vorarlberger Gebietskrankenkasse*, C-347/08, EU:C:2009:561, para. 35.

8.3.6.3 *Action against the insurer: liability insurance; direct right of action*

a) Liability insurance deviates from other forms of insurance in that the injured party does not have a contractual relationship (as has the policyholder, the insured or the beneficiary) with the insurer. Therefore, a third party outside the contract is involved. This justifies a special regime. Articles 12 and 13 do justice to the special nature of liability insurance. These provisions, in particular Article 13, are not easy to understand. The EU Court has had to make a number of decisions to clarify their true meaning. Therefore, and because they are of particular importance for the settlement of international road traffic accidents, we are going to head deeper into this issue.

b) The first provision concerning claims against a liability insurer is Article 12. In the case of liability insurance, the insurer may also be summoned before the court of the place where the harmful event occurred.[13] This competence is the insurance equivalent of Article 7(2) (see para 8.3.5.2, under *b*).
The place where the harmful event occurred must be understood to mean the place of the event which led to the damage, not the place where the damage was suffered.

c) Article 13 provides a number of additional jurisdictional rules for liability insurance.
According to the first paragraph, the insured person has the possibility to summon the insurer – for purposes of indemnification – to the court where the victim's legal action against the insured is pending, providing that applicable legislation permits such third party action. This provision is therefore the insurance equivalent of Article 8(2).

d) Article 13(2) reads:

> "Articles 10, 11 and 12 shall apply to actions brought by the injured party directly against the insurer, where such direct actions are permitted."

This provision has given rise to a certain level of uncertainty.
These problems were primarily caused by the somewhat ambiguous wording of the reference to the Articles 10, 11 and 12. However, questions were also raised about the scope of the provision in light of the objective underlying Section 3, namely the protection of vulnerable participants in social and economic life. This provision deserves greater attention due to its significance for the settlement of traffic damage.

---

13. This may also apply in the case of property insurance or a policy that covers both movable and fixed property if both are affected by the same incident.

Eventually, the EU Court clarified the meaning and scope of Article 13(2) in a number of decisions. However, this was preceded by a somewhat curious attempt by the European Parliament to clarify the reference in Article 13 to Articles 10 to 12 by inserting a recital in the preamble to the 5th Motor Insurance Directive. The recital returns in the preamble to the codified Directive as recital (32).[14]

Before examining the ambiguities and case law of the EU Court further, the following observation is useful: the precondition in Article 13(2) of a direct right of action does not cause problems in the sphere of MTPL insurance. A direct right of action is mandatory throughout the EU due to the 4th Directive, initially only for accidents impacting visiting victims in the sense of that directive, but then also for purely domestic and for Green Card accidents with the 5th Directive. See para 6.3.2.

e) The ambiguity, created by the reference in Article 13(2) to Article 11, can be summarised as follows: is its intention that the injured party

- (only) has the possibility to litigate before the specific courts which are competent to hear the case of the policyholder, the insured or the beneficiary (the limited interpretation), or
- is the underlying principle that they may litigate before the courts of their place of residence (the 'generous' explanation)?

It was initially argued that the term 'beneficiary' should be interpreted to include the injured third party, who after all 'benefits' from a direct action. However, this explanation was not tenable: 'beneficiary' is a term used in life insurance and refers to the person in the contract who is entitled to receive the sums insured. This slightly artificial attempt to accommodate the injured third party has now become superfluous in the light of the EU Court of Justice's case law.

f) As has already been pointed out, European Parliament has raised the issue and made an attempt to remove the problem by inserting a recital in the 5th Directive, which reads as follows in the codified Directive:

> "Under Article 11 (2) read in conjunction with Article 9 (1) (b) of Council Regulation (EC) No 44/2001 of 22 December 2000 on jurisdiction and the recognition and enforcement of judgments in civil and commercial matters, injured parties may bring legal proceedings against the civil liability insurance provider in the Member State in which they are domiciled."

---

14. A very creative method of legislation: a recital in a Directive explaining and possibly amending a Regulation. The EU Court had not yet issued its opinion on the matter, and the possibility that the Court would have ruled differently could not be entirely ruled out. Note that directives are adopted by Parliament and the Council, but Regulations were not at that time. The *Brussels I Regulation* was adopted by the Council alone and not by Parliament. So, it could be argued that Parliament exceeded its mandate.

In a first judgment from 2007, the Court ruled on the matter of the relationship between Article 13(2) and – in particular – Article 12.

The question in this *FBTO Schadeverzekeringen* decision was whether Mr Odenbreit, domiciled in Germany and being the victim of a road traffic accident in the Netherlands for which an insured of Dutch insurance company FBTO was held liable, could start an action against FBTO before the court of his German place of domicile.[15]

The Court came to the following conclusion:

"The reference in Article 11 (2) [currently Article 13(2)] of Council Regulation (EC) No 44/2001 of 22 December 2000 on jurisdiction and the recognition and enforcement of judgments in civil and commercial matters to Article 9 (1) (b) [currently Article 11(1), point (b)] of that Regulation is to be interpreted as meaning that the injured party may bring an action directly against the insurer before the courts for the place in a Member State where that injured party is domiciled, provided that such a direct action is permitted and the insurer is domiciled in a Member State."

Thus, it was clear that (the current) Article 13(2) should be understood in the second (broader) sense. Not only the courts available to policyholders and insureds (and beneficiaries) are available to the injured party, but (also) the court of the injured party's domicile.

g) Were all questions resolved? No. The (Austrian) *Vorarlberger Gebietskrankenkasse* (a regional public health insurance company), which had reimbursed the medical costs of their insured, who was injured in a road traffic accident in Germany, was subrogated in the latter's claim against the German liable party and his vehicle's MTPL insurer. *Vorarlberger* was of the opinion that the *FBTO* decision entitled them to bring the recourse claim against the German liability insurer before the Austrian courts as well. Unfortunately for this health insurer, the Court came to another conclusion, on the basis of the objectives of Section 3 as well as a linguistic interpretation of the wording of Article 11. The Court ruled that subrogated parties such as the *Vorarlberger Gebietskrankenkasse* could not invoke Article 11(2) of the *Brussels I Regulation*.[16] The decision reads as follows:

"The reference in Article 11 (2) [*currently Article 13 (2)*] of Council Regulation (EC) No 44/2001 of 22 December 2000 on jurisdiction and the recognition and enforcement of judgments in civil and commercial matters to Article 9 (1) (b) [*currently 11 (1) (b)*] thereof must be interpreted as meaning that a social security institution, acting as the statutory assignee of the rights of the directly injured party in a motor accident, may not bring an action directly in the courts of its

15. CJEU, Judgment of 13 December 2007, *FBTO Schadeverzekeringen*, C-463/06, EU:C:2007:792 (often also referred to as the '*Odenbreit* decision').
16. CJEU, Judgment of 17 September 2009, *Vorarlberger Gebietskrankenkasse*, C-347/08, EU:C:2009:561.

Member State of establishment against the insurer of the person allegedly responsible for the accident, where that insurer is established in another Member State."

The argumentation underlying this decision is too interesting not to consider in further detail, all the more so because this approach is seen again in other judgments.[17]

On the one hand, the Court reaches their conclusion on the basis of an interpretation of the differences in the Regulation's various language versions as regards the term 'injured party'. On the other hand, the intentions of Section 3 are considered, more specifically the protection of the weaker party.

The relevant paragraphs 29 to 43 can be summarised as follows:

> The Court begins with a reminder that it is settled case law that – in the case of differences between the different language versions of a provision – the different versions must be examined in order to obtain the correct interpretation. The various language versions differ as far as Article 13(2) of the *Brussels I Regulation* is concerned: the German, Spanish, Czech, Danish, Estonian, Italian, Polish, Slovakian and Swedish texts use the equivalent of the term 'injured party'. The French version, on the other hand, uses the word *'victime'*, which, in semantic interpretation, refers to the person who has directly suffered the damage or injury. 'Injured party' is the term used to denote all who, directly or indirectly, have suffered damage. In light of the majority of language versions that have taken the broad concept of 'injured party', the Court concludes that Article 11(2) refers to both the (direct) victim and the indirectly injured party. This would be in favour of the *Vorarlberger Gebietskrankenkasse*. But the Court's reasoning doesn't stop there.
>
> Only now does it arrive at the real question of the referring court: can a social security institution such as the *Vorarlberger Gebietskrankenkasse* rely on Article 13(2)? And the answer to that question is: no.
>
> The Court considers that the *Brussels I Regulation* should have full effect and an autonomous interpretation, and that it is therefore necessary primarily to take into account its system and its objectives. National law cannot be conclusive, since that would jeopardise the uniform interpretation of the Regulation.
>
> In doing so, the Court considers that the principle of the Regulation is that the defendant is called before the courts in the Member State of their domicile without prejudice to Sections 2 to 7 of chapter II. The rules of jurisdiction which derogate from the general principle should not be interpreted as being applicable outside the cases expressly provided for by the Regulation. Section 3 establishes an autonomous system for the judicial division of jurisdiction in insurance cases. The purpose of this section, according to Recital 13 in the preamble, is the protection of the weaker party by rules of jurisdiction that are more

17. Cf CJEU, Judgment of 4 September 2014, *Vnuk*, C-162/13, EU:C:2014:2146, where the same comparison of the different language versions of the codified Directive brought the Court to their judgment.

> favourable to their interests than the general rules. And because a social security institution such as the *Vorarlberger Gebietskrankenkasse* does not need such protection as an insurance professional, it cannot rely on Article 13(2) of the *Brussels I Regulation*.

h) The Court adds an interesting paragraph (44): if the party to whom the victim's claim has been passed by way of subrogation has to be considered as a weaker party itself, then Article 13(2) shall apply. This applies in particular to the heirs of a deceased victim, but as the *MMA IARD* judgment demonstrates, other parties may also invoke Article 13(2) in certain circumstances.[18]

> The facts leading to this decision are as follows: an employer, a public law institution, operates five hospitals and pays an employee's salary after they are involved in an accident. Subsequently, the employer is subrogated in the rights of their employee. The Court bases its decision on its previous jurisprudence in *FBTO* and *Vorarlberger Gebietskrankenkasse*. This shows the importance of the interpretation of the term 'injured party' in that last decision. While *Vorarlberger Gebietskrankenkasse* was not protected under Article 13(2) as an insurance professional, the Court's judgment is favourable to the plaintiff in this case. Again, the Court argues from the necessity of autonomous interpretation of the *Brussels Ia Regulation*. In this context, the Court refers to the opinion of the Advocate General (paragraph 47) that the notion of a 'weaker party' in insurance matters has a broader significance than in the case of agreements with consumers or individual employment contracts:
>
> > "(...) a case-by-case assessment of the question whether an employer which continues to pay the salary may be regarded as the economically weaker party in order to be covered by the definition of 'injured party' within the meaning of Article 11 (2) of Regulation No 44/2001, would give rise to the risk of legal uncertainty and would be contrary to the objective of that Regulation, laid down in recital 11 thereof, according to which the rules of jurisdiction must be highly predictable."
>
> The conclusion is that
>
> > "it must be held that, pursuant to Article 11 (2) of Regulation No 44/2001, employers to which the rights of their employees to compensation have passed may, as persons which have suffered damage and whatever their size and legal form, rely on the rules of special jurisdiction laid down in Articles 8 to 10 of that Regulation."

It therefore seems that only insurance companies miss out on the benefits of Article 13(2) of the *Brussels Ia Regulation*. Whether this would be reasonable in all cases is doubtful, but '*dura lex, sed lex*'.

---

18. CJEU, Judgment of 20 July 2017, *MMA IARD*, C-340/16, EU:C:2017:576.

8.3.6.4 Action of the insurer against the policyholder, insured or beneficiary

Section 3 also contains rules on the legal action instigated by the insurer against the policyholder, the insured or the beneficiary. In the context of this book, these rules will primarily be relevant for claims in which the insurer, under the Motor Insurance Directive, has reimbursed the injured party whilst cover does not apply in the internal relationship between policyholder/insured and insurer: exclusions such as alcohol consumption, driving without a driving licence, contractual deductibles, damage caused intentionally or non-payment of premiums.[19] Such exclusions cannot be opposed to the injured third party, but they are permitted in the internal relationship between insurer and insured. See para 6.2.13.

These rules should also be seen in the light of protecting the weaker party. Article 14(1) allows the insurer to start their action only before the courts of the Member State where the defendant is domiciled, whether the defendant is the policyholder, insured or beneficiary.[20]

The second paragraph confirms beyond doubt that this does not affect the competence of the court before which the original claim was brought – for example, action by the policyholder against the insurer before the court of the place of the accident on the basis of Article 12 – to hear the case of a counterclaim put forward by the insurer against their contracting party.

8.3.6.5 Contractual choice of jurisdiction

A distinction should be made between two situations: the possibility of a jurisdiction clause in the insurance contract and the choice of a particular court in the relationship between insurer and injured third party. Although the latter will not occur frequently, it is not impossible. Article 15 contains rules to which such a choice of jurisdiction between insurer and counterparty is subject.

As far as contractual jurisdiction clauses – policy clauses which regulate the relationship between the insurer and the policyholder, insured or beneficiary – are concerned, such a choice is only possible, according to Article 15(2) and (3), if

> "2) the clause entitles the policyholder, the insured or the beneficiary to submit the case to other courts than those referred to in Section 3;
> 3) policyholder and insurer have their domicile or habitual residence in the same Member State at the time of the contract's conclusion; this also applies (even) if the incident that caused the damage occurs abroad and (apparently) even if the policyholder moves to another Member

---

19. In those jurisdictions where the insurer in case of damage caused intentionally cannot refuse to indemnify the injured third party, as is the case in the Netherlands, for example, see para 6.2.13.7.
20. The term 'beneficiary' is also irrelevant here, it only refers to the person who is entitled to receive payment under a life insurance policy.

State after concluding the contract. The condition is that the Member State whose courts are designated in the agreement shall allow such a choice.
Please note: not only a domicile, but also a policyholder's habitual residence in the Member State of the insurer's residence is sufficient for the applicability of Article 15."

Paragraphs (4) (the policyholder has no domicile in a Member State) and (5) (insurance of certain special and major risks) are not relevant for our subject. Paragraph (4) because it is not applicable in the case of compulsory insurance, and paragraph (5) because MTPL insurance is not one of the risks set out in Article 16.[21]

The first part of Article 15 could be of interest for the position of the injured third party, although jurisdictional choice between victim and insurer will not often occur. The victim may also agree with the insurer on a particular competent court to be designated, but *only* if that choice is made *after* the dispute has arisen. It is to be assumed that this is not the moment when the injured party submits a request for compensation, but only the moment it becomes clear that no agreement on liability or compensation can be reached.

8.3.6.6 The positions of Green Card Bureau, Guarantee Fund and Compensation Body

Section 3 is dedicated to jurisdiction in insurance cases. This raises the question of how to assess the position of the Green Card Bureau, the Guarantee Fund and the Compensation Body. In a relationship with the injured third party, their role resembles that of an insurer. But does this also mean that Section 3 applies?

The EU Court has not yet expressed itself on this matter, so we can only guess the answer. Two different approaches are in our opinion defendable:

- Section 3 is not applicable in the relationship between the injured third party and the Bureau, the Guarantee Fund or the Compensation Body, since Section 3 relates to insurers and the three bodies do not qualify as such, or
- Section 3 is applicable, since the Bureau, Guarantee Fund and Compensation Body can be assumed to have the necessary expertise to handle cross-border road traffic claims and can therefore be regarded as a 'strong' party.

We are inclined to prefer the first interpretation. Our position is based on two arguments: first of all, Section 3 is an exception to the main rule that defendants are summoned before the courts of the Member State of their residence, and it is the Court's settled case law that exceptions to a rule must be interpreted restrictively. Economically and socially, a Bureau, a Guarantee Fund or a Compensation Body may resemble an insurer, but they do not legally qualify as such. A strict – and

21. Directive 2009/138/EC of the European Parliament and of the Council on the taking-up and pursuit of the business of insurance and reinsurance (Solvency II) (recast).

therefore restrictive – interpretation of Section 3 would imply the inapplicability of this Section.

This would perhaps be different in light of the objective of victim protection, which is the basis of Section 3, but in our opinion there is no need for wider jurisdiction: in the case of the Bureau, the injured party can usually litigate before their own courts already. The same applies to actions against the Guarantee Fund. And insofar as the injured party is domiciled in another Member State, they have access to the claims representative – and, in the absence thereof, to the Compensation Body – all in their domiciled Member State. There is, therefore, no need for Section 3 to apply.

8.3.6.7 Rules of the Lugano II Convention relating to insurance matters

The rules on jurisdiction in insurance cases in the *Lugano II Convention* are identical to those of the *Brussels Ia Regulation*. We assume that the Court's case law is also valid in EFTA cases. More specifically, this means that the interpretation of Article 13(2) also applies.[22]

8.3.7 Section 4 – jurisdiction over consumer contracts

As with jurisdiction in insurance cases, the rules of Section 4 are exclusive and autonomous. It is broadly identical to Section 3 and has the same background: protection of the weaker party in economic traffic. See Article 17(1):

> "(…) a person, the consumer, for a purpose which can be regarded as being outside his trade or profession (…)."

Although the rules of Section 4 are only of very limited importance for our topic, they should nonetheless be discussed, if only for the sake of completeness. This limited importance is due to the fact that, in the practice of the handling of road traffic accidents, Section 4 has significance only in the context of so-called 'package travel agreements'. See Article 17(3):

> "this Section shall not apply to a contract of transport other than a contract which, for an inclusive price, provides for a combination of travel and accommodation."

What is a consumer contract? It must, according to Article 17(1), be an agreement concluded

22. This also seems to be the opinion of the German Supreme Court: Urteil des Bundegerichtshofs, 23 October 2012, VI ZR 260/11.

- by a person, the consumer, for a purpose which cannot be regarded as business or professional, and (insofar as is relevant in this context)
- the agreement must have been concluded with a person in the pursuit of their commercial or professional activities in the Member State of the consumer's domicile, or
- with a person who, by any means, directs such activities to that Member State or to several Member States, including that Member State, and the agreement falls within those activities.

A legal action for breach of contract started by the consumer against their counterpart may be brought before the courts of the Member State of the other party's residence (the basic rule that the defendant is summoned before their own courts), but also before the court of the consumer's place of residence, irrespective of the other party's place of residence. See Article 18(1):

> "A consumer may bring proceedings against the other party to a contract either in the courts of the Member State in which that party is domiciled or, regardless of the domicile of the other party, in the courts for the place where the consumer is domiciled."

From the connection with Article 17(1), point (c), it follows that the consumer must be domiciled in a Member State.
Legal action carried out by the other party against the consumer – we're mentioning this only for the sake of completeness – can only be brought before the courts of the Member State in which the consumer is domiciled. Cf. Article 18(2)
In accordance with this section, any counterclaim by the other party may, as in the case of insurance, be brought before the court where the consumer's original claim against the other party was made. See Article 18(3).

Again, the rules governing choice of law are similar to those in insurance cases. See Article 19 and *supra* para 8.3.6.5.

The *Lugano II* rules correspond perfectly with those of the *Brussels Ia Regulation.*

8.3.8 Section 9 – lis pendens – related actions

The example of the journey from Bucharest to Hamburg made by a Dutch bus presented in paragraph 8.3.5.2 shows that several courts may be competent in the same case. If this invites parties to start multiple proceedings against each other before different courts, the result may be incompatible decisions. In order to avoid this undesirable consequence of a plurality of jurisdictions, the Regulation contains rules in Articles 29 and 30 for situations involving identical proceedings between the same parties or related legal actions.

The risk of incompatible judgments in identical or related cases becomes a possibility, as Article 36(1) (in Chapter III – Recognition and enforcement) stipulates that a judgment given in a Member State is recognised in the other Member States without any further formality, and can therefore be enforced.

Article 29 deals with the situation of *lis pendens* or – briefly – identical claims between the same parties before the courts of different Member States. The condition for the applicability of Article 29 is that the proceedings:
- are pending between the same parties,
- have the same cause of action and
- concern the same subject.

In several judgments, the Court of Justice of the European Union has stipulated that these concepts should be interpreted autonomously and are therefore not dependent on (the interpretation of) national law.[23] Let us briefly cover each of these conditions.

The requirement that the legal actions must be between *the same parties* does not mean that they should have the same (procedural) role in the procedures. The plaintiff in one case may very well be the defendant in the other case.

The requirements of *the same cause of action* and *the same subject* are more complicated. 'The same cause of action' means that the legal actions are based on the same facts and on the same legal rules. In the sphere of international road traffic accidents, for example, the same collision and the rules on tort.
'The same subject' refers to the purpose of the procedure, such as reimbursement for damage caused by the accident.

If these conditions are met, the court of the second or further procedure *must* defer its decision until the first court has declared itself competent to hear the case. If it considers itself competent, then any courts requested later will not have jurisdiction.

> Different rules apply in the case of a contractual jurisdiction clause. See Article 31(2). If a case is brought before the court on the basis of a choice of jurisdiction, then all other requested courts should hold the case until the court requested on the basis of Article 25 has decided on its jurisdiction, regardless of the order of requests.

23. See CJEU, Judgment of 8 December 1987, *Gubisch/Palumbo*, C-144/86, EU:C:1987:528 and CJEU, Judgment of 6 December 1994, *Tatry*, C-406/92, EU:C:1994:400.

Article 30 covers a situation of several proceedings which show such coherence that the proper administration of justice requires simultaneous treatment in order to avoid incompatible rulings. The aforementioned *Tatry* Court ruling shows that the notion of incompatibility must be interpreted autonomously and broadly.

The requirements of Article 29 that the parties in the various proceedings are identical, as well as that the proceedings have the same cause of action and the same subject, do not apply here.

Example
An injured party domiciled in Denmark has a road traffic accident in Austria. He brings his claim against the Austrian insurer of the vehicle he holds liable, before the court of his place of residence, on the grounds of tort and using his direct right of action (see Article 13(2)). The Austrian driver, however, who is only insured against third party liability, holds the Danish citizen liable for his damage and starts proceedings against the Danish insurer before the court of the place of the accident, Austria, on the basis of Article 12.
The possibility of both courts deciding that neither of the two (different) defendants are not liable (or that both are fully liable) should be avoided. Article 29 cannot be relied upon, since the parties are not identical.

Article 30 provides for a slightly different solution to this problem than Article 29. Whilst the Austrian court must stay the case until the Danish court has made a decision under Article 29, the Austrian judge *can* decide to defer the case under Article 30. At the request of the parties, they can also refer the case to the other court in Denmark.
For Article 30 to apply, both cases must be pending at first instance *and* both courts must be competent to hear the case.

This means that *Vorarlberger Gebietskrankenkasse* (see paragraph 8.3.6.3, under *g*) would not have benefited from Article 30. Since Article 13(2) cannot be invoked by an insurer, reference to the Austrian court would not have been possible, even if the insurer had started proceedings before the victim did.

The rules in the *Lugano II Convention* on *lis pendens* and related claims are identical to those in the *Brussels Ia Regulation*.

8.3.9 *Final remarks*

This completes our discussion of rules relating to the international jurisdiction of courts under the *Brussels Ia Regulation* and the *Lugano II Convention*. Many of these rules will only be used occasionally in the day-to-day practice of handling and settling cross-border road traffic accidents. The injured party will (usually) be able to appeal to either a Bureau, a Guarantee Fund or a Compensation Body in their own country (and the national rules of jurisdiction will then be applied: proceedings then do not have a relevant international component). However, the next Section of this chapter will show that, due to differences in national material law, parties may have an interest in bringing the case before the courts of another Member State (or non-Member State). And, therefore, we cannot ignore these rules of jurisdiction, even though we realise that the above does not answer the question of jurisdiction in cases where the dispute is outside the formal scope of application of the Regulation and the Convention because no elements of the case have any relation to the EU.[24]
All in all, there is enough reason to proceed to a discussion of the law of conflicts.

8.4 Applicable law

8.4.1 *Introductory remarks*

Each court applies its own, national conflict of law rules. This applies even if these rules have an international or supranational origin: they remain – or rather, become – national law. And despite the EU's interference with conflict of law, there are still differences, even between Member States.

In the following paragraphs, we will mainly focus on three international or supranational legal instruments: the *Rome II Regulation* and the *Hague Convention* on the law applicable to road traffic accidents insofar as non-contractual obligations (tort) are concerned, and the *Rome I Regulation* insofar as the claim has a contractual basis.[25,26,27] *Rome I* and *Rome II* are in their formal scope limited to disputes tried by courts in Member States (insofar as they are not bound by specific conventions such as the *Hague Convention*) and thus do not cover the whole Green Card system (the fact that the applicable law may be the law of a non-Member State notwithstanding). The Hague traffic law convention also includes a number of non-Mem-

24. See *supra* para 8.2.
25. Regulation (EC) No 864/2007 of the European Parliament and of the Council Of 11 July 2007 on the law applicable to non-contractual obligations (Rome II), OJ L 199, 31.7.2007, p. 40.
26. Hague Convention of 4 May 1971 on the law applicable to traffic accidents.
27. Regulation (EC) No 593/2008 of the European Parliament and of the Council of 17 June 2008 on the law applicable to contractual obligations (Rome I), OJ L 177, 4.7.2008, p. 6.

ber States (and some Member States), but doesn't bind all non-Member States under the Green Card system either. Therefore, there is a number of non-Green Card system countries not bound by international rules for which only national rules of conflict are relevant. These countries' law of conflict is not discussed in this book.[28]

Because a non-contractual basis claims arising from road traffic accidents is by far the most common, we will first deal with the rules of the *Rome II Regulation* (para 8.4.2) and the *Hague Convention* (para 8.4.3). *Rome II* applies if the *Hague Convention* is not applicable. This convention is signed not only by non-Member States but also by 13 Member States.[29] Though much less common, the contractual basis – for example, a claim based on a transport contract – will be discussed in paragraph 8.4.4.

The issue of applicable law regarding subrogated claims will be discussed in paragraph 8.4.5. Paragraph 8.4.6 will be devoted to the applicable law for claims against Guarantee Funds and Compensation Bodies.

8.4.2 The Rome II Regulation[30]

8.4.2.1 Material, formal and temporal scope

a) The material scope

According to the first sentence of Article 1(1), the *Rome II Regulation* shall apply to non-contractual obligations in civil and commercial matters in situations involving a conflict of law. Not only acts of tort, but also unjust enrichment, *negotiorum gestio* and *culpa in contrahendo* will fall within the scope of 'non-contractual obligations in civil and commercial matters', as is made clear in Article 2(1).[31] For our subject, these non-contractual relations are obviously not important. The same applies to the legal relationships explicitly exempted from the Regulation's scope in Article 1(2).

The question of demarcation with contractual liabilities is of interest. In our field, this question is mainly relevant in the context of transport or travel contracts. This

28. See paragraph 8.1.
29. The Hague traffic law convention is signed by the following Member States: Austria, Belgium, Croatia, France, the Czech Republic, Latvia, Lithuania, Luxembourg, the Netherlands, Poland, Slovakia, Slovenia and Spain. The other 15 Member States are therefore bound by Rome II. In addition to the Member States mentioned above, the non-Member States Belarus, Bosnia-Herzegovina, Montenegro, Morocco, North Macedonia, Serbia, Switzerland and Ukraine are parties to the Hague Convention.
30. Regulation (EC) No 864/2007 of the European Parliament and of the Council of 11 July 2007 on the law applicable to non-contractual obligations (Rome II), OJ L 199, 31.7.2007, p. 40.
31. The second paragraph of Article 2 also refers to imminent damage. This could apply in the example in paragraph 8.3.5.2 point *b* of the tilted tanker at risk of leaking dangerous substances.

issue will be further addressed in paragraph 8.4.4, but a few comments may be made here: *Rome II* and *Rome I* are linked to one another, so one should also look at *Rome I* for the meaning of a transport or travel agreement. The concept of 'contractual agreement' in this Regulation has an autonomous character. It refers to situations where one party has voluntarily entered into a commitment with another party. In the case of professional paid transport – by taxi or bus – there will be little doubt that a claim based on this legal relationship is contractual in nature. But how should one regard transport that is free of charge, in the context of family or friends or classic hitch-hiking, for example? The qualification of such legal relationships is judged differently, as is demonstrated by comparative law. In some jurisdictions, they fall under the law of contract, while they are considered non-contractual relations in others. See also para 8.4.3.2, under *a)*.

It has to be noted that matters of evidence and procedural law are not governed by the Regulation. The law applicable to the non-contractual obligation according to the Regulation, however, sets out rules which raise presumptions of law or determine the burden of proof. See Article 1(3) and 22.

b) The formal scope

As stipulated in Article 3, *Rome II* has a universal formal scope of application: the law designated by the Regulation is also applicable if it is the law of a non-Member State, even if the case is not linked to any Member State (which appears to be relevant only in the case of a jurisdiction clause; courts in the Member States otherwise have no jurisdiction if the case is not connected with a Member State).

c) The temporal scope

The Regulation applies to events which occurred after 11 January 2009.

This provision is somewhat peculiar. According to the general rules, regulations will enter into force on the twentieth day following their publication in the Official Journal of the EU unless otherwise stated. In the case of *Rome II*, that would be twenty days after 31 July 2007, therefore 20 August of that year.

Article 31 stipulates that the Regulation shall apply to events that occurred after the date of its entry into force. This would mean events occurring after 20 August 2007. Article 32, however, determines something else: the Regulation shall apply to events that occurred after 11 January 2009.

The issue was decided upon by the Court of Justice of the EU in the *Homawoo* case.[32] Mr Homawoo, a UK citizen, sustained personal injuries and other damage in a car accident in France on 29 August 2007, therefore after the date referred to in Article 31 but before the date mentioned in Article 32. The question was of whether the Regulation was to be

32. CJEU, Judgment of 17 November 2011, *Homawoo*, C-412/10, EU:C:2011:747.

applied or not. If not, British law would govern the assessment of damages. But if the Regulation were applicable, French law was to govern the case. The Court ruled that Articles 31 and 32 of *Rome II*, read in conjunction with Article 297 TFEU,

> "must be interpreted as requiring a national court to apply the Regulation only to events giving rise to damage occurring after 11 January 2009 and that the date on which the proceedings seeking compensation for damage were brought or the date on which the applicable law was determined by the court seised have no bearing on determining the scope *ratione temporis* of the Regulation."

This issue is, of course, less relevant with the passing of time. But it is remarkable that the European legislator apparently was confused by their own rules.

8.4.2.2 *Structure of the Regulation; relationship with the Hague traffic law convention*

The Regulation does not contain a separate regime for road traffic accidents so, as this category of non-contractual obligations isn't excluded from its scope, it therefore also governs the applicable law on road traffic accidents.[33] It should be noted, however, that Article 28 creates an exception to this applicability (as well as for product liability).

Article 28 reads as follows:

> "1. This Regulation shall not prejudice the application of international conventions to which one or more Member States are parties at the time when this Regulation is adopted and which lay down conflict of law rules relating to non-contractual obligations.
>
> 2. However, this Regulation shall, as between Member States, take precedence over conventions concluded exclusively between two or more of them in so far as such conventions concern matters governed by this Regulation."

Conventions concluded between Member States and third countries that came into force before 11 July 2007 (the date the Regulation was adopted) shall therefore have precedence over the Regulation. Two such conventions exist: the *Hague traffic law convention* of 1971 and the Hague product liability convention of 1973. Member States and non-Member States are party to both conventions.

33. In the preamble, the Regulation does, however, have a somewhat peculiar recital (33) concerning road traffic accidents. This is discussed in more detail in paragraph 8.4.2.3.

The Regulation instructs the European Commission to carry out a study on the impact of Article 28 of this Regulation on the Hague traffic law convention. However, to our knowledge no such study – which should have been presented to Parliament, the Council and the Economic and Social Committee no later than 20 August 2009 – has (yet) been carried out.

The Regulation opens with provisions on its scope of application, as set out in paragraph 8.4.2.1. The following five chapters are successively devoted to tort (Chapter II), unjust enrichment, *negotiorum gestio* and *culpa in contrahendo* (Chapter III), free choice of law by parties (Chapter IV), common provisions (Chapter V) and a variety of other provisions (Chapter VI); the final provisions in Chapter VII determine *i.a.* the entry into force.
Chapters II, V and VI are of special interest to us, as is Chapter IV to a lesser extent. These will, therefore, be the focus of the following paragraphs.

One further preliminary remark: the rules on conflict of law determine which national law applies to a complex of facts with international links. If the Regulation were simply to refer to 'the law' of a specific state, this would also imply a reference to that country's private international law. As already observed in paragraph 8.1, private international law is essentially also national law.

If the state where the claim is pending (state A) has a rule on conflict of law that implies the applicability of the law of state B and state B's rules on the conflict of law in turn refer to the legal system of another country (such as that of country A, or perhaps even a country C), a potentially unsolvable conflict of applicable legal systems would emerge. Therefore, most modern systems of private international law avoid any such *'renvoi'*. *Rome II* does so directly in Article 24 by excluding private international law from its field of application.[34]

8.4.2.3 Which aspects are governed by the Regulation

Before discussing which law will be applicable in various situations according to the Regulation, we shall first consider which aspects of a non-contractual claim are governed by the applicable law. Article 15 provides the relevant rules.

> "The law applicable to non-contractual obligations under this Regulation shall govern in particular:
>
> a. the basis and extent of liability, including the determination of persons who may be held liable for acts performed by them;

34. The *Hague Convention* does so by referring only to the 'internal law' of the designated country. *Rome I* has a similar solution to this problem as *Rome II*.

b. the grounds for exemption from liability, any limitation of liability and any division of liability;
c. the existence, the nature and the assessment of damage or the remedy claimed;
d. within the limits of powers conferred on the court by its procedural law, the measures which a court may take to prevent or terminate injury or damage or to ensure the provision of compensation;
e. the question whether a right to claim damages or a remedy may be transferred, including by inheritance;
f. persons entitled to compensation for damage sustained personally;
g. liability for the acts of another person;
h. the manner in which an obligation may be extinguished and rules of prescription and limitation, including rules relating to the commencement, interruption and suspension of a period of prescription or limitation."

With respect to (c), reference should be made to recital (33) of the preamble, which is dedicated to road traffic accidents (and is the result of an initiative of the European Parliament). It reads as follows:

> "(33) According to the current national rules on compensation awarded to victims of road traffic accidents, when quantifying damages for personal injury in cases in which the accident takes place in a State other than that of the habitual residence of the victim, the court seised should take into account all the relevant actual circumstances of the specific victim, including in particular the actual losses and costs of after-care and medical attention."[35]

Although aspects of evidence and procedure are not governed by the Regulation according to Article 1(3), the law applicable under *Rome II* shall govern matters of presumptions of law and determine the burden of proof. See Article 22(1).

8.4.2.4 The main rule

The classic conflict rule in private international law with respect to tort is the *lex loci delicti commissi*: the law of the state in which the accident occurred shall be applicable. This is also the main rule of the *Hague Convention* of 1971 (see also para 8.4.3). This principle of *lex loci delicti commissi* is, however, branded in *Rome II* as more or less obsolete. See the preamble, recitals (15) and (16):

> "(15) The principle of the lex loci delicti commissi is the basic solution for non-contractual obligations in virtually all the Member States, but the practical application of the principle where

35. Why this would be necessary especially in road traffic accidents – and not, for example, in the case of accidents involving defective products, environmental accidents that lead to injury or occupational accidents – is unclear to us. But Parliament's interventions do not always lead to clear and consistent legislation.

> the component factors of the case are spread over several countries varies. This situation engenders uncertainty as to the law applicable.
> (16) Uniform rules should enhance the foreseeability of court decisions and ensure a reasonable balance between the interests of the person claimed to be liable and the person who has sustained damage. A connection with the country where the direct damage occurred (lex loci damni) strikes a fair balance between the interests of the person claimed to be liable and the person sustaining the damage, and also reflects the modern approach to civil liability and the development of systems of strict liability."

Rome II opts for the law of the state where the direct damage occurred, the *lex loci damni,* instead of the law of the country of the injurious event. See Article 4(1):

> "Unless otherwise provided for in this Regulation, the law applicable to a non-contractual obligation arising out of a tort/delict shall be the law of the country in which the damage occurs irrespective of the country in which the event giving rise to the damage occurred and irrespective of the country or countries in which the indirect consequences of that event occur."

It is therefore not relevant in which country the injurious event took place, nor in which country or countries the indirect effects of that event manifest themselves. Recital (17) of the preamble clarifies this:

> "(17) The law applicable should be determined on the basis of where the damage occurs, regardless of the country or countries in which the indirect consequences could occur. Accordingly, in cases of personal injury or damage to property, the country in which the damage occurs should be the country where the injury was sustained or the property was damaged respectively."

Example

Take the example of a road traffic accident occurring in Finland, where a Swedish citizen is injured. The damage occurs in Finland. The fact that the Swedish victim returns home and will suffer the consequences of the accident (medical treatment, inability to work, loss of income) in Sweden is not relevant to the question of applicable law: Finnish law will be applicable.[36]

The damage sustained personally by a family member of a person who died in a road traffic accident must also be classified under 'indirect consequences' of that accident. The applicable law under *Rome II* will therefore be the law of the country

36. According to recital (33), the assessment of the damage must take into account 'all the relevant factual circumstances of the victim concerned, in particular with the actual costs of aftercare and medical care'. See *supra* para 8.4.2.3.

where the deceased person suffered the damage, *i.e.* the Member State where the accident took place.[37]

The choice for the *lex loci damni* is of less importance for the day-to-day handling of international traffic accidents than it seems to be. After all, the damage occurs almost always at the moment of the collision and, therefore, the outcome under *lex loci delicti commissi* and *lex loci damni* will almost always be identical. This also implies that there will be little difference between the application of the main rules of *Rome II* and the *Hague traffic law convention*, as will be shown in paragraph 8.4.3.

If any other law than that of the country of the accident is applicable, 'factual and appropriate' account must be taken of the rules of safety and conduct which are in force at the time and place of the event giving rise to the liability. See Article 17.

This is an important rule to be taken into consideration when handling claims arising from road traffic accidents. Even if the applicable law differs from the law of the country where the accident took place, traffic regulations will still be relevant to determine the party liable for the accident. This seems evident but is often neglected in legal disputes. When lawyers and even judges have determined the applicable law, they will still too often apply that law in its entirety, including that law's traffic regulations. This may result in applying traffic regulations to determine liability in a country where these traffic regulations are not applicable at all …

8.4.2.5 Exceptions to the main rule

a) The conclusion that little difference exists between the main rule of *Rome II* and that of the *Hague Convention* is not valid when one of the exceptions to Article 4(1) applies.

Article 4(1) opens with the words 'unless otherwise provided for in this Regulation'. This does not only affect Articles 5 (product liability), 6 (unfair competition and acts restricting free competition), 7 (environmental damage), 8 (infringement of intellectual property rights) and 9 (industrial action), but also the special rules of Article 4(2) and (3).

b) Article 4(2) covers a situation in which the person whose liability is in question and the person who suffers damage are both habitually domiciled in the same country at the time the damage occurs. In this case, the law of that country shall apply.

A few observations in the context of this provision:

37. CJEU, Judgment of 10 December 2015, *Lazar*, C-350-14, EU:C:2015:802.

- Article 4(2) concerns itself with the person whose liability is at issue and the party that suffers the damage. This means that they do not need to be litigants themselves.

> **Example**
> In a dispute between a healthcare insurer and an MTPL insurer arising out of an accident caused by an insured of the latter and where the insured of the health insurer has been injured, the habitual residence of both insureds and not of their insurers is of relevance.

- The question may arise as to how this provision should be applied if there are several injured parties. Take as an example a road traffic accident with several injured parties. In this case, two approaches are conceivable:
  i. the habitual residence of each of the injured parties is determined individually as to whether this is located in the same country as that of the liable party, or
  ii. the provision is applicable only if all parties concerned live in the same country.

The Regulation does not provide a decisive answer.
The first interpretation leads to the fragmentation of the applicable law. Therefore, the second interpretation may seem preferable in our opinion, but it is questionable whether in practice it will always be applied.

- What if, in addition to the directly injured party, other persons also suffer indirect damage, such as family members or an employer who continues to pay the wages of his injured employee? Can they also apply Article 4(2)? We venture to suggest that the concept of 'damage' in the second paragraph should be given the same meaning as in the first paragraph: only the habitual residence of the person who suffers the damage directly is taken into account. Any other interpretation would also lead to the fragmentation of the applicable law.
- The criterion is the habitual residence of the parties concerned at the time the damage occurs. A later move to another country on the part of one or both parties is irrelevant.
- The habitual residence of involved parties is relevant. To this extent, *Rome II* deviates from the *Brussels II* Regulation, for example, which uses the place of domicile (in an autonomous interpretation) as a criterion. What is to be understood as habitual residence? To begin with, it is an autonomous concept specified in Article 23. This provision, however, only provides rules for legal entities and natural persons engaged in the exercise of a profession.

The habitual residence of legal entities according to Article 23(1) is the place of central administration. In the case of an injurious event in the operation of a branch office, agency or subsidiary, the location of that subsidiary, agency or branch office shall be the habitual residence.
The habitual residence of a natural person acting in the course of their business activity is their principal place of business. See Article 23(2).
The Regulation does not contain any indication of the notion of 'habitual residence' for natural persons not acting in a professional capacity. Whether that will give rise to problems is the question: the habitual residence usually coincides with the place of domicile.

- The moment the damage occurs is relevant. The moment of the injurious event is therefore not important here, although both moments will usually coincide in a traffic accident.
- In relation to the Regulation's universal formal scope of applicability, the provision is not limited to Member States. Therefore, in the case of an accident in a Member State where the liable party and the victim are both resident in a non-Member State, the courts of Member States shall apply the law of that non-Member State.

Example
Consider an accident in Germany where a Russian motorist collides with a pedestrian equally domiciled in Russia. If the case were brought before the German court – for example, because the pedestrian appeals to the German Bureau – Russian law will be applicable.

- There is no question of an option for the parties: if the conditions of Article 4(2) are met, paragraph (1) shall no longer be applicable. If they wish to declare other law applicable, they will have to come to agree on a choice of law as referred to in Article 14. See also para 8.4.2.6.

c) Article 4's second exception to the main rule of the first paragraph concerns a closer relationship with the law of a country other than the one whose law would be applicable under the main rule or under the second paragraph's exception. If the circumstances show that the tort has a manifestly closer relationship with another country, the law of that country shall apply. A manifestly closer relationship with another country could, in particular, be based on a previous link between parties that is closely related to the tort/delict, such as an agreement.

The precise meaning of this provision is not immediately clear. Some comments in this regard:

- The regime of Article 4(3) should be regarded as an exception to paragraph (1) and (2). It is obvious that this derogation is to be interpreted restrictively because it would otherwise negatively affect the predictability of the applicable law, and the Regulation serves to pursue this predictability. In particular, the provision may not be used to determine the law that is most closely connected with the legal relationship. Only if all the circumstances of the case indicate one particular legal system is derogation from paragraphs (1) or (2) allowed.
- The link must be 'manifestly closer'. Not just any previously existing agreement can lead to the application of the third paragraph.
- The third paragraph refers to a contract as a possible relevant factor, but other factors are apparently also conceivable. It is not clear what other factors could be taken into consideration. In the case of a contract, it must have existed before the tort. Any contract concluded between the two parties later on obviously does not qualify.
- The court *can* take any such contract, such as a travel agreement, into consideration as a factor within the meaning of paragraph (3), but does not need to do so: 'a manifestly closer relationship (...) *might* be based in particular ... [*italics added by the authors*].' The court has discretionary power.

d) Article 17 plays a role here as well. Whatever law is applicable as a departure from the main rule or from the derogations, traffic and safety rules applicable in the country of the accident must always be taken into account 'factually and appropriately'.

8.4.2.6 Choice of law

Although not a frequent phenomenon in the context of a tort or road traffic accident, it is not inconceivable that parties may agree to the applicability of a particular legal system. Chapter IV of *Rome II* deals with the choice of law.

The main rule – at least where both parties are not in the pursuit of commercial activities – is that choice of law is possible, providing that the agreement is concluded *after* the event giving rise to the damage occurred. In the context of a road traffic accident, this is unlikely to lead to any confusion because the parties have usually had no contact with each other before the accident.[38]

Furthermore, the choice of law must be made expressly or sufficiently clear in the circumstances of the case. What is to be understood by the latter is not clear. Since the choice of law can also be made during the trial, the question arises of whether an undisputed proposition from one of the parties that a certain law applies quali-

38. An exception might be when a passenger is injured in an accident for which the driver of the vehicle is liable (providing there is no contractual relationship between driver and passenger).

fies as a 'reasonable certain choice of law' as referred to in Article 14(1), second sentence.

Obviously, any choice of law cannot prejudice the rights of third parties, as this second sentence also explicitly states.

> It would therefore not be acceptable that the person responsible for the accident and the injured party would agree on the choice for national law, knowing that the application of this law would lead to a higher amount of compensation for the injured party and being aware that the MTPL insurer covering the liability of the tortfeasor's liability, would have to pay.

Moreover, if all the relevant aspects of the event giving rise to the damage are located in another country at the time of the injurious event, the choice of law may not prejudice the application of provisions in the law of that other country, which cannot be derogated from by agreement. This situation will not occur frequently in the context of a road traffic accident. A similar provision is that of the third paragraph: the choice for the law of a non-Member State cannot prejudice the application of mandatory community law provisions if all the relevant elements of the case are located in one or more Member States.

8.4.2.7 *Direct right of action against the insurer*

Article 18 gives a provision regarding the law applicable to the injured party's direct right of action against the liable party's liability insurer. Its meaning is not immediately clear. Article 18 reads:

> "The person having suffered damage may bring his or her claim directly against the insurer of the person liable to provide compensation if the law applicable to the non-contractual obligation or the law applicable to the insurance contract so provides."

Since the direct right of action has been introduced in all Member States under Article 18 of the codified Directive, this provision does not appear to pose many problems at first glance, but appearances are deceiving.[39] The question is: which law is applicable to this direct right of action? And this question becomes relevant as the regime of direct action varies from one Member State to another. As an example, the limitation period varies from one year in Spain to several years in other jurisdictions. And a second, no less interesting question is whether the injured party can choose to base their claim on one or the other.

---

39. We have to bear in mind that Rome II has a much wider scope of application than just road traffic accidents, and that in some countries such a direct right of action does not exist for other types of liability insurance than MTPL insurance.

> **Example**
> Consider an accident in Spain, involving a German victim and caused by a German national driving a Spanish rental car. Both countries have obviously introduced a direct right of action. According to Article 4(2) of *Rome II*, German law is applicable to the German victim's claim against the Spanish insurer (this claim may be brought before a German court on the basis of Article 13(2) of the *Brussels Ia Regulation*). The insurance contract is governed by Spanish law. Based on Article 18 of *Rome II*, would German direct action apply or could the German victim also opt for Spanish law to govern the direct right of action?

Let us start with this last question: in all probability, the injured party will not be entitled to any such choice. A provision in the original commission proposal, in which the injured party was offered this option, did not make it to the final text.[40] But the question still remains: which of the two direct actions applies? The text in Article 18 does not provide clarity.

Various answers are conceivable. It is suggested that the court applies the most favourable regime for the injured party. But the text in Article 18 gives no indication that this is the intended solution.

The most obvious solution, which also corresponds with Article 9 of the *Hague Convention*, would be that Article 18 of *Rome II* only deals with the matter of *whether* the injured party has a direct right of action. Its content and scope are then governed by the regime applicable to the insurance contract.

> **Example**
> In our accident involving the German citizen and the Spanish rental car driven by a German driver, this means that Spanish law determines the content and scope of direct action. The German victim will then have to take the short Spanish limitation period into account.

In our opinion, the defences available to the insurer are also governed by the law applicable to the insurance contract.

40. See COM (2003) 427, p. 42.

8.4.3 *The Hague traffic law convention of 1971*[41]

8.4.3.1 *Introduction*

First of all, it is important to state that the Hague traffic law convention takes precedence over *Rome II* if the proceedings are brought before the courts of one of the signatory countries.

> The following EU Member States are also signatories to the Hague Traffic Law Convention: Austria, Belgium, Croatia, the Czech Republic, France, Latvia, Lithuania, Luxembourg, the Netherlands, Poland, Slovakia, Slovenia and Spain. The other 15 Member States of the EU are therefore bound by Rome II. In addition to the Member States bound by the *Hague Convention*, non-Member States Belarus, Bosnia-Herzegovina, Morocco, Montenegro, North Macedonia, Ukraine, Serbia and Switzerland are also party to the *Hague Convention*. Portugal has signed the Convention but has not followed up any further.

However, it is not enough to simply identify that a country has signed the treaty. Material, formal and temporal applicability should also be established.

The question of whether the applicable law for a road traffic accident claim is governed by the *Rome II Regulation* or by the *Hague Convention* is more than academic: although the outcome will be the same in the majority of cases, frequently enough the answer is different. And this always justifies the effort of making an analysis.

The recommended approach is that we first have to examine the outcome under the Convention and then consider the outcome under *Rome II* every time a signatory country to the *Hague Convention* is involved in any way. And in order to answer this question, one should first establish which court or courts are competent to hear the case.

The *Hague Convention* is not easy to follow, especially in comparison with the *Rome II Regulation*. It has been argued that, in view of this complexity, the *Hague Convention* should not 'override' *Rome II*, and that only the Regulation should be applied by the courts of the Member States.[42] But *Rome II* is also not as simple as it seems at

---

41. Hague Convention of 4 May 1971 on the Law Applicable to Traffic Accidents; the text of this Convention, the list of Contracting States and the Essén Explanatory Report are available on the website of the Hague Conference on Private International Law: https://www.hcch.net.
42. The Convention's complexity was regarded as a problem when *Rome II* was conceived. The reasoning was that individuals could not understand it. We do not believe that this argument is in any way convincing: in the aftermath of a cross-border road traffic accident, no citizen will consult the relevant texts independently and without expert legal assistance. Lawyers should be expected to be able to understand and to apply both the Regulation and the Convention.

first glance, and it is clear from the above that interpreting the Regulation can also be a tricky business.

8.4.3.2 Material, formal and temporal scope of application

a) The material scope

Article 1 of the Convention outlines its substantive scope: civil, non-contractual liability for road traffic accidents, regardless of the nature of the court before which the claim is made. The article then defines the term 'traffic accident': an accident that involves one or more vehicles, motorised or not, that is connected with traffic on a public highway, on land open to the public or on private land to which certain persons have a right of access.

This definition deserves some clarification:

- Like *Rome II*, the Convention is applicable to civil claims. Criminal and administrative claims do not fall within its material scope.
- The notion of 'non-contractual liability' deserves some attention because it is not defined in the Convention. In particular, the demarcation line with contractual liability may pose problems.
  As has already been noted in the context of the *Brussels Ia Regulation*, this question is particularly important in the context of travel contracts.[43] In general, there will be little debate about the fact that professional transport of persons at a charge, by taxi or bus, is to be considered contractual. More doubt is possible in the case of free transport, partly because this type of transport is treated differently in different jurisdictions. It is justifiable, however, to argue that transport that is free of charge – within a family, friends travelling together, but also typical hitchhiking – should be considered as non-contractual.
- How should one view compensation schemes such as those in the Nordic countries, which are not based on tort/delict but on compensation of the victim directly through vehicle insurance? It is reasonable to regard these schemes as outside the scope of the Convention, since compensation is based on an insurance contract and therefore of an inherently contractual nature.
- The *Hague Convention* does not only apply when motor vehicles are involved. A collision between two cyclists, a cyclist and a pedestrian, or a pedestrian and a horse-drawn cart are within its scope of application as well. A sledge, a pram and a trailer – even when not connected to a towing vehicle – are vehicles in the context of the Convention. The same should be stated in the case of an accident involving a pedestrian and a man on horseback, because the horse is being used as a vehicle. On the other hand, a horse being led by its reins is not a vehicle. For the term 'vehicle', see the Essén Explanatory Report on Article 1, No. 3.4.

---

43. See also *supra* para 8.4.2.1 and *infra* para 8.4.4.7.

- The term 'involvement of a vehicle' must be interpreted neutrally. A stationary vehicle may also be involved within the meaning of the Convention. Compare the notion of 'involvement' (*implication*) in the French *Loi Badinter*. This also has non-coloured content. However, at least one of the vehicles concerned must have been in motion. See the Essen report on Article 1, No. 3.5.

For the record, the fact that the *Hague Convention* also applies if a vehicle is purely passively 'involved' in an accident does not, of course, mean that liability is also automatically assumed. The Convention only designates the applicable law, and any liability must be determined in accordance with that law.

- The Convention's applicability is not limited to public highways. Accidents in private areas, irrespective of whether they qualify as roads or not, also fall within its scope, providing that they are open to the public or (even) only for a limited number of persons who have a right to be there. This means, for example, that industrial sites may also fall under the scope if suppliers have a right to enter.

Article 2 excludes six types of legal relationships from the Convention's application, and these are not unimportant. Under Article 28 of *Rome II*, the Regulation will usually be applicable. Should *Rome II* also fail to apply, then the national law of conflict shall govern the question of applicable law.
In the context of cross-border road traffic accidents, the most important exceptions are:

4). recourse claims between liable persons,
5). recourse claims and subrogation insofar as insurance companies are involved and
6). actions and recourse actions by or against social insurance institutions, other similar institutions and public automobile guarantee funds, and to any exemption from liability laid down by the law which governs these institutions.

- Recourse actions between persons jointly liable – for example, in complex accidents involving several liable persons and victims – were regarded as so complicated that they were left outside the scope of the Convention. Not a principled, but a practical choice.
- Insofar as insurers are involved, recourse claims and subrogation are considered to be contractual and therefore fall outside its scope.
- Recourse claims against social security institutions are considered to be public in nature and are therefore also exempt from its scope.
- The same seems to apply in the Convention's rationale for claims against 'public guarantee funds for automobiles'. The Essén Report, Notes 6.1 and 6.2 on Article 2 seems to indicate that this relates to Guarantee Funds operating on the basis of public law. Legal actions against private law Guarantee Funds (the Essén Report mentions those in Germany and

Sweden in particular) are governed by the Convention. Apparently, the claim's public law nature is the reason for this exception. However, the question is whether the public law nature of a Guarantee Fund necessarily means that the injured party's claim is also public in nature.

Example
The situation of the Dutch Guarantee Fund prior to its privatisation in 1989 can serve as an example. Until then, the fund was part of the Ministry of Finance, and therefore came under public law. But the claims of injured parties against the Guarantee Fund have always fallen under private law.

Hence, it will be necessary to assess whether a Guarantee Fund is public within the meaning of Article 2(6) on a case-by-case basis.

b) The formal scope
The *Hague Convention* has a universal formal scope. The law designated by the Convention is applicable even if this is the law of a non-contracting state according to Article 11. To this extent, the formal scope of application is identical to that of Rome II. The place of the accident is not relevant, nor are the places of residence or nationalities of the persons concerned. Even accidents in non-contracting states fall within its formal scope.

c) The temporal scope
Although the Convention does not give any indication as to its temporal scope and national transitional law is therefore decisive, it is to be assumed that it should be applied to accidents which have taken place after its entry into force. Since the Convention's date of entry into force differs from one contracting state to another, the date of entry into force must also be individually determined for each state.
Since the Convention was conceived in 1971, it is tempting to regard the question of temporal scope to be of academic interest, but that would be oversimplifying the matter. Over the last decade, new contracting parties such as Morocco and Ukraine have joined the Convention, with entries into force of 2010 and 2011 respectively. New entrants are not excluded, albeit restricted to non-Member States of the EU on the basis of Article 28 of Rome II. Whether new Member States which are already bound by the *Hague Convention* can remain bound by them if they were to join the EU is an unanswered question. We are inclined to answer this question in the affirmative, but it all depends on the conditions for their accession to the EU.[44]

44. This question could rise with respect to Serbia in the future, regarding its status of candidate Member State.

8.4.3.3 *The methodology of the Hague Convention's referral rules*

The treaty works with 'mechanical' rules of reference: there is a main rule (Article 3) and a number of special rules for specific situations in which the law of another state suggests a closer link with the facts (Article 4 and 5). In contrast with Article 4(2) and (3) of *Rome II*, the courts have no freedom to interpret the facts themselves and thus decide that an exceptional situation exists, the *rationale* being that the Convention gives precedence to legal certainty and to the predictability of the conflict of law process.

An exception to this perhaps rigid system is to be found in Article 9, which concerns the law applicable to the direct right of action. The Convention offers not just one solution, but accommodates the victim by opting for a system of multiple steps: if the law applicable to the accident does not cover a direct right of action, but the law of the state where the accident occurred does, this *action directe* is available to the victim. If neither of these two legal systems contain a direct right of action, but the law applicable to the insurance contract does, then the victim can fall back on that law. But, in fact, this system of steps does not offer any real choice either, as will be demonstrated in paragraph 8.4.3.9.

Unlike in *Rome II*, which seems to depart more from the victim's position in a sense, the starting point for the *Hague Convention* is the offender, the liable person if you will.

In the system of the Convention, the applicable law is 'internal law'. This means that only the substantive law of the named state is applicable, and not (also) private international law.[45] This avoids a *'renvoi'*, the effect that would occur if the Convention referred to the law of state A, whose law of conflicts referred in turn to the law of state B. The situation would become almost unsolvable if state B's law of conflict again referred to the law of state C, or even back to that of state A.

> Renvoi is also excluded in *Rome II*, but using a different approach. Article 24 explicitly excludes the possibility of *renvoi*. See para 8.4.2.2.

8.4.3.4 *The main rule of the Hague Convention: Article 3*

According to Article 3, the main rule of the *Hague Convention* is the applicability of the internal law of the state in whose territory the accident occurred. Theoretically, this main rule is different from the basic rule under Rome II, which declares as applicable the law of the state where the damage occurred. But the result is usually the same in practice when it comes to road traffic accidents.[46]

---

45. That field of law, as set out in paragraph 8.1, should also be included in the term 'national law'.
46. See para 8.4.2.4.

For the record, the decisive factor is not the tort, but rather the accident under the Convention's system. If an accident in country B was caused by the vehicle's brakes being inadequately repaired in country A, then only the accident in country B determines applicable law.

The fact that the *locus delicti* is usually easy and quick to determine is presented as an advantage of this choice for the law of the country of the accident, as this is supposed to facilitate the extrajudicial settlement of road traffic accidents greatly. The counter argument is that, in this regime, the applicable law is unsatisfactory in some situations (some say: in many cases) because it purely depends on coincidence. The rigid choice for the *lex loci delicti commissi* is mitigated, however, by the special rules of Articles 4, 5 and 6.

In the vast majority of cross-border road traffic accidents, the applicable law under the *Hague Convention* will be determined on the basis of the main rule of Article 3. But the special rules of Articles 4 to 6 will apply more often than one might think. Therefore, and because the *Hague Convention* has a compelling regime that does not offer the possibility of choosing between the different solutions, it is necessary to review carefully whether any of the exceptions under Articles 4, 5 or 6 occur in each specific situation.

8.4.3.5 Exceptions to the main rule: Article 4

Article 4 relates to a situation where the relevant facts have a stronger relationship with a different legal sphere than that of the country where the accident took place. The Article, which relates to damage to persons and damage to the vehicles involved (Article 5 is about other material damage), is difficult to unravel but can be illustrated as follows:

a) The accident involves only one vehicle registered in a state other than that of the accident (Article 4, point (a)):

- Liability towards the *driver, keeper, owner or any other person that has any right to the vehicle* shall be governed by the law of the state of registration, irrespective of the habitual residence of the said parties.

Example
A Czech vehicle skids and crashes in Germany because the passenger jerks the steering wheel. The driver is injured and the car damaged. If a Czech court hears the case against the passenger, the compensation claim made by the driver and the owner of the vehicle will be decided on the basis of Czech law. This is still the case if the driver lives in Germany or Slovakia.[47]

- The same applies to liability towards the *victim who was a passenger of the vehicle,* but only if they had their habitual residence in a state other than that of the accident.

Example
Let us consider the same accident, but now with a second passenger. He has his habitual residence in Slovakia, and has also been injured. Czech law is applicable not only if litigation is carried out in the Czech Republic, but also if tried in Slovakia.
If there is a third injured passenger who has their habitual residence in Germany, German law has to apply under Article 3, even if litigation takes place in the Czech Republic
If the case is brought before a German court, then *Rome II* will apply. As a consequence, the law of the country where the damage occurred applies, i.e. German law.

- The law of the state of registration also applies with regard to liability towards a *victim outside the vehicle,* but only if their habitual residence is in the vehicle's state of registration.

Example
Again, let us revisit the same accident. A pedestrian, whose habitual residence is in the Czech Republic, is now also injured. Czech law applies. However, should the pedestrian be a resident of Slovakia or Germany, then Article 3 would again apply and the claim would be governed by German law.

- If there are two or more victims, the applicable law shall be determined for each individually.

---

47. However, if neither the owner nor the holder nor the driver had their habitual residence in the Czech Republic, the exception of Art. 6 applies, as discussed in paragraph 8.4.3.7. Because the registered owner or keeper will generally be domiciled in the country of registration, this situation will not be common.

Example

Applying the *Hague Convention* to the examples given above, the following laws will be applicable to the claim against the liable passenger:

- the driver and owner of the car:	Czech law
- the injured Slovakian passenger:	Czech law
- the wounded German passenger:	German law
- the injured Czech pedestrian:	Czech law
- an injured British pedestrian:	German law

b) Two or more vehicles are involved in the accident (Article 4, point (b)):
The rules under *a*) shall apply, but only if all these vehicles are registered in the same state, which differs from the state where the accident took place.

Example

In the same accident, a second Czech car is now involved (as co-responsible or as a victim). In this case, the same answers apply. If the second vehicle in question were registered in Slovakia, then Article 4 would not apply. The main rule of Article 3 would apply.

c) One or more persons outside the vehicle or vehicles are involved and may be held liable (Article 4, point (c)):
The rules under *a)* and *b* only apply if everyone's habitual residence is in the state of registration. This also applies if they are victims.

Example

Let us assume that the two pedestrians are possibly co-responsible. Because they are not both habitually domiciled in the vehicle's country of registration (the Czech Republic), the main rule of Article 3 applies. If they both reside in the Czech Republic, the answers given above will apply.

8.4.3.6 Exceptions to the main rule: Article 5

Article 4 covered damage to persons and to vehicles, while Article 5 governs the law applicable to claims with respect to other material damage. Three situations are regulated:

a) *Damage to a passenger's property or to goods entrusted to them and transported in the vehicle (Article 5(1)):*
Liability towards that passenger is governed by the law which is applicable according to Article 3 or 4.
b) *Damage to other goods transported by the vehicle (Article 5(2)):*
Liability for this damage is also governed by the law applicable to the vehicle owner's liability.
c) *Damage to goods outside the vehicle or vehicles (Article 5(3)):*
Liability for this damage is governed by *lex loci delicti commissi*, unless it concerns damage to a victim's personal property outside the car. If, on the basis of Article 4, the law of the vehicle's state of registration applies to liability towards this victim, then this law also applies to any damage to this property.

Article 5 cannot be applied without first checking the applicability of Article 4.

The terms 'habitual residence' and 'the vehicle's state of registration' deserve some attention.
'Habitual residence' is an autonomous concept. It is broader than that of residence and will have to be filled in with facts. A certain length of stay is an element, but also the intentions of the person concerned. An – even somewhat prolonged – stay in a country for holidays or study would probably not qualify, but a short stay for the purpose of completing immigration formalities can be qualified as 'habitual residence'.

The notion of 'territory of the vehicle's state of registration' is a formal notion. If there is a defect in the registration (the registration does not correspond to the vehicle; see Article 1(4), point (*d*) of the codified Directive and para 6.2.5.5), the vehicle will probably be regarded as not registered in that state and Article 6 will have to be applied.

8.4.3.7 Unregistered vehicles: Article 6

This provision distinguishes between two situations that lead to the same outcome. In the first, the vehicle in question does not bear a registration plate (or is registered in more than one state). The second situation is one where the vehicle is registered in a certain state, but neither the owner, the holder nor the driver has their habitual residence in that state at the time of the accident. In these situations, the law of the state in which the vehicle is normally stationed supersedes the law of the country of registration.

In the first situation, there is no state of registration and no clear link with one state or another. In the second case, there is insufficient connection with the state of registration, and the state in which the vehicle is normally stationed replaces the state of registration.

> **Example**
> The second situation might occur in the case of a vehicle registered in Bulgaria but with a Romanian owner, if the driver is also domiciled outside of Bulgaria.

The Convention distinguishes between the state of registration and the state in which the vehicle is normally stationed. So if neither the owner, keeper, nor driver has their habitual residence in the state of registration, the meaning of the term 'normally stationed' is not identical to the term 'normally based' in the codified Directive. The Directive defines the concept of 'normally based' with the concept of registration.

> **Example**
> Imagine a Moroccan citizen, who buys a vehicle in France and causes an accident in Spain while the car is still registered in France. If the case is brought before a court in Spain, which would apply the *Hague Convention*, the Spanish court would have to assess where the vehicle is normally stationed. Apparently not in France. Morocco? Spain? The Convention offers no easy answer.

8.4.3.8 Which aspects are governed by applicable law?

The *Hague Convention* determines the law applicable to civil, non-contractual liability for road traffic accidents. But which aspects of this liability in particular are governed by the applicable law? Article 8 provides the relevant rules: the applicable law shall determine, in particular:

"1. the basis and extent of liability;
2. the grounds for exemption from liability, any limitation of liability, and any division of liability;
3. the existence and kinds of injury or damage which may have to be compensated;
4. the kinds and extent of damages;
5. whether a right to damages may be assigned or inherited;
6. the persons who have suffered damage and who may claim damages in their own right;
7. the liability of a principal for the acts of their agent or of a master for the acts of their servant;
8. rules of prescription and limitation, including rules relating to the commencement of a period of prescription or limitation, and the interruption and suspension of this period."

A few comments on some of these aspects:

- The applicable law determines the basis and extent of liability. Article 7, however, explicitly stipulates that the rules relating to the control and safety of traffic in force at the place and time of the accident are to be taken into account when determining liability. This is of particular importance, as the law of a state other than that of the accident will apply on the basis of Article 4, 5 or 6. See also *Rome II* Article 17 and para 8.4.2.4.
- The applicable law also governs the basis and extent of the damage to be compensated. The *Hague Convention* has no such approach as in *Rome II*, preamble, recital 33, stating that, 'in cases in which the accident takes place in a State other than that of the habitual residence of the victim the court should take into account all the relevant actual circumstances of the specific victim, including in particular the actual losses and costs of after-care and medical attention'.

It is often argued that the *Hague Convention*'s strict rules in this area are its weakness.

- A complex aspect of this provision is (5). The applicable law determines whether the right to compensation can be transferred. However, this does not mean that the transferred claim is subject to the same law. After all, according to paragraph (4), (5) and (6) of Article 2, the law applicable to recourse claims between liable persons, recourse claims and subrogation involving insurers and (recourse) claims by or against institutions of (in short) social security are not governed by the Convention. In the case of Member States, *Rome II* will therefore govern the applicable law on such claims. See *Rome II*, Article 19.

8.4.3.9 The direct right of action and applicable law

The rules covering the direct right of action under the Convention differ from those of *Rome II*. Unlike the Regulation, the Convention introduces a system of steps, a 'ladder' as it were. See Article 9.

In reading this article, a distinction should be made between two aspects: (1) the question whether the injured party has a direct right of action at their disposal and (2) the question of the regime, the content, of that *action directe*.
First of all, the availability of direct action:

The first rung on the decision ladder is whether the injured party possesses an *action directe*, if the law applicable under Article 3, 4 or 5 contains such an action.
If – and only if – the answer to that question is negative, the second rung will come into play: if, on the basis of Article 4 or 5, the applicable law is that of the vehicle's state of registration and that law does not contain an *action directe*, the injured person can nevertheless exercise such an action if allowed by the law of the country where the accident took place.

And then the third rung on the ladder: if that law does not provide for a direct right of action, but the law applicable to the insurance contract does, then the injured party may exercise that right.

It is important to point out that the injured party cannot choose. If the first rung leads to the availability of a direct right of action, the decision process will stop there. The same is true if the second step offers *action directe*.

In specific terms, this system means that the injured party has two *'repêchages'* if the law of the state of registration is applicable and that law does not provide for a direct right of action. The victim will first have a second chance under the law of the country where the accident took place and if that law offers no relief, there is a third possibility on the basis of the law applicable to the insurance contract.
If, under Article 3, the *lex loci delicti commissi* is applicable and that law does not recognise an *action directe*, the victim only has one second chance, namely the law applicable to the insurance contract.

The availability of a direct right of action thus being established, the question arises of its content. In principle, the law governing the *action directe* under Article 9 also governs its content, such as the conditions under which it can be exercised and the defences available to the insurer. However, the matter of its scope, the sum insured, is not covered. Neither is the extent of liability.
The aspect of prescription deserves separate attention. From the Essén Explanatory Report's note 11 on Article 8, it appears that the limitation period, including that of the *action directe*, is governed by the law applicable to liability and not by the law which determines whether a direct action is available under Article 9.

This may lead to the peculiar situation that the law applicable to the insurance contract entails a direct right of action to the injured party, whose right is, however, subject to the law of the country where the accident took place. The injured party cannot, however, choose: the regime of Article 9 is rigid.

8.4.4 *The Rome I Regulation*[48]

8.4.4.1 *Introductory remarks*

Rome I, the Regulation which governs the law applicable to contractual obligations, is only of limited importance in the context of this book, namely only in the case of a transport or travel contract. Only then will there be any damage during road traffic which may also lead to compensation based on breach of contract. Although the

48. Regulation (EC) No 593/2008 of the European Parliament and of the Council of 17 June 2008 on the law applicable to contractual obligations (Rome I), OJ L 177, 4.7.2008, p. 6.

basis for compensation will be non-contractual liability in most cases, we cannot avoid a brief discussion of *Rome I*, if only for the sake of completeness. We will also discuss the law applicable to subrogated claims.

Rome I and *Rome II* are closely linked and cannot be interpreted separately.
Rome I is the successor to the Rome I Convention, a parallel treaty from 1980 that dealt with the same matter.[49] This explains why *Rome I*, although from a later date than *Rome II*, is referred to by a 'lower' Roman numeral.

Lastly, it is important to note that two Member States have declared themselves not bound by the Regulation: Denmark and the United Kingdom. They remain bound by the *Rome I* Convention.[50] See recitals (45) and (46) in the preamble.

8.4.4.2 Material, formal and temporal scope of application

a) *The material scope of application*
The substantive scope is that of contractual obligations in civil and commercial matters, according to Article 1(1). Tax, customs and administrative matters are explicitly excluded from its scope.
The concept of a 'contract' has an autonomous character. In the jurisprudence of the Court of Justice, a 'contract' must be understood to mean a legal relationship in which one party voluntarily entered into a commitment with another party. See also para 8.4.3.2.
In the second paragraph of Article 1, a number of contractual relationships are excluded from the scope of *Rome I*. Under item *e)*, arbitration agreements (of interest in relation to the arbitration and mediation rules of the Council of Bureaux) and agreements on the choice of court (a matter governed by the *Brussels Ia Regulation*) are of some importance.
b) *The formal scope of application*
Like *Rome II* and the *Hague Convention, Rome I* has a universal scope: the law designated by the Regulation applies even if it is the law of a non-Member State according to Article 2.
c) *Temporal scope of application*
The Regulation is to be applied to agreements concluded after 17 December 2009. See Article 28.

49. Convention on the law applicable to contractual obligations, 19 June 1980, also referred to as the Rome I Convention.
50. It is not clear whether the United Kingdom will still be bound by the Rome I Convention after 'Brexit' has become a reality. Since this is a parallel treaty that the signatory States signed individually, a separate decision has to be made by the UK to step out of this Convention as well.

8.4.4.3 *Structure of the Regulation*

Chapter II of the Regulation contains uniform rules for the determination of applicable law. The starting point of Article 3 is the assumption that parties to the contract have made a valid choice for a given legal system. Article 4 then provides rules in the absence of a (valid) choice of law. For a number of specific agreements, Articles 5 – 8 provide for specific rules: contracts of carriage (Article 5), consumer contracts (Article 6), insurance contracts (Article 7) and individual employment contracts (Article 8).[51] Article 9 gives priority to provisions of particular mandatory law in the field of political, social or economic structuring, for example, which are of such importance to a country to safeguard its public interests that they should be applied even if other law is applicable to the contract.

Article 12 sums up which aspects of the contract are governed by the applicable law. Article 14 deals with assignment and (contractual) subrogation, while Article 15 regulates the law applicable to legal subrogation.

Chapter III, entitled 'other provisions', contains a description of the notion of 'habitual residence' in Article 19 that is essentially identical to that of Article 23 of *Rome II*. *Renvoi* is excluded in Article 20 in precisely the same way as in Article 24 of *Rome II*. See para 8.4.2.2 and 8.4.3.3. Article 24 stipulates that the Regulation replaces the *Rome I* Convention, but that this does not apply to those Member States which do not accept *Rome I*: Denmark and the United Kingdom. See para 8.4.4.1.

8.4.4.4 *Aspects governed by the Regulation*

Article 12 determines which aspects of the contract are governed by the applicable law:

"a. interpretation;
b. performance;
c. within the limits of the powers conferred on the court by its procedural law, the consequences of a total or partial breach of obligations, including the assessment of damages insofar as this is governed by rules of law;
d. the various ways of extinguishing obligations, and prescription and limitation of actions;
e. the consequences of the contract's nullity."

---

51. Note that the Commission has been instructed to present a study on the law applicable to insurance contracts by 17 June 2013 at the latest. A search on the internet has not led to results and did not even reveal that such a study has even been started.

8.4.4.5 *The basic principle: freedom of choice of law (Article 3)*

A basic principle in most, if not in all, modern European legislation is the freedom of contractual parties to shape their relations. This also applies to the possibility of choosing the law applicable to international contracts.

It is, therefore, only logical that the starting point of the *Rome I Regulation* in its Article 3 is the applicability of the law chosen by the contracting parties. Even a choice of legislation that has no link with any of the parties in the contract nor with elements of the contract itself will in principle be valid. Should, however, all relevant elements of the contract be located in one (other) country, then the parties' choice of another law shall not prejudice the mandatory rules of that country's law. And if all (other) relevant elements of the contract are situated in one or more Member States, then provisions of community law that cannot be contractually derogated from, shall not be prejudiced either.

The choice can be made explicitly or implicitly. In the case of the latter, the choice must be clearly demonstrated by the terms of the contract or the circumstances of the case, such as the reference to specific provisions in a national law. The choice for a specific jurisdiction can also be an indication that the contracting parties intended to make a choice for the *lex fori.*

8.4.4.6 *Applicable law in the absence of choice (Article 4)*

Parties in an international contract will not always have made a choice regarding applicable law. Article 4 then provides rules to resolve this situation, unless the provisions of Articles 5 – 8 lead to another law being applicable.

In its first paragraph, the applicable law is given for a series of contract types, such as contracts for the sale of movable goods, for the provision of services, and distribution contracts.

Contracts not listed in paragraph (1) (or mixed contracts falling within the definition of more than one category) will be governed by the law of the country where the party required to carry out the contract's characteristic performance has their habitual residence according to the second paragraph.

> When the contract stipulates the payment of a sum of money in exchange for something else, the payment of that sum is not the characteristic performance. This could be relevant for the question of which law will govern the relations between the handling and the guaranteeing Bureau, assuming that the contract binding the two is not to be characterised as a contract for the provision of services.

Should it, however, be clear from all the circumstances of the case that the contract is manifestly more closely connected with a country other than the one indicated in paragraph (1) or (2), the law of that other country shall apply. See para (3).

> It must be *manifest* from *all* the circumstances of the case that the contract is more closely connected with the law of another country. Since paragraph (3) is an exception to the principle rules of paragraph (1) and (2), it is to be assumed that a strict interpretation should apply. A (merely) predominantly closer connection to the law of another country would, therefore, not be sufficient. The same conclusion must be drawn if the law of more than one country is involved, even if most elements point in the direction of one of them.

If the applicable law cannot be determined on the basis of the previous paragraphs, then the contract will be governed by the law of the country with which it is most closely connected. This is obviously an open norm. It is hard to imagine a contractual relationship in the context of road traffic accidents where this provision would be relevant.

8.4.4.7 Applicable law in contracts of carriage (Article 5)

The European legislator felt that the general rules above are not satisfactory for a number of specific types of contract, either because the character of the contract requires more specific solutions to take different situations into account or because one of the contracting parties deserves more protection than the other. A combination of these motives is also a possibility. Contracts of carriage are an example of one such combination.

Rome I contains specific provisions for contracts of carriage, for consumer and insurance contracts and individual labour contracts. In the context of this book, which is dedicated to (the insurance aspects of) cross-border road traffic accidents, Article 5 on contracts of carriage is the most relevant, as well as Article 6 in the context of package travel contracts.

Article 5 is applicable to contracts of carriage for goods and persons, with the exception of package travel contracts, which are governed by Article 6.

A package travel contract, according to Directive (EU) 2015/2302, is a contract that combines at least two types of travel services for the purpose of the same trip or holiday.[52] The Directive distinguishes the following three types of travel services: (a) carriage of passengers; (b) accommodation; (c) rental of motor vehicles.

In principle, Article 5 recognises the autonomy of contractual parties to choose the applicable law. In paragraph (1), it determines the applicable law for contracts for the *carriage of goods* in the absence of such a choice. That law shall be the law of the country of the carrier's habitual residence, providing that the place of receipt or the place of delivery or the consignor's habitual residence is also situated in that country. If this condition is not met, the applicable law shall be the law of the country that contains the contractually agreed place of delivery for the goods.

The rules for the *carriage of persons* are different and more complex, and also reflect a desire to protect the weaker party. The second part of paragraph (2) restricts the options to designate the applicable law in the contract, a restriction that will hardly be noticed in practice.[53] Parties may opt for the law of the country in which

a. the passenger has his habitual residence; or
b. the carrier has his habitual residence; or
c. the carrier has his place of central administration; or
d. the place of departure is situated; or
e. the place of destination is situated.

The law of the country of the passenger's habitual residence will govern the contract in the absence of a contractual clause, providing this country is also the country of the place of departure or destination. Should this condition not be fulfilled, then the law of the country of the carrier's habitual residence will govern the contract.

As is the case in Article 4(3), an exception is made when it is clear from all the circumstances of the case that the contract, in the absence of a choice of law, is manifestly more closely connected with a country other than the one indicated in paragraph (1) or (2).

52. Directive (EU) 2015/2302 of the European Parliament and of the Council of 25 November 2015 on package travel and linked travel arrangements, amending Regulation (EC) No 2006/2004 and Directive 2011/83/EU of the European Parliament and of the Council and repealing Council Directive 90/314/EEC, OJ L 326, 11.12.2015, p. 1.

53. In practice, the passenger will almost always be faced with the law of the country of the carrier's habitual residence. Article 6 gives more protection to consumers in general and to persons who have entered into a package travel contract. See para 8.4.4.8.

8.4.4.8 *Consumer contracts (Article 6)*

In the context of this book, Article 6 will only be relevant for package travel contracts, so we will therefore focus solely on this type of contract. For the definition of a package travel contract, see para 8.4.4.7. Other forms of contracts of carriage are governed by Article 5.

Article 6(1) states that, if the contract is concluded by a natural person for a purpose which can be regarded as being outside their trade or profession (a consumer) on one hand and another person acting in the exercise of their trade or profession (a professional), the law of the country of the consumer's habitual residence will govern the contract, providing that the professional:

a. pursues their commercial or professional activities in the country of the consumer's habitual residence, or
b. by any means, directs such activities to that country or to several countries including that country,

and the contract falls within the scope of such activities.

> The condition under (b) means that the online sale of package travel may fall within the scope of Article 6(1).
> Should conditions (a) and/or (b) not be met, then the applicable law shall be determined on the basis of Articles 3 and 4. An American citizen on holiday in Europe deciding to book a package tour with a company that is only active in Europe will not have the protection of Article 6. See Article 6(3).

In line with the general principles of *Rome I*, there is a certain freedom to choose the applicable law in consumer contracts. This does include package travel contracts, but this choice is more limited than in other types of contract. Choosing a different law may not deprive the consumer of the protection afforded by the imperative rules of the law which would have been applicable on the basis of paragraph (1) in the absence of a choice. See Article 6(2).

8.4.5 *Subrogation and recourse actions*

8.4.5.1 *General remarks*

So far, we have analysed the *Rome I* and *Rome II Regulations* as separate instruments. In practice, both Regulations are closely linked in several respects. First of all, their respective scopes – both in the field of law applicable to obligations – are complementary to a large extent. In *ERGO Insurance* and *Gjensidige Baltic*, the European Court of Justice confirmed its settled jurisprudence that a 'contractual obligation' (under the *Brussels Ia Regulation* but also under *Rome I*) designates a legal obligation freely consented by one person towards another and that (under the *Brussels Ia Regulation* but also under *Rome II*) 'matters relating to tort, delict and quasi-delict' includes all actions which seek to establish the liability of a defendant and are not related to a contract.[54] That being said, claims may be brought both on a contractual and a non-contractual basis regarding one and the same accident.

In the following two paragraphs, we will first discuss the recourse of the injured party's insurer – a comprehensive or casco, health insurer or social security institution – against the liable party and their insurer (para 8.4.5.2). We will then cover the recourse in multiple liability situations. More than one party may be held liable for one and the same accident and may have a right of recourse against other potentially liable parties and their MTPL insurers after one of the parties (or their MTPL insurer) has compensated the injured party (para 8.4.5.3).

In all of these circumstances, the question must be answered which law will govern these relationships in an international context.

8.4.5.2 Recourse of a first party insurer against a liable party or their insurer

First, a matter of terminology: in this paragraph, we use the term 'first party insurer' to refer to other types of cover than third party liability insurance contracts, more specifically casco or health insurance policies or social security indemnifications. The term, therefore, encompasses a wider category of insurance cover than the same term in paragraph 6.2.7, where it merely indicates a specific type of motor vehicle insurance, especially the traffic insurance schemes in some of the Nordic countries.

A first party insurer having indemnified their insured on the basis of either the insurance contract or a legal obligation, may want to exercise a right of recourse against a third liable party. Which law governs that relationship in a cross-border accident?

Article 14 of *Rome I* deals with the situation of contractual subrogation: the relationship between the subrogated party and the debtor is governed by the law that applies to the contract between the assignor and assignee under this Regulation. In other words and translated into insurance terms, the question of whether the insured's claim against the liable party is subrogated to their (first party) insurer depends on the law applicable to the (first party) insurance contract, and this applicable law must be established on the basis of Rome I.

Article 15 deals with legal subrogation, and the outcome is the same in principle: the question whether the (social security) institution that has paid social security

54. CJEU, Judgments of 21 January 2016, *ERGO Insurance*, C-359/14, EU:C:2016:40 and CJEU, Judgment of 21 January 2016, *Gjensidige Baltic*, C-475/14, EU:C:2016:40 (joined cases).

benefits to a person injured in a road traffic accident is subrogated in the rights of the injured party against the liable party, is governed by the law that applies to the social insurer's obligation towards the injured party.

8.4.5.3 The law applicable to contractually or legally subrogated claims

When more than one party can be held liable for the consequences of an accident, the injured party may choose to start legal proceedings against any single one or all of them. This choice will depend on issues of legal jurisdiction, the content of applicable law (which may be different by virtue of the differences between *Rome II* and the *Hague Convention*) or the burden of proof.

A party that indemnified the injured party may have a right of recourse against other parties liable for the same accident. In road traffic accidents, the subrogated party is usually an MTPL insurer of one of the vehicles involved in the accident. Article 20 of *Rome II* provides an answer to the question of the law applicable to the claims subrogated as a consequence of one party having compensated the victim and having a right of recourse against other liable parties.

The insurer that compensated their insured (for example, on the basis of a health, casco or occupational disability insurance contract), will be subrogated in the rights of their insured against the liable party or parties. The same may be the case with an MTPL insurer having compensated the third party victim of an accident when other parties than their insured may be held liable. It is also possible that the MTPL insurer has a right of recourse against their own insured in the case of a deficiency in the contract. A right of recourse may be based on legal subrogation in other situations, more specifically with social security institutions.

Since subrogation may be based on tort and on a contract at the same time in the context of road traffic accidents, both *Rome I* and *Rome II* (possibly also the *Hague Convention*) will play a role.

The question of their mutual application was the subject of two joint decisions of the European Court: *ERGO Insurance* and *Gjensidige Baltic*.[55]

> The facts leading to these two decisions were largely similar. In both cases, an accident took place in which a lorry, normally based in Lithuania, combined with a trailer which also was normally based in Lithuania, caused an accident in Germany. Both lorries and trailers were properly insured against third party liability.

55. CJEU, Judgments of 21 January 2016, *ERGO Insurance*, C-359/14, EU:C:2016:40 and CJEU, Judgment of 21 January 2016, *Gjensidige Baltic*, C-475/14, EU:C:2016:40 (joined cases). See also para 8.4.5.1.

> In both cases, the German Bureau, having indemnified the German injured party, received reimbursement from the Lithuanian insurers. The MTPL insurers of the lorries turned to the insurers of the trailers for reimbursement of 50% of the amounts claimed by the German Bureau, since both insurers – of lorry and trailer – have to bear half of the damage *in solidum* under German jurisprudence.

The question raised by the referring Lithuanian courts was essentially which law governs the relationships between the two insurers, and more specifically whether those relationships are governed by *Rome I* or Rome II.

> In the *Gjensidige Baltic* case, the referring court also wanted to know whether Article 14 of the codified Directive contains a conflict of law rule as referred to in Article 23 of *Rome I* and 27 *Rome II*. The Court's answer was negative, since nothing in the wording or the objectives of the Directive seems to suggest that it is intended to lay down conflict of law rules.[56]

Apparently – but not surprisingly! – a simple answer cannot be given. It is useful to paraphrase the relevant paragraphs of the joint decisions (the authors have highlighted the essential parts of the text in italics in order to make it more accessible):

> *It is clear that*, within the meaning of the Rome I Regulation, *contractual obligations exist between the insurers and the owners or driver of the tractor unit and the owners of the trailer respectively*. However, there is *no contractual undertaking between the two insurers.*
> *The existence of any right of the insurer of a tractor unit*, the driver of which caused an accident, *to bring an action for indemnity against the insurer of a trailer* once the victim has been compensated *cannot be inferred from the insurance contract, but is based on the premise that the owner of the trailer will concomitantly incur liability in tort, delict or quasi-delict in relation to the same victim*. This would constitute a 'non-contractual' obligation within the meaning of Article 1 of the Rome II Regulation. Therefore, it is in light of the provisions of that Regulation that the law applicable to the obligation must be determined.
> *The law applicable to any such non-contractual obligation is that of the country in which the damage directly resulting from the accident is suffered*. According to Article 15 (a) and (b) of the Rome II Regulation, that law will determine the basis and extent of liability and the grounds for any division of that responsibility.
> Therefore, *the law of the place of the direct harm determines the debtors of the obligation to compensate the victim and*, if appropriate, *the respective contributions of the trailer's owner and of the owner or driver of the tractor unit to the damage caused to the victim.*

56. Decision, para 40; see also para 6.2.10.4.

> The *obligation for an insurer to compensate the damage caused to a victim arises* not from the damage caused to the latter but *from the contract between the insurer and the insured party who is liable.* Such *compensation is therefore based on a contractual obligation* and, therefore, the law applicable to such an obligation must be determined in accordance with the provisions of the Rome I Regulation.
> *Whether the insurers of those two kinds of vehicle were bound* in accordance with those contracts *to compensate the victims of an accident caused by those vehicles must be examined in light of the law applicable to the contracts insuring the tractor units and to the contracts insuring the trailers coupled to them respectively.*
> *Regarding the issue of whether the insurer of a tractor unit who has compensated a victim has a right to bring an action in subrogation against the insurer of the trailer* in some circumstances, *Article 19 of the Rome II Regulation distinguishes between matters subject to the tort/delict regime and those subject to the contractual regime.* This provision particularly applies to a situation in which a third party, namely an insurer, has compensated the victim of an accident, the creditor of an obligation in tort/delict of damages owed by the driver or owner of a motor vehicle, in order to discharge the duty to satisfy that obligation. *Article 19 of the Rome II Regulation provides that* the issue of *any subrogation of the victim's rights in this case is governed by the law applicable to the obligation of the third party, namely the civil liability insurer, to compensate that victim.*
> Hence, *the insurer's obligation to cover the civil liability of the insured party and the conditions under which the insurer may exercise the rights which the victim of the accident has against the persons responsible for the accident depend upon the national law governing that insurance contract,* which is determined in accordance with Article 7 of the Rome I Regulation.
> *However, the law applicable to determining the persons who may be held liable and the allocation of responsibility between them and their respective insurers remains subject to Article 4 et seq. of the Rome II Regulation* in accordance with Article 19.
> In particular, *it must be held that if,* according to the law applicable by virtue of those provisions of the Rome II Regulation, *the victim of a road traffic accident caused by a tractor unit coupled with a trailer has rights against both the owner of the trailer and its insurer, the insurer of the tractor unit,* after compensating the victim, *has a right of action against the insurer of the trailer since the law applicable to the insurance contract* in accordance with Article 7 of the Rome I Regulation *provides for the insurer's subrogation to the victim's rights.*

In summary, and applied to cross-border road traffic accidents:
- The *law applicable to the non-contractual obligation* – the accident, to be determined on the basis of *Rome II* – governs the question of whether and from whom an injured party is entitled to compensation.
- The *law applicable to the insurance contracts* of the parties involved – to be determined on the basis of the *Rome I Regulation* – determines whether the MTPL insurer is obliged to indemnify the injured party. If this is the case, that law also determines whether the insurer has been subrogated in the rights of the injured party after having indemnified the injured party.

It seems to us that this decision, which was given in a case of two insurers of two coupled (motor) vehicles, also has relevance in other situations where more than one potentially liable and insured parties are involved, such as an accident involving two motor vehicles and an injured third party.

As to the question of the law applicable to the non-contractual obligation, the decision only refers to *Rome II* but it seems to us that the decision would be the same in a situation where not *Rome II* but the *Hague Convention* has to be applied.

Example
As an example, let us take an accident in the Netherlands, involving a German and a Dutch motor vehicle, in which a Dutch pedestrian is injured. If the case were brought before a Dutch court, the question of the law applicable to the accident would have to be decided on the basis of the *Hague Convention* (that law would be Dutch law). Whether the insurers of the Dutch and the German vehicle will have to indemnify the injured party must be decided by the law applicable to the respective insurance contracts (to be established on the basis of *Rome I*, in all likelihood Dutch and German law respectively). And each of these two legal systems also decides whether the respective insurers are subrogated in the rights of the injured party against the respective insured parties.

In the context of the *Hague Convention*, one has to bear in mind that the Convention shall not apply to recourse actions and to subrogation insofar as insurance companies are concerned according to Article 2(5). See para 8.4.3.2. And, apparently, so does Rome II.

8.4.6 *The law applicable to claims on Guarantee Funds and compensation bodies*

8.4.6.1 *Introduction*

In the previous paragraphs, we gave an extensive description of the conflict of law rules, such as they can be found in the *Rome I* and *II* Regulations and the Hague Traffic Law Convention. The focus lay on the relationship between the injured party and the liable party, and their relationship with the MTPL insurer. One aspect has, however, been neglected: the question of the law applicable to claims against a Guarantee Fund or a Compensation Body.

This is not an unimportant question. Whereas the applicable law will not be in dispute in the majority of the accidents for which a Guarantee Fund provides cover, since the liable uninsured motor vehicle will normally be based in the Member State of the accident and the victim's domicile will be in the same country, the question will come up in several situations. When a Compensation Body has indemnified a victim on the basis of Article 24 or 25 of the Directive, questions of applicable law will be unavoidable.

Guarantee Funds may have to intervene:
- if a vehicle originating from a non-Multilateral Agreement country has an accident in a Member State without being provided with a valid Green Card;
- if a vehicle which is exempted from compulsory insurance under Article 5(2) has an accident in another Member State.

Compensation Bodies will have to handle and settle claims resulting from accidents in other Member States:
- if the injured party receives no offer for compensation, nor a reasoned reply from the insurance company or their claims representative within three months of the date when the injured party presented their claim;
- if the insurance company has not appointed a claims representative in the injured party's Member State of residence;
- if the insurer of the liable vehicle cannot be identified within two months;
- if the vehicle which caused the accident cannot be identified within two months.

In all of these situations, two questions arise:
- which law applies to the injured party's claim against the Guarantee Fund or the Compensation Body which handles and settles their claims; and
- which law applies to the recourse action – based on subrogation – by the handling Guarantee Fund or Compensation Body against the debtor Guarantee Fund or Compensation Body (in the Member State where the accident took place or where the insurance company is established)?

These questions are all the more relevant due to the differences in protection offered by Guarantee Funds and Compensation Bodies. Not only will the law on liability and on compensation differ from one Member State to another, the funds and bodies may have a subsidiary role, certain injured parties may not have a claim against the fund or the body as opposed to direct victims, and the amounts covered may be different.
These questions will be discussed in the following paragraphs. Paragraph 8.4.6.2 will be devoted to an analysis of the legal relationships between the parties involved in the accident. Paragraph 8.4.6.3 will deal with the applicable law in relation to claims against and from Guarantee Funds and Compensation Bodies.

8.4.6.2 The legal relationships between parties involved in the accident

In order to find the law applicable to the relationships between injured party, liable motorist and the Guarantee Funds or Compensation Bodies in their dual capacity as a handling and a guaranteeing entity, an analysis of their legal relationships is required.

It is obvious that the relationship between liable motorist and injured party will be based on tort.[57]

The relationship between the injured party/victim and the Guarantee Fund in case of an accident caused by an uninsured or unidentified vehicle will be based on a legal provision to be found in the MTPL law of the country where the accident took place, with the tort acting as its trigger. In the absence of a voluntary commitment between injured party and Guarantee Fund or Compensation Body, there is no contract.

The foundation of the claim by the handling Compensation Body against the guaranteeing entity (this being either the Guarantee Fund of the Member State where the accident took place, the Guarantee Fund of the Member State where the uninsured liable vehicle is normally based or the Compensation Body of the Member State where the insurance undertaking which issued the policy is established) can be found in the Directive's Article 24(2) and 25. In the situation of Article 24 (the insurance company or its claims representative has not given a reasoned reply within three months or the insurance company has failed to appoint a claims representative), the Directive states that this provision becomes effective after the Compensation Bodies have concluded an agreement regulating *i.a.* the reimbursement procedure. Such an agreement is not foreseen in the context of Article 25 (unidentified or uninsured vehicles) but the Guarantee Funds and the Compensation Bodies have nonetheless concluded such an agreement. For the agreements between Compensation Bodies and Guarantee Funds, see *supra* para 5.6.3 and 5.6.4. The conclusion may, therefore, be that the legal relationship between the handling Compensation Body and the guaranteeing entity (be it Guarantee Fund or Compensation Body) is contractual in nature.

8.4.6.3 Applicable law in relation to Guarantee Funds and Compensation Bodies

In Member States which are not bound by the *Hague Convention*, the *Rome II Regulation* governs the matter of motorist liability. In general terms, the law of the country in which the event giving rise to the damage occurred will be applicable. In Member States which are signatories to the *Hague Convention*, the law will have to be established by applying that Convention. Usually, the law of the country where the accident occurred will be applicable.

57. Since a claim will only seldom be based on a contract, we will not discuss this variant.

The injured party's claim against the Guarantee Fund or the Compensation Body in the Member State of their domicile can only be qualified as non-contractual. Therefore, *Rome II* or – providing that the Guarantee Fund is not public in nature, see para 8.4.3.2, *a)* – the *Hague Convention* will govern that relationship as well.

The claim 'in second instance' between the handling Guarantee Fund or Compensation Body and the guaranteeing Guarantee Fund or Compensation Body may find its foundations in a contractual relationship, the agreements referred to in paragraph 5.6.3 and 5.6.4. The law applicable to that recourse in second instance must be established on the basis of *Rome I*.

There is no case law of the European Court of Justice dealing with these issues. However, the decisions of the European Court of Justice in the *ERGO* and *Gjensidige* cases seem relevant.[58] In these decisions, the Court made a distinction between questions of liability for the accident and the recourse actions between the various parties that compensated the victim and that may have a right of recourse against other entities.

Example

In practical terms, the *ERGO* and *Gjensidige* approach would mean the following:

a) ***Accident in Spain, victim resident in Spain, vehicle (e-bike) normally based in the Netherlands and exempt from compulsory insurance under Article 5(2) of the Directive***
The victim will address the Spanish Guarantee Fund, which will handle the accident as it was caused by an uninsured vehicle. The law applicable to liability issues will be Spanish law (although presumably not on the basis of the *Hague Convention* but of *Rome II* since the Spanish Guarantee Fund is a public law entity; see the *Hague Convention*, Article 2(6) and *supra* 8.4.3.2, under (*a*)).
Spanish law will also govern the matter of the liability of the Spanish Guarantee Fund, including aspects such as subsidiarity, amounts covered, admissible exceptions, limitations and exclusions.
The Spanish Guarantee Fund will have a right of recourse against the Dutch Guarantee Fund, based on the Directive (the agreements between Compensation Bodies and Guarantee Funds not being applicable to this situation). The law applicable to this right of recourse will have to be established on the basis of *Rome II*, Article 19. The law which governs the Spanish Guarantee Fund's obligation to compensate the victim will also govern the existence and scope of the subrogation. Spanish law will therefore be applicable to this aspect.

58. See *supra* para 8.4.5.3.

b) ***Accident in Spain, victim Italian tourist, vehicle normally based in Spain and insured;***
insurer fails to provide reasoned reply or has not appointed a claims representative
The law applicable to the accident will be Spanish law (in view of the public nature of the Spanish Guarantee Fund based on *Rome II*)).
The Italian victim will address the Italian Compensation Body, which – once the 2-month period set out in Article 24(1), fourth paragraph has expired without the insurance undertaking or its claims representative having taken the necessary steps – will handle the claim. Since *Rome II* will govern this relationship, the law of the country where the event giving rise to the damage occurred will apply: Spain. The victim's claim against the Italian Compensation Body will, therefore, be governed by Spanish law on MTPL insurance, which will define its limits and boundaries.
The Italian Compensation Body's claim for reimbursement against the Spanish Compensation Body will be based on the Agreement between the Compensation Bodies, which in turn will have to be interpreted in the light of *Rome I*. In the light of Article 14 of that Regulation, Italian law will govern the matter of whether the Italian Compensation Body is subrogated and to what extent in the rights of the injured party against the liable motorist and the insurance company.

c) ***Accident in Spain, Italian victim, vehicle normally based in Spain but uninsured***
The law applicable to the accident will be Spanish law (according to *RomeII*).
The Italian victim will address the Italian Compensation Body, which will handle the claim. Since *Rome II* will govern this relationship, the law of the country where the event giving rise to the damage occurred will apply: Spain. The Italian victim's claim against the Italian Compensation Body will, therefore, be governed by Spanish law, which will define its limits and boundaries, including subsidiarity, amounts covered, admissible exceptions, limitations and exclusions.
The Italian Compensation Body's claim for reimbursement against the Spanish Guarantee Fund will be based on the Agreement between the Compensation Bodies and Guarantee Funds, which in turn will have to be interpreted in the light of *Rome I*. In the light of Article 14 of that Regulation, Italian law will govern the matter of whether the Italian Compensation Body is subrogated and to what extent in the rights of the injured party against the liable motorist and the Spanish Guarantee Fund.

d) ***Accident in Spain, Italian victim, vehicle unidentified***
The law applicable to the accident will be Spanish law (according to *Rome II*).
The Italian victim will address the Italian Compensation Body, which will handle the claim. Since *Rome II* will govern this relationship, the law of the country where the event giving rise to the damage occurred will apply: Spain. The Italian victim's claim against the Italian Compensation Body will, therefore, be governed by Spanish law, which will define its limits and boundaries, including subsidiarity,

amounts covered, admissible exceptions, limitations and exclusions. The Italian victim may, therefore, not have a claim against the Italian Compensation Body, since the Spanish Guarantee Fund excludes damage to property if no significant bodily injury occurred in the same accident.

The Italian Compensation Body's claim for reimbursement against the Spanish Guarantee Fund will be based on the Agreement between the Compensation Bodies and Guarantee Funds, which in turn will have to be interpreted in the light of *Rome I*. In the light of Article 14 of that Regulation, Italian law will govern the matter of whether the Italian Compensation Body is subrogated and to what extent in the rights of the injured party against the Guarantee Fund.

e) ***Accident in Spain, Italian victim, vehicle normally based in Portugal and insured; Portuguese insurer fails to provide reasoned reply or has not appointed a clams representative***

The law applicable to the accident will be Spanish law (according to *Rome II*). The fact that the liable vehicle is normally based in Portugal makes no difference in this respect.

The Italian victim will address the Italian Compensation Body, which – once the 2-month period set out in Article 24(1), paragraph 4 has expired without the insurance undertaking or its claims representative having taken the necessary steps – will handle the claim. Since *Rome II* will govern this relationship, the law of the country where the event giving rise to the damage occurred will apply: Spain.

Contrary to the situations described under *b), c) and d)* above, the Italian Compensation Body will handle the claim on behalf of the Portuguese Compensation Body. The law to be applied will have to be established on the basis of the *Rome II Regulation* (Italy not being bound by the *Hague Convention*) and, therefore, Spanish law on MTPL insurance will govern the scope of intervention by the Italian Compensation Body, including possible subsidiarity, amounts covered, admissible exceptions, limitations and exclusions.

The victim's claim against the Italian Compensation Body will, therefore, be governed by Spanish law, which will define its limits and boundaries.

The Italian Compensation Body's claim for reimbursement against the Portuguese Compensation Body will be based on the Agreement between the Compensation Bodies, which in turn will have to be interpreted in the light of Rome I. In the light of Article 14 of that Regulation, Italian law will govern the question whether the Italian Compensation Body is subrogated and to what extent in the rights of the injured party against the liable motorist and the insurance company.

f) ***Accident in Spain, Italian victim, vehicle normally based in Portugal but uninsured***

The law applicable to the accident will be Spanish law (based on *Rome II*).

The Italian victim will address the Italian Compensation Body, which will handle the claim on behalf of the Portuguese Guarantee Fund. Since *Rome II* will govern this relationship, the law of the country where the event giving rise to the damage occurred will apply: Spain. The Italian victim's claim against the Italian Compensation Body will, therefore, be governed by Spanish law, which will define its limits and boundaries, including subsidiarity, amounts covered, admissible exceptions, limitations and exclusions.

The Italian Compensation Body's claim for reimbursement against the Portuguese Guarantee Fund will be based on the Agreement between the Compensation Bodies and Guarantee Funds, which in turn will have to be interpreted in the light of *Rome I*. In the light of Article 14 of that Regulation, Italian law will govern the matter of whether the Italian Compensation Body is subrogated and to what extent in the rights of the injured party against the liable motorist and the Guarantee Fund.

The consequence of this approach is that a Guarantee Fund may have to provide wider cover than required by its domestic legislation under certain circumstances. In other circumstances, it may benefit from the more limited scope of legislation in other countries. Not only would this solution be consistent with the jurisprudence in the *ERGO* and *Gjensidige* cases, but an additional benefit would also be that the applicable law will be the same whether the claimant addresses the claim to the Compensation Body of their Member State of residence or against the Bureau of the Member State where the accident occurred. Forum and law shopping would thus be made less attractive.

9 Future Developments

9.1 Introduction

Throughout the previous chapters, we examined the gradual improvement of the legal position of a victim suffering damage from a road traffic accident in the period between 1949 and today. The Green Card system started protecting the victims of accidents that were caused by foreign vehicles but that occurred in their own countries. The European legislator further improved this protection scheme by way of the various Motor Insurance Directives, now codified in one single legal instrument. And yet, the European Union is elaborating a new Directive, aimed at an even stronger improvement of the victim's position.

In this chapter, we will focus on a number of current and future evolutions that are taking place and that may substantially influence road traffic in a modern world. We will examine how the risks related to such road traffic are being – or could be – covered by insurance.
We will first focus on the geographical scope of the main protection schemes analysed in this book: the Green Card system and the Motor Insurance Directive. In which countries may these protection schemes be expected to apply in the future? This question will be answered in paragraph 9.2. Subsequently, we will give a short analysis of the European legislator's plans regarding the amendment of the existing Motor Insurance Directive (para 9.3). In paragraph 9.4, we will briefly discuss the technological evolutions that are taking place in the car manufacturing industry and, more particularly, the influence of these evolutions on road traffic safety and on rules of liability and insurance. We will also briefly discuss society's changing perceptions of motor vehicles and car ownership and the way in which these changing attitudes have an impact on MTPL insurance (para 9.5). Some conclusive remarks will be formulated in paragraph 9.6.

9.2 Geographical scope

In our earlier chapters, we analysed the geographical scope of both the Green Card system (para 3.2.2) and the Motor Insurance Directive (para 3.5.4, 4.2, 5.2.2 and

6.2.8), explaining where both protection schemes are currently applicable. In this paragraph, we will examine whether this geographical scope may change in the months or years to come.
In paragraph 3.5.4, we described the geographical scope of the *Green Card system* as defined by the Council of Bureaux: limited to the countries situated to the west of the Ural Mountains and the Caspian Sea as well as to the countries bordering the Mediterranean Sea.[1] This limitation results in the following countries being potential future participants in the Green Card system:
- Countries situated to the west of the Ural Mountains and the Caspian Sea: Armenia, Georgia and Kazakhstan;
- Countries bordering the Mediterranean Sea: Algeria, Egypt, Lebanon, Libya and Syria.

A number of these countries have already expressed their interest in possible future participation in the Green Card system: Algeria, Armenia, Georgia and Kazakhstan. Whether their Bureaux will indeed become members of the Council of Bureaux will depend on the fulfilment of a number of conditions that are to be assessed by the Application Committee of the Council of Bureaux.

The *system of deemed insurance cover* (see para 3.2.1 and 3.5) is dependent on the participating countries' signing of the Multilateral Agreement. Today, the Multilateral Agreement is subscribed to by the 31 countries participating in the European Economic Area as well as by Andorra, Serbia and Switzerland.[2] Any Bureaux of the countries participating in the Green Card system may theoretically become a signatory of the Multilateral Agreement, providing that a number of conditions is respected. Recently, the Bureau of Bosnia and Herzegovina became a signatory of the Multilateral Agreement. For the system of deemed insurance cover to become applicable in that country, a formal decision of the European Commission is still necessary. In accordance with Article 8 of the codified Motor Insurance Directive, that decision shall fix the date from which a control of a valid Green Card shall no longer be necessary.

The *Motor Insurance Directive* applies in the 31 countries that are part of the European Economic Area. The European Union may still be enlarged in the years to come with new Member States. At this moment, the following countries have the official status of 'candidate countries', which means that accession negotiations

1. It is useful to recall that the non-European parts of European States such as Turkey and the Russian Federation are also covered by the Green Card system.
2. On 1 March 2019, the European Economic Area comprises of Austria, Belgium, Bulgaria, Croatia, Cyprus, the Czech Republic, Denmark, Estonia, Finland, France, Germany, Greece, Hungary, Iceland, Ireland, Italy, Latvia, Liechtenstein, Lithuania, Luxembourg, Malta, the Netherlands, Norway, Poland, Portugal, Romania, the Slovak Republic, Slovenia, Spain, Sweden and the United Kingdom.

with the European Union are taking place: Albania, Montenegro, North-Macedonia, Serbia and Turkey. Two other countries, Bosnia-Herzegovina and Kosovo, have the status of 'potential candidate countries'.

The decision of the United Kingdom to leave the European Union (*Brexit*) and the continuing uncertainty about the United Kingdom's future relationship with the European Union imply that the Council of Bureaux faces a number of challenges regarding the UK Motor Insurers' Bureau's (MIB) participation in the Green Card system and the applicability of the Motor Insurance Directive within the territory of the United Kingdom.

Two different aspects have to be taken into consideration in respect of the abolition of border checks on the insurance of motor vehicles:

- the EU's perspective (the decision of the European Union under Article 8(2) of the codified Directive that motor vehicles normally based in specific third countries when entering the territory of the EU shall be treated as EU vehicles) and
- the aspect of inter-Bureaux Agreements (the signing of the Multilateral Agreement by the Bureau of the non-European country and the Bureaux of the European Union).

The United Kingdom leaving the European Union makes the UK a third country and, as a consequence, a decision by the European Commission as referred to above is required in order to put UK vehicles on an equal footing with EU vehicles. In the absence of such a decision, UK vehicles will have to be checked for the presence of a valid Green Card. It is merely logical that the same applies to EU vehicles wishing to enter the territory of the UK, although this conclusion cannot be drawn based on the wording of the Directive.

The fact that the United Kingdom is leaving the European Union has, however, no direct consequences for the validity of the United Kingdom's Bureau's adherence to the Multilateral Agreement. This means that, as long as MIB continues to be a signatory to this Agreement, accidents caused by EU vehicles in the UK and, similarly, accidents on the territory of one of the Member States for which UK vehicles are responsible, will continue to be guaranteed by the EU Bureaux or the UK Bureau respectively, irrespective of whether the vehicle was insured or not.

In context of Brexit, the following observations can be made:

- All the Bureaux that have signed the Multilateral Agreement (including MIB) have expressed their willingness to continue their cooperation based on that Agreement. This means that cooperation between MIB and other signatory Bureaux of the Multilateral Agreement will continue to be based on deemed insurance cover after Brexit. Based on Section III of the Internal Regulations, claims will be handled on the basis of a vehicle's normally based status and no Green Card will be required for a claim to be addressed to the participating Bureaux;

- Even if a Green Card will continue not to be required for the claims handling process between signatory Bureaux of the Multilateral Agreement, the physical existence of a Green Card may be necessary for vehicles wishing to travel between the United Kingdom and the European Economic Area after Brexit. Today, the European Commission has not yet adopted a decision as referred to in Article 8(2) in relation to the United Kingdom, which means that, theoretically, a Green Card may be required when crossing the border between the United Kingdom and the countries participating in the Multilateral Agreement after Brexit. In the absence of such a decision from the Commission, it remains difficult to imagine how the physical existence of a Green Card will be checked in practice at the numerous border crossing points between the United Kingdom (Northern Ireland) and the Republic of Ireland;
- After Brexit, the Motor Insurance Directive will no longer apply in the territory of the United Kingdom. The same also goes for provisions on the protection of visitors, since the Directive – in principle – only provides safeguards for victims suffering an accident in a *Member State* other than their *Member State* of residence (see chapter 5). As explained in paragraph 5.8, the Council of Bureaux has elaborated agreements allowing the extension of the protection of visitors scheme to third countries, albeit in a more limited way. MIB has invited the Bureaux and Guarantee Funds of the countries of the European Economic Area to conclude such Protection of visitors Agreements. However, since these are voluntary agreements, their subscription remains in the hands of the individual Bureaux and Guarantee Funds.

9.3 The European legislator's plans regarding a new Motor Insurance Directive

In paragraph 3.5.1, we referred to the European Commission's proposal for a new Motor Insurance Directive. On 24 May 2018, the Commission proposed to amend the existing Motor Insurance Directive on the following five points[3]:

1. The scope of the Directive, the risks to be covered under MTPL insurance and the definition of the use of a vehicle;
2. The risks due to uninsured driving and checks on insurance;
3. Insurer insolvency and the protection of injured parties in the case of an insurance undertaking's insolvency or lack of cooperation;

3. Document COM(2018) 336 final, 2018/0168 (COD).

4. Minimum amounts of cover;
5. Claims history statements.

These points were analysed in more detail throughout the book, whenever the specific subjects of the proposed amendments were discussed.

We also mentioned the European Parliament's report in which a number of additional modifications to the Motor Insurance Directive are proposed. These additional changes were also described in several paragraphs of the previous chapters, depending on the subject of the proposed amendments.

Most of the proposals included in the texts published by the European Commission and the European Parliament aim to bring further improvements to the situations of insured persons, drivers and, most importantly, victims of motor vehicle accidents. The further developments of this legislative proposal must therefore be followed up.

Since the Directive is a piece of legislation to be adopted jointly by the European Parliament and the Council of the European Union, the legislative process is subject to cooperation between the European Commission, the European Parliament and the Council of the European Union. The Directive not being adopted before the European elections of May 2019, it may be hoped that the initiative and the legislative procedure will be resumed shortly after the elections in order to realise the intended improvements.

9.4 The influence of technological developments

9.4.1 *Introduction*

For a number of years, the automotive industry has been rapidly implementing important technological advancements to motor vehicles, thus improving both the vehicle user's comfort and road safety.
While these technological evolutions are constantly taking place, they do at the same time present a number of challenges for insurers, insured persons and victims of road traffic accidents. The aim of the following paragraphs is not to describe all the technological developments taking place in the automotive industry, but rather to analyse their potential impact on the MTPL insurance sector. We will consecutively focus on connected vehicles (para 9.4.2) and on (semi-)autonomous vehicles (para 9.4.3) before asking ourselves how connected vehicles could, in the longer term, present an alternative to the paper-based Green Card as an international insurance document (para 9.4.4).

9.4.2 Connected vehicles and detection systems installed in vehicles

The internet, the internet of things and the permanent possibility of connecting technological devices allow vehicles to be almost permanently connected with other devices and service providers. This connectivity allows better interaction between vehicles and of vehicles with the outside world, and opens up a wide variety of opportunities to improve the safety of motor road traffic.

Connected vehicles enable initiatives such as e-call, resulting in an automatic alert signal being sent by the vehicle from the moment it detects a serious impact or an accident. In this way, the emergency services can instantly be notified and informed of the vehicle's exact position, even if the driver is no longer able to send an emergency message or if no witnesses are present to do so. As a result, new technologies can help save numerous lives on public roads.

The advanced technology installed in vehicles also improves the way in which vehicle software can analyse the driver's behaviour in traffic and detect external obstacles. Based on this data, the vehicle can send out warning signals to the driver in order to avoid collisions. Examples of such applications that improve road safety are: forward collision warning, lane change warning, blind spot warning, emergency brake light warning and all other kinds of systems that may contribute to lowering the number of minor or significant collisions.

Vehicle connectivity and detection systems not only result in a constant exchange of data, they also allow the storage of data relating to a vehicle's movements and manoeuvres. This data can be useful in analysing the circumstances of an accident or in determining liabilities following an accident. But the data may also be useful in evaluating an insured person's driving and, as a consequence, in assessing the driver's risk from an insurance perspective. Inevitably, the question arises of who owns the data stored in and by the vehicle. Is it the car manufacturer, the vehicle owner or driver who owns the data and decides on what can be done with it? If it is the driver who owns the data, are this data then protected as personal data? Is it the driver who can decide with whom to share the data? Are insurers allowed to ask for the data to be shared with them? And would drivers be willing to share data about their driving with insurers in exchange for a lower insurance premium? Could the collection of data by insurers result in a mass exclusion of 'bad insurance risks'? And could the availability of such data help insurers to identify and fight insurance fraud?

We are deliberately limiting ourselves to formulating a number of questions but refraining from seeking answers. The answers to the many questions that vehicle connectivity may give rise to are not part of this book's scope of study. We only wish to list some of the many questions in order to illustrate the way in which new technologies may influence the future of road safety, MTPL insurance products and the protection of road traffic accident victims.

9.4.3 *Semi-autonomous and autonomous vehicles*

Vehicle connectivity and detection systems as described in the previous paragraph not only facilitate constant data exchange. This permanent interaction may also enable vehicle technology to react on the basis of the information exchanged. A brake light warning system, in combination with an estimation of the distance to the vehicle in front, may automatically activate the braking system in the vehicle in question. Cameras and other devices to identify obstacles outside the vehicle may help in designing parking assist systems. All these developments and interactions may gradually result in more and more driving manoeuvres being executed automatically by the vehicle instead of the driver. In this way, we move closer to semi-autonomous or even autonomous driving, where the driver's input will be reduced or even excluded.

Vehicle autonomy exists across many levels and variations. The lowest level is where the entire driving process remains in the hands of the driver, who is to have complete control over the vehicle, and where the driving technology has no automatic interventions. In fact, this lowest level equals a total absence of vehicle autonomy. Many variations of semi-autonomous driving exist at the intermediate level. Certain driving manoeuvres are hereby performed by the vehicle technology but the driver must at all times be able to take over and re-gain control of the vehicle. The time interval within which the driver should be able to take back control may vary from instantly to a few seconds. The highest level would be an entirely autonomous vehicle, where no manipulation is required of the driver and where the presence of a driver may even no longer be necessary.

Although tests are already being carried out with entirely autonomous vehicles, it is not expected that vehicles will become entirely driverless in the very near future. Long-distance travel along straight motorways may offer more opportunities for autonomous driving, but this is less suitable for traffic in towns and cities. The complexity of roads and traffic does not yet allow autonomous vehicles to be operational across the entire network of public roads at this time.

Whatever the level of autonomous driving, these evolutions again present important challenges to the insurance industry and to the protection mechanisms for victims of road traffic accidents.

Comparable to the influence of connected vehicles, autonomous driving will most probably contribute to a reduction in accidents, hopefully resulting in better road safety as well as fewer personal injuries and fatal accidents. At the same time, this damage reduction may result in lower MTPL insurance premiums. But the high level of technology in the vehicles may also increase the cost of repairing material damage to vehicles involved in an accident, resulting in higher damage costs. This may then have the opposite impact, resulting in higher MTPL insurance premiums. But apart from damage costs and insurance premiums, questions of liability will inevitably arise as well. In what way can the driver be held exclusively liable if the accident is (partially) due to a failure in the technology's design? Will the answer to this question be the same in jurisdictions where the liability for road traffic accidents does not rest with the driver but with another person, such as the keeper or owner of the vehicle (as can be found in Switzerland), or where the obligation to compensate the victim lies with the insurer (either under a scheme of first party insurance such as those in Finland, Norway and Sweden or under legislation such as the *Loi Badinter* in France)? Will this lead to issues of product liability, therefore resulting in the portion of liability arising from the defective product no longer being covered by MTPL insurance? If vehicles become entirely autonomous (in the longer term), will there still be room for MTPL insurance cover or will there be a full shift from MTPL insurance towards product liability? And how will car manufacturers respond to this increased risk of product liability? Will they have this potential product liability risk insured or would they prefer to cover (part of) this risk themselves? And even if autonomous driving may result in a decrease in the number and severity of accidents, there is still a risk of mass amounts of comparable or identical accidents due to faults in vehicle technology.

Again, a long series of questions arises and, again, it is not our intention to find answers to all these questions. But it is important to emphasise the substantial differences that exist between the level of protection offered by MTPL insurance regulation on the one hand and the protection provided by product liability schemes on the other. The protection mechanisms created by MTPL insurance regulation (to a large part harmonised at the European level by way of the Motor Insurance Directive) are specifically designed not only to protect drivers and insured persons but also to defend the interests of road traffic victims. And, more particularly, cross-border road traffic victims are especially protected via the Green Card system and the Motor Insurance Directive. It would be a considerable step backwards for the position of victims – and therefore completely unthinkable – if these protection mechanisms were to be entirely replaced by a product liability regime without at least equal protection of victims being guaranteed.

9.4.4 *The future of the Green Card*

The Green Card system was developed in the late 1940s and has applied since the early 1950s. In those days, it was obvious that an international proof of insurance would be a paper document. Today, more than 65 years later, technological development provides much easier and safer ways to issue official documents. Since all vehicles are normally included in national databases, linking these databases with insurance data allows real-time checks of the international insurance cover that exists for a specific motor vehicle. Moreover, such checking mechanisms would prevent the fraudulent counterfeiting of Green Cards.

In fact, maintaining the paper form for an official document like a Green Card today seems to be an anachronism.

Nevertheless, there are certain impediments that make it difficult to replace the paper Green Card with a digital document:

- The Green Card system is a cooperation of 47 Bureaux, active in very divergent insurance markets. All these individual markets must be capable and willing to invest in a common digitalised system allowing the monitoring of international insurance cover. It is a huge challenge to have all these markets on the same page and convince them to make the necessary investments;
- Green Cards not only need to be verified by insurance companies and claims handling offices. Since they are a guarantee document enabling entry into a country's territory, they must be checked at border checkpoints. Each border checkpoint needs to be equipped with the necessary technology to check the Green Card on whatever (digital) carrier it is displayed. Moreover, the Green Card also needs to be checked after an accident has occurred. This means that the necessary technological means must be available (together with sufficient internet connection) at all possible locations where an accident can take place to verify the insurance status of the vehicle involved in the accident.

The Council of Bureaux is reviewing the possibility of replacing the paper Green Card with a more modern carrier, but the above-mentioned challenges have to be taken into account in order to implement any such replacement. It may therefore be expected that it will still take some time for an entirely digitised Green Card to be introduced in all the countries participating in the system.

9.5 The concept of car ownership in a changing society

Throughout the 65 years of the Green Card system, the presence, importance and reputation of motor vehicles has dramatically changed and is still in full evolution today. While car ownership was still reserved for a minority of the population in the early days of the Green Card system, it has become almost standard in modern society for every household to have one or more motor vehicles at their disposal. But with the growth of car ownership, the negative side effects have also increased. This has harmed the reputation of motor vehicles as a means of transport. Air pollution, noise, traffic congestion, road traffic accidents causing material damage and personal injury have all changed the perception that society has of motor vehicles. More recently, the discovery of the mass manipulation of environmental protection systems by certain car manufacturers ('dieselgate') has brought further harm to the reputation of motor vehicles in society. The car is no longer perceived as the ultimate provider of individual freedom, but also as the cause of multiple negative effects on society.

As a result of these evolutions, a car no longer has the same status it enjoyed for many years. Younger generations see the motor vehicle as a useful means of transport but certainly not the sole method of getting from one place to another. It is just one of the many transport options that are available in modern society. As a result, car ownership is seen as an expensive means of providing oneself the opportunity to move. Especially in an urban environment, the many disadvantages of owning a car (including the necessity of having a place to park the car) have encouraged people to explore new forms of car ownership. Car sharing has become a popular alternative to the individual ownership of a motor vehicle.

At the same time, such new forms of car ownership still present challenges to the MTPL insurance industry. How should insurers cover the risks related to the use of vehicles if they don't know the identity and risk of the potential users of the vehicles they want to cover? Where and how will the vehicle be used and, most importantly, by whom?

Cars as a means of individual transport will most probably continue to exist for at least a number of years or decades. However, perceptions change and the individual ownership of vehicles may lose ground to the benefits of other ways of using cars. The insurance industry will have to be creative to cope with the challenges presented by these evolutions.

Another aspect is the increasing popularity of private leasing. Here, the lease company is owner of the vehicle and, as a consequence, the obligation to insure the vehicle rests in principle with the lease company. This would mean that the insurance market may, if this phenomenon increases, be confronted with only a few powerful buyers instead of a multitude of small individual vehicle owners. Will they establish their own insurance undertakings, a decision already made by several lease companies? What consequences will this development have for the availability of cover in countries other than the country of the vehicle's registration?

Will these few big buyers (try to) influence the decision making process of the Bureaux? How will they influence claims handling, taking into account that they will also centralise the nominations of correspondents and claims representatives? This question will become even more pressing if car manufacturers also act as lessors, a development which would become more likely in the light of a shift from MTPL insurance to product liability as described above. Again: questions and no answers. Food for thought.

9.6 Conclusion

In this chapter, we have attempted to describe a few developments that may influence the future of the Green Card system, the Motor Insurance Directive, the daily practice of offering MTPL insurance and, most importantly, the protection of consumers and the injured parties of motor road traffic accidents. Without any doubt, we have not identified all the possible factors that may in the near or far future form the reality of MTPL insurance and victims' protection. Many more challenges may present themselves to motor insurers, claims handling offices, Green Card Bureaux, Compensation Bodies, Guarantee Funds, Information Centres, lawyers, courts, representatives of injured parties and the injured parties themselves.
Whatever the future landscape of MTPL insurance and cross-border road traffic may bring, it may be hoped that any future evolutions and legislative initiatives will always take into consideration and be designed in favour of the two objectives that the Green Card system and the Motor Insurance Directive have tried to promote and reconcile:

- the facilitation of cross-border motor road traffic and
- the protection of cross-border road traffic victims.

10 Conclusions

After the first UNIDROIT attempts and based on positive experiences in the Nordic countries, the Green Card system tries, as of the late 1940s, to reconcile the following two important principles to the benefit of society:
- the facilitation of motorised cross-border road traffic;
- the provision of a satisfactory level of protection for victims of accidents caused by this motorised cross-border road traffic.

Step by step, the European Union incorporated the protection provided by the Green Card system into the creation of a single market. By means of the Motor Insurance Directives, the European legislator gradually extended the protection offered to consumers and the injured parties of accidents. Guarantee Funds were entrusted with the task of protecting victims of accidents caused by the use of uninsured or unidentified vehicles. Claims representatives and Compensation Bodies were introduced to help the injured party in their own Member State of residence to obtain compensation for damage caused by an accident that occurred in another Member State. Information Centres were established to support the injured party in identifying the vehicle that caused the accident and the insurer covering that vehicle. Moreover, the system of 'European passporting' gave consumers the opportunity to insure their vehicles with European insurers operating in other Member States by way of the Freedom to Provide Services or the Freedom of Establishment.

All in all, the regulation of MTPL insurance offers a fairly extended level of protection to consumers and injured parties today. This is the case in the geographical zone where the Green Card system applies, and this protection is even more comprehensive in the European Economic Area. Moreover, the gradual harmonisation of rules on private international law in the European Union contributes to this high level of victim protection, as is demonstrated in chapter 8.

However strong the level of protection may be, a limited number of deficiencies still exist in European or international rules, leading to a lack of protection for injured parties. This is particularly the case for accidents caused by vehicles insured with an insurer in a state of insolvency, as follows from paragraph 4.3.6 and 7.4.5. It is to be hoped that the European Commission's proposal for a new Motor Insurance Directive will, once adopted, offer satisfactory protection for injured parties suffering damage from an accident caused by a vehicle that is insured with an insolvent MTPL insurer.

Rapid evolutions in motor vehicle technology mean that the MTPL insurance industry is facing new challenges. The appearance of new means of transport such as e-bikes, connected and (semi-)autonomous vehicles requires appropriate answers from the MTPL insurance industry and from (supranational) legislators in order to maintain a sufficient level of consumer and victim protection. The question of whether these new types of vehicles (should) fall within the scope of the definition of 'motor vehicles' should consistently be answered before they receive authorisation to be used on public roads.

Even if our overall conclusion is that injured parties of cross-border road traffic accidents benefit from a relatively satisfactory level of protection, we are of the opinion that this protection may be endangered by the complexity of the system and by a lack of sufficient knowledge. The combination of different rules and divergent levels of protection depending on the geographical area where the accident occurred leads to an extreme level of complexity. The Green Card system exists in two variants: cooperation between Bureaux based on the existence of a valid Green Card and cooperation based on deemed insurance cover. The Motor Insurance Directive has added various actors and rules to this complexity with the creation or recognition of Guarantee Funds, claims representatives, Compensation Bodies and Information Centres. Moreover, the rules on MTPL insurance are subject to the jurisdiction of the Court of Justice of the European Union, which is regularly invited to decide on the interpretation of certain provisions.

It would be an illusion to think that the average consumer is able to follow all these complex rules on MTPL insurance. This is also not necessary.

The challenge is, however, to make sure that there is a sufficient number of people professionally involved in cross-border MTPL insurance, aware of and experienced in the rules applicable to cross-border MTPL insurance in all countries participating in the Green Card system. The management and employees of insurance companies, Green Card Bureaux, Compensation Bodies, Guarantee Funds and Information Centres, claims handling offices, lawyers, judges, people representing injured parties in a professional capacity, loss adjusters and all others claiming to be professionally active in the sector of cross-border road traffic insurance and claims handling processes have an obligation to make themselves acquainted with the rules and protection mechanisms related to road traffic accidents. They can only contribute to the correct insurance and adequate compensation of victims if they have sufficient knowledge of the protection schemes, their technicalities and their application in daily practice. Moreover, in order to be experienced in the international claims handling process, each and every professional needs to be confronted with a sufficient number of claims. Experience is the result of practice. Therefore, a certain specialisation is necessary. Hence, in our opinion, the handling of cross-border claims should preferably be centralised in a specific department or with dedicated members of staff in the above-mentioned organisations.

Adequate technical knowledge and sufficient comprehension of the system are indispensable in order to apply the rules on cross-border road traffic claims so as to achieve the required level of quality. The authors of this book sincerely hope to have contributed, if even to a small extent, to the dissemination of this necessary knowledge and hope that the users of this book have been able to enrich their knowledge or to have taken some inspiration from it.

About the authors

Luk De Baere worked for seven years in the foreign claims department of a Belgian insurance company. Since October 2011, he occupies the post of Legal Manager at the Secretariat of the Council of Bureaux in Brussels.

Frits Blees was the Managing Director of the Dutch Guarantee Fund and Green Card Bureau since the early 1990s, until his retirement in 2017. In his professional capacity, he has been active within the Council of Bureaux as a member and chairperson of various Committees and Working Groups. He holds a PhD degree from Erasmus University Rotterdam.

The authors of this book are or were closely involved in the daily activities of the Council of Bureaux. The ideas and opinions expressed in it are however their own and cannot be attributed to the Council of Bureaux.

Annex 1 - List of Member countries of the Green Card system

Country	Abbreviation / country code	Year of adherence to Green Card system	Bureau competent for the territory (only if different from the country name)	Status in Green Card system (situation on 1 March 2019)
Albania	AL	1992		4
Andorra	AND	1996		3
Austria	A	1954		1
Azerbaijan	AZ	2016		4
Belarus	BY	2003		4
Belgium	B	1949		1
Bosnia and Herzegovina	BIH	1996		4 (Multilateral Agreement signed in 2019)
Bulgaria	BG	1971		1
Croatia	HR	1992		1
Cyprus	CY	1996		1
Czech Republic	CZ	1949		1
Denmark	DK	1949		1
Estonia	EST	1992		1
Finland	FIN	1949		1
France	F	1949		1
Germany	D	1951		1
Greece	GR	1949		1
Hungary	H	1960		1
Iceland	IS	1970		2
Ireland	IRL	1949		1
Islamic Republic of Iran	IR	1976		4
Israel	IL	1968		4
Italy	I	1953		1
Latvia	LV	1998		1
Liechtenstein	FL		Swiss Bureau	2

Country	Abbreviation / country code	Year of adherence to Green Card system	Bureau competent for the territory (only if different from the country name)	Status in Green Card system (situation on 1 March 2019)
Lithuania	LT	2003		1
Luxembourg	L	1949		1
Malta	M	1985		1
Moldova	MD	1997		4
Monaco	MC		French Bureau	3
Montenegro	MNE	2012		4
Morocco	MA	1969		4
Netherlands (the)	NL	1949		1
North-Macedonia	MK	1994		4
Norway	N	1949		2
Poland	PL	1958		1
Portugal	P	1953		1
Romania	RO	1965		1
Russia	RUS	2009		4
San Marino	SM		Italian Bureau	3
Serbia	SRB	1954		3
Slovak Republic	SK	1949		1
Slovenia	SLO	1992		1
Spain	E	1953		1
Sweden	S	1949		1
Switzerland	CH	1949		3
Tunisia	TN	1969		4
Turkey	TR	1964		4
Ukraine	UA	1997		4
United Kingdom of Great Britain and Northern Ireland	GB	1949		1
Vatican City State (Holy See)	VA		Italian Bureau	3

1: Bureau = signatory of the Multilateral Agreement; European Union Member State;

2: Bureau = signatory of the Multilateral Agreement; State participating in the European Economic Area;

3: Bureau = signatory of the Multilateral Agreement; State is neither a Member State of the European Union, nor participating in the European Economic Area;

4: Bureau is not a signatory of the Multilateral Agreement; cooperation with Bureaux in the Green card system is based on Section II of the Internal Regulations.

Case Law

Jurisprudence of the Court of Justice of the European Union

Jurisprudence of the EFTA Court

Printed by Libri Plureos GmbH in Hamburg,
Germany

9 789462 369580